D1357659

WASHINGTON at Home

Jane Freundel Levey, Assistant Editor
Bill Rice, Photo Researcher
"Partners in Progress" by Mark H. Dorfman

Produced in cooperation with the Columbia Historical Society

Consulting Editors:
J. Kirkpatrick Flack,
and Howard Gillette, Jr.

Windsor Publications, Inc.
Northridge, California

WASHINGTON at Home

An Illustrated History of

NEIGHBORHOODS IN THE NATION'S CAPITAL

Kathryn Schneider Smith

EDITOR

Windsor Publications, Inc.—
History Books Division
Managing Editor: Karen Story
Design Director: Alex D'Anca

Staff for *Washington at Home:*
Project Manager: Karl Stull
Photo Manager: Loren Prostano
Copy Editor: Rita Johnson
Assistant Manuscript Editor: Jeffrey Reeves
Production Editor, Corporate Biographies: Phyllis Gray
Editor, Corporate Biographies: Brenda Berryhill
Senior Proofreader: Susan J. Muhler
Editorial Assistants: Didier Beauvoir, Thelma Fleischer, Alyson Gould, Kim Kievman, Michael Nugwynne, Kathy B. Peyser, Pat Pittman, and Theresa Solis
Sales Representatives, Corporate Biographies: C.W. Hoddinott, Stephen Hung, and Diane Murphy
Layout Artist, Corporate Biographies: Robaire Ream
Layout Assistant, Editorial: Deena Tucker

Designer: Christina L. Rosepapa

Library of Congress Cataloging-in-Publication Data

Washington at home.
"Produced in cooperation with the Columbia Historical Society."
Bibliography: p. 356
Includes index.
1. Washington (D.C.)—History.
2. Washington (D.C.)Description. 3. Washington (D.C.) Social life and customs.
I. Smith, Kathryn Schneider. II. Columbia Historical Society (Washington, D.C.)
F194.W34 1988 975.3 87-37280

ISBN: 0-89781-205-0

Published 1988
Printed in the United States of America
First Edition

Windsor Publications, Inc.
Elliot Martin, Chairman of the Board
James L. Fish III, Chief Operating Officer
Hal Silverman, Vice President/Publisher

***Title page:** Artist's version of Washington City in 1833 provides a view of the capital from the other side of the Eastern Branch, now called the Anacostia River. The Capitol Hill neighborhood of today is seen on the opposite shore, with the Navy Yard on the riverbank and the Capitol in the background. Courtesy, The Kiplinger Collection*

***Page six:** Map of Washington D.C. neighborhoods, 1988. By Larry Girardi*

CONTENTS

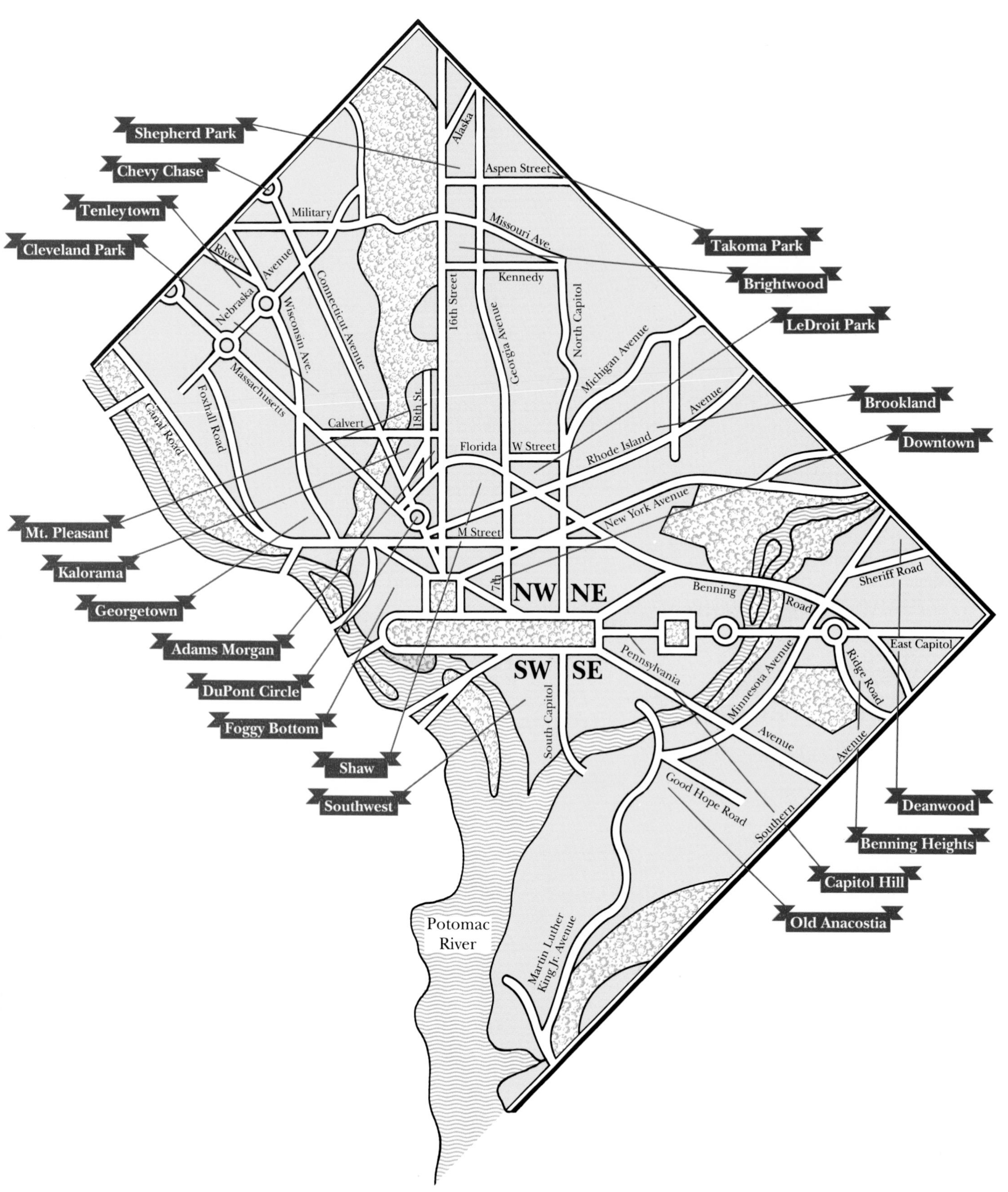

Shepherd Park
Chevy Chase
Tenleytown
Cleveland Park
Takoma Park
Brightwood
LeDroit Park
Brookland
Downtown
Mt. Pleasant
Kalorama
Georgetown
Adams Morgan
DuPont Circle
Foggy Bottom
Shaw
Southwest
Deanwood
Benning Heights
Capitol Hill
Old Anacostia
NW
NE
SW
SE
Potomac River
Alaska
Aspen Street
Military
Missouri Ave.
River
Avenue
Nebraska
Wisconsin Ave.
Connecticut Avenue
16th Street
Kennedy
Georgia Avenue
North Capitol
Michigan Avenue
Massachusetts
Foxhall Road
Canal Road
Calvert
18th St.
Florida
W Street
Rhode Island
Avenue
New York Avenue
M Street
7th
Benning
Road
Sheriff Road
East Capitol
Pennsylvania
Minnesota Avenue
Ridge Road
Avenue
Avenue
South Capitol
Good Hope Road
Southern
Martin Luther King Jr. Avenue

PREFACE

This book is about communities, written by a community. The authors of these essays have a common inspiration—their fascination with Washington's local history. They come to their subjects from a variety of backgrounds. They are architectural, social, political, and urban historians, preservationists, neighborhood activists, and journalists. Some teach in the area's universities, others are independent consultants, a few manage their own public-history businesses. Still others work in unrelated fields and consider history their avocation. But all are committed to an increased understanding of the little-known residential history of Washington, D.C.

Washington at Home gathers under one cover the research conducted by these historians over the last 10 years or so, research that is part of the nationwide renewal of interest in local history, inspired by the nation's bicentennial. The questions being asked by historians in the relatively new fields of urban and social history are also reflected in these essays—questions that focus on how cities grow and on the ways that people of all races and ethnic backgrounds have lived together in the urban setting. Pieces of new research on Washington have emerged in walking tours, pamphlets, exhibit catalogs, historic-district applications, and scholarly theses, but the information has until now remained scattered and not easily available.

While *Washington at Home* represents the most comprehensive look at Washington neighborhoods to date, the editors and authors are all aware that much has been left out. The neighborhoods were chosen for a combination of historical and practical reasons. Historically, they represent the oldest and most generally recognized places in the city; in fact, all but two originated before the twentieth century. Together they help to tell the story of each phase in the nineteenth-century growth of the city. As a practical matter, these were also the neighborhoods where painstaking and time-consuming research was already complete or under way, including: the digging in census and tax records, the poring over real estate maps, the locating of lost community records, and the interviewing of longtime residents who are a vital means to recover the origins and the spirit of a small place. The major reason some neighborhoods are missing from this collection, especially twentieth-century neighborhoods, is that much work remains to be done.

Given the restraints of time and space, these brief essays cannot tell the complete story of any of these places. Rather they attempt to capture the essence of a neighborhood, according to each author's insights, experience, and research. The essays vary in style as well as in content. Some focus more on physical development than others; some dwell on early history, others on post-World War II developments.

The authors and editors also recognize how personal the idea of neighborhood can be. This becomes particularly clear when one tries to find agreement on specific boundaries. Most of these neighborhoods have edges that are to some extent historically determined—by subdivision maps, by school boundaries, by community organizations, by distinctive architecture, and the like. For the physical boundaries to have any meaning, however, they must reflect the personal experiences of a community—networks of people who acknowledged some common bonds as they worked with the home and school association, promoted community playgrounds and libraries, and planned block parties and community festivals. A neighborhood is after all a state of mind. Its existence depends on the belief held by some that small places within the city still have meaning and importance in a mobile and changing world. With a bow to neighborhoods as very personal places, this book suggests boundaries in the text but draws no hard lines on the accompanying maps.

Washington at Home is sponsored by the Columbia Historical Society, founded in 1894 to collect, preserve, and teach the city's history. The society and the authors and editors of this book consider it a beginning and not an end. As Washingtonians who are aware of the neglect of our local city realize, we have much to do to recapture its rich history. It is our hope that *Washington at Home* will inspire further interest in collecting still-scattered papers, photographs, and other materials, in doing oral history, and in creating support for a new scholarship that will build on the story presented here.

The authors and editors are all grateful to the community of Washingtonians who have helped with this book in many ways, from checking facts to reading manuscripts to turning up previously unknown photographs. With great appreciation, their names are listed in the Additional Acknowledgments.

I want to add my personal thanks to Mark G. Griffin, who initiated and generated the support for this project, to Howard Gillette, who became a true mentor , to Jim Flack for all his thoughtful comments, and to Bill Rice for his untiring efforts as photo researcher. I am also indebted to Roxanna Deane, Kathryn Ray, and G.R.F. Key of the D.C. Library's Washingtoniana Room; to Larry Baume of the Columbia Historical Society, as well as the society library's volunteers; and to Antoinette Lee and Robert Truax, all of whom were, as always, generous with their time and knowledge. Particular recognition is due to Emily Medvec for her dedication to this project; to Hajna and Tamas DeKun for their very special photographic services; to Linda Christenson for her help with photo research; to Susan Klaus and Keith Melder for reviewing the final draft with fresh eyes.

The authors gave extraordinary time and care to this project, as did Jane Levey, whose expertise made putting all the pieces together possible. I am enormously grateful for their consistent enthusiasm, their patience, and their good humor, as well as that of my own family—Sam, Nat, and Ben—who never fail me.

Kathryn Schneider Smith
December 1987

1778
1943
AMERICANS
will always fight for liberty
TAXICABS
RAILROAD TICKETS
PULLMAN TICKETS
TAXICABS
TELEPHONES
INFORMATION
TICKET OFFICE OPPOSITE SIDE
TRAIN ARRIVALS · TRAIN DEPARTURES ·

INTRODUCTION

Kathryn Schneider Smith

Above: Today a strip of upscale stores and restaurants that draws people from throughout the metropolitan area, M Street, N.W., in 1948 was lined with small businesses serving a local clientele. This view looks west from Wisconsin Avenue. Courtesy, National Archives

Facing page: Union Station swarmed with service personnel, war workers, and visitors in March 1943, when as many as 100,000 people passed through the station every 24 hours. Washington, D.C., grew by leaps and bounds during World War II, as it has during every other national crisis. Courtesy, Library of Congress, Prints and Photographs Division

Washington, D.C., is among the best known and the least understood of American cities. Images of marble-columned buildings and well-known politicians flash across the nation's television screens every evening. The monuments that dominate the central city are symbols familiar since childhood. Beyond the marble, however, is another city whose history is hidden even from its own residents—a city of homes, schools, small businesses, and religious institutions. Perhaps surprising to those who see it only from afar, Washington is a city of neighborhoods—and many neighborhood residents have considered it their hometown for generations. *Washington at Home* takes a look at the history of this hidden city.

Within these 21 chapters lie the pieces of a shared past. The authors focus on the particular history of one neighborhood, yet the reader will repeatedly encounter issues and events affecting all Washingtonians. Thus, themes emerge that throw new light on the whole sweep of Washington history—the story of a local community uniquely involved with the fortunes of the nation.

Neighborhoods in Washington, D.C., were shaped by some of the same forces that created distinctive communities in other large American cities. Foremost were the transportation innovations of the last half of the nineteenth century—the streetcars and commuter railroads that offered the public the option, for the first time, of living farther away from their employment than they could conveniently walk. The old pedestrian city—where people of all races, ethnic backgrounds, and economic levels had lived intermixed—began to separate into a city of different parts as white people with the financial means left the increasingly crowded and unhealthy central city for new suburban developments along the streetcar and railroad lines. Although this did not happen as swiftly or completely as in the more dense and ethnically diverse industrial cities of the North, many of the Washington neighborhoods we recognize today have their roots in this common nineteenth-century phenomenon.

In other ways, Washington neighborhoods were affected by the peculiar origin and unique role of the city as the nation's capital. The visionary and large-scale plan drawn for the capital by Pierre L'Enfant, for example, fostered the emergence of separate communities in the city's great open spaces. The fact that the city was denied a locally elected government for more than 100 years also encouraged strong community identities as influential neighborhood associations performed functions assigned to city politics in other places. Most significantly the timing of neighborhood development in Washington paralleled the spurts of growth of the federal establishment, which evolved from a government of relatively limited powers, employing only about 130 clerks in 1800, to a world power supported by a bureaucracy of about 276,000 employees during World War II.

The 21 neighborhood histories are presented in the order of their chronological beginnings and are grouped by the city's phases of development. The present-day neighborhoods of Georgetown, Capitol Hill, Foggy Bottom, and Southwest, combined with the old downtown along 7th Street, represent the earliest phase—a period when the magnificent plans for a grand capital city were most at odds with reality.

Unlike the American cities that grew from tightly clustered settlements located at convenient places for trade, the District of Columbia began as a mostly undeveloped 10-mile square, set down in a rural landscape by Congress in 1791. Within it were two small tobacco-trading port towns: Alexandria, with about 5,000 people, and Georgetown, with about 3,000. Georgetown, crude though its amenities were, became the center of commercial and social life in the capital's earliest days. Alexandria, because of its location across the Potomac, never actually functioned as part of the District; its economy suffered until 1846, when Congress heard the pleas of its citizens and agreed to return the entire trans-Potomac portion of the District to Virginia.

Within the 10-mile square, the federal government created a new town, just across the Rock Creek valley from Georgetown, named the City of Washington. It was designed on a grand scale by Pierre L'Enfant, a French architect and engineer known to George Washington since the Revolutionary War. Although vast, considering there was little population to fill it, the city's land area comprised only a portion of the District, occupying what now lies south of Florida Avenue and Benning Road. L'Enfant used topographical features to define his city, with Rock Creek as the western boundary, the Potomac River to the south, and the Eastern Branch, today known as the Anacostia River, on the east. His northern boundary followed the old wagon road from Georgetown to Bladensburg, Maryland, winding its way along the base of the hill that rises above present-day Florida Avenue, for many years called Boundary Street. L'Enfant's boundaries—the major rivers, the chasm of Rock Creek, and the separation of high land from low—both defined and symbolized significant social and political divisions within the city for most of its history.

L'Enfant's large-scale plan for Washington City encouraged the emergence of separate communities from the beginning as a small population of only about 3,000 spread out across the city's great open spaces. James Sterling Young argues in his analysis of the early federal government in Washington that the federal city was clearly laid out to represent geographically the separation of powers upon which the Constitution rested. Indeed, legislators did cluster near the Capitol, and those with executive business, near the President's House. A third settlement formed, not around the judiciary, which had not yet attained status equal to the other branches of government, but rather on the Eastern Branch near the Navy Yard, where L'Enfant had envisioned the new city's industrial section. The Navy Yard settlement and the one just behind the Capitol building eventually merged into today's Capitol Hill neighborhood.

Other population clusters in early Washington City reflected its commercial needs. Wharves to serve the new city sprang up in the Southwest section. Virtually cut off from the city to the north by the Washington Canal, which followed the present-day course of Constitution Avenue, Southwest was referred to as "the island." Its port activity drew a largely working-class population—a distinction it carried until the 1950s. A small light-industrial community also grew up along the Potomac River in Foggy Bottom, between the President's House and Georgetown. Foggy Bottom's workers labored in a glass-blowing factory, a brewery, a boatyard, and a lime kiln. The area served as one of the city's few industrial centers into the twentieth century. Shops and stores sprang up around the city's Center Market at 7th and Pennsylvania Avenue, N.W., and spread north along 7th Street to create an early commercial community.

From its beginnings Washington had a large black population, part slave, part free. The black population comprised 29 percent of the total in 1800; the number fluctuated between a quarter and a third of the total until the mid-1950s, when blacks became a majority in the District. While not physically divided from the white population in the nineteenth century, blacks formed a strong separate social community centered on their own churches and schools. Descendants of this early community, many of whose leaders are memorialized in the names of schools and other institutions, remain in the city today.

As many of these essays reveal, Washington also had a significant white ethnic population, though it was small compared to that of Philadelphia or New York, where thousands of industrial jobs were available. Irish and Germans clustered in Foggy Bottom; Germans, both Jewish and Christian, formed the nucleus of the city's early commercial core on 7th Street.

These scattered communities of the early city, however, hardly fulfilled the dream of a capital city that would symbolize the nation's highest ambitions and ideals. The federal government was primarily responsible for the failure. In their ambivalence about the need for a strong central government, the early Congress contributed almost nothing to the city's construction; they had neither the money nor the will. Washington City's streets remained almost entirely ungraded, unpaved, and unlit. The founders never intended for the city to rely on the federal presence for its livelihood. Yet the waterway that was to balance the city's economic life and tie Washington's commercial fortunes to the vast untapped market of the Ohio River valley—the Chesapeake and Ohio Canal—fell short of its trans-Appalachian goal due to a lack of capital. By the Civil War it was clear that the city's commerce was almost totally eclipsed by competition from Baltimore. Even the government remained small; its three branches employed only about 2,000 on the eve of the Civil War. While a few wealthy and socially prominent families expressed their commitment to the city's future by building houses in Washington, most members of Congress, and the powerful and well-to-do who wished to influence them, only came to town for the congressional season. They stayed in hotels and boardinghouses and then returned to their homes elsewhere.

Throughout the antebellum period the area of the District outside Washington City and Georgetown remained countryside, dotted with small farms and the estates of the gentry. Improvements in transportation, however, foreshadowed developments to come. Private investors built turnpikes to connect the capital with Rockville and Frederick, Maryland; the crossroads towns of Tenleytown and Brightwood sprang up at tollbooths along their routes into Georgetown and Washington City, respectively. The location of bridges also shaped the growth of the early city. In 1854 the first suburb of Washington City—Uniontown, now called Old Anacostia—was laid out at the eastern end of the Navy Yard Bridge because the bridge made that area so convenient to jobs at the Navy Yard.

The Civil War marked a watershed in the city's history. The mobilization and maintenance of the Union army necessitated a strong federal government; consequently, the ranks of federal employees swelled to about 7,000, including women for the first time. A circle of forts was constructed to defend the capital's vulnerable location just across the Potomac from the Confederate state of Virginia. Entrepreneurs flooded the city to take advantage of new commercial opportunities created by the war, and journalists from other cities for the first time took up residence to report full-time on events in the capital. While the District saw military action only once (at Fort Stevens in Brightwood, in 1864), every section of the city was affected.

At war's end the city was in shambles. Because local government historically lacked adequate tax revenues to pave L'Enfant's wide streets and avenues, and the federal government saw no reason to help, the city's streets were woefully inadequate. The heavy traffic of the war had only added to the strain. Furthermore, the thousands of war workers who remained to administer the peace, and the newly freed slaves—as many as 40,000—overwhelmed the city's capacity to house and meet the social needs of its population. In order to escape the seemingly insurmountable problems of the current site, moving the capital elsewhere was seriously proposed. St. Louis was suggested as a more central location in the rapidly expanding nation.

The city's reaction to this possibility set the stage for its postwar growth. A new citizens' reform group pressed for a more efficient and centralized local government to replace the still-separate governments of Georgetown, Washington City, and Washington County. In 1871 all three were abolished in favor of a bicameral territorial government, with the lower house elected by the citizens. The governor and upper house of the legislature were appointed by the president of the United States. Thus in control, the federal government agreed to give the city $6 million to modernize under the auspices of a board of public works.

Onto the stage of Washington history strode Alexander "Boss" Shepherd, an energetic individual of great personal charm who, as the most influential member of the board of public works and later as District governor, transformed the city in just three years. He graded and paved streets, laid miles of sewers and gas mains, planted trees, and installed more than 3,000 streetlights. However, he spent not $6 million but almost $20 million, and his methods of record-keeping along with his favoritism to friends, typical of big-city boss operations at the time, earned him two congressional investigations.

While Congress never formally accused Shepherd of wrongdoing, it chose to repudiate his role by abolishing the territorial government in 1874 and instituting instead a governing body of three appointed commissioners. The District would not have a locally elected government again until 1974. The end of territorial government was seen by many as a way to void completely the voting rights of the city's recently enfranchised black citizenry, the first of many setbacks that would slowly undermine other rights blacks had gained in the city during Reconstruction. Once Congress had taken full control of city affairs through the Organic Act of 1878, it agreed for the first time to grant a regular federal payment to the District government to compensate for the tax money lost on the city's nontaxable federal land—an amount that remained 50 percent of the local budget until World War I.

In spite of its loss of democratic rights, the city emerged in the late 1870s with a fresh image. Its smoothly paved and well-lighted streets and broad avenues gave it a new appeal; the commitment of regular federal funds seemed to guarantee the city's future. Furthermore, Shepherd's improvements opened many new areas of Washington City for development. He had, in fact, added to the landscape many streets that previously existed only on paper in the L'Enfant Plan. The capital had become respectable.

The population, which had swelled from 75,000 to 131,000 in the 1860s, jumped to 177,000 by 1880. New transportation technology—public horsecar lines created during the Civil War—shaped the city's post-war growth. Entrepreneurs developed new sections of the reborn capital along these horsecar routes, both inside and outside the boundaries of Washington City. The third group of neighborhood essays describes this period of dramatic growth.

In 1865, for example, Samuel Brown of Maine subdivided his hilltop acreage within reach of the 14th Street line. He called it Mount Pleasant, attracting a group of new government employees from New England. A little later, in 1873, a group of investors laid out LeDroit Park, a more ambitious planned suburb just beyond Boundary Street on the 7th Street Metropolitan horsecar line. Romantic cottage-style houses set in landscaped grounds along streets named for trees epitomized a new suburban ideal. In Washington, as in other growing American cities at the time, residents were beginning to look for a way out of the increasingly crowded and unsanitary conditions of the urban core, seeking the ambience of the country but also convenient access to jobs in the city. Deanwood, in far-Northeast Washington, began as three small subdivisions in this period, sited along a new steam-railroad line in open countryside across the Eastern Branch.

Public transportation had a revolutionary impact on the way the city was organized. In the premodern city, the humble and the rich lived side by side, as did black and white, although their social worlds were separate. With the arrival of the streetcar, the city began physically to separate by race and, to some extent, by economic level—a segregation that would become more pronounced by the early twentieth century. This separation was also encouraged by the city's new water supply, piped downriver from Great Falls in conduits completed in 1862. The Northwest section, nearest Georgetown, was the first to be served reliably and began to attract the well-to-do. Dupont Circle grew up in the 1870s around one of Shepherd's newly paved circles and quickly became the favored address for the white elite.

On the other hand, the near-Northwest neighborhood now called Shaw experienced the beginnings of the racial segregation that would increasingly force blacks of all economic levels into the only housing made available to them. This segregation was eventually to become institutionalized through restrictive housing covenants. By necessity, Shaw became the center of black enterprise; its main thoroughfare, U Street, developed into the major black business and entertainment street in the city. At the same time older neighborhoods such as Capitol Hill, whose population had been mixed by race and class since its earliest days, increasingly attracted white, middle-income government workers who were more willing to buy houses after 1883 when civil-service reform made their jobs more secure. Pockets of the city's oldest and least desirable housing, much of it in interior alleys in such neighborhoods as Southwest and Foggy Bottom, were left increasingly to the poor.

The 1880s set the stage for the next phase of city growth. The federal government's enlarged role in American life engendered new Washington-based agencies, including the Bureau of Labor (1884), the Interstate Commerce Commission (1887), and a reorganized Department of Agriculture (1889). The Smithsonian Institution and new scientific commissions attracted astronomers, geologists, meteorologists, and other scientists to the capital. Government jobs offered more opportunities for women and for blacks than elsewhere in the nation. By 1891 black workers accounted for one out of ten federal employees; in 1893 about three in ten were women. Federal employment tripled in a decade from 7,800 in 1880 to 23,000 by 1890. Confidence in the city was high. Almost everyone from the $900-a-year government clerk to the millionaire developer saw opportunities in Washington real estate. The strength and civic consciousness of the city's businesses were reflected in the formation of the Washington Board of Trade in 1889.

Added to these ingredients for growth in the late 1880s were more transportation innovations—new Baltimore and Ohio commuter railroad lines into the city and the electrification of the city's streetcars, making them much faster and more reliable than the horse-powered version. Consequently, the city leaped across its old boundaries. More ambitious and more distant suburbs sprang up along the transportation routes in the county and beyond, including Brookland and Takoma Park along the commuter railroad lines, and Chevy Chase and Cleveland Park along the electric-streetcar route out Connecticut Avenue. Some of the developers were descendants of longtime residents, such as the Brooks family, who subdivided their homestead. Others were new entrepreneurs: Senator Francis Newlands of Nevada, for example, operated with large dreams and enormous capital to acquire 1,700 acres and create Chevy Chase, as well as the bridges and streetcars needed to take people there.

These neighborhoods also grew in a social sense as, once again, the unique character of the federal city shaped its residential development. New communities needed paved streets, water systems, and other city amenities, but the developers only partially supplied them. Lacking an elected city government to hear their needs, citizens formed neighborhood organizations as early as the 1870s to lobby the District commissioners and the congressional District and Appropriations committees for city services. White groups called their organizations "citizens' associations." Blacks, being excluded from membership in the white organizations, formed their own groups somewhat later, using the designation "civic associations." Such organizations served to create local solidarity through their activities and also reinforced the identities of the neighborhoods whose names they carried.

By the 1890s the embarrassment over conditions in the nation's capital had turned to pride. In contrast to its past image as a neglected backwater, the city began to be thought of as a model and was used as a proving ground for some of the newest ideas of the emerging city-planning movement. In an effort to bring order to the haphazard development of the county, Congress passed the Highway Act of 1893, which extended the original L'Enfant Plan for Washington City to the rest of the District. In 1898 the act was revised to excuse previously laid-out subdivisions from compliance. Soon afterwards the city became a model for the City Beautiful Movement, inspired by the World's Columbian Exposition of 1893, held in Chicago.

The Senate's McMillan Commission, organized in 1901, brought the key men responsible for the Chicago fair to Washington to develop a new plan for the city in honor of its centennial. As carried out in the twentieth century, the McMillan Plan eventually produced an enclave of gleaming federal buildings and monuments centered on the Mall, making a physical distinction, for the first time between the federal city and its residential areas. The plan also led to the establishment of those parks and parkways that give the city its characteristic green openspaces today.

New developments faltered during the nationwide financial panic of 1893, and some stood still between 1893 and 1898, awaiting the final version of the Highway Act in case previously laid-out streets had to be moved. But by the turn of the century suburbs had mushroomed as new streets and sewer and water systems carried out the plans of the Highway Act. Sixteenth Street and Connecticut Avenue, for example, were paved to the District line, and such prestigious neighborhoods as Meridian Hill and Kalorama emerged along their courses. By 1907 the grand and graceful Taft Bridge spanned the chasm of Rock Creek at Connecticut Avenue, a major improvement over the lightweight-iron truss bridges that private developers had created at Massachusetts Avenue in 1888 and Calvert Street in 1891.

Changing transportation technology continued to affect Washington's growth. In the 1920s automobiles came within reach of the middle-class pocketbook for the first time, and once again the impact could be seen on the map. Since neighborhoods had developed along public transportation routes, the city's populated sections appeared as nodes on the spokes of a wheel. In the 1920s and 1930s the wedges in between, not served by the streetcar, began to fill in with such developments as Burleith, Wesley Heights, and Spring Valley in Northwest. Once again government growth was the spur, as the New Deal agencies brought federal employment to an unprecedented 139,000 by 1940. The most remote sections of the District, particularly in far-Northeast and far-Southeast across the Anacostia River, remained open space until World War II, when a burgeoning city, now a world capital, finally required the entire land area of the District to house its population. The capital city not only completely filled out the District after the war, it spilled over its boundaries, so that today it is the hub of a metropolitan area of more than 3 million people spread across multiple political jurisdictions in Maryland and Virginia.

The last group of neighborhoods in this book represents Washington's neighborhoods in the postwar period. Only Benning Heights, constructed for the most part after the war on the District's far-southeastern border with Maryland, is an example of actual physical growth. The Shepherd Park and Adams Morgan chapters illustrate another form of neighborhood-building—the emergence of a renewed sense of social community as older neighborhoods changed their identities and their names.

Neighborhood consciousness has deepened in Washington's recent history as its older developments adapted to, and sometimes fought, rapid changes in the capital after the war. As the walls of legal segregation fell after World War II with Supreme Court decisions declaring restrictive housing covenants (1948) and school segregation (1954) unconstitutional, the social fabric of many Washington neighborhoods changed dramatically. Middle-class whites—some pulled by new suburban housing, others pushed by school and neighborhood desegregation—began an exodus to the suburbs. Middle-class blacks settled into District neighborhoods formerly closed to them. Many black and white Washingtonians found common goals as they sought to build integrated neighborhoods in such places as Brookland, Capitol Hill, Mount Pleasant, Takoma Park, and Shepherd Park. The Shepherd Park chapter examines the particularly successful tactics of Neighbors, Inc., in achieving this goal.

A sense of neighborhood also deepened as residents fought threatening physical developments. The oldest central-city neighborhoods all faced massive change from post-World War II urban renewal programs designed to attack urban decay with clearance and rebuilding, using the nation's capital as a test case. In a program meant to show the way for the nation, Southwest Washington was almost totally leveled in the 1950s; Foggy Bottom was overwhelmed with large-scale, high-rise redevelopment. Citizen efforts to forestall a similar fate for Shaw were organized in the 1960s by the Model Inner City Corporation. Washington neighborhoods showed their greatest civic strength, however, in David-and-Goliath encounters over the massive freeway proposals of the 1950s and 1960s, virtually halting the highways slated to run through such places as Cleveland Park, Brookland, and Takoma Park.

In recent years, history itself has served to build a sense of community. In the 1950s and 1960s the movement to preserve the city's historic architecture spread from Georgetown to Foggy Bottom to Capitol Hill. In the 1970s the movement broadened to include not just architecture but also the preservation of neighborhoods as historic communities, as their residents began to apply for official recognition as historic districts. At this writing there are 18 Washington neighborhoods listed on the National Register of Historic Places. Awareness of local history influenced the naming of stations on the new subway system; for example, the Tenleytown stop is a revival of a historic name.

The historical importance of neighborhoods in the city's political life was reinforced in 1973 when Congress granted the city a locally elected government for the first time since 1874. Included in the legislation was a provision for Advisory Neighborhood Commissions, a measure that placed Washington in the vanguard of a growing national recognition of the importance of strong neighborhoods in large American cities.

The essays that follow, the most comprehensive collection of Washington neighborhood research to date, trace the historical role of the city's residential communities in the context of city history summarized above. In their variety, and in their interrelated detail, the essays provide a new perspective on a city that is not only the nation's capital; it is also, and has been for many thousands of people since 1791, a hometown.

Well-known street musician Bob Devlin sets up his one-man band on Pennsylvania Avenue, N.W., with the Old Post Office building and the United States Capitol for a backdrop. Photo by Rick Reinhard

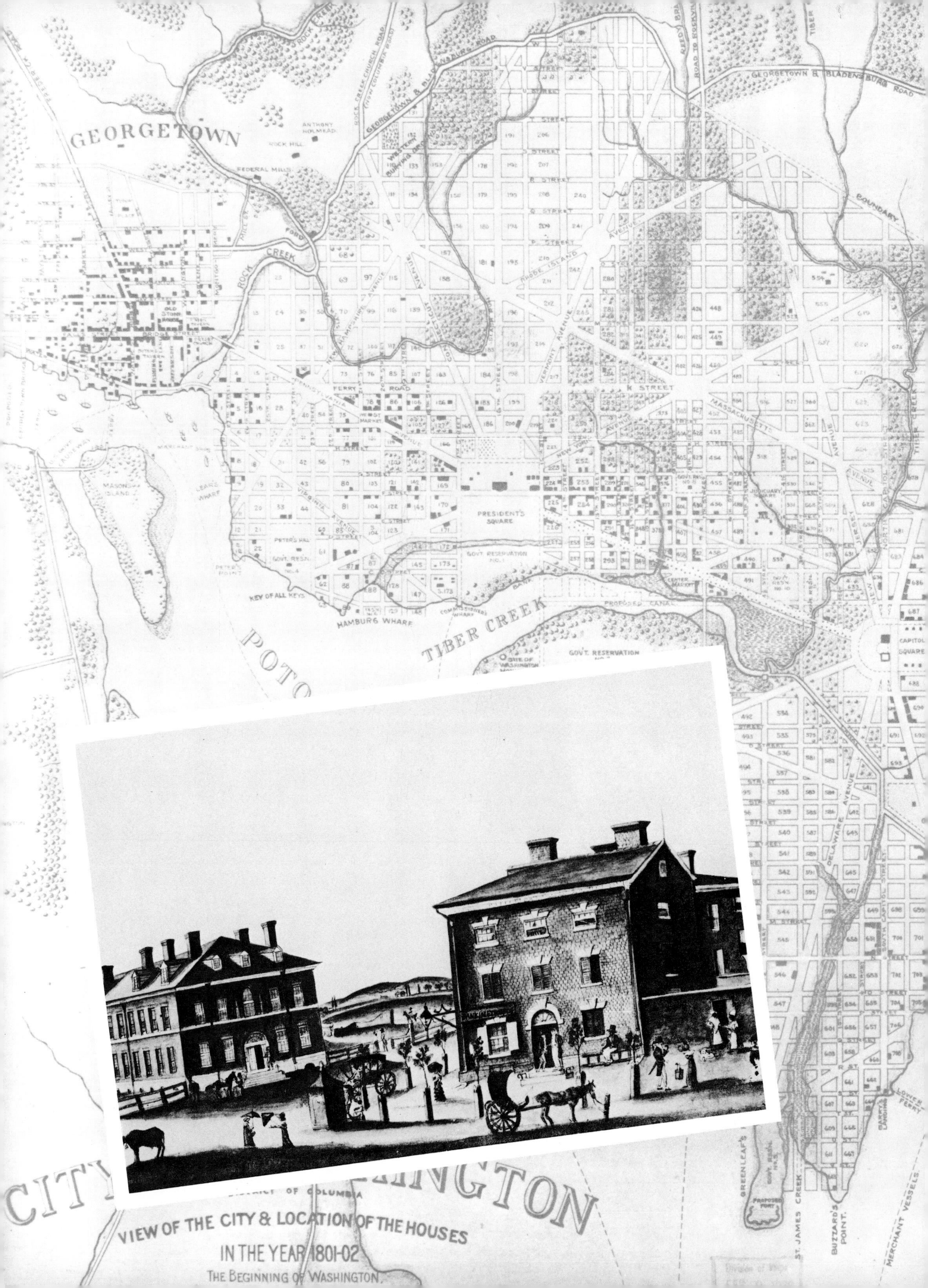
GEORGETOWN
ROCK CREEK
GEORGETOWN & BLADENSBURG ROAD
ROCK HILL
FEDERAL MILLS
ANTHONY HOLMEAD
MASONS ISLAND
LEAR'S WHARF
PRESIDENT'S SQUARE
GOVT. RESERVATION NO. 1
KEY OF ALL KEYS
HAMBURG WHARF
TIBER CREEK
POTO
K STREET
MASSACHUSETTS
NEW YORK AVENUE
VERMONT AVENUE
RHODE ISLAND AVENUE
PENNSYLVANIA
VIRGINIA AVENUE
NEW HAMPSHIRE AVENUE
CONNECTICUT
FERRY ROAD
BOUNDARY
CAPITOL SQUARE
DELAWARE AVENUE
SOUTH CAPITOL STREET
NEW JERSEY
GREENLEAF'S
ST. JAMES CREEK
BUZZARD'S POINT
MERCHANT VESSELS
LOWER FERRY
CITY OF WASHINGTON
DISTRICT OF COLUMBIA
VIEW OF THE CITY & LOCATION OF THE HOUSES
IN THE YEAR 1801-02
THE BEGINNING OF WASHINGTON.

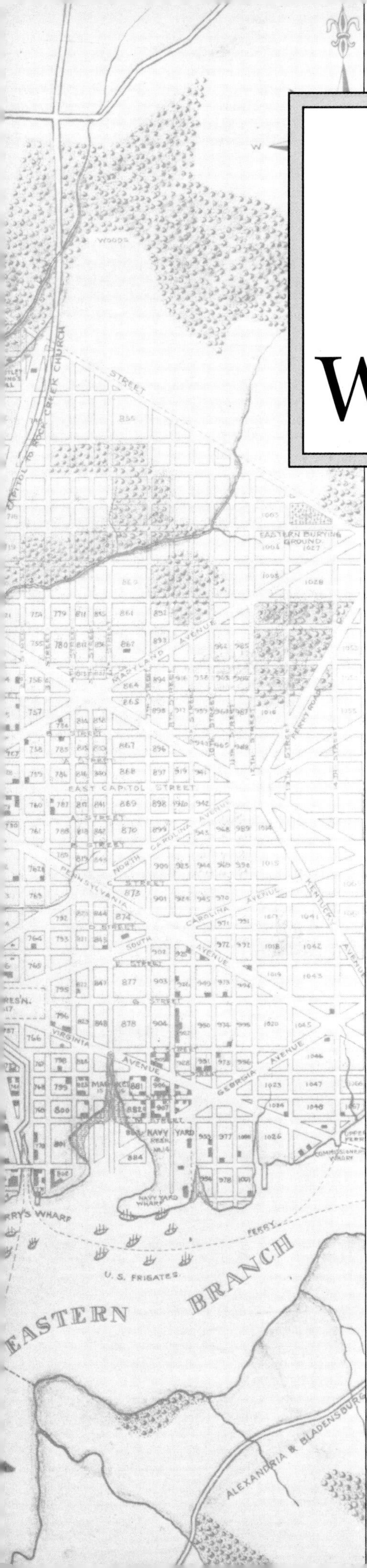

PART ONE

GEORGETOWN AND WASHINGTON CITY

The early District of Columbia contained not one city but three: the two tobacco port towns of Alexandria and Georgetown, and the federal city designed by Pierre L'Enfant, named Washington City. Outside these towns, the District also encompassed farmland and forest, called Washington County on the Maryland side of the Potomac River and Alexandria County on the Virginia side.

The federal government spent little on its new capital city. Although the founders encouraged the visionary plan for Washington City designed by Pierre L'Enfant in 1791, the money for its realization was not forthcoming. The grand avenues drawn on the map remained for many years unpaved and unlit. Connections between the scattered settlements within the District were so bad that shortly after the government moved to the Potomac in 1800 a group of congressmen on their way home from a dinner party got lost in the trackless wilderness, near what is now called Haines Point. It was morning before they found their way through the bogs and gullies to their residences on Capitol Hill, just a mile away.

Georgetown and the separate communities that grew up in early Washington City—such as Foggy Bottom, Southwest, Capitol Hill, and the old 7th Street downtown—are now the oldest urban neighborhoods in the capital. Alexandria returned to Virginia in 1846. Although these neighborhoods took on somewhat different characters, they were all mixtures of rich and poor, black and white residents, whose homes were located, by necessity, within walking distance of their places of work.

Left: Buggies, pedestrians, and cows shared the corner of 15th and F streets, NW, in this watercolor painted between 1816 and 1822. Open countryside is visible behind the U.S. State Department, left, and the bank at the right, a building once known as Rhodes Tavern that stood on this corner until its demolition in 1985. Courtesy, New York Public Library

Map drawn by Artemas Harmon; 1931. Courtesy, Library of Congress, Map Division

1

GEORGETOWN

PORT TOWN TO URBAN NEIGHBORHOOD

Kathryn Schneider Smith

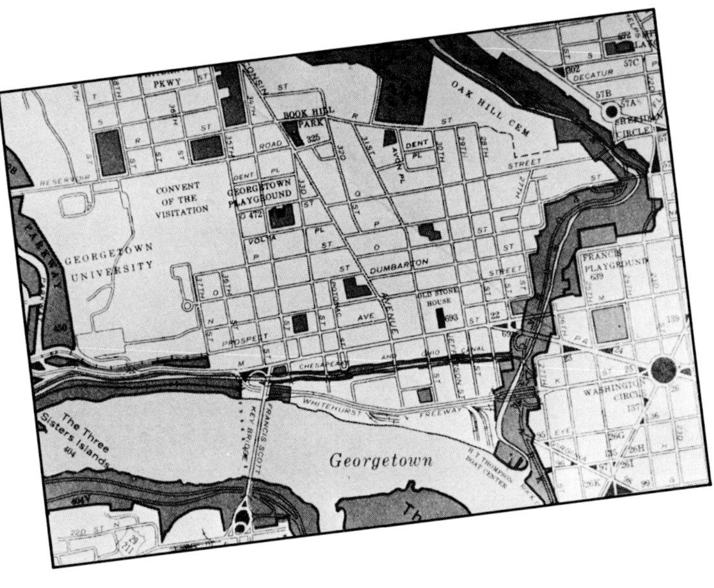

The intimate scale of most Georgetown streets sets it apart from other, later Washington neighborhoods. Photo by Paul Jaffe

Map: Park System of the National Capitol and Environs. National Park Service 1962. Courtesy, D.C. Public Library, Washingtoniana Division

In Georgetown red-brick houses huddle alongside tree-lined brick sidewalks. Visitors know they are entering a distinctive place from any approach. It is a scene known nationwide, for its houses have been home to many of the nation's social and political elite, its character saved by one of the country's most publicized preservation efforts.

Georgetown is Washington's oldest neighborhood, a once independent town predating the federal capital itself by more than 50 years. It is seen by some as socially and physically set apart from the rest of the city. It is home to a homogeneous white and well-to-do population, with clear boundaries on three sides: the Potomac on the south, Rock Creek on the east, and Georgetown University on the west. At the same time the widest range of Washingtonians flock to its shops, restaurants, and lively streets and take pleasure in a place that is truly local, truly their own, in a city where federal buildings and activities most often claim center stage.

This tension arising from being separate—yet central to the city's local identity—is not new. For most of the nineteenth century Georgetown was in the anomalous position of having its own locally elected government and its own competitive economy while still being part of the District of Columbia. Later, its citizens struggled to maintain a local identity while at the same time developing an integral role in the life of the city and the region. Then, for a time in the early twentieth century, it was considered a social backwater, its waterfront an industrial dumping ground, its old-fashioned character an embarrassing reminder of an outdated past. Today its low-rise streetscapes, small-town

The approximate equivalent of K Street today, this riverside road carried the business of the port of Georgetown circa 1800, when the federal capital moved to its new location on the Potomac. Courtesy, Library of Congress, Prints and Photographs Division

ambience, and Potomac River waterfront have become amenities enjoyed by people from all over the metropolitan area.

The people of Georgetown's past have been similarly varied. The homogeneity of today's population is only a recent phenomenon. In fact, Georgetown's story includes people of every race and occupation: merchants, craftsmen, and laborers as well as government employees; black and white; European immigrants and natives of Tidewater Maryland and Virginia.

This story began almost 250 years ago. Georgetown was one of a number of Maryland and Virginia Tidewater towns created in the mid-eighteenth century to provide inspection stations and shipment facilities for tobacco, the area's major crop. Long before, native Americans had discovered it as a good place for trade. Situated just below the Great Falls of the Potomac, it had the advantage of being as far inland as one could go by boat from the ocean. Its location was crucial for the first European traders also. By 1740 tobacco merchants from Glasgow, Scotland, and Whitehaven, in northwestern England, had focused on the future site of Georgetown. When a 1745 Maryland law required the official inspection of tobacco, the warehouse of Scottish merchant George Gordon, southwest of the present-day intersection of Wisconsin Avenue and M Street, was designated for that purpose. By 1751 a small cluster of buildings had sprung up around the warehouse, and a group of merchants decided to petition the Maryland General Assembly for permission to lay out a town. The 60 acres included in the original site were bounded approximately by present-day N Street on the north, Jefferson Street on the east, and 34th Street on the west.

The tobacco merchants dominated Georgetown in the eighteenth century, fueling its economy, creating a social elite, and initially running the town with appointed commissioners. Robert Peter was among the most prominent, a Glasgow native who had come to America as a representative of John Glassford and Company, that town's biggest tobacco importer. In 1789, when the town was granted a charter by the Maryland legislature, Peter was elected the first mayor. His son would marry a step-granddaughter of George Washington and live in elegance at Tudor Place, as would six generations of that family until the 1980s.

Another early and prosperous merchant was Benjamin Stoddert, who built Halcyon House, one of the grand Georgian homes of the eighteenth century that still stand in the 3400 and 3500 blocks of Prospect Street. From these houses he and others could watch the activity on the riverbanks, an area more built up at this time than once believed. Archaeologists have recently uncovered evidence of eighteenth-century warehouses, wharves, and cobblestone paths to the river beneath the twentieth-century landscape. The only warehouse associated with the tobacco trade that remains is that of the prominent business of Francis and A.H. Dodge at the foot of Wisconsin Avenue.

This fanciful Italianate house, designed in 1850 by Andrew Jackson Downing and Calvert Vaux, reflects the affluence of its first owner, the successful Georgetown merchant Francis Dodge, and later Governor Alexander Shepherd. Pictured here in about 1888, it still stands at 30th and Q streets, N.W. Courtesy, Columbia Historical Society

There were high hopes for this area among colonial leaders in the eighteenth century. A plan by the Ohio Company sponsored by George Mason as early as 1749 would have made the Georgetown site the entrepot for trade with the entire trans-Appalachian West by improving navigation on the Potomac. In 1785 the idea was revived by the Patowmack Company, with George Washington as president, and by 1802 five sections of canal had been built to circumvent obstacles to navigation.

It is thus not surprising that the area around Georgetown should have been considered a leading contender for the federal capital, a site that could have become a commercial as well as political center. When the District of Columbia was created in 1791, Georgetown and Alexandria, its competitor in the tobacco trade across the Potomac, were enclosed within its boundaries.

Washington City, the new town designed by Pierre L'Enfant, existed for the most part on paper. In the first years of the capital, Georgetown and Alexandria were the only well-established communities within the District, Georgetown with about 3,000 people and Alexandria with about 5,000. Alexandria was inconvenient, separated from Washington City by the Potomac River; in 1846 it would retrocede to Virginia. It was Georgetown that provided housing and daily necessities for the new capital. Abigail Adams, for example, was obliged to send someone daily to Georgetown to do the marketing. The highly regarded Dr. Stephan Bloomer Balch of Georgetown welcomed people of all denominations from Washington City and Georgetown to his Bridge Street Presbyterian Church. Georgetown College, founded in 1789 as the nation's first Catholic institution of higher education, was the new capital's only center of intellectual life.

Initially Georgetown benefited from its new status; the population jumped from 3,000 in 1800 to more than 8,000 in 1830. By the 1820s, however, it began to suffer from competition with its new neighbor across Rock Creek as well as with Alexandria. Washington City was growing faster, from 3,000 in 1800 to more than 18,000 in 1830. The construction of the Long Bridge from Virginia into the federal city, located where the 14th Street Bridge is today, had been hotly contested by Georgetowners who favored a bridge at the Three Sisters site just above their town. As predicted, the Long Bridge carried most Virginia business to Washington City rather than Georgetown, and its low construction caused silt from upstream to fill in the shipping channel to Georgetown, a problem that would persist throughout the century.

Concurrently, the tobacco trade sputtered and died. Soil exhaustion, damage to crops in the War of 1812, and navigation problems all contributed to its demise. The trade had peaked in 1792 and 1793 but was effectively finished with the death of the last of the large merchants, John Laird, in 1833. Though coastal shipping of wheat and other commodities continued, by the 1820s most of the international trade had been lost to Alexandria, with its more favorable position below the Long Bridge. Between 1830 and 1840 Georgetown's population dropped from about 8,000 to about 7,000, and the town submitted a petition for retrocession to Maryland, hoping affiliation with that state would help its economic position.

The local economy was saved, however, by a revival of the old dream of an improved waterway to the West. On July 4, 1828, the first spade of dirt was turned by President John Quincy Adams for the Chesapeake and Ohio (C&O) Canal, with Georgetown as its terminus. By 1850 it was completed to Cumberland, Maryland—short of its trans-Appalachian goal but long enough to make Georgetown a local and regional transshipment center for wheat, coal, lumber, and other commodities. By the 1850s coal dominated the trade; wooden trestles were constructed at the west end of the waterfront to carry the cargo from canal boat to sailing ship. The Pickrell, Libbey, and Wheatly families all developed significant lumber businesses on the riverbanks to the east. The waterpower created by the approximately 30-foot drop from canal to river combined with the influx of wheat to create another economic staple, milling. By 1860 there were 22 flour dealers and seven millers.

Until 1871 Georgetown existed for the most part politically, socially, and economically independent of the District of Columbia, of which it was a physical part. The town elected its own mayor and council. Unlike the new and more transient Washington City, Georgetown could claim some old families and social traditions that dated back to the eighteenth century. The fashionable Georgetown Assembly regularly attracted the cream of society to dances in the Pompean Hall of the Union Hotel. On Bridge Street (M Street) residents could do their banking, have their shoes made and fixed, and shop for food and clothing, harnesses, and feed. There were more than 80 such businesses listed in the 1850 census.

This Tidewater town was Southern in its population and social patterns. In 1810, the first year for which figures by race are available on Georgetown, 35 percent of the popula-

A Metropolitan line horse-drawn streetcar rounds the corner from O Street onto Wisconsin Avenue, N.W., around 1892. Streetcars brought shoppers from the farms and new suburbs of Virginia and Montgomery County, Maryland, to Georgetown, which served as a market town for the region at that time. Courtesy, Columbia Historical Society

tion was black, about two-thirds in slavery. By 1860 the percentage had dropped to 22 percent, and about one-third were in bondage. In a pattern that was also typical of Washington City, some blacks were able to achieve freedom through manumission, purchase, or other means before the Civil War. Despite legal and social restrictions, some members of the free black community managed to move from service and labor to craft, commercial, and professional occupations and to property ownership. One of the most successful was Alfred Lee, a feed dealer at 29th and M streets, who left his two sons more than $100,000 in real estate upon his death in 1868.

The black community formed its own strong institutions, such as Mt. Zion United Methodist Church, the oldest black congregation in the District, founded in 1816. Its church register notations suggest the trials of the community: "sold off," "lost," "taken away," "escaped." The black population, slave and free, was interspersed residentially with the white population before the Civil War in a pattern typical of Southern towns. In the late nineteenth century many blacks would settle in larger enclaves southeast of 28th and P streets, an area that came to be called Herring Hill, and on the other side of Wisconsin Avenue west of 33rd Street.

The coming of the Civil War brought severe strains to Georgetown, as it did to the entire District. Military activities disrupted shipping on the Potomac, and Confederate guerrillas vandalized the Maryland and northern Virginia stretches of the canal. Miss Lydia English's Georgetown Female Seminary, Georgetown College, the Union Hotel, and three Georgetown churches were commandeered for hospital space. As historian Mary Mitchell described in her study of Civil War Georgetown, the largely Southern population of the town engendered sharply divided loyalties. Even families were torn by the war; the son of William A. Gordon, the chief clerk of the U.S. Quartermaster Corps, for example, fought in the Confederate Army.

The end of Georgetown's governmental autonomy had roots in the Civil War. It soon became clear after the war that the three governments in the District—in Georgetown, Washington City, and Washington County—could not deal efficiently or effectively with the vast social and physical problems of the postwar capital. In 1871 Congress created one territorial government for the District, ending the separate franchises of Georgetown and Washington City. Although the idea at first met with vociferous objections from Georgetowners who valued their independence, the actual transition took place with surprisingly little turmoil.

The loss of its own government notwithstanding, Georgetown continued for approximately the next two decades to cling to its own social identity and customs and to maintain its own local economy. The town had a rich social life, regularly reported in the *Evening Star,* which ran the town's news under the name "Affairs in West Washington" in the 1880s but later beat a retreat and restored the older "Affairs in Georgetown" heading. There was an unparalleled number of clubs and societies devoted to literary pursuits, music, sports, civic betterment, bicycling, and any other interest one might pursue. There were the dances of the Georgetown Assembly, founded about 1810, and the Ladies German Club, as well as five dancing academies open to those of less prominence socially. A vast array of Masonic orders attracted as many as 200 to regular events. There were excur-

Members of the Potomac Boat Club, one of many social and recreational organizations in nineteenth-century Georgetown, pause for the camera in 1886. The schooners of the ice and coal trade are lined up at the Georgetown wharves in the background. Courtesy, Columbia Historical Society

sions and picnics up and down the river, sporting events on Analostan (now Roosevelt) Island, and rowing competitions out of the waterfront boat clubs.

The C&O Canal had its most successful years in the 1870s; historian Walter Sanderlin termed this the "golden age" of the canal. About 500 canal boats brought coal, limestone, flour, and other raw materials to the many waterfront industries in Georgetown. The cluster of mills, cooperages, iron foundries, and lime kilns, fertilizer manufacturers, carriage builders, and blacksmiths made the Georgetown waterfront one of the District's few centers of manufacturing. A Northeast coast trade in coal and ice beginning in the 1880s added new business to the waterfront. Sailing schooners brought ice from Maine rivers and returned with Cumberland coal that had come down the canal.

Meanwhile the number and variety of businesses along M Street grew. Many were run by European immigrants such as the Nordlinger brothers, Wolf and Isaac, who ran clothing and shoe stores across the street from each other in the 3100 block of M Street amid a cluster of Jewish merchants from Germany and France. There were also many Irish families on the street, often proprietors of saloons and groceries. In 1888 the Aqueduct Bridge, a privately owned venture since the 1830s, reopened as a public thoroughfare, without the tolls that had hindered trade with Virginia. Led by M Street businessmen, Georgetown celebrated with a massive parade featuring displays of 58 trades on 400 wagons pulled by 800 horses.

The prosperity of the town was reflected in the number of new houses erected late in the century, as many as 400 in the last decade, adding a fine array of Victorian structures to the Colonial and Federal scene, particularly north of P Street. The opening of the Curtis Public School in 1875 was a matter of great community pride; it also housed the town's first library, a gift of George Peabody, and the Linthicum Institute for the schooling of young workers.

It was the 1890s that saw Georgetown begin to shift in character from a small town to an urban neighborhood. First of all, its local economy, based on the transshipment of goods by canal boat and sailing ship and on the products of mills powered largely by waterwheels, had become outmoded in an age of railroads and steam. Many attempts by town leaders to get a rail line to the waterfront had been frustrated by Congress and the District commissioners, who seemed to discourage improvements that would help Georgetown compete with Washington City. Another example of this was the dredging of the Washington Channel in Southwest Washington in the 1880s, which created a protected

Power production and other industrial uses had taken over the Potomac riverfront by 1920, replacing its historic function as a port. The building materials and barges in the foreground are associated with the construction of Key Bridge, completed in 1922. Courtesy, National Archives

In 1935, when these boys created their own entertainment around a sidewalk tree box, Georgetown was like a comfortable small town, although generally considered unfashionable. Courtesy, Library of Congress, Prints and Photographs Division

harbor behind Hains Point. The Georgetown harbor, more exposed to damaging floods and ice floes, was now clearly inferior.

When Georgetown was hit with a massive flood in 1889, the vulnerability of its outdated economy became clear. The raging waters smashed boats and broke through the walls of the C&O Canal, putting hundreds of canal boatmen and waterfront craftsmen and laborers out of work. The C&O Canal Company went bankrupt, and control of the canal passed to none other than its major rival, the Baltimore and Ohio (B&O) Railroad, which had little interest in seeing the canal reopened with dispatch. It was two years before the C&O was in full operation again, and never again did it run at a profit. Some businesses such as the Borden Coal Company closed immediately after the flood. Several flour mills changed hands and then closed one by one, leaving only one flour mill and a paper mill by 1913.

By about 1915 the Georgetown waterfront was playing a very different role in the city. This shift was part of a larger pattern that emerged as the city grew to fill the District boundaries; different sections came to serve different urban functions. The center of old Washington City became the commercial downtown; the new suburban developments along the streetcar lines became the most desirable residential areas; the Southwest harbor became the District's major port; the railroad yards in Northeast Washington, the hub for transporting coal, lumber, produce, and other commodities once partially handled by Georgetown. By default, the waterfront of powerless Georgetown came to be given over to some of the city's least desirable functions: power production, meat rendering, and the storage of stone and other construction materials. A spur of the B&O Railroad finally came to K Street in 1911, but it was too little and too late to save the old town's role as transportation center. Smokestacks had replaced ships' masts on the skyline. In 1920 the city's first zoning ordinance labeled the Georgetown waterfront "industrial."

At the same time the old houses of Georgetown, many of which had no indoor plumbing or central heating, came to be considered out of style and uncomfortable, the neighborhood dowdy and unfashionable, a backwater in the suburban growth all around it. Georgetown was the hub of a network of new electric streetcars; four lines began to run out of town in all directions in the 1890s. Many Georgetowners went looking for more modern living arrangements in the suburbs of Virginia across the Aqueduct Bridge and elsewhere in the District. M Street, like the waterfront, began to serve more citywide and regional functions, as the streetcars made it a shopping street for the rural and suburban areas of Maryland, Virginia, and the District that did not yet have local services of their own.

Those who lived in Georgetown in the 1920s and 1930s remember it as a place considered unfashionable and run-down, but with a mixture of people, nearby shops and services, and an appealing quality of small-town living. A number of prominent old families remained. While suburban growth and new transportation patterns were encouraging the segregation of people by race and by class elsewhere in the city, Georgetown retained the intermixed population characteristic of Southern towns. The grand houses of the wealthy and elite stood side by side with the rowhouses of the middle class and the little wooden houses of the poor, occupied by both races. Black and white were physical neighbors, but their relationships were proscribed by social conventions. The black population did not increase, remaining between 20 and 30 percent as it had since 1830. However, the mixed nature of the population, both racial and economic, must have added to the sense that the place was out of date, as the separation of white from black, middle class from poor, and residential from commercial, was becoming the modern ideal.

But it was not long before newcomers to Washington rediscovered the charm of Georgetown's buildings and small-town character. According to a study by Dennis Gale, the roots of the preservation movement in Georgetown go back as far as the early 1920s when a group of homeowners, concerned about apartment and possible high-rise development near the new Q Street Bridge, took the first citizen action to protect the town's ambience. The move was led by Bernard Wyckoff and John Ihlder, new residents and employees of the national Chamber of Commerce who were familiar with the new tool of zoning. It took only a month for a small group of new residents and the old families they organized to push through a zoning amendment prohibiting construction over 40 feet high in Georgetown. Ihlder would later head the city's low-income-housing efforts as director of the Alley Dwelling Authority.

It was the New Deal, however, that spurred the preservation movement as highly educated, idealistic newcomers, attracted by Georgetown's low prices and charm and unconcerned about its social status, descended on the old town in droves in the 1930s. At 3238 R Street Benjamin Cohen, Thomas Corcoran, and other members of the Roosevelt Brain Trust met to fashion the social legislation that would revolutionize the federal government's role in American life. Among the newcomers were middle-level government employees as well as the socially elite; 117 Georgetown residents made the social register in 1929, according to Gale, and by 1932 the number had risen to 688.

By the late 1930s the focus had changed from remodeling to restoration. Led by the Progressive Citizens' Association, which was founded in 1926 by Etta Taggart and other women, the Georgetown community began to look for legal ways to protect the neighborhood's historic architecture. The war interrupted the movement, but in 1948 Eva Hinton and Harriet Hubbard spearheaded a successful rezoning that promoted residential uses in Georgetown. In 1949 Dorothea De Schweinitz drafted a bill to make Georgetown a historic district; a year later the Old Georgetown Act was passed by Congress. The law required that all exterior changes, demolitions, and new construction be reviewed by a panel of architects to be selected by the Fine Arts Commission.

The intensified restoration of buildings that followed ran parallel to a continued decline in the black population: 22 percent in 1940, 13 in 1950, 3 in 1960. It was a shift directly opposite that of the rest of the city, which changed from 28 percent black in 1940 to 54 percent in 1960. Pauline Gaskins Mitchell, one of the few black residents remaining today, recalls that black tenants were "ousted," while

many black homeowners chose to take advantage of attractive offers and moved elsewhere. Her own family roots in Georgetown go back more than 100 years. She has chosen to stay, but, according to Mitchell, her family is one of only about 15 black households that remain as of this writing.

While the Old Georgetown Act of 1950 has preserved the physical character of the town above M Street, protracted citizen battles over the future of the waterfront to the south ended with a court decision allowing high-rise, mixed commercial and residential buildings on the streets leading to the riverbank. Since the late 1970s modern construction has come to dominate the waterfront. While some old commercial buildings have been remodeled for reuse at the center of new developments, only pockets of its historic

Above: These late-eighteenth-century buildings at 30th and M streets, N.W., were saved by Historic Georgetown, Inc., a citizen group formed for that purpose in 1951. City street grading in the 1870s required the addition of a story at the bottom of the buildings, which originally were two stories. Courtesy, D.C. Public Library, Washingtoniana Division, c. Washington Post

Right: By 1949 the Georgetown waterfront south of M Street, N.W., right, had a mixture of industrial, commercial, and residential uses, an area then untouched by the preservation movement gaining strength to the north. The elevated Whitehurst Freeway, center, cut through this section in that year. Courtesy, National Archives

ambience remain. The elevated Whitehurst Freeway, constructed in 1949 parallel to the river above K Street, has also compromised the area's historic character.

As old family businesses, some having operated for two and three generations, closed along M Street and Wisconsin Avenue in the 1950s, they began to be replaced with antique shops and clothing boutiques. As the young, single population of Georgetown increased in the 1960s, so did the number of restaurants, bars, and trendy shops.

A lively street scene developed as shoppers and strollers mixed with Georgetown University students, hippies, vendors, and street musicians on M Street and Wisconsin Avenue. By the 1980s Georgetown had become a social center, especially for the young of the city and region. At the same time, exceptionally high real estate values changed its residential character; most young singles and families were priced out of the market, as were many small service businesses.

Georgetown's popularity as a shopping and entertainment mecca also brought traffic problems, and some blamed the congestion on Georgetown's lack of a subway stop. While many believe this omission was the result of active Georgetown opposition, the decision not to include the neighborhood in the system was a mixture of Georgetown ambivalence, economics, and technical concerns. The neighborhood was divided; local organizations took no stand for or against a subway. Metro planners and the influential National Capital Planning Commission did not advocate a Georgetown stop either. In the early 1960s, when the system was being designed, Georgetown was still an area of small specialized shops without the employment to merit a station, the planners believed. Furthermore, making a 90-degree turn to cross the Potomac from Foggy Bottom to Rosslyn, Virginia, by way of Georgetown, posed a serious technical problem. Whatever the key factors, an increasingly busy commercial Georgetown faces the 1980s without a link to the city's most modern public transportation system.

Thus, after several centuries of history, the old port town turned urban neighborhood continues to bear a strong identity. It may be considered by some a place set apart, but it has also become a symbol of the local aspects of life in a city dominated by national images. When the Washington Redskins win a major victory, it is at the city's oldest intersection, Wisconsin Avenue and M Street, and not somewhere downtown or on Capitol Hill, that residents spontaneously choose to celebrate.

A variety of shops and restaurants in nineteenth-century commercial buildings such as these on Wisconsin Avenue above M Street, N.W., attract strollers and shoppers from all over the metropolitan area. The street leads to the Potomac River in the distance. Photo by Paul Jaffe

2

CAPITOL HILL

THE CAPITOL IS JUST UP THE STREET

Ruth Ann Overbeck

Ornamental brickwork, made with the smooth machine-made bricks popular after the Civil War, embellishes many of the late nineteenth century rowhouses on the Hill. Courtesy, Washington Post, reprinted by permission of the D.C. Public Library

Map; Park System of the National Capital and Environs. National Park Service, 1962. Courtesy, D.C. Public Library, Washingtoniana Division

Capitol Hill—the very words conjure up a lofty seat of government. In Washington, D.C., however, the words mean not only the heights crowned by the nation's Capitol but also the adjoining neighborhood that occupies the broad expanse east of the Capitol building. Some say the Hill's boundaries have never extended past the three or four blocks nearest the Capitol, but documents dated as early as 1870 tagged privately owned buildings a mile east of the Capitol as "Capitol Hill." Other sources declare that the community encompasses all the land east of the Capitol, from the shoreline arc of the Anacostia River to the end of the Hill's northern descent—almost four square miles.

The neighborhood's close relationship with the nation's seat of power has continued in various forms throughout its almost 200-year history. Its residents have ranged from the workmen who built the Capitol to Thomas Jefferson, from congressmen to Navy Yard craftsmen. Many residents have had no association at all with the federal government, except for living with the Capitol as a backdrop for their daily lives. Although federal activities on the Hill have expanded to claim some of its oldest buildings, the neighborhood has survived its proximity to power. Its largely nineteenth-century buildings remain intact to house a varied population in a comfortable residential neighborhood just steps from the Capitol of the nation.

When it was selected as the location of the Capitol building in 1791, Capitol Hill was farmland. Descendants of the Rozier-Young-Carroll family had owned much of the area for almost a century. The family had farmed the land

For this jogger on East Capitol Street, the nation's most familiar symbol is just part of the daily scene. Photo by Emily Medvec

with slaves, but beginning in 1770 had attempted to attract developers to it. Daniel Carroll "of Duddington," as he was known, stood to profit most from the arrival of the federal government. Pierre L'Enfant, the Frenchman credited with the federal city's design, called a sharp rise on Carroll's land "a pedestal awaiting a monument" and reserved it for the Capitol. His plan faced the Capitol eastward, toward the pedestal's broad top. Consequently, land speculators such as George Walker, a Scottish merchant who lived in Philadelphia, assumed that much of the city's residential and commercial development would occur on the hilltop and invested accordingly.

The Capitol was slow to rise, however, and the community around it lagged as well. There was little money available, and there were too few skilled men and laborers in the District to build the Capitol, much less a whole city. Maryland and Virginia supplied many of the construction workers for the Capitol, native and foreign-born whites, free and enslaved blacks. Others came from the Northern states and from Europe. These men, with or without their families, joined the old rural population to constitute the Hill's first community. Most newcomers chose to live within walking distance of their work; some lived right on the Capitol grounds in wooden barracks. Others moved into private houses that were little better than shanties. The houses of master craftsmen, supervisors, and surveyors usually were more solid, most often two-story frame buildings with steep gable roofs. Whether frame or brick, the buildings

Above: The descendants of Daniel Carroll gathered on the steps of Duddington, the family mansion, for a rare 1862 photograph. Courtesy, Library of Congress

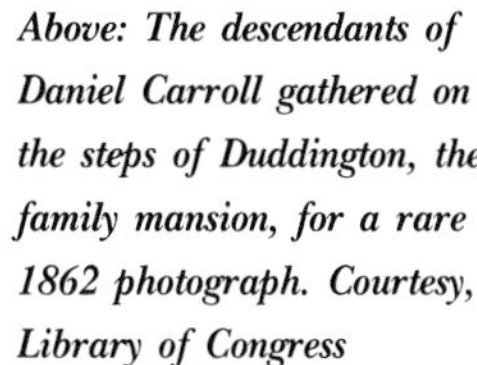

Below left: These croquet players were photographed on the lawn of The Maples in the late nineteenth century when it was the home of journalist Emily Edson Briggs. Built between 1795 and 1797 by William Mayne Duncanson, it stands today as Friendship House at 619 D Street, S.E. Courtesy, Junior League of Washington

This is the first known photo (a daguerrotype) of the Capitol. Attributed to John Plumbe, Jr., it shows the east front about 1846. Courtesy, Library of Congress, Prints and Photographs Division

tended to look alike, with multipaned windows flanked by shutters, rectangularly paneled wooden doors, and shingled roofs.

In keeping with his prominence as one of the capital city's original landowners, Carroll built Capitol Hill's first mansion, named Duddington. While Duddington was under construction, L'Enfant discovered that it projected onto the street line of his proposed New Jersey Avenue. He ordered it removed, but Carroll resisted. L'Enfant's decision to raze the building himself, in one of a series of disputes with the District commissioners, contributed to his being fired as the city's chief engineer. Carroll rebuilt the Georgian-style brick mansion nearby, and it became a gathering place for a fledgling Washington society. Within two decades, however, Carroll was disillusioned by the city's failure to live up to his expectations and spent the rest of his life as an embittered recluse.

Only a handful of other Hill residents could afford mansions like Carroll's. These Englishmen, who had amassed fortunes in the East India trade, established wharves along the Eastern Branch (now the Anacostia River) to develop a new, Washington-based East India trade. Most faded into obscurity before they could give substance to their plans, but two of them, Thomas Law and William Mayne Duncanson, made their mark in the new city. Law married one of George Washington's step-granddaughters, lived on the Hill, and erected at least 10 of its buildings. Law had three young Anglo-Indian sons who came with him from India, the first Hill residents known to descend from ancestors who were neither western Europeans nor Africans. Their Indian mother remains a mystery.

Duncanson enjoyed such enormous wealth when he arrived in the federal city that his servants wore full livery and his wine cellar reputedly rivaled that of his friend Thomas Jefferson. By 1800, however, his ill-fated real estate investments led to bankruptcy. He died a few years later, almost a pauper. Today only The Maples (now Friendship House), Duncanson's mansion built in 1795-1797 six blocks southeast of the Capitol, remains as physical evidence of the East India group's presence on the Hill.

In 1799 Capitol Hill gained a second nucleus: the Navy Yard. George Washington personally approved its site on the Eastern Branch's west bank, almost two miles above the river's confluence with the Potomac. Sheltered from the view of ships coming up the Potomac, the site was presumed to provide U.S. warships the element of surprise necessary to defend the federal city against invasion by sea. The yard's other purpose was to build those warships, and it quickly earned the reputation as one of the town's most reliable employers. Because it hired whoever had the needed skills, many black and immigrant craftsmen and laborers achieved financial independence working there.

When the federal government moved to the District of Columbia in 1800, only one wing of the Capitol had been built. A Connecticut congressman described it as a shining object in dismal contrast to its surroundings. Congressmen and Vice President Thomas Jefferson took rooms at the few boardinghouses and taverns scattered in the "dismal" blocks nearest the Capitol. Later, as president, Jefferson located the U.S. Marine Barracks near the Navy Yard and then added to the Hill's ethnic diversity by sending to Italy for musicians to be members of "the President's Own"—the U.S. Marine Band.

By 1810 gable-roofed houses, shops, smithies, a farmers' market, the Masonic Naval Lodge (#4), and Episcopal, Presbyterian, and Methodist congregations were flourishing on the Hill. They dotted a crescent of development that swept generally southeast from the Capitol to the Navy Yard and Marine Barracks. The heaviest concentration of buildings surrounded the Navy Yard, because of its year-round employment opportunities. A mile farther east, the public alms house and Congressional Cemetery took shape. Private schools for white children, including one sponsored by the Masons, opened near the Navy Yard. In 1807 three former slaves—George Bell, a carpenter, and Moses Liverpool and Nicholas Franklin, caulkers at the Navy Yard—established a school for black children. And in 1808 the city established Eastern Academy for impoverished white children living east of the Capitol. Despite a growing population,

Private citizens, influential Hill residents among them, financed this structure to house Congress and encourage the federal government to stay in Washington after the British burned the Capitol in 1814. It was a political prison when this Civil War period photo was taken. The Supreme Court now stands on this site. Courtesy, National Archives

empty blocks far outnumbered those with even one building on them. This open land was available to anyone, regardless of race, color, or creed, who had the money to buy or lease it.

Congress' cyclical sitting, after fall harvest and before spring planting, punctuated time for the Hill. In August 1814 the British almost ended these cycles. When they invaded Washington by land instead of by sea, the British soldiers' first stop was Capitol Hill. They burned and looted the Capitol and camped on its grounds. The commandant of the U.S. Navy, acting on orders, set fire to the yard and the ships being built there. Most civilians either fled the city or added to the chaos. Some who lived near the Navy Yard became so angry with the failure of the government to protect their lives, their homes, and their jobs that they looted the few buildings within the yard that had escaped the flames.

Washington's failure to defend itself rankled Americans everywhere. Congress met in September and immediately proposed moving the capital from Washington City to some "more convenient and less dishonored place," as Congressman Charles J. Ingersoll later wrote. Thirty-eight local citizens, including Daniel Carroll and Thomas Law, acted quickly. Using their own funds, they erected a large brick building on the site now occupied by the Supreme Court and offered it to Congress. The federal government decided to stay, and Congress used the "Brick Capitol" until it moved back to the U.S. Capitol across the street in 1819.

Capitol Hill spent the years from 1820 to 1850 in relative quiet. Its population grew; residents formed a Roman Catholic church and the Methodists split into two congregations, one white, one black. East Capitol Street, however, the street that led straight east from the Capitol's principal door, remained so undeveloped that part of it was used for horse races. Numerous families augmented their incomes by selling vegetables raised on nearby empty lots at local markets. The Eastern Branch proved too shallow for the new ship designs, so the Washington Navy Yard turned increasingly to armament design and manufacturing. The remodeled Brick Capitol joined the boardinghouses that served the Congress in its seasonal sittings.

Newcomers to the Hill in this period included both white and black Americans as well as a wave of German, Irish, and southern European immigrants, all of whom came to seek a new life in the capital. Many were talented building artisans and craftsmen who worked on the Capitol's expansion in the 1850s and 1860s. Some found jobs elsewhere or went into business for themselves. Antonio Sousa of Portugal chose the Marines. He and his Bavarian-born wife, Elizabeth, gave Capitol Hill a citizen of the world: their son John Philip Sousa, the "March King," wrote "Stars and Stripes Forever" and many other internationally known compositions.

With the advent of the Civil War, the Union Army commandeered every public building, including the Capitol, and many private ones as well. The government built a temporary hospital on East Capitol Street near today's Lincoln Park. The old Brick Capitol became a prison for Southern soldiers, contrabands, spies, cashiered Union officers, and as many as 200 political prisoners at a time. Wartime needs also led to Washington's first horse-drawn streetcar lines in 1862, one of the three linking the Navy Yard, the Capitol, and the White House.

Many Washingtonians sympathized with the South. When the Episcopal bishop of Washington ordered his clergymen to read a prayer of thanksgiving for the District's deliverance from the Confederates' blockade and siege in 1861, some flatly refused. Perhaps the most ironic refusal came from the Reverend J. Morsell of Christ Church near the Navy Yard—then the official congregation of the Marine Barracks. Nonetheless, throughout the war Christ Church's bell tower served as a Union lookout post.

At the Navy Yard the men manufactured armaments and refitted and repaired ships as they docked. The submarine U.S.S. *Monitor* thrilled the Navy Yard and the entire neighborhood when it arrived on October 2, 1862, for alterations and repairs. William F. Keeler, the submarine's paymaster, wrote, "The 'Monitor' & her officers are the lions of the day . . . no caravan or circus ever collected such a crowd."

Washington's wartime prosperity and population boom brought new investors to the Hill. Wealthy Philadelphia tugboat manufacturer and speculator Stephen Flanagan built a row of 16 attached houses a block off East Capitol Street and a mile east of the Capitol. Called Philadelphia Row, the buildings had flat fronts of innovative machine-made "pressed" bricks. The bricks' smooth surfaces and crisp edges contrasted visibly with the coarser texture of older ones and would replace them in most construction on the Hill, and across the city, after the war. Flat roofs invisible from the streets, modest brackets at the cornice line, four-panel doors, and larger windowpanes further distinguished Philadelphia Row from its Hill forebears. The row's location, well outside the old crescent, anticipated by at least 30 years a new center of population for the Hill.

During the early 1870s the city government provided funds for a new public market and placed it equidistant from the Capitol and the Navy Yard but outside the original crescent of development. German immigrant Adolph Cluss was selected to design it. The handsome red-brick Eastern Market stood almost alone at first, but new buildings filled countless lots by 1900. Many were the first ever built on their site; some replaced earlier structures.

Most of the new buildings were two- or three-story single-family residences for Washington's growing middle class, a signal that the same forces that shaped Washington's post-Civil War suburbs also changed Capitol Hill. The city was growing rapidly as the federal government increased in importance and required more workers. At the same time new public transportation networks allowed some people new options in choosing a residence; they no longer had to live within walking distance of their work. In Washington as in other American cities at this time, residential areas began to separate by race and by class, and neighborhoods became more uniform. Northwest Washington increasingly attracted the most affluent. Capitol Hill appealed to the middle-income home buyer, a growing category of people in Washington ever since the Civil Service Reform Act of 1883 ended the whims of the spoils system and made government employment more secure.

Thus the men who built the Capitol Hill houses during this era, most Hill residents themselves, tended to aim their projects at the white middleclass market. The neighborhood's established black families, such as George Bell's descendants, persisted in their pre-Civil War houses or in new ones they built on individual lots. Most of the post-Civil War developers' long

The main entrance to the Navy Yard dominated the intersection of 8th and M streets, S.E., in the late nineteenth century. The Navy Yard was created in 1799 both to help defend the capital and to construct the nation's warships. Courtesy, Columbia Historical Society

With the appearance of some authority, these Navy Yard employees posed amidst the machinery in the late nineteenth century. The world's largest armament manufacturer by 1890, the Yard was one of Washington's few heavy industries. Courtesy, D.C. Public Library, Washingtoniana Division

rows, however, were closed to them for at least half a century.

Between 1875 and 1895, Charles Gessford, one of the city's prolific builders, built more houses on the Hill than anyone else. A Maryland native, Gessford began his building career in Washington as a carpenter's apprentice, then made the transition from carpenter to builder and speculator. He excelled at building marketable rowhouses. Once he found a house "formula" that worked, he repeated it over and over, usually with a square-cornered projecting bay that stretched from ground to sky, always in red pressed brick, and often with stone trim. Gessford further enhanced his most expensive houses with stained-glass window and door transoms and slate roofs.

Capitol Hill's young set socialized at Augustus C. Taylor's drugstore at 2nd and Maryland Avenue, N.E., in 1906, all dressed up either for a special occasion, or for the photographer. Courtesy, Columbia Historical Society

While residences accounted for most of the Hill's new buildings, for about 30 years the Hill sprouted churches, one every third block or so. German Catholics led the way in 1868 with St. Joseph's, two blocks from the Capitol. In 1882 Calvin Brent, Washington's first black architect, designed Mt. Jezreel Baptist Church for a black congregation whose members resided primarily in the old crescent between the Capitol and the Navy Yard. Black members of St. Peter's Catholic Church, who had been excluded from full participation in the church, were granted their own parish, St. Cyprian's, in 1893. Most churches in the neighborhood and in the city had separated into black and white congregations long before.

Although most of the Hill's nationally known, nineteenth-century residents were men, journalist Emily Edson Briggs was an exception. After moving from Iowa to Washington in 1861 with her husband, she wrote an anonymous letter to the *Washington Chronicle* protesting the newspaper's allegations that women government clerks were inefficient. That letter led to a newspaper career that lasted for 40 years and included hundreds of nationally published columns written under the pen name "Olivia." When she became a widow in 1872, Briggs bought Duncanson's old mansion, The Maples, and resided there until she died, in 1910.

By 1898 the Navy Yard had become the world's largest ordnance production and engineering-research center. It remained one of the city's largest employers for almost 50 years. Its demand for unskilled labor helped a new immigrant group establish an American foothold; the old buildings outside its walls provided affordable housing. Capitol Hill's new eastern European Jewish population sold kosher food, opened haberdashery stores, and formed the Southeast Hebrew congregation, all within four blocks of the Navy Yard's main gate.

Construction fell off dramatically

during the depression of 1893. When it began to pick up momentum in the first decades of the twentieth century, developers concentrated on empty land north and east of the older sections. At first, red brick was still the material of choice, but the bayfront facades were swept almost clean of ornamentation. Front doors contained a single expansive pane of beveled-edge glass, and concrete steps took the place of iron. By World War I fashion dictated flat fronts, often with a roofed porch jutting from the front of each house. New materials came with the new styles: rough-surfaced bricks in pale shades of yellow and gray, topped with red tiled roofs.

The Hill's population swelled to the bursting point from the onset of World War I through World War II. Although the area gained a few new shops and apartments in this period, many of the Hill's streets retained their first buildings. Some dramatic changes took place, however, near the Capitol. From the 1870s the Hill had suffered some attrition of its earliest buildings, most of it at the behest of the federal government. Thomas Law's and Daniel Carroll's buildings near the Capitol fell to make room for congressional office buildings and the Library of Congress, and the Supreme Court occupied the site of the old Brick Capitol. Also, one of the Hill's oldest remaining residences, The Maples, underwent major alterations in 1937 to become the headquarters of Friendship House. The agency had originated elsewhere in 1904 to provide social services to the Navy Yard area's working poor "latchkey" children, and to non-English-speaking immigrants.

Most of the Hill's late eighteenth- and early nineteenth-century buildings remained unchanged, however, and began to catch the eye of the early restoration movement after World War II. By 1949, for example, Justice William O. Douglas had bought one of Capitol Hill's historic houses. Foggy Bottom and Capitol Hill were the first of Washington's neighborhoods to follow in the footsteps of the earlier preservation movement in Georgetown.

Early restoration took place within a mile east of the Capitol and coincided with major changes in the demography of the Hill in its largest definition. Its middle-class population, black and white, began to move away, lured by suburbia, VA loans, and newer housing in neighborhoods farther from the center of the city, some newly opened to blacks by the 1948 Supreme Court ruling declaring housing covenants unconstitutional. Many of these people had held blue-collar jobs with good wages at the Navy Yard, but these jobs became less plentiful when the yard stopped manufacturing weapons after the war. At the same time, low-income families, mostly black, who had been displaced by the Southwest Urban Renewal project, moved into the Hill's older run-down

The elaborate Italian Renaissance-style Library of Congress, completed in 1897 at the western edge of the Capitol Hill neighborhood, looms over the tree-shaded streets of the community The partially-clothed statue of George Washington on East Capitol Street, left, was later removed to the Smithsonian because it was offensive to turn-of-the-century sensibilities. Courtesy, National Archives

Shops along Pennsylvania Avenue, S.E., serve employees of the nearby offices of Congress as well as residents of the Hill. The original Library of Congress building is seen in the background. Photo by Emily Medvec

houses or into public housing on the Hill's fringes. Adding to the mix were the young families and singles, mostly white and upwardly mobile, who began to invest in and restore the houses between the Capitol and Lincoln Park. By 1960 the economic and racial mix had tipped to one that was less middle-class black and white to one that included more low-income black and middle- to upper-income white.

By the 1970s the Hill had acquired a reputation for civic activism, as new residents, dedicated to urban living, organized to shape their community. Their achievements were legion. Successes included defeat of federal projects to turn East Capitol Street into a boulevard of federal offices and to split the community with a freeway. Persistence integrated some public schools, revitalized Eastern Market and the police station, and defeated plans to construct the tallest high rise in the city at Pennsylvania Avenue and 14th Street. Residents also established annual events such as the House and Garden Tour, begun in 1957 by the Capitol Hill Restoration Society, the city's longest continuous tour. Church banners have led the annual Easter parade sponsored by the Capitol Hill Group Ministry for more than 20 years, and some 55,000 people annually attend Market Day, sponsored by Friendship House, and the Octoberfest, organized by The Capitol Hill Association of Merchants and Professionals. In 1976 residents gained historic district status for a large portion of the neighborhood nearest the Capitol, one of the largest districts in the nation with more than 8,000 primary buildings.

Capitol Hill today continues its history of diversity. It has single-family houses, condominiums, and group homes. It has shops, places of worship, and institutions. Although the area of the Hill nearest the Capitol has become increasingly white and middle- to upper-middle-class, the residents of the entire neighborhood represent every race and almost every nation. It is still a place where a U.S. senator, a former national president of the Young Republicans, three generations of welfare recipients, a retired letter carrier, an electrician, an artist, attorneys, journalists, and Hill staffers all live on one block. It is a rare mixture of people with very local, as well as national and international, concerns. It is in some ways an urban neighborhood like any other—except that the Capitol is just up the street.

AUTO
REPAIR
SERVICE
619

3

7th Street Downtown

An Evolving Commercial Neighborhood

Alison K. Hoagland

Handsome residences such as this brick row house that still stands at 617 H Street, N.W., were very near the 7th Street commercial corridor. Courtesy, Columbia Historical Society

Map; City of Washington, 1848. Courtesy, Library of Congress

Washington's downtown presents many faces. To some it is a place of business: blocky new office buildings of glass and concrete, filled daily from nine to five with workers. To others it is a place for shopping, with glitzy department stores and modest, single-purpose small businesses. To yet others it is home, a neighborhood filled with older brick rowhouses. Indeed, downtown has always been a neighborhood, although much more so in the nineteenth century, when shopkeepers and government clerks of necessity lived close to their places of work. With the introduction of the horsecars in the 1860s and electric streetcars in the 1880s, however, downtown became more commercial as many people moved away from their work to quieter locations. The impact on downtown was dramatic and is reflected in the changing fortunes of its buildings and the constantly changing character of its resident population.

Downtown is geographically centered north of the Mall between the White House and the Capitol. Three major streets, Pennsylvania Avenue and F and 7th streets, traverse this district. The most impressive boulevard, Pennsylvania Avenue, runs at an angle from the Capitol to the White House and lies in the lowest part of downtown, near the former Tiber Creek. Stretching through the heart of downtown, F Street is situated on a distinct ridge, a feature that made it one of the area's earliest passable streets. Sev-

Today a treasured landmark on Pennsylvania Avenue halfway between the White House and the Capitol, the Old Post Office was threatened with demolition almost as soon as it was built in 1899. It was finally saved in the early 1980s. Courtesy, National Archives

enth Street extends from the rolling hills of distant Maryland over the hillocks of downtown, finally descending to the lowlands of Pennsylvania Avenue, and then across the Mall to the Potomac River wharves.

In the nineteenth century Pennsylvania Avenue was the most important commercial address in the city, but so few buildings remain from this period that its historic character has been lost. Today F Street is the primary commercial street of downtown, but until the 1880s it was best known as a fine residential street and did not reach its prime as a shopping area until the 1920s. But it is 7th Street that was developed from the start as a commercial street, still is commercial today, and retains much of its historic ambience. Part of the neighborhood that grew up to support it survives today east of 7th Street, north of G Street.

Seventh Street was one of the most important thoroughfares of the early city. Farmers from Maryland and Washington County, outside of the L'Enfant city, brought their goods into town and to the waterfront via 7th Street. Until 1845 Pennsylvania Avenue, N.W., was the only paved street in the city, and that was done at federal expense. In 1845, however, 7th Street was paved with cobblestones from Virginia Avenue, S.W., to H Street, N.W., making it the first street paved by city authorities. In 1862 the first three horsecar lines opened, and one of these ran on 7th Street. On May 12, 1890, when this line was converted from horsecars to cable cars, the line ran three-and-a-half miles from Fort McNair in Southwest to Boundary Street (now Florida Avenue). At the streetcar's northern terminus was a resort known as the Maryland House, which was demolished in 1914 for the construction of Griffith Stadium, the

Outdoor food stands such as this one photographed about 1910 spilled out into the streets adjacent to Center Market, the city's largest public market that stretched from 7th to 9th streets along the south side of Pennsylvania Avenue, N.W. Courtesy, D.C. Public Library, Washingtoniana Division

The Center Market at the foot of 7th Street on Pennsylvania Avenue, N.W., drew a diverse crowd to its indoor and outdoor stalls. This young man is offering his wares to Secretary of Agriculture Henry C. Wallace and his wife in 1922. Courtesy, Library of Congress, Prints and Photographs Division

city's American League baseball field. With the introduction of the automobile, 7th Street continued to be a thoroughfare, and today, less visibly, the Yellow and Green lines of Metrorail follow the historic pattern underground.

The reason for much of this activity on 7th Street, particularly at 7th and Pennsylvania, was the construction of Center Market in 1801. Center Market served as the city's produce supply center and, according to historian Washington Topham, "was probably the principal factor in the drawing of business interests away from the vicinity of the Capitol." By 1870 more than 100 businesses operated in the market, with another 40-odd in the immediate vicinity. The sidewalks near Market Square generally measured 30 feet in width to accommodate the vendors and shoppers. Market days were Tuesdays, Thursdays, and Saturdays. Yokes of oxen brought farm products from the east by way of Pennsylvania Avenue, while farmers bringing goods down 7th Street often stopped overnight at James Shreve's livery stable on 7th between H and I. Another large public market on 7th Street, Northern Liberty at Mt. Vernon Square, operated from 1846 to 1872, adding to the street's importance as a commercial thoroughfare.

In 1870 Center Market was destroyed by fire but was immediately rebuilt. Designed by the prominent German-born architect Adolph Cluss, the enormous new turreted brick structure that filled two city blocks opened in July 1872. After expansion in the 1880s the market had indoor stalls for 1,000 vendors and outside space for 300 farm wagons; it was open six days a week, from dawn until noon. Center Market continued to offer fresh meat, poultry, fish, and vegetables until it was removed in 1931 for construction of the National Archives Building.

The location of important federal buildings along 7th Street insured the development of downtown as an office and residential district as well as a commercial center. Blodgett's Hotel, constructed in 1793 at 8th and E streets, was used as the U.S. Post Office and Patent Office from 1810 until the hotel burned down in 1836. In that year construction started on the Patent Office, which today houses the National Museum of American Art and the National Portrait Gallery. When it was finished in 1867 the Patent Office covered the blocks bounded by 7th, F, 9th, and G streets. Simultaneously, the General Post Office was built on the block just to the south, bounded by 7th, E, 8th, and F streets. Besides influencing temporary construction workers to settle nearby, the finished offices encouraged further settlement by people who wanted to live close to their work.

Before the Civil War, Washington's commercial and residential buildings were similar in appearance: two- or three-story brick buildings, two or three bays (windows) wide, with a gable roof or, by the 1850s, a flat roof. Often only the storefront would give away a commercial building's purpose. Shopkeepers usually lived above their stores.

Most early downtown residents earned a living as merchants, clerks, and building tradesmen. The merchants, such as William M. Shuster, who ran a dry goods store at 38 Market Space and lived at 617 H Street, owned shops of all sorts on the busier streets or in the market houses. Government clerks worked in the government offices nearby: in 1853 Horatio King was a principal clerk in the Post Office and lived at 707 H Street. With the amount of construction occurring downtown, it is not surprising that builders also lived there, such as James Towles, who according to the city directory lived and worked at 807 H Street as a "measurer of carpenter's and builder's work in general, and real estate agent." Living in brick rowhouses with gable roofs and with entrances several steps above the street, such middle-class merchants, clerks, and building craftsmen were responsible for the construction of Washington.

Not everyone was a homeowner,

Seventh Street, N.W., was in transition in 1867. The handsome Federal-style DeKrafft house had been converted to commercial use, and a cast-iron-fronted office building, the May Building, was under construction next door at 7th and E. Courtesy, Library of Congress, Prints and Photographs Division

Above: Mon Soey Lee occupied the former Mary Surratt house at 604 H Street, N.W., in 1981, where his Soey Sang Long Grocery had been in business for 40 years. Courtesy, D.C. Public Library, Washingtoniana Division, c. Washington Post

Right: Mary Surratt was hanged for her part in the conspiracy to assassinate President Abraham Lincoln, plotted in this placid row house. Once run as a boardinghouse by Mrs. Surratt, the structure stands today at 604 H Street, N.W., as a typical example of a pre-Civil War downtown residential building, with its gable roof and raised side-hall entrance. Courtesy, Columbia Historical Society

however. Because of the part-time nature of Congress and general uncertainty about the viability of the capital before the Civil War, boardinghouses were a common form of residence. One of the more notorious boardinghouse proprietors was Mary Surratt, who was hanged for conspiracy in the assassination of President Lincoln. But in many ways her circumstances and boardinghouse were typical. The Surratts owned a plantation and a tavern in Maryland, and after the death of her husband and the outbreak of the Civil War, Mary Surratt, in reduced circumstances, moved to their house in Washington, at 604 H Street, and began renting rooms. One account of the testimony at her trial reveals the way her house, a typical gable-roofed brick rowhouse, was used:

A narrow three-story and attic structure, it had a high, outside flight of stairs leading up to the front door, and sat back from the street behind a row of large trees. On the street floor a hall led to the dining room and beyond it to the kitchen. On the second

The center of the downtown German community's spiritual life was St. Mary's Catholic Church at 5th and H streets, N.W., where confessions were heard in German until about 1961. Taken about 1900, this view down 5th Street shows the congregation's second church building, which was built in 1890. The rectory was to the left, and the gable-fronted school building, to the right, was replaced by a new one in 1906. Courtesy, Library of Congress, Prints and Photographs Division

floor Mrs. Surratt's room was actually the back parlor, separated from the parlor in front of it only by folding doors . . . On the third floor . . . the Holahans had the front bedroom, directly over the front parlor, their daughter sleeping in a small room close by. Weichmann slept in a room back of the Holahans'. In the attic . . . Miss Anna Surratt and her cousin, Olivia Jenkins, slept when the latter was in town. Miss Fitzpatrick slept with Mrs. Surratt. When John H. Surratt was in town, he slept with Weichmann.

The formal entrance to parlors on the second floor, with the dining room and kitchen on the first floor, is characteristic of these rowhouses.

By the time of the Civil War, downtown was nearly completely built up and the frontage of 7th Street had few gaps. Very few of these pre-Civil War commercial buildings remain, however; instead, the buildings in the 7th Street area today date largely from the latter half of the nineteenth century. These residential and commercial buildings were taller and more ornamented than before the war, with elaborate cornices of wood, cast iron, or pressed metal. As the building styles changed, so did their occupants: a growing minority of German immigrants began to make its presence felt on 7th Street.

In 1850 only 11 percent of Washington's population was foreign born, but of that group nearly 30 percent was from Germany. By 1860 the foreign-born population had risen to 17 percent, 26 percent of whom came from Germany and Austria. The German community was not concentrated in downtown; in fact, there were thriving communities in Foggy Bottom and Southwest. But Germans tended to work as dry goods merchants and craftsmen, and because of that many congregated near 7th Street.

The impact of German merchants on downtown is well illustrated in the 700 block of 7th Street between G and H streets. The east side has been completely demolished, but the west side retains an ensemble of three- and four-story brick commercial buildings that have changed little since the last was built in 1913. The names of the original owners reflect the German community: Herman Gasch, August and Henry Schmedtie, Henry Sievers, Frederick Schmeir. Their businesses, too, were typical: jewelers, dry goods retailers, grocers, confectioners, furniture merchants. This pattern continued up 7th Street.

Typical of these new German merchants was Anton Eberly, who opened his stove and home furnishings store in 1868 at 718 7th Street, where he also lived. In 1881 he built a new store, one that proudly bore his name, on the same site. That same year he started construction on a three-story house two blocks away at 740 5th Street, where he moved in 1883 and lived until his death in 1907. Active in the German community, Eberly served as the first treasurer of the Saengerbund, a singing society founded in 1851, and remained involved for the next 50 years.

The German community's spiritual life found expression in St. Mary's German Catholic Church, still in existence at 5th and H streets. The land was donated by early Washington mayor John P. Van Ness specifically for the erection of such a church, probably to attract Germans, who had a reputation for being industrious and hardworking, to a part of the city where Van Ness owned land he wished to develop. The original church was replaced in 1890 by a handsome stone structure designed by E. Francis Baldwin of Baltimore. A school, rectory, and orphanage were built next to it, indicating this German-language church's community involvement. Although Sunday announcements in German were discontinued during the anti-German fervor of World War I, at which time the German-born priest of St. Mary's was banished from the city, confessions were heard in German as late as 1961.

Three synagogues in a six-block area indicated a sizable Jewish minority. In the mid-nineteenth century the Jewish population was largely of German origin and maintained close ties to the Christian Germans. In 1860 there were fewer than 200 Jews in Washington out of a total population of 75,000, but by 1910 there were more than 5,000. In 1860, 29 of the 51 employed males were merchants, which explains their settlement near the commercial core of 7th Street.

The Washington Hebrew Congregation was founded in 1852 and 11 years later bought a church building from the Methodist Episcopal Church, South, on 8th Street between H and I, on land that had been donated to the Presbyterians by John P. Van Ness. The church underwent several alterations in 1863 and again in the 1880s, until it was replaced in 1897 by the present onion-domed structure. In 1869 a second Jewish congregation was formed, Adas Israel, which built its synagogue at 6th and G streets in 1876. After 30 years of growth this congregation built a new, vaguely Byzantine-style synagogue two blocks north at 6th and I streets. The old synagogue, when threatened with demolition in 1969, was moved to 3rd and G streets, where it serves as the Lillian and Albert Small Jewish Museum of Washington.

Albert Small, who was born in 1902 at 725 5th Street, recalled the importance of Adas Israel:

The neighborhood was our whole lives in those days. The synagogue was the focal point. We went to school at Seaton, and we took music lessons in St. Mary's, across the street from our house. We used to help in the family stores two blocks away. I did belong to a Herzl Club in the YMHA at 11th and Pennsylvania but that was about the only time we left the neighborhood . . .

Small's father, Isidore, had a hardware store at 713 7th Street. Open from 8 a.m. to 6 p.m., and 8 a.m. to 10 p.m. on Saturdays, "It was a fairly well-ordered store. In those days, everybody had some of their merchandise outside, for show." Albert Small described the area: "Seventh Street was a wide street. It had streetcar tracks. Everyone kept about the same hours. The temple played a very predominant part in their lives. Almost all of the merchants were Jewish." He also noted that the area around St. Mary's was predominantly German, except for Washington Street, which ran through the block that the Government Accounting Office building now occupies, whose residents were black.

Some Jewish merchants were immensely successful. Max and Gustave Lansburgh, sons of one of the first cantors at Washington Hebrew Congregation, came to Washington from Baltimore in about 1860 and started a dry goods store on 7th Street between H and I, moving to 406 7th Street in 1866. In 1882 they moved up the block and developed their business into one of the major department stores in early twentieth-century Washington. Other German and German-Jewish department stores included Saks and Co., at 7th and Market Space (1867-1932); Kann and Sons, at 8th and Market Space (1886-1975); and the Hecht Co., at 7th and F (1896-1985).

By the turn of the century 7th Street had become the commercial core of Washington. Samuel Dodek, who was born in 1902 and whose father had a clothing store on 7th Street between H and I, recalled:

It was probably the leading business street in those days. F Street hadn't been developed, and Connecticut Avenue was a residential area. This was the business street. Kann's department store was there, Hecht's, and the Patent Office, and the Public Library, the Carnegie Library. That was the center of business, and the library was the center of culture, because Washington's degree of culture, in those days, just went about as far as the library.

Germans were by no means the only ethnic group in downtown, but because of their visibility as merchants they had the most impact. One estimate of immigrants in 1880 in downtown puts the number of German and eastern European Jews at 700, all other Germans at 1,100, and Irish at 1,050. The Irish, who often served as hard laborers in Washington, settled in a marshy area called "Swampoodle," northeast of Massachusetts and New Jersey avenues.

In 1920 Russians, both Jews and Gentiles, formed the largest immigrant group in Northwest Washington, reflecting the recent upheavals in their homeland. Eastern European Jews flocked to a thriving downtown community in Washington, where the predominantly eastern European congregation, Chai Adom, had been founded in 1886. In 1906 Chai Adom purchased the Assembly Presbyterian Church at 5th and I streets. The congregation, renamed Ohev Sholom, replaced the steeple of the picturesque wooden church with a dome. One observer saw

W.B. Moses attracted well-heeled clients such as this Mrs. Proctor to his drygoods emporium in the central business corner of early Washington, the intersection of 7th and Pennsylvania Avenue, N.W., just across from the busy Center Market. Courtesy, Columbia Historical Society

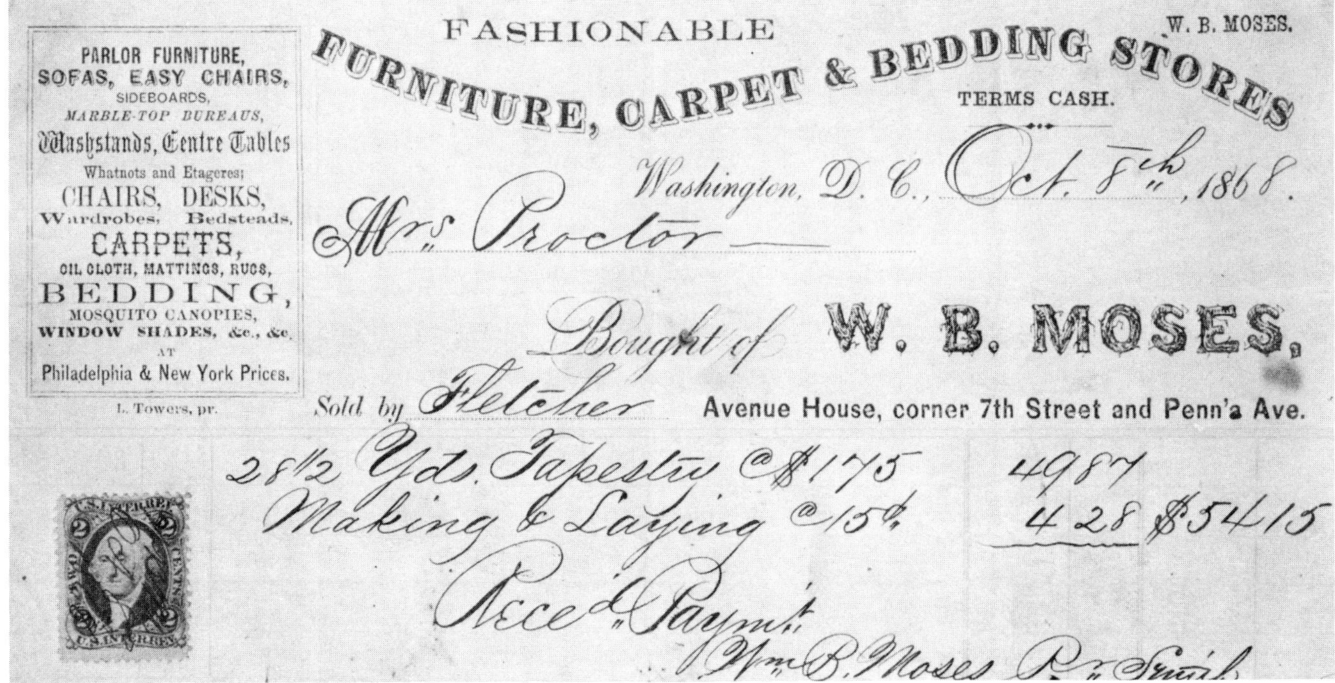
PARLOR FURNITURE,
SOFAS, EASY CHAIRS,
SIDEBOARDS,
MARBLE-TOP BUREAUS,
Washstands, Centre Tables
Whatnots and Etageres;
CHAIRS, DESKS,
Wardrobes, Bedsteads,
CARPETS,
OIL CLOTH, MATTINGS, RUGS,
BEDDING,
MOSQUITO CANOPIES,
WINDOW SHADES, &c., &c.
AT
Philadelphia & New York Prices.
L. Towers, pr.

FASHIONABLE
FURNITURE, CARPET & BEDDING STORES
W. B. MOSES.
TERMS CASH.

Washington, D. C., Oct. 8th, 1868.
Mrs Proctor
Bought of W. B. MOSES,
Sold by Fletcher
Avenue House, corner 7th Street and Penn'a Ave.

28½ Yds. Tapestry @ $1.75 — 49.87
Making & Laying @ 15¢ — 4.28 — $54.15

Recd Paymt
Wm B. Moses Pr Smith

Awnings extending across the entire sidewalk enlivened the pre-World War I streetscape of the 700 block of 7th Street, N.W., north of F, providing shade as well as advertising space. The street was a home as well as a business address for many shopkeepers in the late nineteenth and early twentieth centuries. Courtesy, Columbia Historical Society

a marked split between the Jewish communities of established Germans and the more recent arrivals from eastern Europe. Leon Shinberg noted that the Jewish community was bordered by K, Q, 5th, and 9th streets, "with 8th Street and 9th Street being predominantly the German-Jewish community, and 7th Street and east of 7th Street being the eastern European Jewish community."

Italian immigrants, who numbered only about 100 in 1880 in downtown, surged to 1,464 in 1920 in Northwest alone. Italian laborers succeeded the Irish as inhabitants of Swampoodle, but many Italians also served as food and produce merchants throughout the city. The first Italian Catholic Church, Holy Rosary, was established in 1914 at First and H streets, N.W. The church building was constructed in about 1920, four blocks away at 3rd and F, not far from the 7th Street corridor, indicating that Italians lived near it, if not in it.

Blacks constituted a little more than a third of the population in Northwest Washington in 1910 and 1920, and they appear to have been concentrated east and north of the 7th Street corridor. Pervasive segregation prohibited blacks from shopping in the major stores downtown. Consequently, secondary black-oriented shopping areas appeared on the periphery of downtown, including one on upper 7th Street between Massachusetts and Florida avenues. Here, black- and white-owned businesses were intermingled, serving a largely black clientele. By 1923 the only nonsegregated places were the trolleys and buses, Griffith Stadium, and the public library, which had opened on Mt. Vernon Square in 1903. As one of the few places in Washington that were not segregated, the library served an important role for blacks. One black scholar recalled that only because he was able to read and study alongside whites in the public library did he avoid hating all of white America.

By the turn of the twentieth century, successful merchants were beginning to move out of downtown, leaving their businesses on 7th Street and commuting from in-city suburbs such as Mount Pleasant, Petworth, and Brightwood. As the Germans prospered and moved on, their houses became home to Italians, Greeks, and then blacks. After World War II, downtown businesses desegregated. Hecht's opened its lunchroom to all races in November 1951, and other department stores as well as drugstores along lower 7th Street followed suit. At the same time desegregation of public schools made downtown less appealing to whites as a residential area. As a result downtown became an increasingly black neighborhood and shopping district; three synagogues became black Baptist and African Methodist Episcopal churches. The riots of 1968 proved to be the final push for faltering businesses: after the riots prominent stores such as Lansburgh's and Kann's closed, as whites found fewer reasons to shop downtown. Widespread demolitions and the moving of Hecht's to 12th and G streets in 1985 have further decimated the shopping activity on 7th Street. Today new development favors high-rise offices in previously low-scale commercial and residential areas. There is one ethnic group, though, that is anchoring the residential nature of downtown, at least for the moment, and that is Washington's Chinese community.

Washington's Chinatown had been established on the north side of Pennsylvania Avenue east of 4 1/2 Street in the 1880s. In 1890 there were 91 Chinese, and in 1892 the Toc Sing Chung grocery store opened. While Chinese restaurants and laundries were scattered all over the city, only Chinatown had Chinese stores. Although the population grew to several hundred by 1930, there were no more than 15 women, because the Chinese Exclusion Act of 1882 prevented wives of Chinese laborers from joining their husbands. The Chinese community developed its own social structure, and by 1930 it was dominated by two tongs, organizations that served as family associations, fraternal organizations, and benevolent societies. The importance of the tongs to a community of men who were facing overt racism and were deprived of their families cannot be overrated.

The year 1931 brought crisis to the community as its Pennsylvania Avenue neighborhood was obliterated to make way for a proposed municipal center. The tongs took the lead in relocating. On Leong Tong, the larger of the two tongs, with about 200 members, operated secretly through real estate agents and was able to obtain space on the 600 block of H Street for all 11 of the businesses operated by its members. Hip Sing Tong, On Leong's 50-member rival, which had at first threatened to move elsewhere, eventually followed suit and the new Chinatown was born. When the new location was announced, reaction was immediate and negative. Area businessmen circulated a petition in opposition, and one was quoted in the newspaper, "It is not that we object to their coming because they are Chinese. It is just that we don't feel they will bring any business here."

Besides bringing new and distinctive business to the 7th and H streets area, Chinatown continued to serve as the nucleus for a larger Chinese community. In 1936 the Chinese population in Washington numbered about 800, with 145 laundries and 62 restaurants scattered throughout the city. But only Chinatown had a distinctly Chinese atmosphere and appearance, achieved partly through the Chinese ornamentation applied to existing buildings. The On Leong Tong, which was renamed the On Leong Merchants Association at the time of the move, again led the way. The organization bought a double building at 618-20 H Street and added a pent tile roof over the first floor, a balcony at the second level, and a tile roof above the third floor. Other buildings have been similarly remodeled.

Today Chinatown continues to serve as the hub of a much larger metropolitan-area Chinese community, estimated at 30,000. Chinatown is home to an elderly male population as well as to recent immigrants who traditionally work in unskilled restaurant jobs until they achieve a more established life in the suburbs. The presence of about 500 Chinese in Chinatown has allowed the residential nature of this neighborhood to survive.

The Chinese, then, are only the most recent in a long line of ethnic groups who have made their mark on downtown Washington. From the generally white, Anglo-Saxon stock of middle-class Americans who originally built downtown, to immigrant Germans and eastern Europeans who favored mercantile occupations and thus chose to live in the city's commercial core, to black Americans who were not permitted a fair role in downtown until the mid-twentieth century, to the Chinese who have developed a thriving commercial area and lively neighborhood, downtown has seen many changes. Each successive group has left its impact in the form of buildings that, if they are permitted to remain, reveal an important part of Washington's past.

4

Foggy Bottom

Blue-Collar Neighborhood in a White-Collar Town

Suzanne Sherwood Unger

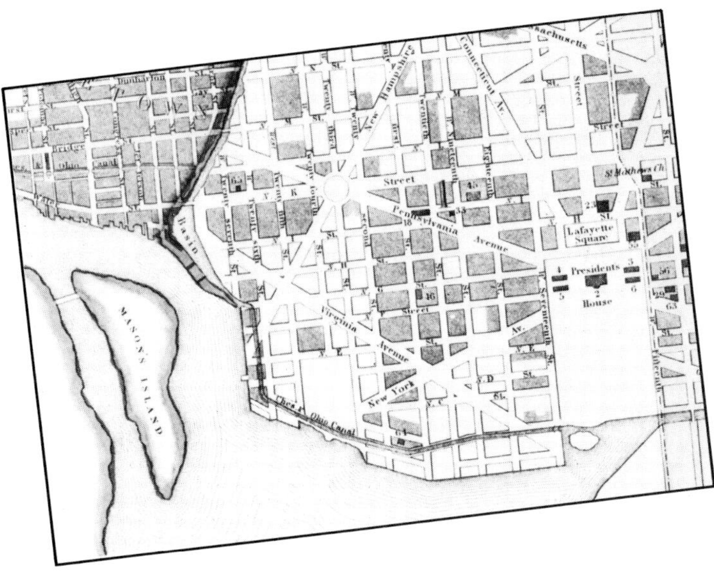

Restored brick row houses of nineteenth-century, blue-collar Foggy Bottom line the 900 block of 25th Street, N.W. Courtesy, D.C. Public Library, Washingtoniana Division, c. Washington Post

Map; City of Washington, 1848. Courtesy, Library of Congress

Washington, D.C., evokes images of the powerful few. Yet most here, as elsewhere, have led anonymous lives. It is primarily a white-collar town, the major industry and employer being government. The perception also is that Washington's white population was and is homogeneous. The country's ethnic, blue-collar cities lie farther north and west.

Before the Kennedy Center, the Watergate complex, the highways and condominiums, Foggy Bottom was a low-income neighborhood for nearly 100 years, a place where many residents worked at a variety of industries located on the edge of the Potomac River. Early on, German and Irish immigrants lived in Foggy Bottom, and many blacks moved in later.

As in most other neighborhoods, Foggy Bottom's boundaries are somewhat amorphous and have changed over the years. The Foggy Bottom described here is the area bounded by Pennsylvania Avenue to the north, 23rd Street to the east, the Potomac River to the south and west, and Rock Creek to the west. The area east of 23rd Street where the George Washington University campus is situated is also known as Foggy Bottom, but its history and the people who have lived there are somewhat distinct from the section west of 23rd Street. These residents were more likely to be middle class, as the larger, substantial houses in "east Foggy Bottom" attest.

In 1765 Jacob Funk, a German immigrant who lived in Frederick, Maryland, bought and subdivided into 234 lots the area roughly between 19th and 24th streets from H Street to the river. Most lots, if they sold at all, were

Above: This wooden house in the 400 block of 20th Street, N.W., photographed in 1934 and since demolished, was one of the earliest houses in Foggy Bottom, possibly built as part of the first colonial-era settlement on the site called Hamburgh. Courtesy, Columbia Historical Society

bought for speculative purposes, and little land was actually developed prior to the formation of the District of Columbia in 1791. Funk's most lasting contributions to Hamburgh, also known as "Funkstown," were a brick house built in a German style between the future 22nd and 23rd streets and a church at what would be 20th and G streets where the Concordia United Church of Christ stands today. The former church held services in German for many years, long after Hamburgh had become part of the District of Columbia and was known as Foggy Bottom.

Pierre L'Enfant placed two important public sites in this part of the city. One of his formal circles became Washington Circle, at the intersections of Pennsylvania and New Hampshire avenues and 23rd and K streets. The second site, at what was then the riverfront between 23rd and 24th streets, was officially titled "Reservation Number Four" and locally known as Camp Hill. The 1792 engraving of the L'Enfant Plan shows battlements on this site, and over the years it has served a succession of military purposes, even though Thomas Jefferson, himself an accomplished architect, at one time suggested placing the Capitol on Camp Hill. L'Enfant, however, preferred Jenkins Hill, now Capitol Hill, and George Washington agreed.

Samuel Claggett Busey, a resident who recorded his recollections of the city in 1895, wrote that troops were encamped on the hill during the War of 1812. In 1844 the Naval Observatory, the first major scientific establishment built by the federal government, went up on this site. The first observatory building still stands today, housing offices of the Naval Medical Command.

Because of Foggy Bottom's proximity to the river and Rock Creek,

Right: These government scientists took a break before departing from the Naval Observatory on Camp Hill for the far Pacific to measure the Transit of Venus across the sun in December 1897. The astronomical event had last occurred 105 years earlier and would allow astronomers to determine the distance from the earth to the sun. Courtesy, Columbia Historical Society

which were wider and deeper than they are today, many of the neighborhood's early activities developed along the edge of the water, where wharves and warehouses were located. Two businesses established at this time attracted a number of the Germans who influenced Foggy Bottom's early history. In 1807 two brothers, George and Andrew Way, Jr., started a glassblowing factory called the Glass House, situated on the river at the foot of 22nd Street. Residents of the time recalled that sometimes the Way brothers opened the Glass House to the public, and the Bohemian glassblowers made special toys and singing bottles for visitors. The second business was a brewery established in 1796 at B Street (now Constitution Avenue) between 21st and 23rd streets, beginning a long tradition of beer making in this section of Foggy Bottom that continued well into the twentieth century.

In this early period Foggy Bottom must have been an odd mix of rural and urban. Despite the commercial activity along the water, city directories indicate all of Foggy Bottom included only 40 households in 1822, 41 in 1830, and 60 in 1843. There were no churches west of 23rd Street. Residents had to haul water from one of the two springs in the area and go to Georgetown across Rock Creek to shop.

Published reminiscences of former residents include memories of hunting and fishing along the river, sledding and ice-skating in the winter, and cockfights on F Street between 21st and 23rd. George Washington Parke Custis, who lived in Arlington House across the Potomac, frequently held picnics on the grounds of his estate. People from Foggy Bottom would cross the river in boats to hear Custis play the violin and tell stories about his step-grandfather, George Washington.

Foggy Bottom residents were fairly evenly divided among the skilled, professional, commercial, and unskilled classes. Christian Hines, who lived in Foggy Bottom at this time, wrote in his 1866 account of the city that in 1800 Foggy Bottom included a carpenter, an architect, a pump borer, and a stone cutter.

In addition to the people who lived near their work at the wharves and industries along the water, a few notable and well-to-do residents lived along K Street, a thoroughfare between Georgetown and the President's

Camp Fry on 23rd Street south of Washington Circle, and others like it, brought the Civil War into the city. The early equestrian statue of George Washington by Clark Mills, bringing up the rear of the parading Union troops, was erected in the circle in 1860. Courtesy, Columbia Historical Society

House. Near the bridge across Rock Creek from Georgetown, Georgetown merchant Robert Peter built six three-story houses in 1797 for his sons on three blocks along K Street between 24th and 27th streets. The area had been part of his estate named Mexico that stretched along Rock Creek and the Potomac at the western end of Foggy Bottom. Robert Peter's son Thomas was married to Martha Washington's granddaughter, and George Washington visited the Peters in 1798 in their Foggy Bottom residence.

In 1803 Thomas Peter's house and the one next door were rented to Anthony Merry, the British minister to the United States, who lived there until 1806. Merry described Washington as a "commons which is meant to be the city of Washington." He wrote that the houses were "mere shells . . . with bare walls and without fixtures of any kind, even without a pump or well."

In the 1840s another British minister, Henry S. Fox, chose to live in the neighborhood. His house was located southwest of Washington Circle. Sarah Vedder in *Reminiscences of the District of Columbia or Washington City Seventy-Nine Years Ago, 1830-1909,* wrote of Fox:

He was a very tall man, over six feet and carried his head leaning to the side, never raising his eyes or noticing anyone, his chin covered with his cravat, and as surly looking as one could imagine. He never appeared on the street before six o'clock and slept all day and sat up all night, with twelve wax candles to light his study. No visitor was admitted before eight in the evening. The children all ran if they saw him coming, and thought him a terrible giant, ready to eat them on short notice.

She also recalled that Fox had an aversion to shaking hands with women and used this as an excuse for not giving receptions, although he did attend official functions himself. According to Vedder, he died in 1846 of an opium overdose in the Foggy Bottom house.

The origin of the name Foggy Bottom is as murky as the neighborhood was in its early years. The name was probably first used during this period when so much of the area, especially to the south, was swampy, a bottomland prone to fog.

The construction of the Chesapeake and Ohio (C&O) Canal, beginning in 1828, was a spur to the neighborhood's nascent commercial and industrial character. By 1850 the canal was complete from Georgetown, just across Rock Creek, to Cumberland, Maryland, and a connecting canal ran along the Potomac River edge of Foggy Bottom to the entrance to the Washington Canal just south of the White House. The city directories record that the number of households jumped from 58 in 1850 to 175 in 1860. Almost half (42 percent) of these residents were described as unskilled, whereas in previous decades only 9 to 18 percent were typically placed in this category. Although the Glass House had closed its doors by 1833, a number of new businesses began. In 1859 a business on the site of the Glass House was producing lamp black and roofing cement. There were three lime kilns, a shipyard, a wood yard, an icehouse, and by 1860 a factory producing plaster, ammonia, and fertilizer.

The most prominent Foggy Bottom businessman during these years was Captain William Easby, a Yorkshireman who had worked at the Navy Yard and received an appointment by James Monroe to the Riflemen of the Second Legion, First Brigade of the District of Columbia Militia in 1824. When Andrew Jackson became president in 1829, Easby left his Navy Yard job to start the shipyard in Foggy Bottom, taking advantage of its proximity to the C&O Canal, begun the year before. A bondholder in the canal project, Easby was closely connected with the canal's contractor. He also owned one of the lime kilns and the icehouse.

In 1856 the Washington Gas Light Company built a gas storage facility at the intersection of Virginia and New Hampshire avenues. The large, unsightly facility dominated Foggy Bottom's landscape for the next 100 years and contributed to the more industrial character of the neighborhood during the latter half of the nineteenth century.

The Civil War brought new activities, sights, and sounds to Foggy Bottom. Simon Newcomb, who worked at the Naval Observatory, recalled in *Reminiscences of an Astronomer* "that across the Potomac, Arlington Heights was whitened by the tents of soldiers from which the discharges of artillery or the sound of fife and drum became so familiar that the dweller almost ceased to notice it."

He also remembered the two-mile walk to and from his home through the streets of Foggy Bottom. "After a rain, especially during winter and spring, some of the streets were like shallow canals . . . night-swarms of rats, of a size proportional to their food supply, disputed the right of way with the pedestrian."

Military horse corrals were located at the foot of 22nd and 21st streets, near the river. In 1861 when a corral burned, horses stampeded through the streets. Camp Fry, established south of Washington Circle along 23rd Street, housed invalid soldiers, members of the Veteran Volunteer Corps who guarded government buildings.

After the war, horsecars offered wealthier residents an opportunity to move away from the central city. This left the neighborhood to less affluent residents who could not afford the luxury of a house in the suburbs and the cost of a daily streetcar commute. Further, the trend in industrial development that began before the Civil War continued apace afterwards, providing greater incentive for unskilled and skilled laborers to move to Foggy Bottom. In the nineteenth century many of these laborers were newly arrived immigrants, and contemporary accounts always describe Foggy Bottom as an Irish and German area. Harold D. Langley, in *Saint Stephen the Martyr Church and the Community 1867-1967,* quotes one resident as saying that the neighborhood was entirely German and Irish and that members of each group traded only with their fellow countrymen. This exclusivity was true also in their work and social life.

The congregation of St. Stephen the Martyr Church, at the corner of Pennsylvania Avenue and 25th Street, was predominantly Irish. German Catholics attended another church farther away. Members of the black community in Foggy Bottom established St. Mary's Episcopal Church on 23rd Street between G and H streets in 1867. Originally members of the Church of the Epiphany at 13th and G streets, the congregation grew to the point in 1886 that it could afford the services of James Renwick, architect of the Smithsonian "Castle" and the original Corcoran Gallery. He designed the distinguished church that stands on this site today.

Many of the German residents worked at the two breweries at the south end of Foggy Bottom. In the 1870s John Albert started a brewery that later became the Abner Drury Brewery, and Christian Heurich established the Heurich Brewery. The Heurich Brewery originally stood at 1229 20th Street, and in 1895 it was moved to a new, all-brick, fireproof building at 25th and Water streets. The structure stood solidly at this site until 1961, when it was blown up to make way for the access ramp to the Theodore Roosevelt Bridge.

The Irish, on the other hand, worked at the Washington Gas Light Company gasworks. Between 1887 and 1903 the facility was enlarged to include an even bigger tank at 26th and G streets. The Irish workers lived near their jobs, many settling south of Virginia Avenue in a section called Connaught Row. They fielded their own baseball team, the Emerald Athletic Club, and a football team, the Irish Eleven. By the 1880s the West End Hibernian Society had been established at 19th Street and Pennsylvania Avenue.

Besides the breweries and gasworks Foggy Bottom businesses included the Godey Lime Kilns, established in 1864 on Rock Creek at 27th Street by William H. Godey. A competitor, Knott and Moler, also converted limestone transported via the C&O Canal from Harper's Ferry. There were also coal dealers, J. Maury Dove at the foot of F and G streets and James A. Tumelty at Pennsylvania Avenue and 26th Street; a moving firm, Littlefield Alvord at 26th and D; and the Arlington Bottlers at 27th and K. All were more or less dependent on the river and the canal as a source of cheap transportation.

Not surprisingly, the housing in this neighborhood was modest. Narrow, brick rowhouses predominated, typically only one room wide and two rooms deep, without basements. Some of these houses were built on alleys instead of streets. Central Washington had many inhabited alleys such as those in Foggy Bottom, where hudreds of families lived in narrow rowhouses hidden inside the large city blocks, often accessible only by a narrow passageway. Poor sanitation and crowded conditions in such places made them the target of social reformers by the late nineteenth century. In 1892 Congress banned construction of houses on alleys less than 30 feet wide without sewers, water, or light as well as on all blind alleys, but it is estimated that about 1,500 people were already living in Foggy Bottom alleys by this time.

The neighborhood's fortunes began to change around 1900. The increased use of rail service diminished the importance of the canal and river to local business. Coal consumption declined as customers switched to gas and oil. Foggy Bottom's lack of rail connections placed it in a poor position to compete with the Northeast railroad yards, and a number of businesses moved or closed. Many Foggy Bottom residents moved also, following jobs to other locations. The breweries might have continued except for the advent of another untimely blow to local industry, Prohibition. The Abner Drury Brewery limped along making soft drinks until 1922. The Heurich Brewery survived but never regained the success it had achieved before World War I. After reopening in 1933, the brewery closed permanently in 1960.

By 1950 Foggy Bottom could still have been described as a low-income residential area, but it was not the same neighborhood it had been 50 years earlier. The industrial activity was less vital. Housing conditions were substandard. A 1944 survey by the Washington Housing Association revealed that of 186 dwelling units in the blocks bounded by Virginia and New

The Christian Heurich Brewery stood for 61 years on the Foggy Bottom waterfront. This delivery man from the Littlefield, Alvord and Company Express awaited his cargo in about 1915. Courtesy, Library of Congress, Prints and Photographs Division

This happy group on an Easter hike in 1915 posed among the artifacts of a failed port and craft economy—an old canalboat on Rock Creek, right, and the abandoned Godey Lime Kilns in the background. Courtesy, Library of Congress

Hampshire avenues and 23rd Street, a quarter had no water and a fifth had no electricity. Almost 90 percent of these dwellings were rental properties. As elsewhere in the city, this substandard housing had fallen to those with the least freedom of choice. The neighborhood was now predominantly black.

Despite the efforts of government to improve housing conditions in Foggy Bottom, it was private redevelopment on both a small and a large scale that succeeded in doing so. Two events following World War II created a climate favorable for private redevelopment. First, the U.S. Department of State moved to a new building at 23rd and D streets in 1947. The proximity of the State Department made Foggy Bottom attractive to some department employees. Second, and also in 1947, the Washington Gas Light Company dismantled the gas-manufacturing plant, two large tank holders, and other equipment. The last tanks were removed in 1954, along with any remaining physical disincentive to development for middle- and upper-income markets. Further, in Washington as elsewhere, the river's edge was becoming more attractive as people developed an appreciation for the waterfront as a recreational and cultural amenity.

Private development soon followed with the construction of Potomac Plaza, an eight-story complex of offices and apartments near the former site of the gas tanks. A vigorous

Facing page: Workmen at the Christian Heurich Brewery in Foggy Bottom enjoy their four o'clock beer in 1956, with the image of the founder behind them. Courtesy, D.C. Public Library, Washingtoniana Division

small-scale redevelopment effort began simultaneously as individuals and small companies bought the little brick rowhouses and renovated them, including many of those in the alleys. Renovation of this kind had been going on in Georgetown since the 1930s; the second manifestation of this process in the city, today called gentrification, took place in Foggy Bottom in the 1950s. The physical changes came with a social price. As property was improved, poor residents were forced to move because of rising rents, rapidly changing Foggy Bottom from a predominantly black neighborhood in 1950 into a white, middle-income area by 1960.

Large public projects also were planned for the neighborhood during the 1960s, specifically the Theodore Roosevelt Bridge, the Inner Loop Highway, and the John F. Kennedy Center for the Performing Arts. The investments of those carrying on small renovations were threatened by these large-scale projects. Local residents formed the Foggy Bottom Restoration Association and sought the help of the Redevelopment Land Agency (RLA) and the National Capital Planning Commission (NCPC). Through these agencies the association hoped to participate in the planning process and, as a result, protect its interests.

The developers of the larger private projects, however, opposed public involvement, fearing interference and costly delays. The NCPC did indeed discourage all types of redevelopment because of uncertainties about the location of the Inner Loop and George Washington University's future plans. The RLA considered making Foggy Bottom an urban renewal area. Yet a preliminary study showed so much renovation and redevelopment had occurred that the area was barely eligible for funding. Further, opposition to RLA's plans grew as time went on. Thus, both agencies eventually declined to use the urban renewal process as a means of developing a plan for Foggy Bottom. In other words, a neighborhood plan could not be developed until after key land-use decisions were made for the neighborhood by more powerful agencies seeking sites for highways and a performing arts center.

In the end the Restoration Association members succeeded in having the Inner Loop moved from the center to the west side of the neighborhood, but could not prevent the 1958 zoning decision allowing high-rise development in Foggy Bottom. It was a time when highway and urban renewal projects had powerful advocates and neighborhood activism was in its infancy. Many renovated houses were destroyed by the highway, and large-scale buildings such as the Kennedy Center and the enormous Watergate complex were set down incongruously amid the small buildings of the nineteenth-century, working-class neighborhood. The recent expansion of the George Washington University campus just on the other side of 23rd Street has added more high-density construction to the area.

Hotel and high-rise development continues in Foggy Bottom, but parts of the earlier, blue-collar neighborhood remain in the form of the quaint, brick, laborers' houses near 25th and I streets. If the earlier inhabitants of these houses returned today, they no doubt would be shocked to see how their modest homes have become the architectural gems of the 1980s. They would be even more shocked to learn how much they are worth.

5

SOUTHWEST WASHINGTON

WHERE HISTORY STOPPED

Keith Melder

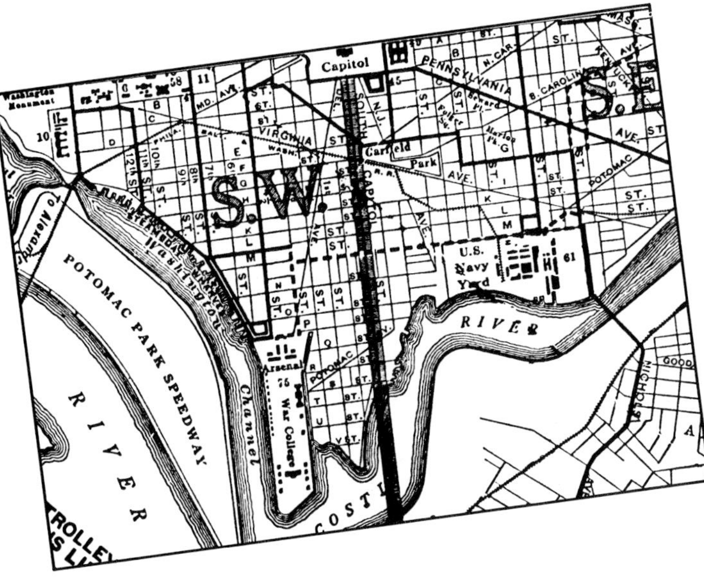

Gordon Parks captured this young sentinel at the edge of a Southwest alley for the Farm Security Administration in 1942. Inhabited alleys hidden at the center of city blocks often functioned like small villages, hardly known to outsiders. Courtesy, Library of Congress

Map; 1924 District Transportation Routes. Courtesy, Robert Truax

The Southwest Washington neighborhood represents a paradox: it is at the same time one of the city's oldest and one of its newest sections. A visitor to Southwest today, unless aware of its historic background, will assume that the neighborhood developed recently. But the area known as Southwest is old, not new; its glowing modernity is evidence of one of the city's most traumatic neighborhood histories.

Known by the Indians who occupied the Potomac basin thousands of years before Englishmen arrived, seen by Captain John Smith in 1608, and settled by Marylanders in the late seventeenth century, Southwest Washington was included in the federal city in 1790 and developed gradually from that time until the mid-twentieth century. Then suddenly, shortly after World War II, the process of gradual change came to a halt. Old Southwest was physically destroyed, leveled, and replaced with a brand-new and radically different physical environment. A handful of graceful late eighteenth- and early nineteenth-century buildings remain, incongruously reminding visitors that something else was here earlier.

Southwest Washington is part of the original Washington City designed by Pierre L'Enfant. Because of its accessible waterfront, the section appealed to L'Enfant and developers alike. For strategic reasons the planner designated the southernmost part of Southwest as a military site, and since 1794 Greenleaf's Point has served as a fort, a military arsenal, and a federal prison. Today this site, one of the nation's oldest military posts, is known as Fort Lesley J. McNair and houses the National Defense University.

Early private development in Southwest was oriented toward the river. Rough wharves and maritime structures provided access for shipping and stopping points for regular passenger packetboats and ferries. Beginning in the 1790s, for more than a century travelers could book passage on vessels bound downriver for Alexandria and points beyond. Fishermen brought their catches into Southwest for sale to Washingtonians. The slave trade also flourished here for many years.

Real estate developers believed that with easy access to the river Southwest would become a popular location for homes and businesses. One of the city's earliest real estate tycoons, James Greenleaf, built several speculative ventures including a rowhouse project, the "twenty buildings." Never finished, owing to the speculator's bankruptcy, the buildings stood in ruins for many years, symbolizing the city's vanquished hopes for early prosperity. Wheat Row, dating from 1793-1794, Washington's oldest standing rowhouse group, remains on 4th Street. Several individuals constructed elegant houses such as these, but after the late 1790s individual cottages and simple frame rowhouses dominated the area.

The low scale of the old Southwest neighborhood is evident in this 1946 view of the wharves and tree-sheltered residential streets clustered at the base of the city's monumental center. Courtesy, D.C. Public Library, Washingtoniana Division, c. Washington Post

Southwest early became a neglected, unfashionable neighborhood. The Washington City Canal in 1815 cut the area off from downtown and the more fashionable Northwest. Thereafter known as "the island," Southwest was home to a diverse population, including many low-income residents. Commerce in bulky goods such as fuel, building materials, and armaments, as well as its trade in foodstuffs and slaves, set the neighborhood off from the federal establishment and provided employment for tradesmen and laborers. Many households kept pigs, chickens, and other livestock.

Before the Civil War Southwest housed numerous black people. Enslaved and free blacks coexisted in the District from its founding, and by 1830 more than half of all blacks were free. The city's free black community comprised respected, energetic laboring people, as well as ministers, teachers, and businessmen. One of the leaders in Washington's free black community, Anthony Bowen, lived in Southwest on E Street between 9th and 10th, where he maintained a mission and day school for neighborhood young people. During the 1850s he worked with the Underground Railroad, the network of people who helped fugitive slaves escape from the South. Bowen met escaped slaves at the 6th Street wharf in Southwest and assisted them on to Philadelphia and other points north where they could be absorbed and hidden from slave-catchers. In 1848 a group of Washington slaves attempting to escape on the ship *Pearl* were captured and returned to Southwest in a notorious incident roundly condemned by national abolitionists.

During and after the Civil War the neighborhood flourished and grew, expanding from 10,000 to about 18,000 people between 1860 and 1870. From its docks hundreds of shiploads of arms, supplies, and troops were launched down the Potomac to wage war on Richmond, Virginia. A busy gun and powder factory operated at the armory on Greenleaf's Point. The war changed the neighborhood's population. Thousands of newly freed slaves settled in Southwest; 18.5 percent of the population was black in 1860, 37.3 percent in 1870.

Southwest's population nearly doubled between 1870 and 1900 as thousands of new rowhouses were built and commercial enterprises expanded. Hundreds of tiny, very low-rent rowhouses sprang up along alleys hidden within city blocks. Such inhabited alleys were like small villages, intimate communities occupied by black families, hardly known to outsiders. Although impoverished, they nourished strong protective institutions and rich Afro-American folk traditions.

Although the City Canal was abandoned and filled in the 1870s, the "island" remained set apart by another physical barrier, the Baltimore and Potomac Railroad, built along Virginia and Maryland avenues between 1856 and 1870. Around the same time, however, new streetcar lines tied Southwest to the rest of the city.

Among newcomers to the neighborhood in the 1880s and later were European immigrants, including numerous Jewish families from Germany and eastern Europe. Jews engaged in retail trades, establishing lively rows of small shops along 4 1/2 (now 4th) and 7th streets. They operated dry goods, tailoring, butcher, and bakery shops, and after 1900 specialized in family run "mom-and-pop" grocery stores. By the 1890s Jewish immigrants were holding religious services with a cantor and rabbi, Moses Yoelson. In 1906 they dedicated a synagogue, the Talmud Torah congregation. One of the rabbi's sons, Al Jolson, became a leading American entertainer. In explaining his success, Jolson recalled his youth on the streets of old Southwest where he traveled with a "tough gang" and learned Afro-American dialects.

As in other parts of the city at this time, a pattern of racial segregation developed. Black residents, formerly

This quiet scene at the Washington Arsenal on Greenleaf's Point in 1862 belies the fact of a nation at war. The arsenal was the site of a busy gun and powder factory where an accidental explosion killed 21 women workers during the Civil War. Courtesy, National Archives

P.J. Fitzgerald's Drug Store at 901 4 1/2 Street, S.W., anchors the corner of this important, primarily Jewish commercial street about 1900. Courtesy, Library of Congress, Prints and Photographs Division

living in several sections of Southwest, were increasingly concentrated east of 4 1/2 Street, and whites dominated the neighborhood west of that artery. Geographer Paul A. Groves argues that Southwest was one of Washington's first fully segregated neighborhoods: "The development of a black residential area in Southwest was a *fait accompli* by 1897. As a result, the Southwest was residentially divided."

In retrospect the years between 1895 and 1930 may be thought of as the "golden age" of residential Southwest. The population peaked at nearly 35,000 around 1905. Community institutions reached their fullest development, with a rich assortment of houses of worship, voluntary associations, social agencies, schools, and activities for young and old, black and white. The Jewish population grew from 30 to 190 families and supported a host of institutions, including the synagogue, social service agencies, and the Hebrew Free Loan Association. The city's first social settlement house for whites, the Barney Neighborhood House, opened in 1900, followed a few years later by the Southwest Neighborhood House for blacks. Southwest began to seem like a self-contained small city, offering work and services for most of its inhabitants. An old-timer remembered: "Southwest was a little town in those days. The streets were paved with bricks and lined by tall stately elm trees, like European towns. Everyone knew each other. Whether there was good news or bad news, we all shared the joys and the sorrow."

But Southwest's strong social ties concealed many problems that developed after 1900. Relentlessly competing for scarce space, federal agencies—the Bureau of Engraving, Department of Agriculture, and others—spread into residential areas, replacing streets of dwellings with massive office buildings. Private commercial interests also expanded. Blocks of warehouses, markets, and freight yards

For more than a century, produce of all kinds was shipped to the Southwest harbor and often marketed there. The young rowers admiring this boatload of watermelons were photographed in 1933. Courtesy, Library of Congress, Prints and Photographs Division

Flanking the imposing U.S. Capitol, turn-of-the-century Southwest was densely built with small wooden and brick working-class houses. For years the contrast of regal and ramshackle tempted many reform-minded photographers. Courtesy, Library of Congress, Prints and Photographs Division

also spilled over into residential sections.

These changes increased noise, congestion, and dirt, making the area less desirable for residents who could afford to move elsewhere. Absentee landlords, especially owners of the alley houses, reduced maintenance, diminishing the quality of low-income housing. Population fell to 32,000 in 1920 and 24,000 in 1930, and the ratio of black to white increased. With a mixture of commerce and poverty, Southwest gained a reputation as run-down, dirty, crime-ridden, and "blighted"—a slum area.

Southwesters complained of neglect from the city. Harry Wender, a city activist and member of the Southwest Citizens' Association, for years called for better city services in his section. "Truly an orphan among communities," he wrote, "its problems have never seemed to concern anyone with sufficient interest or influence to attempt their solution." Parks, schools, and public services were never adequate. Wender recalled the battle when the white Citizens' Association and the black Civic Association joined to have the "obnoxious" 4 1/2 Street repaired and renamed 4th Street. "We got the cobblestones removed and the street paved. We got the street widened and lights put up. Then we put on the biggest celebration in the history of the city . . . It was the first time that Negroes and whites paraded together in the history of Washington."

In the 1930s federal authorities became concerned about conditions in Southwest. They labeled the neighborhood a neglected slum, a disease-ridden, crime-infested eyesore in the very shadow of the Capitol. Photographers from government agencies and the mass media enjoyed capturing images of dilapidated alley shanties and their inhabitants with the Capitol dome in the background. City planners and federal housing reformers agreed that conditions in Southwest needed to be radically changed. But what should be done?

Federal authorities already had ample experience in planning Washington's neighborhoods. L'Enfant's plan of 1791, the McMillan Plan of 1901-1902, and the massive Federal Triangle development of the 1920s and 1930s all had demonstrated the federal government's ability to shape the national capital. Moreover, New Deal housing reformers and planners had faith in the ability of federal power to improve housing for low-income people. In the 1940s the government set out to find more radical solutions to so-called urban blight. Experts invented a process called urban renewal and chose Southwest Washington to be its first national laboratory.

In 1946 Congress chartered a new city agency, the Redevelopment Land Agency (RLA), with ample powers to condemn, redesign, and rebuild whole neighborhoods. Another law, the National Housing Act of 1949, offered federal subsidies for slum clearance, redevelopment, and low-rent public housing for cities across the nation. Neighborhoods could be planned and "renewed" with little assent from their inhabitants.

By 1950 the pressure for urban renewal in Southwest was irresistible. A critical planning document of 1950 described Southwest as "obsolete." "The character of the buildings is so bad that partial rehabilitation is not justifiable economically," wrote a federal commission. More than two-thirds of the residents were low-income blacks. The city's newspapers, led by the *Washington Post,* called for radical change. In a dramatic series of articles titled "Progress or Decay? Washington Must Choose!" the *Post* called for a "bold approach" in reconstructing blighted areas, Southwest especially, to reverse "white flight" to the suburbs and rebuild the city's tax base.

Control of the neighborhood's destiny had passed entirely out of the hands of Southwest's inhabitants. Because Congress and local officials ruled the District of Columbia in a kind of benevolent dictatorship, their professional planners easily took charge of the neighborhood. Faced with several

The Smithsonian Castle presides over an unpaved B Street, S.W., in this 1863 photograph by Matthew Brady. Today known as Independence Avenue, the street marks the northern boundary of the Southwest neighborhood as it meets the grand expanse of the Mall. Courtesy, National Archives

The stores on the 600 block of 4th street, SW, awaited demolition by the Redevelopment Land Agency in 1957 when Bernard Green posed in front of his liquor store, the last to remain open on the street. Courtesy, D.C. Public Library, Washingtoniana Division

alternatives, including one option to maintain the area's character and many of its existing buildings, the RLA chose to rebuild totally, creating a mixture of stylish high-rise towers and new town houses, with many open green spaces. Old houses and businesses —even many old streets—would disappear.

What would happen to the many low-income blacks in Southwest? Critics cited evidence of racism in the planners' bold design, which clearly implied that poor blacks would be removed and replaced by affluent whites. Officially, some black people were expected to return after reconstruction, to be housed in new public housing projects. However, many poor people would have to move permanently, like it or not, to "other" locations.

Some observers, concerned with the human implications of uprooting people against their wishes, raised questions. Reporter George Beveridge of the *Evening Star* asked: "To what extent must the area provide for needs of its present residents?" A clergyman was more blunt, writing to the *Post:* "The plan is 'bold' as tyranny is bold; and 'dramatic' as tyranny is dramatic," a "turning of our Nation's Capital, the citadel of democracy, into the city of the rich."

While arguments raged, urban renewal moved forward. In addition to the residential renewal, highway engineers evolved plans for a dramatic new six-lane highway, the Southwest Freeway, which would displace blacks from existing rowhouses. Despite lawsuits and planning disputes, the RLA started acquiring property for clearance in December 1953. In spring 1954 the RLA began demolition, knocking down a group of alley houses, "a sore

The small frame houses of old Southwest such as these at 9th and E streets, many without modern conveniences, housed a tightly knit, largely black community in 1950. Federal authorities saw it as a slum and a blight on the capital, and planned its demolition through urban renewal. Courtesy, Columbia Historical Society

The Fairbrother Elementary School at 500 10th Street, S.W., succumbs to the wrecker's ball on February 3, 1960, as employees of the nearby Briggs Sausage Company look on. Courtesy, D.C. Department of Housing and Community Development

spot of crime, illegitimacy, refuse, and disordered lives," according to the *Post.* By late in the year, with many buildings gone, an aged black store owner assessed the results for the *Washington Star:* "Well, it seems like they're handin' out a passel o' joy and a passel o' sorrow."

In the meantime, the planners won an important victory in the Supreme Court. An opinion prepared by Justice William O. Douglas declared D.C. urban renewal to be constitutional. Denying the contention of Southwest business people that the condemnation of their property was unfair or arbitrary, the Court found that upgrading housing and the urban environment was as much within the municipal police power as more traditional applications of that power.

And so, between 1954 and 1960 most of the old Southwest disappeared. Eliminating the old was easier than building the new, however. While plans for new neighborhood designs had to be reviewed, revised, and sometimes reversed, the most difficult problems concerned human beings. Faced with having to rehouse and reorient more than 15,000 poor black people, public agencies experimented with new social programs. In 1958 RLA social workers introduced a "human redevelopment" plan to teach homemakers about their improved and more complex household environments, as well as their unfamiliar social surroundings.

On the whole these efforts at human engineering were less than successful. Sociologist Daniel Thursz, in a 1966 study of displaced Southwest families, found "a substantial amount of dissatisfaction" among the people interviewed. Families had suffered a social loss: "The fact is that they had friends and felt a part of a community which had been theirs for many years . . . It was home . . . They . . . resent more than ever before the forced disintegration of the social milieu which was theirs in the old Southwest."

About a quarter of those displaced from Southwest handled their own problems of readjustment. But even these residents—mostly white and middle class—seldom moved willingly, because they had chosen Southwest for its convenience and its location near the river. Many had invested substantially in their homes and felt unfairly compensated for condemned property. Thirty years and more have passed since the old Southwest disappeared, but few old residents remember their experience of urban renewal with much happiness.

History stopped for Southwest Washington in the early 1950s. History began again in the late 1950s as the neighborhood was reconstructed. The new Southwest includes L'Enfant Plaza at the northern edge—office buildings, a hotel, and an underground shopping mall. Federal office buildings crowd the area between Independence Avenue and the Southwest Freeway, neatly arranged like giant filing cases. Along the waterfront a handsome promenade lined with new restaurants and parking lots replaces the old docks, warehouses, and markets. Offering a hint of the old disorder and vitality, a waterfront outdoor fish market remains among sleek buildings. The Arena Stage has successfully operated for more than 25 years.

Ironically, today's residential Southwest retains some of the old contrasts. To the east of 4th Street, which was formerly the segregated black section, sit many blocks of public housing projects—tall towers and low town houses. Although some structures are abandoned, others are densely occupied by low-income residents. All share the barren, unkempt look of so many public housing projects. West of 4th—the former main street of Southwest—are complexes of handsome apartment towers and modern town houses, built in varied styles. A leading 1965 architectural guidebook to Washington comments about their designs: "This is Washington's showplace of contemporary building, and perhaps it will in the future constitute an outdoor museum of the architectural cliches of the two decades following World War II."

Planners expected that the new Southwest's focus would be a shopping center and mall that replaced small shops along 4th and 7th streets. But in the late 1980s Waterside Mall, patterned after suburban shopping centers of the 1960s, remains half-tenanted and lifeless. A large supermarket and a liquor store are its busiest operations. While affluent Southwesters apparently prefer to drive elsewhere to shop, the less well-off in nearby public housing units have little choice but to shop in this streamlined but dreary mall.

The new Southwest has undeniably handsome features. Still, the absence of the variety found in other areas, where buildings were constructed at different times, makes Southwest look like a suburb. A reporter in 1973 found residents commenting "on the sterility of the renewal area, on its lack of soul."

In the larger context of recent local history, the story of Southwest is not unique. Since 1950 the affluent have displaced the poor throughout inner-city Washington—but without wholesale, traumatic removal and rebuilding. Instead, on Capitol Hill, in Georgetown, and in parts of near-Northwest, a process of restoration and gentrification occurred. Yet poor blacks, forced out of these sections by rent increases and real estate developers, moved just as surely as they had to when removed by urban renewal. Whether desirable or not, these changes diminished the values and practices of intimate face-to-face community life, as remembered in old Southwest.

The Southwest story illustrates the peculiar function of Washington as a federal laboratory for urban experimentation. Just as the 1901-1902 McMillan Plan to rebuild, beautify, and create a planned model city on the Mall served as a precedent for later federal planning in the 1920s and 1930s, Southwest's urban renewal—its old-new, lost-and-found neighborhood—taught Americans the advantages and disadvantages of dramatic urban change.

Captain Clyde Parker of Onacock, Virginia, offers two fine crabs to a customer at the Southwest waterfront fish market in 1959. Courtesy, D.C. Public Library, Washingtoniana Division, c. Washington Post

Milkhouse Ford
Brookville Road
Rockville Road
River Road
TENNALLYTOWN
Chesapeake and Ohio Canal
Distributing Reservoir

PART TWO

EARLY SETTLEMENTS IN WASHINGTON COUNTY

The high rolling hills above Washington City and Georgetown and the area across the Eastern Branch (now the Anacostia River) remained undeveloped until after the Civil War. This rural part of the District, known as Washington County, was occupied by farms of various sizes and the grand estates of the well-to-do.

A few settlements sprang up in this rural landscape before the Civil War, all along transportation routes into Georgetown and Washington City. Tenleytown clustered around the tavern of John Tennally at one of the District's earliest intersections—the juncture of a tobacco-rolling road between Georgetown and Frederick, Maryland (now Wisconsin Avenue) and the road to Harper's Ferry (now River Road). When the Georgetown-to-Frederick road became a paved turnpike in 1827, Tenleytown was enhanced by its new status as a toll stop. Brightwood sprang up around another toll booth on the main route from Washington City to Frederick, the 7th Street Turnpike built between 1818 and 1822 (now Georgia Avenue).

The location of bridges also affected the way Washington grew, and Uniontown, now called Old Anacostia, is an early example. The first suburban planned development outside of Washington City and Georgetown, it was laid out across the Eastern Branch in 1854 at the foot of the bridge to the Navy Yard, the District's only large industrial employer.

Left: Pioneer photographer Mathew Brady captured this scene at the eastern end of the Navy Yard Bridge, near Uniontown, in the 1860s when most of the District was still rural countryside. Courtesy, National Archives

Map; 1861, A. Boschke. Courtesy, Library of Congress

WISCONSIN MARKET

6

TENLEYTOWN CROSSROADS

Judith Beck Helm

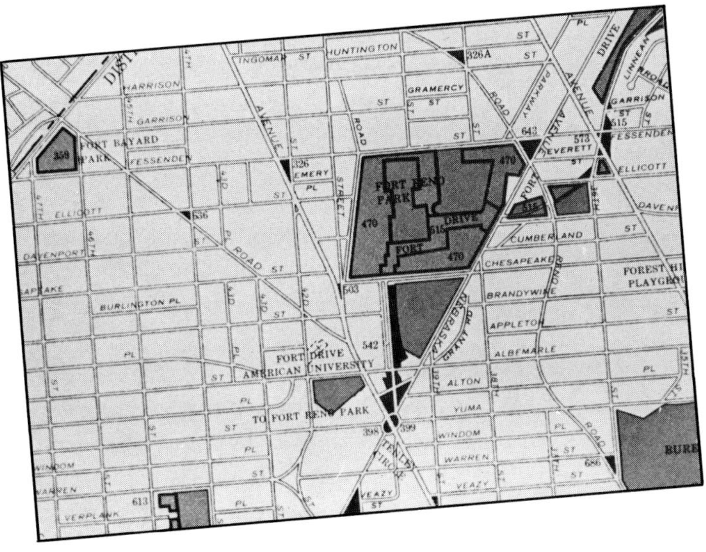

David Tievsky posed beside the produce of the family-owned Wisconsin Market in 1926. Courtesy, Marvin Tievsky and George Tievsky, M.D.

Map: Park System of the National Capitol and Environs. National Park Service 1962. Courtesy, D.C. Public Library, Washingtoniana Division

Tenleytown has been a village within the District of Columbia since before the War of 1812. Its location at the intersection of two major country roads outside Washington City began to attract settlers as soon as the District was created, in 1791, and for many years its inns and taverns were favored stopovers for travelers to Georgetown and the federal city.

Tenleytown's identity as a nineteenth-century crossroads village has only recently been rescued from oblivion. As the city grew around it, the twentieth-century developments of American University Park, North Cleveland Park, Chevy Chase, and Friendship Heights erased the place from the map and from people's minds. It was the resurgence of interest in local history, sparked by the nation's Bicentennial celebration, and the publication of a history of Tenleytown in 1981 that resurrected the name. Its rediscovered past reveals a place that has been shaped by the city's transportation patterns from its earliest days to the present. Today it is a crossroads again, a busy stop on the Metro subway system, a stop named Tenleytown.

The center of the village has always been what is now Wisconsin Avenue, above and below its intersection with River Road. The landmarks today are Sears, Hechinger's, and the new Tenley Point building. Earlier landmarks, however, were Tennally's tavern, a tollgate and tollhouse, the Tennally-Lightfoot house, the Tennallytown Inn, the Gloria Point house, and even the police Substation-Tenleytown, called Sub-T. All of these are now gone.

Tenleytown has never had exact boundaries, nor was it ever incorporated as a village, but it is approximately between Upton Street on the south and Fessenden Street on the north. This is a relatively limited area now, but a

Above: Tom Paxton, whose family bore one of turn-of-the-century Tenleytown's 12 common surnames, built these two houses in the 1880s. Situated in the 4400 block of Grant Road, N.W., these houses still stand today. Courtesy, National Park Service

Right: Dr. Robert W. Scholl, cigar in hand, leans against the wire fence of his pharmacy on Wisconsin Avenue and Grant Road, N.W. Courtesy, Estate of Marjorie Scholl

hundred years ago Tenleytown was the post office for farmers as far east as Rock Creek, and beyond River Road and Western Avenue on the west.

Tenleytown grew up along one of the District's oldest thoroughfares. Wisconsin Avenue began as an Indian trail that wound uphill from the Potomac River. The trail became a passage through the countryside for the earliest English settlers, and by the mid-eighteenth century it was a well-traveled route between Georgetown and points to the north and northwest. This route came to be known as the Georgetown to Frederick Road. Maryland farmers rolled their tobacco in barrels called hogsheads along its descent to the warehouses on the Potomac.

This route became the first military road in colonial America. In 1755 the British were planning an expedition against the French at Fort Duquesne, to be led by General Edward Braddock. To aid the movement of troops, Governor Horatio Sharpe of Maryland ordered the construction of a 12-foot-wide road from Rock Creek to Wills Creek, beyond Cumberland. This "Braddock Road" followed the present-day route of Wisconsin Avenue to a point just north of what would become Tenleytown, veering right onto today's 41st Street and then onto Belt Road, both of which predated River Road and the upper section of today's Wisconsin Avenue. It resumed the route of Wisconsin Avenue just north of the District line, and then angled left onto Old Georgetown Road to a point just south of Rockville. The construction of this road in 1755 encouraged travel to and from the port of Georgetown and benefited the area that would become Tenleytown.

The oldest name associated with the area cut through by the road to

Frederick was not Tenleytown, but Friendship. In 1713 Thomas Addison and James Stoddert received a patent of more than 3,000 acres from Charles Calvert, Lord Baltimore, which they named Friendship. This land grant extended from today's American University campus on the south to Bethesda on the north. Stoddert claimed the northern half, above today's Fessenden Street, and Addison claimed the southern portion. Twelve years later, in 1725, Joseph Belt patented Cheivy Chace, adjoining the northern half of Friendship. Belt Road, which winds through this area of the District today as a narrow roadway, is named for this early landowner.

Addison's grandson, John Murdock, was the first to build a homestead on the Friendship patent, in about 1760. This house, facing southeast with a view of the Potomac and Georgetown, was at the crest of a hill on today's American University campus. The old Murdock house was torn down before 1918. John R. McLean, publisher of the *Washington Post,* would later use the name Friendship for his lavish, early twentieth-century estate just south of Tenleytown, and the more euphonious name has subsequently been perpetuated in many ways in the area. Friendship Heights, for example, is used to refer to the area just north of Tenleytown.

The place that would become Tenleytown was established as an important crossroads site with the construction of River Road for horse-drawn vehicles by Jacob Funk about 1779. This was the same Jacob Funk who founded and promoted Hamburgh, a small German community on the Potomac east of Georgetown, today called Foggy Bottom. Funk's River Road began at the Georgetown to Frederick Road and continued west until it paralleled the Potomac River on its way to Great Falls, Seneca, and Harper's Ferry.

Around 1790 John Tennally opened a tavern on the road to Frederick at the new River Road intersection. It became a landmark in this undeveloped rural area, and the fork in the road came to be referred to as Tennally's Tavern. In 1791 Tennally's Tavern was included within the boundaries of the new District of Columbia.

John Tennally must have died by 1800, for he was not recorded in that year's census. His sister, Sarah Tennally, lived for many years, however, at the top of the hill near the present-day Hechinger's store, in a house torn down in the 1950s. There are continued references to Tennally's Tavern in land records after 1800, as well as the first references to a place called Tennallytown. What is now Wisconsin

The oldest commercial building still standing in Tenleytown, constructed in the late 1880s, housed Scholl's Pharmacy when this picture was taken about 1920. It originally served as O'Day's general store and the post office. Courtesy, Estate of Marjorie Scholl

The left-hand side of this house, "The Rest," was begun in 1801 by Charles Jones for his sister, Sarah Love; the tower was added much later by the Magruder family. It stands today at 4343 39th Street, N.W., as the oldest house in Tenleytown. Photo by John Russo. Courtesy, Judith Beck Helm

Avenue came to be known in the nineteenth century as the Tennallytown Road.

Henry Riszner built a new tavern at Tennallytown, south of the River Road fork, around 1805. It probably replaced the old tavern as a stagecoach stop. Dolley Madison stopped at Tennallytown on her flight from the British invasion of Washington in 1814 and encamped with the army there. There is no evidence that she slept in the inn, as some sources have claimed.

The Tennallytown Road and its continuation to Frederick became a well-traveled road, a southeastern link in the Great National Road to the west completed as far as Wheeling, Virginia, by 1818. Its surface, however, was infamous for its poor quality, deeply rutted when dry and impassable with mud in the rainy season. Tales told by stagecoach riders between Georgetown and Frederick show they traveled always in fear of capsizing when careening down a steep hill or crossing a creek, and their worst fears often came true.

As a result, enterprising local landowners formed the Washington Turnpike Company and, beginning about 1827, widened and paved the road to Frederick. The company erected a series of tollhouses in 1829, one at Tennallytown, to cover the cost of improvements. The Tennallytown tollgate was at the top of the hill in the village, just north of the River Road turnoff. By 1840 the original route along Belt Road had been changed to the shorter but steeper route of present-day Wisconsin Avenue from Brandywine Street to the District line.

In the first half of the nineteenth century the well-favored land in this area was held by a very few, mostly interrelated families. Of the old estate houses, only three are still standing: The Rest, built for Sarah Love in 1806, now a private home at 39th and Windom streets; Highlands, begun by Charles Nourse in 1817, now the Sidwell Friends School on Wisconsin Avenue; and Dumblane, built in the 1830s for Clement Smith, until recently also a school at 42nd and Warren streets.

In the 1850s a new and larger Tennallytown Inn was built on the west side of the Tennallytown Road. It served as an overnight stopping place for horse and coach travelers, especially farmers and merchants going to and from Georgetown and Washington City. The ground floor doubled as a dining room and saloon. Later owned by German brewer Christian Heurich, it was torn down in 1939 and replaced with the present Sears, Roebuck and Co. building.

Tennallytown's location made the village central to the Civil War defenses of Washington in 1861. A hill northeast of the crossroads town, adjacent to Belt Road, was the highest elevation in the city, 430 feet above sea level. A fort was hastily erected there around the farmhouse of Giles Dyer.

It was named Fort Pennsylvania because it was built and manned by soldiers from that state. A year later Fort Pennsylvania was the largest fort protecting the capital, with the heaviest artillery and the greatest number of soldiers. Its name was later changed to Fort Reno in memory of a Union major general, Jesse Lee Reno. The strength of Fort Reno was never challenged by the Confederate Army. Instead it was Fort Stevens, commanding the 7th Street Turnpike entrance to the city, that was attacked in the summer of 1864 in the only Civil War battle fought in the District. Fort Reno provided backup support in the defeat of Confederate Major General Jubal Early's invasion.

The village was never the same after the four years of army occupation. The Dyer family, again the owners of the fort site, subdivided it and sold lots at very reasonable rates, creating the first real development in Tennallytown. Many black people settled at Fort Reno; the development provided homes for many newly freed slaves.

Fort Reno subsequently became a predominantly black community. It was served by three churches, Rock Creek Baptist, Saint Mark's AME, and Saint George's Episcopal; by the Jesse Lee Reno grammar school; and by a few stores. From 1872 to 1906 the area was listed in the city directories as Reno City, but residents rarely used the word "city." By 1894 there were about 60 houses on the old fort site. Many of the small shacks built just after the war had been replaced by more substantial houses. The community was a secure and healthy place, especially when compared to the more crowded conditions in the downtown sections of Washington. Relationships between the races were generally good, with black and white families well known to one another and in many cases interdependent.

This early electrified streetcar linked city (Georgetown) to suburb (Tennallytown) via Wisconsin Avenue, N.W., in the 1890s then called the Tennallytown Road.. Its motorman piloted commuters from M Street to the District line. Courtesy, Gladys Smith Clemons

The streetcars came clanging through Tennallytown from Georgetown on the way to Rockville in 1890, following almost the same route traveled by stagecoaches a century earlier. The construction of the trolley line north from Georgetown closed the distance between Washington and Tennallytown and opened up adjacent land for development. In 1895 Congress officially ended the legal distinction between Washington City, Georgetown, and Washington County, of which Tennallytown was a part. The village was about to be absorbed by the growing capital.

By the turn of the century the village was largely a working-class community, although there were still a few wealthy residents, including the phenomenally rich John R. McLean at Friendship. The homes of most were simple frame cottages, some with Victorian details popular when they were built in the 1880s. A number of these still stand, particularly along Grant Road and 41st Street. Most local men were farmers, butchers, marketmen,

The 15 children of patriarch C.H.M. Walther and his second wife, Sophronia, gathered along with their families on the sturdy porch of his Murdock Mill Road home. Walther, seated at center with his wife at his right, headed the largest of Tenleytown's numerous large families in 1915. Courtesy, Mary Frances Brown

storekeepers, stone masons, laborers, carpenters, policemen, or streetcar motormen. Most whites were of English or German heritage, but there were Irish and Italian families as well. They were hardworking, churchgoing, family-oriented people, as secure in their small-town community as were most of their counterparts in turn-of-the-century America.

Churches were central to community life, and it was unusual for someone not to be a member of any church. There were four white churches in Tennallytown. Mt. Zion Methodist Episcopal was the first, begun in 1840 and later renamed Eldbrooke Methodist. Saint Ann's Roman Catholic parish was established in 1867 by the Jesuits of Georgetown College, and Mt. Tabor Baptist (now Wisconsin Avenue Baptist) was founded in 1870. Saint Columba's Episcopal Church was created as a mission of Saint Alban's in 1874.

Families in turn-of-the-century Tennallytown tended to be large and intertwined. There were 12 common surnames in the village early in this century, and almost all white residents were related to one or more of these families: Burrows, Riley, Robey, Hurdle, Harry, Perna, Poore, Shoemaker, Chappell, Paxton, Queen, and Walther. C.H.M. Walther of Murdock Mill Road had the largest family in Tennallytown. He was the father of 14 children by his first wife, although only six lived to maturity, and nine by his second wife.

Among some critics the village had a bad reputation because of its taverns, frequently the scenes of gambling, drunkenness, and fights. About

Today's northwest corner of Van Ness Street and Wisconsin Avenue, N.W., had a distinctly rural appearance as late as 1928 when this photograph recorded Harper's filling station and its surroundings. The road at the left was then Loughborough Road; it was later moved and renamed Van Ness Street. The three houses seen on Loughborough still stand on Van Ness Street. Courtesy, Johnson's Flower and Garden Centers

once a year someone was shot or stabbed. Such people, however, were a minority, accepted by the majority as "local color." After all, they were their fellow parishioners, customers, and relatives.

Disagreement about the spelling of Tennallytown (Tenallytown, Tenley-Town, Tennellytown, Tenleytown) was finally resolved in the twentieth century. Certainly members of the Tennally family had pronounced their name with three syllables, for the earliest records all have an *e* or an *a* between the *n*'s and *l*'s. But Tennallytown was not only misspelled; it was also mispronounced. When Oliver Wendell Holmes, Jr., was stationed in the village during the Civil War, he wrote to his mother, "We are at Ten Alley Town." This mistaken accenting of the second syllable was another good reason for the spelling to be changed. The local post office was Tennallytown until 1920, when Tenleytown was decreed by the city post office to be the correct spelling henceforth.

Tenleytown had begun to lose its identity before World War I, however, as large and affluent developments such as Cleveland Park, Chevy Chase, Friendship Heights, University Park, Wisconsin Avenue Heights, and Armesleigh Park grew up around it. Realty brochures for these first developments advertised the desirability of this elevated, beautiful, and undeveloped area. Reacting to the working-class identity of the name Tenleytown and ignorant of its history, real estate agents referred to the area as Friendship. By 1940 that name had replaced Tenleytown on the neighborhood post office.

The new residents were white, middle-class people with high aspirations for their new neighborhoods. They formed citizens' associations to press for civic improvements. The Northwest Suburban Citizens' Association was formed in 1892; in 1928 its name was changed to the Friendship Citizens' Association. By 1940 this group had successfully lobbied for new schools, paved streets, city services, an increased police force, and a library. Citizens' groups with similar aspirations were at work nearby. The Chevy Chase Citizens' Association was formed in 1909, and in 1920 it embraced the Connecticut Avenue Association. American University Park Citizens organized in 1927, and the Devonshire Downs (North Cleveland Park) Citizens in 1926.

When the newcomers looked at Fort Reno, however, they did not like what they saw—"colored people" as well as whites living in an odd variety of tired old houses, some dilapidated. The streets were not paved; chickens were running loose. Many of the Reno residents still had a horse and a cow, or even a goat. The whole image of Fort Reno, as quaint as some may have considered it, was offensive to those whose concept of beauty was red-brick or freshly painted white frame houses, neat fences, sidewalks and curbs, and closely mowed grass.

In the late 1920s and the 1930s, with the approval and encouragement of the civic associations, local and federal agencies took actions that resulted in the eventual demolition of all of the Fort Reno houses and the scattering of their residents. Land and houses were taken by eminent domain for a new water reservoir and tower in 1928 and 1929, for Alice Deal Junior High School in 1931, and for Woodrow Wilson Senior High in 1935. In 1930 Congress approved the acquisition of the fort site for a park, part of a larger plan to turn all the city's Civil War fort sites into recreation centers connected by a circular Fort Drive. The landowners of Fort Reno, white and black, protested to no avail. By 1939 almost all of the Reno community was gone.

The late 1930s and early 1940s brought major changes to the neighborhood, and once again it was a shift in transportation technology that created them. Automobiles were now within the price range of the average citizen, and planners and entrepreneurs made an effort to accommodate them in Tenleytown. The paving of Nebraska Avenue from American University to Military Road connected Tenleytown more directly with Chevy Chase and Connecticut Avenue. Tenley Circle, at the intersection of Nebraska Avenue, Wisconsin Avenue, and Yuma Street, was paved in 1936 and became a busy bus and streetcar connection.

Chain stores opened and began to attract shoppers who drove there from beyond the immediate neighborhood. In 1940 a large Sears, Roebuck and Co. department store with a parking lot on the roof took the place of the old Tennallytown Inn. Its automotive center off River Road was crowded with cars from all over Northwest Washington. Across the street, just north of Sarah Tennally's old house, was a new ultramodern Giant Food Shopping Center, which also had parking space on the roof. A Peoples Drug Store opened in 1939 next to the Masonic Lodge on Wisconsin Avenue. Four old houses were torn down just south of the library for a Kresge's variety store in 1941.

The new chain stores had a dramatic effect on the neighborhood. While some small local stores benefited from the increased business, others could not compete. Three years after Peoples Drug Store opened, for example, "Doc" Winslow Gauley was forced to close his Tenleytown Pharmacy. At the same time traffic increased on Wisconsin Avenue. A traffic light was installed at Albemarle Street to protect bus riders and the children walking to Saint Ann's and Janney schools. The small-town atmosphere disappeared; no longer did people recognize everyone on the street.

The character of Wisconsin Avenue was further altered when the Tenleytown-Friendship streetcar line, No. 30, took its last run in 1960. It was the last overhead trolley in the District. Wisconsin Avenue from Georgetown to the District line was repaved, and buses replaced the streetcars that had served the area for 70 years.

The new six-lane street began to carry even more traffic as the Wisconsin Avenue corridor became an entertainment as well as a shopping strip. In 1965 the K-B Cinema opened on Wisconsin Avenue near Harrison Street, the first movie theater in the Tenley-Friendship area. By 1979 it had been joined by the Outer Circle 1 and 2, the K-B Studio 1-2-3, the Jenifer Cinema I and II, and the Tenley Circle Theatres. Restaurants, bars, and fast-food outlets followed. Financial institutions also multiplied: by 1978 there were ten savings and loans and seven banks along the avenue from Warren Street to Western Avenue.

Traffic continued to increase, stoplights multiplied to one every three or four blocks, and the River Road and Wisconsin Avenue intersection became a bottleneck. According to an early 1970s article in the *American Motorist,* Wisconsin Avenue in Tenleytown was one of the busiest city streets in the nation at that time. A Metro tabulation of 1973 indicated there were 35,000 cars daily on the two-block stretch of Wisconsin Avenue between River Road and Tenley Circle.

The neighborhood's historic significance in the city's traffic patterns continued in the 1970s as construction began for a stop on the city's new subway system across the street from Sears. The new station opened in 1984. By this time there was renewed interest in the neighborhood's history, and local citizens' associations, led by Harold Gray of Palisades, successfully lobbied the Metro Board to name the station with the area's historic name, Tenleytown, rather than Tenley Circle, as had been proposed.

The subway station has brought increased property values and rising pressures for maximum-height office and commercial buildings. Despite organized citizen protest, new construction is under way and traffic continues to increase. The residential area is attracting ever-more-affluent buyers. As house prices have escalated, fewer moderate-income people can afford to live in Tenleytown. In the 1980s, however, the neighborhood has not yet lost its heterogeneity, only because many houses have been inherited by the working-class sons and daughters of old-time residents.

What is it that makes a modest frame bungalow sell for more than $200,000 in 1987? Location. To live on a quiet, treelined street in a relatively crime-free neighborhood, within walking distance of schools, stores, and the subway, is for many people the best of all possible urban worlds.

Although Tenleytown is now a thoroughly urban place, a few reminders of its village past remain. The oldest commercial building stands at Grant Road and Wisconsin, having housed a succession of local small businesses. The small frame houses of the past century still line the oldest streets, and Grant and Belt roads follow their narrow, irregular paths through the area. Its historic name resurrected by the recently published history and the subway stop, Tenleytown continues its historic crossroads role in an urban setting, but with a new awareness of its past.

Below left: "Doc" Gauley presided over his full-service drugstore in 1939. Situated at Wisconsin Avenue and Grant Road, N.W., Gauley's Pharmacy succeeded O'Day's general store and Scholl's Pharmacy at this location. Its "soda jerks" dispensed ten-cent ice cream sodas. Courtesy, Gladys Morders

Bottom: When Giant Food opened this ultramodern store in 1939, its rooftop parking lot lured commuters from beyond the immediate neighborhood. On Wisconsin Avenue just south of Brandywine Street, N.W., the store is recognizable as the Hechinger's of today. In 1942 its windows boasted of "tender juicy rib roast for 27 cents per pound." Courtesy, Library of Congress, Prints and Photographs Division

OYSTERS 15c
FRIED
TABLE
NO SMOKING
No 10
2012
DAIRY
BRIGHTWOOD 10
10
OYSTERS
SOUP 10
STEW 15

7

BRIGHTWOOD
FROM TOLLGATE TO SUBURB

Katherine Grandine

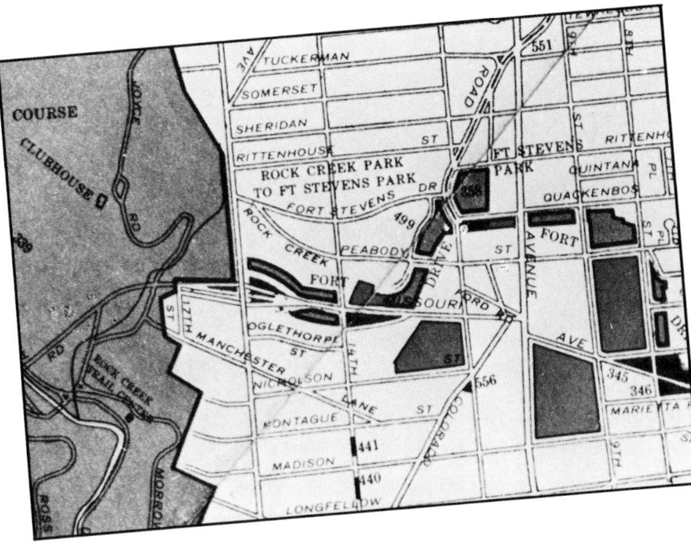

Fried oysters were 15 cents a half dozen when this Brightwood Railway Company trolley carried its young passenger up 7th Street, N.W., in the early 1890s. Overhead trolley lines such as this one were allowed only outside the boundary of old Washington City; south of Florida Avenue, an underground conduit provided the electric power. Courtesy, Robert A. Truax

Map: Park System of the National Capitol and Environs. National Park Service 1962. Courtesy, D.C. Public Library, Washingtoniana Division

During the eighteenth century the Brightwood area was largely uninhabited. Although attractively situated in rolling hills above the Potomac River and well watered by streams and springs, the region was isolated from Georgetown, the nearest city, by Rock Creek. The first recorded settler in the area was James White, who by 1772 had built a log cabin and owned 536 acres of royal patent land. White's descendants continued to live in the area until the 1950s and saw their isolated farm transformed first into a crossroads community, then finally into a suburb of the nation's capital.

In 1790 the area that would become Brightwood was included in the District of Columbia. The new capital city required a transportation network linking it to other towns in the region, so in 1810 Congress granted a charter to construct a system of turnpikes from Washington City to the District line. One of the roads extended 7th Street northward, paralleling Rock Creek to the District line, then turning west to Rockville, Maryland. Although delayed because of high costs, the 7th Street Turnpike was finally constructed between 1818 and 1822. Its importance was soon evident, and in 1825 local chronicler John Sessford reported travel along the road was "very considerable." Tollgates were constructed along the new turnpike; one of these was located three miles north of the Washington City boundary near the White homestead. This tollgate became the nucleus of the crossroads community later to be called Brightwood.

The 1855 Washington County assessment listed 31 property owners along the turnpike from Rock Creek Church Road to the District line. Most had small parcels; only six owned more than 100 acres. The area was racially mixed: five of the 31 landowners were black (four of these

Panic gripped Brightwood in July 1864 as Confederate troops advanced down the 7th Street Turnpike, now Georgia Avenue, N.W. Union troops at Fort Stevens, pictured here, prevented Confederate General Jubal Early from entering the city. The only fort in the District to see action during the Civil War, Fort Stevens has been partially reconstructed at 13th and Quackenbos Street. N.W. Courtesy, National Archives

were women). It is clear the majority were engaged in agriculture, for they were assessed the value of their horses and cows. Six of the 31 were slaveholders, but only two held more than one slave. The most expensive property in the area was the tollgate itself, valued at $250 an acre, with a building valued at $4,000. Most of the other property holders had buildings valued at less than $1,000, and the median value of the surrounding acreage was $80.

Three of these property owners, at least, had strong ties to Washington City: Thomas Carbery, William Cammack, and John Saul. Thomas Carbery owned Norway, a working farm, near the District line. In Washington he managed a successful business shipping and selling building materials. He was also active in public affairs, serving as mayor (1822-1823), city council member, and justice of the peace.

The county acreage of both William Cammack and John Saul directly sustained their city businesses. Cammack, who owned property just south of the intersection of Rock Creek Church Road and the 7th Street Turnpike, was a truck gardener who supplied fruits and vegetables to a local hotel. He was credited with greatly improving the quality of produce generally available in the city. John Saul, whose greenhouses were located near Crittenden Street, was a horticulturalist born in Ireland. Saul came to Washington in 1851 to supervise the improvement of public grounds under the direction of Andrew Jackson Downing, the noted American landscape architect. After Downing's death Saul made Washington his home and became nationally known as an importer and grower of evergreens, ornamental trees, fruit trees, shrubs, and greenhouse plants.

The remains of Fort Stevens at 13th and Quackenbos streets, N.W., the site of the only Civil War battle fought in the District of Columbia, provide a serene setting for the reveries of this mother and child. Photo by Linda Wheeler

Settlement in the Brightwood area was linear, stretching along the 7th Street Turnpike. Nonresidential activities were clustered in three places. Oak Grove, near the District line, offered a post office and a blacksmith shop. Crystal Spring Race Track, with a hotel and tavern, was a recreational center for the city. The third cluster grew up around the tollgate near the intersection of Milkhouse Ford and Piney Branch roads. Here were located, besides tollgate, a road house operated by Lewis Burnett, four dwellings, a hotel, Emory Methodist Episcopal Church, founded in 1832, and an enclave of black landowners in an area called "Vinegar Hill." This crossroads would become the center of Brightwood.

Brightwood was named in 1861 when Lewis Burnett was appointed as local postmaster and relocated the post office to his road house on the corner of Milkhouse Ford Road and the turnpike. "Brighton" was the first name chosen for the new post office. However, it was the same name as a post office in northern Montgomery

The Union Army commandeered this substantial building, home of prosperous businessman Matthew Gault Emory, for a signal station linking nearby Fort Stevens to Washington City. By the 1880s it had become a boardinghouse, sheltering some of the first Brightwood residents who commuted to jobs in the city. Courtesy, Columbia Historical Society

County, Maryland. The mails became so confused that the name was modified to "Brightwood" at the suggestion of Lewis Burnett and Archibald White. This name was widely adopted and came to designate a larger area than the one known as Brightwood today, including places now called Shepherd Park, Brightwood Park, and Petworth. Today a much smaller area, bounded by Aspen and Kennedy streets on the north and south and Georgia Avenue and Rock Creek Park on the east and west, is generally perceived as Brightwood.

As the community of Brightwood developed its own identity, the nation found itself engaged in the Civil War. The federal government turned Washington into a major training, equipping, and supply center for Union troops. For its defense, the Army Corps of Engineers constructed a ring of forts and supporting batteries in the hills surrounding the city. One of these, Fort Massachusetts, was constructed near the middle of Brightwood in August 1861 as an earthwork fortification built on land owned by Betty Thomas, a free black woman who earned her living as a dairywoman. A signal station to link the fort to Washington City was established across the street from the fort in the house that had been recently acquired by Matthew Gault Emery. In September 1862 Military Road was built to connect the western portion of the ring of forts, becoming the third road to intersect the turnpike in the middle of Brightwood.

Because it defended a major turnpike, the fort in Brightwood was enlarged and armed with 17 guns and mortars in 1863. At the same time, it was renamed Fort Stevens to honor Brigadier General Isaac I. Stevens, who died leading Union troops to victory at Chantilly, Virginia, in 1862.

Fort Stevens was the scene of the only Civil War battle fought in the District. In 1864 Confederate Major General Jubal A. Early marched his troops into Maryland and attacked Washington from the north. On July 11 Confederate cavalrymen rode down the 7th Street Turnpike and were deployed as skirmishers. Panic gripped the city as conflicting rumors circulated about the strength of the attacking force. Before the Confederate infantry could arrive to seize the fort, Union troops and volunteers were rushed in to strengthen it. Skirmishing continued throughout the day as the Confederates reconnoitered and assessed the possibility of an assault.

Meanwhile, Brightwood residents frantically protected their lives and property. As the Confederates advanced south along the turnpike, residents packed what they could and fled for safety. At the same time Confederate sharpshooters took up strategic field positions, and both sides prepared for battle.

On July 12 Union troops cleared the immediate area around the fort to ensure an unobstructed field of fire on the advancing Confederates. This required the destruction of barns and houses of many who lived in the middle of Brightwood. Betty Thomas, upon whose land the fort was built, lost her house; its basement was needed for ammunition. Later that day President Abraham Lincoln, who came to watch the battle from the fort's parapets, reportedly consoled Betty Thomas for the loss of her house, saying he knew it was hard but her reward would be great. There is no record that any monetary reward came her way. President Lincoln himself was in danger as he stood exposed to enemy fire until ordered by the commanding general to take cover or be placed under arrest.

At the end of the day the Confederates retreated up the turnpike toward Silver Spring. The next morning it was discovered that Early had withdrawn his troops into Virginia. The Confederate threat to Washington was at an end. Soon after the battle an official Battleground Cemetery was established a mile north of Fort Stevens, today located near Georgia Avenue and Van Buren Street. In it were interred the bodies of 40 Union soldiers who died in the battle.

After the battle Brightwood residents began to rebuild their battered community, constructing homes and a church. Fort Stevens, abandoned after the war, was left to decay on Betty Thomas' land, near present-day Quackenbos and 13th streets. It would never be forgotten, however, and the site was preserved later through the efforts of local residents.

The local community was strengthened after the war. A one-room public school for white children was constructed on Military Road in 1866, and at about the same time a public school for black children was built near Vinegar Hill. In 1873 a group of men organized the Stansbury Lodge of the Ancient Free and Accepted Masons. Later that year the group built a meeting hall near the center of Brightwood.

After the war the 7th Street Road continued to be one of the most important transportation routes to and from the city. Sometime between 1865 and 1871 Brightwood residents, annoyed by the continuing presence of the tollgate that made local travel expensive, extended Piney Branch Road parallel to the 7th Street Turnpike (now a small section of 12th Street), neatly circumventing the tollgate. In 1871, when all parts of the District were unified under one territorial government, Congress authorized the city government to acquire the turnpike and maintain it as a free public highway. Shortly thereafter 7th Street Road was macadamized and the tollgate removed.

More modern transportation also came to 7th Street with the introduction of regular public horsecar service. In 1862 the 7th Street line began to run from the wharves in Southwest to N Street in Northwest, one of the first three regular horsecar routes in the city. By 1873 it was extended to a point just south of Rock Creek Church Road, directing growth toward the Brightwood area.

Alexander R. Shepherd, the most powerful member of the territorial board of public works, must have recognized the potential of the area, for he chose Brightwood as the site of his country estate, in an area that would be subdivided as Shepherd Park. Shepherd acquired part of the Carbery-Lay property and constructed an elaborate wood-frame house valued at $15,000. It was by far the most expensive house in the neighborhood. The second-most-expensive dwelling—assessed at $7,000—was the country house of Matthew Gault Emery, a prosperous businessman and the last mayor of Washington (1870-1871) before the reorganization of the city government.

In 1880 Brightwood remained rural but had increased substantially in population. It now included 146 households, 86 white and 60 black. Although racially mixed, the black and white populations tended to settle in different areas. Blacks congregated in Vinegar Hill along Rock Creek Ford Road (formerly Milkhouse Ford Road) and Military Road. This remained the highest concentration of black landownership. Another group of blacks lived along Shepherd Road east of Brightwood Avenue, a new name for 7th Street Road. The white population settled along Brightwood Avenue and Piney Branch Road.

Among the white residents in Brightwood there seemed to be a general stability; 45 percent of the white households had lived in the District for more than 20 years. Many of the black members of the community, however, were newcomers; only 10 of the 60 black household heads had lived in the District before the Civil War. It is estimated that almost 40,000 new freedmen came to Washington from the South during and after the war, and this influx may explain the new families in Brightwood.

Brightwood residents in 1880 still seemed more oriented to the local community than to the federal city. About 26 percent were directly employed in agricultural activities, and more than 50 percent were employed in occupations that could have been locally supported. Only 20 percent held jobs that were definitely outside the community, including 22 families who boarded in the area. This was one of the first indications of suburbanization that became more pronounced in Brightwood between 1880 and 1910.

Throughout the late nineteenth century the growing population of the District pushed northward from old Washington City as developers laid out new suburbs along 7th, 14th, and 16th streets. In 1887 Myron M. Parker and Brainard H. Warner, both important local businessmen who would become leaders in the Washington Board of Trade, developed Petworth, just south of Brightwood. They purchased and subdivided the former estate of that name, once the home of the wealthy and aristocratic John Tayloe, builder of the Octagon House in the city. Petworth was planned to have many amenities that would appeal to well-to-do residents. The developers purposely designed Petworth with a grid system crossed by diagonals in a conscious effort to extend L'Enfant's plan into the county, setting it apart from other early suburbs such as LeDroit Park, where the street plan was designed to make it appear separate from the central city. Parker also obtained a charter for the Brightwood Railway Company in 1888 and promised the most up-to-date streetcar service, using new experimental technology.

The opening of Petworth enhanced the growth potential of Brightwood. Petworth grew slowly, however, and represented the last major interest that members of the Washington Board of Trade would show in real estate along Brightwood Avenue. The force behind Brightwood's suburban development was a group of men who had less capital and more modest ambitions, and who worked through a local citizens' association.

In 1891, angered when the Brightwood Railway Company's new streetcar system failed, local residents organized the Brightwood Avenue Citizens' Association. They demanded a workable streetcar system and the extension of the line farther along Brightwood Avenue. The new association, whose membership included residents from all along the avenue, also pursued local development through standing committees that focused on streets, roads, bridges, railroads, law and order, police and lights, and sanitation. This neighborhood association, like those in other areas, lobbied the city commissioners and Congress on behalf of local interests to compensate for the lack of a locally elected government.

Other real estate investors, encouraged to take advantage of services already provided to Petworth, opened new subdivisions in Brightwood. These parcels had to be small because of Brightwood's fragmented pattern of landholding. Most landowners had 40 acres or less, and older members of the farming community were reluctant to sell.

The first subdivision to be platted was 82 acres owned by Archibald White, a descendant of James White, the first resident in the region. White sold the property in 1891 for what he thought would be a university. The purchaser, however, ran into financial difficulties, and a disappointed Archibald White watched as his land was divided into smaller and smaller building lots. The new development, called Brightwood Park, consisted of about 33 city blocks with an average lot size of 50 by 150 feet. By 1894, a total of 34 frame houses had been constructed at an average assessed value of $1,190.

Diller B. Groff, a builder who resided in central Washington, owned the majority of lots and sold them directly to individuals or real estate agents. Groff built some of the houses himself and managed to dispose of them quickly; he rarely had more than one or two houses assessed to him per general assessment. William W. Herron and Daniel Ramey, real estate agents in central Washington, promoted the suburb and played leading roles in the Brightwood Avenue Citizens' Association.

In 1893 an Act of Congress officially extended the street plan of old Washington City, as designed by L'Enfant, to the entire District. A straight grid pattern was imposed on the community, and older roads were shifted, straightened, and widened, erasing much of the early physical identity of Brightwood. However, it is still possible to find remnants of the older roads such as Shepherd Alley, Rock Creek Ford Road, and 12th Street.

The social as well as the physical identity of old Brightwood changed as new residents, no longer tied to agriculture or the local community, moved in. During the first decade of the twentieth century, other subdivisions opened as older residents retired from farming or died, leaving heirs uninterested in continuing to operate the family farm. By 1907 Whitecroft, Saul's Addition, North Brightwood, and Peter's Mill Seat had opened. "Brightwood" came to designate a smaller and smaller geographic area as each new suburb developed its own separate physical and social identity.

In 1910 there were 459 households in Brightwood, about three times as many as in 1880. A little less than half of the residents lived in the subdivision of Brightwood Park. The proportion of blacks in the community had dropped dramatically, from 41 percent of all households in 1880 to only about 15 percent in 1910. Less than 5 percent of the residents remained involved in any agricultural activity; most worked in Washington City or in the wider community.

Between 1900 and 1916 the Brightwood Citizens' Association continued to pursue urban amenities under the leadership of Louis P. Shoemaker. A descendant of several locally prominent families, Shoemaker was a real estate agent. After 350 acres, including his family homestead, were purchased for Rock Creek Park, Shoemaker moved to Brightwood and aided the development of that area. He brought political skill to the citizens' association and succeeded in interesting influential District commissioners and congressmen in the development of the region. As evidence of his endeavors, Walter Reed U.S. Military Hospital (now Walter Reed Army Medical Center) was opened in 1908 near Brightwood. In hopes of more congressional support, residents supported a bill changing the name of Brightwood Avenue to Georgia Avenue. Unfortunately, the Georgia senator they had hoped would intercede for them died soon after.

By the time of Shoemaker's death in 1916, the stage was set for the total absorption of old Brightwood into greater Washington. Residents no longer saw themselves as part of a rural community but as part of suburban Washington, entitled to city services paid for at public expense. It was left to other developers to build up the area.

One of these was Harry Wardman, an immigrant from England and one of the most colorful developers in the history of Washington, D.C. Wardman (1872-1938), described in his *New York Times* obituary as the "man who overbuilt Washington," arrived in the city in 1895. During his career he built hundreds of single-family dwellings, rowhouses, and commercial, office, and apartment buildings. At his death, in 1938, it was estimated that between one-eighth and one-tenth of the city's residents lived in buildings constructed by him.

Wardman worked in Brightwood three times during his long and prolific career. In 1897-1898 he began by building six wood-frame houses on the corner of 9th and Longfellow streets in Brightwood Park. These houses were freestanding, single-family dwellings set close together on small lots. Wardman returned to Brightwood after World War I when then-Secretary of Commerce Herbert Hoover challenged local developers and builders to relieve the District's postwar housing shortage. Wardman accepted the challenge and built more than 500 houses in the Brightwood area in the 1920s. After losing everything in the crash of 1929, Wardman started again in Brightwood and was still building there when he died in 1938.

Real estate maps show most of Brightwood fully developed by 1945. Only the site of Fort Stevens and the Emery Mansion remained open space. Georgia Avenue became Brightwood's commercial street. Single-family or semidetached houses dominated the area, but the low-rise apartment buildings that appeared in the mid-1920s foreshadowed the future density of the neighborhood. More apartment buildings and rowhouses, replacing older, single-family houses, were constructed during the late 1930s and 1940s.

Brightwood remained predominantly a community of whites from the 1920s through the 1960s. Many of these people were Jews who moved north along the 7th Street and Georgia Avenue corridor from their earliest homes in Southwest and downtown. Before 1960 the largest proportion of the black population remained north of Military Road, in the vicinity of Vinegar Hill, the traditional enclave of black land ownership. By 1970, however, the black population of Brightwood as a whole outnumbered the white. Similar racial shifts occurred in many neighborhoods of the city at this time.

Although twentieth-century development has made Brightwood an urban community, Brightwood's nineteenth-century past can still be found tucked away in remnants of the older street patterns, wood-frame houses of the earliest phase of suburbanization, and occasionally even an older farmhouse such as the Yost house on Madison Street near 14th. The site of Fort Stevens and the Battleground Cemetery still exist, memorials to Brightwood's Civil War experience. The neighborhood's history is taught through programs in the Brightwood Elementary School. However, the strongest link between the old and the new Brightwood is the continuing concern of local residents to ensure, through active local organizations, the quality of their neighborhood.

William Work opened one of the first businesses in the Brightwood Park subdivision in this 1902 building that still stands at Longfellow Street and Georgia Avenue, N.W. seen here as it looked in 1910. Courtesy, Columbia Historical Society

8

OLD ANACOSTIA

WASHINGTON'S FIRST SUBURB

Howard Gillette, Jr.

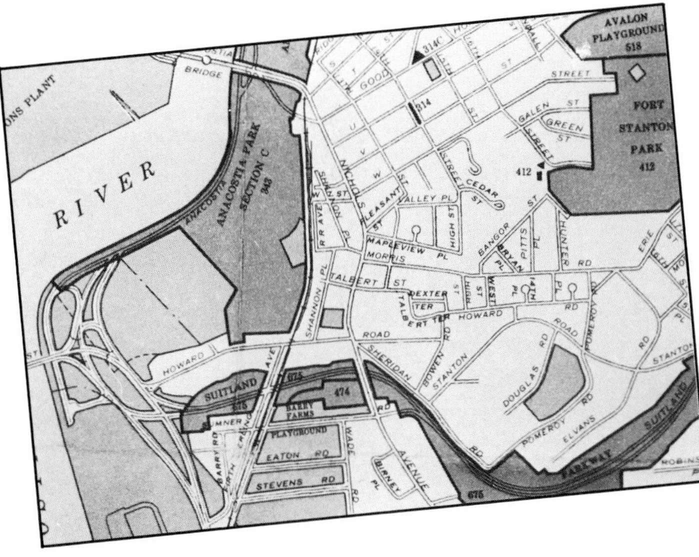

The famous abolitionist Frederick Douglass was a resident of Old Anacostia. In addition to his national activities on behalf of equal rights, he served Washington, D.C., as a member of the Territorial governor's council, and U.S. marshal. Courtesy, Howard University, Moorland-Spingarn Research Center

Map: Park System of the National Capitol and Environs. National Park Service 1962. Courtesy, D.C. Public Library, Washingtoniana Division

Uniontown, or "Old Anacostia" as it is sometimes known, holds the distinction of being both Washington's first suburb as well as a microcosm of the changes of the modern city. As the first development outside Washington City, laid out across the Eastern Branch (Anacostia River) in 1854, it differed from the streetcar-inspired, middle-class suburbs such as LeDroit Park that followed after the Civil War. Uniontown preceded public transportation; its developers hoped to attract a working-class population that would walk to jobs at the Navy Yard, just across the river. Like later suburbs, however, it counted as its chief asset easy access to both city and country.

Uniontown's isolation from the rest of the city soon turned to detriment, as innovations in public transportation and modern city services were slow to arrive. At first offering the best of suburban and urban living, Uniontown could not claim either for long, as its proud and active citizenry, despite its best efforts, alternately faced neglect and active harm from actions taken by the city as a whole. Its fate was shared over time by many of the communities of far Southeast that developed around it.

Washingtonians disagree on the extent of today's Anacostia. The name was originally applied to a new post office located at the foot of the Navy Yard Bridge in 1849, on the land laid out as Uniontown just five years later. Many local residents insist that the name Anacostia may be properly applied, therefore, only to Uniontown and the adjacent Barry's Farm (now Barry Farms) that developed shortly thereafter. Through common usage, however, as well as the most recent government and historical studies, the name Anacostia has come to refer to all the communities of far Southeast that lie east of the Anacostia River and south of Pennsylvania Avenue, S.E., distinguishing its oldest settlements of Uniontown and Barry's Farm as "Old Anacostia."

Originally identified on a 1612 map drawn by Captain John Smith as the Indian village of Nacochtanke, the area ultimately drew its name from the latinized derivation of that Indian name—Anaquash(a)-tan(i)k—meaning a town of traders. In 1793 Thomas Jefferson suggested that Andrew Ellicott add to his map of Washington the words "or Annokostia" to his designation of the Eastern Branch of the Potomac. The river would continue to be called the Eastern Branch, however, until the early twentieth century.

Tobacco growers and merchants, drawn to the area because of its advantages for shipping in the eighteenth century, carved out large estates within the bounds of Maryland's Prince George's County. Maryland ceded this territory to the new District of Columbia at Jefferson's insistence, as he argued that control of the area beyond the Potomac and the Eastern Branch was necessary to help defend the new capital in the event of attack. When such a threat actually materialized in the War of 1812, however, the District militia virtually abandoned the area to the British by retreating back into Washington City, literally burning the bridges across the Eastern Branch behind them to buy a little more time to shore up their inadequate defenses. During the Civil War the city built a string of forts at the outer perimeter of the eastern portion of the District to stave off any possible attacks from the Confederates, but the attitude that the area was more buffer than a part of the city proper compromised its chances for development.

Although Pierre L'Enfant anticipated that the Eastern Branch would afford the new District its most advantageous port, both man and nature conspired against his expectations. In 1815 the District constructed the Washington Canal across the city to connect the Eastern Branch to the Potomac River near Georgetown, but there were continual problems in keeping it open. Soil depletion and the steady silting of the Eastern Branch also dampened the potential for trade on the eastern side of the city. Largely as a result, the land east of Washington City failed to attract commerce.

One of the few communities to develop there in the early part of the nineteenth century was the village of Good Hope, situated on a hilltop overlooking the Eastern Branch. A tavern, blacksmith shop, stable, and a few other small businesses helped make the area a convenient way station on the route from the surrounding countryside into the city. The founding of the Allen African Methodist Episcopal Church in 1850 reflected the importance of the area's growing free-black community.

By mid-century circumstances favored the establishment of quite a different kind of community, Washington's first conscious suburban development. In the first place, the Navy Yard in Washington City—very accessible from eastern Washington by way of the Navy Yard Bridge—had become the city's largest and steadiest industrial employer. In addition, in 1853, the federal government purchased a large tract south of the area that would become Barry's Farm for a new mental hospital, at the urging of health reformers, including Dorothea Dix. It was clear this Government Hospital for the Insane, later renamed St. Elizabeths, would also provide new local employment.

In 1854, three newcomers to the city saw an opportunity and formed the Union Land Association to purchase and develop 100 acres of a 240-acre farm near St. Elizabeths. They laid out lots in a grid around a tree-lined esplanade. In all, the area covered 15 square blocks, bounded by Harrison Street (Good Hope Road) to the north, Jefferson Street (W Street) to the south, Taylor Street (16th Street) to the east, and Monroe Street (Martin Luther King, Jr. Avenue) to the west.

Advertised as "situated in the most beautiful and healthy neighborhood around Washington," the Uniontown settlement was to combine the best of urban form in graded streets and paved gutters with the natural benefits of country living. Covenants restricted residence not just to native-born whites but decreed as well that there be no pigs or soap-boiling. The racial restriction was directed at potential buyers at the Navy Yard who reportedly complained of the growing presence of blacks in Capitol Hill neighborhoods adjacent to the yard. The restriction on industry signaled the first effort to protect a suburban Washington area from nuisances then traditionally relegated to the periphery of the built-up city. It would be officially known as Uniontown from 1865 to 1886, when Congress enacted legislation to return the name "Anacostia" because the name "Uniontown" was so popular in many parts of the country after the Civil War.

Although the developers sold 350 lots quickly, and one of their number, John Van Hook, established a distinguished residence on Cedar Hill high above the fledgling community, cutbacks in the work force at the Navy Yard and competition from other developers in the city proper dampened growth. While most of the lots had been sold by 1860, only a few had been built upon, mostly near the main streets of Monroe and Harrison. When further financial difficulties generated by the panic of 1873 resulted in the failure of the Union Land Company, Van Hook was forced to sell his Cedar Hill property. Ironically, the buyer was the District's most prominent black man, Frederick Douglass, who managed to purchase the home, despite his own financial problems brought on by the failure of the Freedmen's Bank, with the help of a loan from an abolitionist friend.

While Uniontown remained a predominantly white community, it was joined by a black settlement nearby on a 375-acre farm originally owned by James Barry between Uniontown and St. Elizabeths. Bought by the Bureau of Refugees, Freedmen and Abandoned Lands (the Freedmen's Bureau) during Reconstruction to accommodate some of the thousands of freedmen who swelled Washington's black population during and after the war, Barry's Farm came to be known as a model for the self-help philosophy of the nascent Republican party. The bureau sold one-acre lots at prices between $125 and $300, providing enough lumber to build a standard two-room house. Payments were to be made in 24 installments, and more lumber could be purchased if necessary. Whole families worked hard to buy into the area, and by 1868 all but 59 of 359 lots had been sold and a community of some 500 families established, complete with a new Baptist church and a school for 150 pupils. The Freedmen's Bureau could report that year that the area had low-rent housing, work training, adequate educational facilities, and an effective street system. In recognition of their political allies, residents gave their streets the names of the radical Republican leaders most sympathetic to their cause: Sumner, Stevens, and Wade.

Pedestrians stroll along Nichols Avenue, S.E., in Hillsdale around the turn of the century. The community began life as Barry's Farm when it was created by the Freedmen's Bureau just after the Civil War. Courtesy, Library of Congress, Prints and Photographs Division

When the future of the District's governance became an issue after the war, Anacostians were torn between the desire to enhance the new powers offered them through ward politics and the promises a consolidated territorial government might bring in the form of better services for their isolated community. As was to be the case so often in later years, the hopes that lay with territorial government were dashed, as Alexander Shepherd used his powers both as the most powerful member of the Board of Public Works and later as governor to build up the Northwest sector of the city on the other side of the river. The end of territorial government brought the loss of both political power and hope for better services. Much of Southeast Washington remained underdeveloped and country-like well into the twentieth century.

The late arrival of a streetcar line was typical of Anacostia's lag in services. The Anacostia and Potomac River Street Railway brought horsecar service across the 11th Street Bridge in 1875; horsecars had begun serving the city west of the river 13 years earlier.

This was the scene on Independence Day, 1917, along the 2200 block of Nicholas Avenue, S.E. Courtesy, Library of Congress, Prints and Photographs Division

The old wooden Pennsylvania Avenue Bridge had burned in 1845 and was not replaced until growing citizen demands finally won a new, iron-and-masonry crossing in 1890. The bridge spurred the first new development since Barry's Farm, as Colonel Arthur Randle created Randle Highlands (also known as East Washington Heights) at its Anacostia terminus and then brought the first electric streetcar across the river to serve it. He brought another streetcar line out Nichols Avenue to serve his other 1890s development, Congress Heights, at the southern tip of Anacostia.

There would be no more large developments in far Southeast until World War II. Randle Highlands, Congress Heights, Uniontown (now Old Anacostia), and Barry's Farm/ Hillsdale (now Barry Farms) carried on in the manner of small towns, surrounded by open spaces. Many residents kept gardens on their large lots and sold the produce in central Washington. Although a few prominent Washingtonians lived in the area, such as D.C. Budget Director Walter L. Fowler as well as Frederick Douglass, most residents worked at blue-collar or laboring jobs. The Navy Yard continued to be a major employer, as were the small businesses in Hillsdale and Anacostia that served the local community. A few, such as Curtis Brothers Furniture Store and Greenwood Moving and Storage, would become known citywide. Many other residents, however, traveled to work at low-paying jobs in the central city.

The black and white communities grew separately, developing their own businesses, churches, and other institutions. Eight public elementary schools were built in far-Southeast between 1881 and 1910, six for white children and two for black. The area would not have a secondary school, however, until 1935, when Anacostia High School was built to serve the white community; black students had to travel across the river to high school until Anacostia High was integrated in 1955.

Lacking elected government representation, citizens here as in other city neighborhoods organized to present their needs to the appointed city commissioners. White Anacostians formed the Anacostia Citizens' Association in 1882, and blacks formed the Barry's Farm/Hillsdale Civic Association. These organizations lobbied for services that had come to communities across the river more easily: sewer and water mains, electric lines, and adequate public transportation. Despite their efforts, far Southeast continued to lag behind the rest of the city. An article from an 1891 edition of the *Evening Star* reported that "the streets of Hillsdale have the appearance of being neglected by the authorities and inconvenience and discomfort are experienced by the residents as a consequence. The taxpayers are becoming restive under this neglect. Howard Avenue, for instance . . . which is occupied by many residents on either side, is a mere country lane, not even provided with a sidewalk. Water lines were delayed because residents could not afford the cost of installing the pipes from the street." A petition circulated by the Congress Heights Civic Association in 1907 seeking help in combatting the pollution of local wells by the Anacostia River claimed that 79 percent of all District appropriations over the previous 10 years had been spent on the area west of the Capitol.

By 1920 all of far Southeast south of Pennsylvania Avenue had a population of 7,000, still less than 2 percent of the District population of 438,000. The area grew rapidly in the next decade, however, as the development of Twining City and the growth of Randle Highlands and Congress Heights doubled the population by 1930. In the midst of growth, community cooperation remained high. Under the prodding of Dr. George Havenner as president of the Anacostia Citizens' Association, the District commissioners authorized the conversion of the swampy Anacostia flats into a park, and the city added a reservoir at Fort Stanton Park.

The city's housing policies of the mid-twentieth century altered dramatically Anacostia's social composition. During World War II a Federal Housing Administration rental program, directed toward relieving housing congestion in the city at large, stimulated the quick construction of a number of garden apartments in far Southeast. To these were added 943 units of public housing. The shift from single-family to multiple units was subsequently expanded with the addition of 1,300

The Birney Public School was 10 years old when its students visited this Kennebeck Ice wagon in 1899. This photograph was one of a documentary series by Frances Benjamin Johnston to show off the D.C. Public Schools at the Paris Exposition of 1900. Courtesy, Library of Congress, Prints and Photographs Division

Above: These brick houses stand on Branch Avenue, near Alabama Avenue, S.E., in Hillcrest, one of a number of far-Southeast neighborhoods developed in the twentieth century. Photo by Emily Medvec

Right: Cows graze peacefully in the Anacostia marshes southeast of the Capitol around 1882. These wet lowlands were dredged and filled early in the twentieth century, creating Anacostia Park. Courtesy, National Archives

public housing units in the 1950s and 1960s, as planners attempted to find new homes for those displaced across the river by redevelopment and highway construction. This new density not only strained transportation, but play areas were sacrificed, and other services were neglected. Although residents of Barry Farms managed to block a potentially disruptive redevelopment plan for their neighborhood in 1948, the construction of the Suitland Parkway severed their community from the rest of Anacostia.

Even triumph had its costs. Residents of far Southeast worked for seven years to see the end of segregated education; plaintiffs from the Sousa Elementary School in the Benning Heights case, *Bolling v. Sharpe,* were included in the 1954 *Brown v. Board of Education* Supreme Court case that accomplished that end. Victory was short-lived, however, as their schools quickly resegregated after whites first protested integration and then fled the area. Far-Southeast's white population dropped from 82.4 percent in 1950 to 67.7 percent in 1960 and 14 percent in 1970.

Such dramatic change had its effect in communities like Uniontown, where segregation had been the norm even after Frederick Douglass' arrival. Some institutions, like St. Teresa's Catholic Church at 13th and V streets, made the adjustment. Having told its black members to meet in the basement in the early part of the century, thereby causing a good portion of the parishioners to join other churches, in the 1960s St. Teresa's adapted to the neighborhood's new demography. It incorporated black musical forms and then installed a black priest, the Reverend George Stallings; its transformation gained it a new role in the predominantly black community around it. In contrast, the Emanuel Episcopal Church across the street refused to cooperate with the growing black Episcopal church nearby, St. Philip the Evangelist, and ultimately lost the support of the community. In 1982 the church was deconsecrated, and the building has since been restored and taken over by a black Baptist congregation.

By the 1960s and 1970s some areas in far Southeast had remained healthy residential neighborhoods that attracted middle-income people and professionals, including the city's mayor, Marion Barry. However, other sections of Anacostia, in its broadest sense, became dumping grounds for unwanted activities, and residents had to struggle with the problems they brought. They included an overwhelming amount of low-income housing, the Blue Plains sewage-treatment plant, and a number of other nuisance

Children clowned for the camera in 1981 outside the Anacostia Neighborhood Museum, opened in an old theater on Martin Luther King, Jr., Avenue by the Smithsonian Institution in 1967. The museum has since moved to a building designed for its purposes at 1901 Fort Place, S.E. Courtesy, Anacostia Neighborhood Museum

The history and architecture of Uniontown were attracting newfound attention in the 1970s when this family posed for a Washington Star *photographer outside their home on U Street, S.E., one of the oldest and finest early houses of Uniontown still standing. Courtesy, D.C. Public Library, Washingtoniana Division, c. Washington Post*

facilities. In Old Anacostia a number of businesses along Nichols (now Martin Luther King) Avenue left for the suburbs, including Curtis Brothers Furniture, whose trademark giant chair continues to serve as a local landmark. Even the prospect of a subway stop seemed remote, as the city and Prince George's County officials bickered over the location of the trans-Anacostia River route.

In the 1980s valuations of Washington real estate repeatedly listed far-Southeast properties as among the lowest in the city. From 1970 to 1980 the area lost 30 percent in population, even as it climbed in percentage of blacks to 98.3 and in the percentage of female-headed families and youngsters. Overall, educational and income levels lagged well behind the city average, and crucial services suffered from a cut of $538 million in the first three years of the Reagan administration. But even as Anacostia's situation seemed bleakest, a series of community initiatives marked a positive turn.

Public improvements accelerated in the area after the opening of Ballou in 1960, the first senior high school east of the river since the building of Anacostia High School in 1935. At the instigation of James Banks, a native of Barry's Farm and a Washington housing activist, local zoning was changed to limit the construction of new garden apartments, and sidewalks were built around existing units to help control soil erosion. In 1967, the Smithsonian Institution, responding to pressure from Washington's black community, opened the Anacostia Neighborhood Museum on Nichols Avenue. Headed by John Kinard, a former minister and program officer at the D.C. Office of Economic Opportunity, the museum opened in the old Carver Theater to a crowd of 10,000 people.

Also central to the new hopes for Anacostia was the decision to identify the Uniontown area as a historic district. Although there were some fears that such designation would bring the kind of displacement that appeared to accompany rising property rates in historic districts elsewhere in the city, supporters of the effort led by the Neighborhood Housing Services (NHS) organization, located in Anacostia in 1972, argued that the potential benefits of increased pride in community through home improvements were worth the risk. By providing assistance to residents in purchasing their homes as well as by demonstrating restoration techniques, NHS helped improve the physical quality of at least one section of Old Anacostia.

In addition to seeking housing improvements, community leaders sought the revitalization of Old Anacostia's commercial area. Following the disastrous riots of 1968, they formed the Anacostia Economic Development Corporation (AEDC) in December 1969. Although the organization had some trouble realizing its goal to introduce better housing to the area, it did manage to direct attention to the potential revitalization a new Metro subway stop might offer. Working with a planning team based at George Washington University in 1972, AEDC challenged plans to route the Green Line through the Good Hope Road corridor and directly to Suitland, bypassing the primary development-potential and service-dependent area of Old Anacostia. By 1976 the Metro board had agreed, but Prince George's supporters of a new route farther south managed through court action to bring construction to a halt. Anacostians went to court themselves, and in 1983 they formed the Anacostia Coordinating Council

The patriotic passengers on this Fourth of July float await their turn in a holiday parade about 1917 in Old Anacostia. Courtesy, Library of Congress, Prints and Photographs Division

(ACC), with the immediate objective of separating the Anacostia Metro station and tunnel from the stalemate in Prince George's County. Acknowledging in its mission statement Anacostia's historic neglect, the ACC nonetheless declared its intention of building on a distinctive heritage to identify those resources that could become significant factors in the area's rebirth. Speaking for the ACC before the city council in November 1984, John Kinard testified, "For too many years Anacostia has been the forgotten part of the National Capital. Now, with the coming of Metro, we are working to help our community rejoin the city."

The ACC helped generate 30,000 signatures on a petition to unblock construction of the Anacostia station and tunnel and succeeded in getting clearance for their construction while the details of the Metro route in Prince George's County were worked out. Working again with George Washington University's Department of Urban and Regional Planning, the council subsequently proceeded to prepare Anacostia's first development-concept plan, "Old Anacostia: A Capital Gain," to guide actual development stimulated by new Metro construction. It successfully challenged the design of a McDonald's restaurant planned for the historic district and has worked with several community-development corporations to secure new public agencies and private buildings on Martin Luther King Avenue.

The recent redevelopment of the old Curtis Brothers property on Martin Luther King Avenue and the location there of the D.C. Lottery and Charitable Games Board offers promise for a rebirth of Old Anacostia's commercial area. In 1986 Mayor Barry designated a large part of Anacostia as one of three Development Zones for the city, into which the city has plans to target $160 million over a period of five years. Another major retail/office complex is planned for 2100 Martin Luther King Avenue by yet another community-development corporation.

A walk through Old Anacostia today reveals its mixed history. Frederick Douglass' home, now a historic site operated by the National Park Service, sits in relatively isolated splendor above the urban neighborhood. Many of the buildings in the area are run-down, and open lots that might offer some relief from the urban setting are often strewn with junk. And yet, despite the signs of decay in boarded-up buildings, there are signs of revitalization as well. Older houses are being renovated. Churches of all kinds attract followers to their services. A farmer's market and the historic esplanade offer public spaces for gathering. More important, the people of Old Anacostia maintain a tradition of civic commitment, struggling with their problems in the effort to make Washington's first suburb an urban neighborhood that can work in the twentieth century.

METROPOLITAN
BRANCH
R.R.
Harewood Road
SOLDIERS HOME
Rock Creek Church Road
Bunker Hill Road
Brentwood Road
WASHINGTON BRANCH
MT OLIVET CEMETERY
SEVENTH STREET TURNPIKE
Piney Branch Road
GLENWOOD CEMETERY
PROSPECT HILL CEMETERY
COLUMBIA INSTITUTION FOR THE DEAF AND DUMB
SCHUTZEN PARK
HOWARD UNIVERSITY
MT PLEASANT
PLEASANT PLAINS
MT PLEASANT VILLAGE
MERIDIAN HILL
ROCK CREEK
CAPITOL & BOUNDARY.
27
METROPOLITAN

PART THREE

A NEW IMAGE FOR THE CAPITAL

Washington's fortunes changed with the Civil War—a conflict that made it clear the country needed a strong federal government and a more modern and attractive capital city to represent and serve it. The war left the District in shambles, both physically and socially, and serious suggestions that the capital be moved elsewhere forced some dramatic improvements. A more efficient, consolidated territorial government replaced the three separate governments of Georgetown, Washington City, and Washington County in 1871. Alexander "Boss" Shepherd led the territory's board of public works in a massive modernization project in the early 1870s, literally pulling the city out of the mud. Its new smoothly paved, tree-lined, and well-lit avenues realized for the first time some of the grandeur envisioned by the city's founders.

The District's population had almost doubled to about 132,000 during the wartime decade of the 1860s, as federal employment more than tripled. During the 1870s it jumped again to almost 178,000 as entrepreneurs, new government employees, and others began to see new opportunities in the capital.

Shepherd's improvements and a new public transportation system, a network of horse-drawn streetcar lines begun in 1862, combined to shape the way the city grew. Open places within Washington City, newly served by paved streets and sewer and water lines, began to fill out along the streetcar routes, including the neighborhoods we know today as Dupont Circle and Shaw. At the same time developers laid out the first commuter suburbs outside the city boundaries, such as Mount Pleasant and LeDroit Park.

The District's first steam railroad suburb also dates from this period. In 1873 members of the Sheriff-Lowrie-Dean family subdivided their farm across the Eastern Branch to take advantage of a stop on a new Southern Maryland Railroad Company line. Although unsuccessful at first, Deanwood foreshadowed, along with the city's horsecar suburbs across the river, a trend toward suburbanization that would accelerate in the next decade.

Left: Metropolitan Railroad Company employees pose in 1864 with one of the first horsecars to run in the District of Columbia, as it stood on Boundary Street (Florida Avenue, N.W.) between Connecticut Avenue and 18th Street. Courtesy, D.C. Public Library, Washingtoniana Division

Map; 1873, Washington City/ Post Civil War. Courtesy, Kathryn S. Smith

9

Dupont Circle

Fashionable In-Town Address

Linda Wheeler

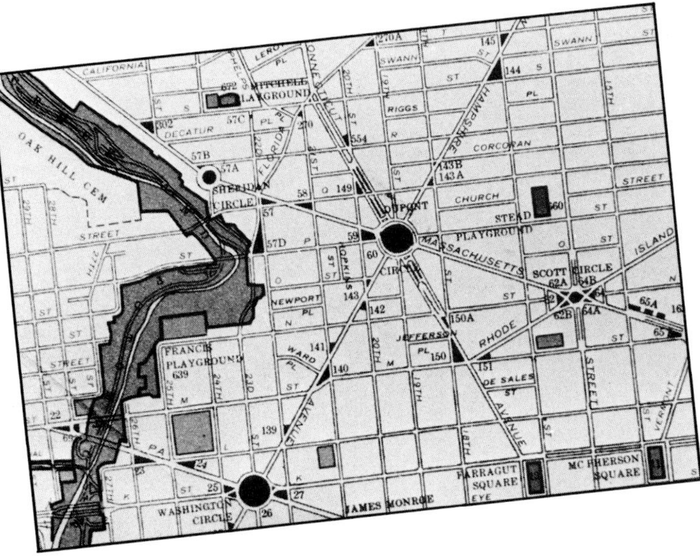

The Romanesque tower of the Christian Heurich mansion has been a landmark at 20th and Sunderland Place, N.W., just off Dupont Circle since its completion in 1894. It is now a house museum and the headquarters of the Columbia Historical Society. Courtesy, Columbia Historical Society

Map: Park System of the National Capitol and Environs. National Park Service 1962. Courtesy, D.C. Public Library, Washingtoniana Division

A little more than a century ago the neighborhood now known as Dupont Circle was an undeveloped area on the outskirts of the growing city of Washington, D.C. The banks of Slash Run, a tributary of Rock Creek that meandered through the area, were dotted with slaughterhouses and farmers' gardens.

Today Dupont Circle is perhaps the city's most cosmopolitan residential neighborhood, with space for only the smallest of gardens and no room for a slaughterhouse. Every residential block in this popular neighborhood is crowded with substantial rowhouses, a mix of old and new apartment buildings, and a generous sprinkling of historic mansions, many of which now house embassies. The commercial streets and avenues that crisscross the neighborhood are filled with restaurants, banks, office buildings, movie theaters, art galleries, and a variety of upscale stores. At its center is Dupont Circle, an element in L'Enfant's original design for the city, now appropriately graced with a white marble fountain honoring Civil War hero Rear Admiral Samuel Francis Du Pont. The circle was called Pacific Circle in the 1880s because it was the westernmost sector of the city; a statue to Du Pont that preceded the fountain was erected in 1884. Today its many benches and landscaped grounds constantly attract crowds from nearby stores, houses, and office buildings.

The evolution of this area—from countryside to the city's most fashionable address at the turn of the century to the present lively, downtown neighborhood—parallels the emergence of Washington as a sophisticated world capital.

From the time the city was created, visitors and residents alike complained about its muddy and unlit streets

Among the mansions dominating Dupont Circle in the early 1920s were the 55-room, three-story home of the Joseph Leiter family at the right and the similarly grand home of Eleanor "Cissy" Patterson, editor and publisher of the **Washington Times Herald**, *on the left. Courtesy, Library of Congress, Prints and Photographs Division*

and its ragged appearance. During the entire antebellum period, members of Congress and the socially prominent for the most part lived in the capital only during the winter season when Congress was in session and when society became briefly interesting. Most lived in boardinghouses and hotels without making a permanent commitment to the city. Dupont Circle at this time was well outside the populated area of Washington City and completely undeveloped, even though the Circle and its avenues and streets appeared on the published maps of the day.

It was the vast civic improvements completed by the board of public works in the early 1870s that opened this area for construction, and its fortunes were closely tied to the most prominent figure in that effort, Alexander "Boss" Shepherd, de facto head of the board. He chose to build his own home not far from Dupont Circle at the corner of Connecticut Avenue and K Street, and his critics maintained that he favored his new neighborhood over other, more established areas such as Capitol Hill and Georgetown as he decided where streets would be graded, paved, and lit, sewers laid, and trees planted.

Indeed, the board did pour many improvements into the central city and the undeveloped land just to the north. It converted Slash Run into a covered sewer, thus eliminating the unhealthful marshes along its course through the neighborhood. It replaced a low, covered bridge across Rock Creek at P Street with a more modern metal-truss

Elegant gatherings at the British Legation, left, at the corner of Connecticut Avenue and N Street, N.W., lent prestige to Dupont Circle in the 1890s. This view looks up Connecticut Avenue toward the Circle. The turreted mansion in the background is Stewart's Castle. Courtesy, D.C. Public Library, Washingtoniana Division

bridge in 1871, thus improving connections between Dupont Circle and the older and much more developed neighborhood of Georgetown. The open space at the intersection of Massachusetts, New Hampshire, and Connecticut avenues and 19th and P streets was fenced in to form a federal park within the traffic circle, and Connecticut Avenue was paved as far north as Boundary Street (now Florida Avenue). In 1874 the Metropolitan Railroad Company laid tracks along Connecticut Avenue as well, making the circle even more accessible and the neighborhood more desirable.

The buildings Shepherd built for himself in 1873, by which time he had become the governor of the District's territorial government, were a row of three grand stone houses just five blocks south of Dupont Circle. His home in the corner building was lavishly decorated with curtains made of Belgian lace and walls covered with scarlet and blue satin. Known as Shepherd's Row, the three houses were subsequently occupied by prominent government officials as well as the Russian and Chinese legations, remaining at the center of Washington social life until the 1920s, when K Street began to develop as a commercial corridor.

The area immediately attracted investors of great wealth. The most prominent were part of a group called the California Syndicate, including mining industrialist Curtis Hillyer, California miner Thomas Sunderland, and Nevada Senator William M. Stewart, who also had mining interests in the West. Unlike their pre-Civil War predecessors, this group of socially elite and politically powerful people now saw the Shepherd improvements and the growing national importance of the federal government as reasons to invest in the capital.

Stewart was the boldest. As early as 1873 he decided to use some of the fortune he had amassed as a gold prospector to build an extravagant Second Empire mansion on the practically empty circle at the intersection of Massachusetts and Connecticut avenues, now the site of the Riggs National Bank. It seemed so out of place in this still-remote part of the city that it was derided as "Stewart's Folly." It was designed by prominent architect Adolph Cluss, who was also responsible for the massive Center Market and many other important buildings in the city. Stewart's Castle, as it was also called, boasted a five-story entrance tower and a carriage porch. James Goode in his book on the lost buildings of Washington, *Capital Losses*, has documented this lavish home and many others that once stood near the Circle. Stewart's wife purchased furniture for the house while traveling in Europe, and the couple was known for their extravagant parties. A newspaper reporter of the day said attending receptions at the mansion "makes one feel like Marco Polo at the Court of Kublai Khan."

The upkeep of the house plus a huge staff of servants and a stable of Thoroughbred horses was such a financial drain that the family lived in the house only for brief periods.

Above: The Chinese minister and his staff conduct business in the Dupont Circle mansion built by Nevada Senator William M. Stewart in 1873. Stewart found the mansion a financial drain and by the 1890s was renting it to the Chinese—one of a number of foreign legations that clustered about the Circle. Courtesy, Columbia Historical Society

Right: The solitary reader appears lost among her possessions in her late nineteenth-century Victorian parlor at 2153 Florida Avenue, N.W., on the edge of Dupont Circle. Courtesy, Library of Congress

Eventually Stewart sold the house to Senator William A. Clark, another millionaire miner, who tore it down in 1901, intending to build a more modern mansion on the site. However, the lot remained vacant until 1924, when the present Riggs bank was built.

In 1874 another significant structure went up near the Circle, and along with Stewart's Castle it helped create the impression that Dupont Circle was a coming neighborhood. British Minister Sir Edward Thornton decided in 1872 that renting various Washington residences for the British Legation was uneconomical. Unable to acquire a site on Capitol Hill, Thornton took a chance and bought a site in the undeveloped Dupont Circle area. The land, at the west side of Connecticut Avenue at N Street, was purchased from Sunderland, one of the original land speculators. Designed by Washington architect John Fraser, the legation was, like Stewart's Castle, an ornate Second Empire structure. It served as Thornton's offices and home.

The legation and the elegant activities that took place there greatly increased the prestige of this undeveloped area. Guests arriving at the legation passed through an iron fence framed by ornate gas lamps and entered the building under an impressive porte cochere. Entering the tiled vestibule, visitors were confronted with a grand staircase and a portrait of the 18-year-old Queen Victoria. A hand-carved mahogany balcony made in England encircled the entire second floor, and the ballroom floor was covered with the rug Queen Victoria had walked upon when she opened the Crystal Palace exhibit in 1851. The building was razed in 1931 after the British Embassy moved from Connecticut Avenue to its present address on Massachusetts Avenue.

These two elegant buildings stood in sharp contrast to their surroundings, for the neighborhood did not immediately develop as an enclave of elite residents. In fact, the imposing buildings were flanked by mostly vacant lots dotted with a few crude shanties. Recent research by Walter Albano has revealed that over time tradesmen, servants, and laborers chose Dupont Circle as home along with the diplomats, government officials, and professionals. In the mid-1870s most new residents built modest frame houses, and by 1880, Albano writes, the area consisted of modest brick and frame structures as well as a few "imposing brick buildings standing in splendid isolation." Just over half of the 1880 population of 3,100 comprised working-class people described in the census as black or mulatto. About 250 immigrants from Ireland, Germany, and Great Britain were counted among the white residents.

By 1885, however, real estate agents were promoting the "West End," as the area was then known, as a place of wealth and fashion. By 1892, it was clear the character of the neighborhood was beginning to reflect their descriptions. The population had doubled, and more substantial houses were being built. As mansions slowly filled in the vacant lots around the Circle and along Massachusetts and New Hampshire avenues, well designed rowhouses in brick or stone became the dominant architecture of the numbered and lettered streets in the neighborhood. Many of the rowhouses, built by speculators, were purchased by professional people who could afford to pay from $4,000 to $8,000 for the substantial houses. The Queen Anne style, with its large main gables, bay windows, chimneys of various designs, and polychromatic materials, was the most popular. Most of these buildings still stand, for example on the 1700 block of Q Street and the 1400 block of 21st.

The racial mix of the neighborhood also had shifted, so that now the white population outnumbered the black. Indicative of the changing social class of the neighborhood, Albano pointed out, was that the number of families with servants had soared. In 1880 only 10 percent had live-in help; by 1900, 40 percent were in that category. The assessed value of real estate in the area rose dramatically during these years. Stewart's house, for example, which was assessed at 35 cents a square foot in 1874, was rated at $3.25 just 16 years later. By 1900 Dupont Circle had earned its reputation as a fashionable, upper-middle-class neighborhood attractive to the financially successful. Other missions had joined Great Britain in the area, among them China, Austria-Hungary, Spain, and Switzerland.

The neighborhood remained one of the most fashionable addresses in the nation's capital throughout the early twentieth century, even though new suburban development within the District was luring the well-to-do away from many other locations in L'Enfant's old Washington City. The neighborhood attracted a black elite as well. Just before World War I black professionals began to move into the northeastern portion of Dupont Circle, particularly along U Street. One block in particular, the 1700 block, attracted so many distinguished residents that it came to be known as "Strivers Row." A recent unpublished oral history of Dupont Circle by Mara Cherkasky includes the reminiscences of many black residents who remember that block. Inez Brown recalled "the block as being very beautiful . . . people had their yards and their hedges and their

Above: The statue of General George B. McClellan commands this 1910 scene of Connecticut Avenue, N.W., south of Columbia Road. The wooded area at the left is now the site of the Washington Hilton Hotel. Courtesy, Library of Congress, Prints and Photographs Division

Right: The controversial Dupont Circle streetcar underpass, seen in this view down Connecticut Avenue from Florida Avenue, N.W., functioned for only 11 years until 1961, when the streetcars were replaced by buses. The low scale of this popular commercial street has been largely preserved into the 1980s by local residents. Courtesy, National Archives

shrubbery and their trees and flowers, and it was just very attractive and very desirable." Black laborers and domestics lived in this area, too, but they settled on the short, narrow streets such as Seaton Street that had smaller two-story rowhouses.

While Dupont Circle has always included both black and white residents, Cherkasky's research reveals two very separate communities, the black residents increasingly clustered in the northeast section above T Street. The two different social worlds did not mix, and by the 1940s two different community associations made the division highly visible. The Dupont Circle Citizens' Association, all white, was formed in 1922, and the Midway Civic Association, all black, began in 1939.

For outsiders, however, the neighborhood was characterized by the elaborate mansions of the very wealthy white elite. Some of these people began to die or leave the area in the 1920s and 1930s, and by the 1940s their enormous homes either had found new uses or were destroyed. The story of the Leiter Mansion, built in 1891 on a pie-shaped piece of land on the north side of the Circle between New Hampshire Avenue and 19th Street, reflects the twentieth-century evolution of such properties.

Built by Chicago department store and real estate magnate Levi P. Leiter, the white-brick, three-story, 55-room mansion with its massive Ionic-columned porte cochere dominated Dupont Circle for 56 years. Leiter's social ambitions brought him and his family to Washington in 1883, when they first rented the Blaine Mansion that still stands at 20th and Massachusetts, one block west of the circle. An extremely wealthy family, they split their time between their Washington, Chicago, and Lake Geneva, Wisconsin, homes and travel in Europe.

Leiter's son, Joseph, continued in business in Washington after his father's death in 1904, entertaining on a grand scale. "Anticipating Prohibition, he stocked the cellar with $300,000 worth of the choicest liquors and wines. The magnificence of the Leiters' parties was exceeded in the 1920s only by the complete reckless abandon of the McLeans," wrote James Goode in *Capital Losses*. He noted that McLean and his wife, Evelyn Walsh McLean, who lived at Friendship, their estate just west of Cleveland Park, once spent $40,000 on a dinner party for 48 guests just prior to World War I.

The Leiter mansion was also known as the home of the "Dancing Class" in the decades between the two world wars. As the *Evening Star* explained in a 1967 article about the Dancing Class, its "purpose was implied by its name, a class where Washington's smart set could learn the latest dances." Membership was limited to "who you were and where you were born," according to Leiter's daughter, Nancy, who was a young child when her parents' house was the site of the dances.

The Leiter mansion was well suited as a gathering place for this socially exclusive club. Nancy Leiter, who later married C. Thomas Claggett, Jr., in the house in 1940, recalled that the elegant ballroom opened onto a long hall with the library at one end. The space could accommodate 350 to 400 people. She vividly remembered her mother's frequent entertainments and "still can see the gold chairs being whipped out for a party."

At the beginning of World War II the family rented the house to the federal government for office space. In 1943 they hired a firm to appraise the property and its future use. They were told that Dupont Circle was undergoing a change that did not enhance the value of their property: the socially prominent and ultra-wealthy were leaving, and the neighborhood was becoming more middle-class. In addition, many of the departing families were trying to sell their mansions, creating a glut on the real estate market that further lowered their value. The Leiter house was sold in 1947 and was soon demolished; its site is now occupied by the Hotel Dupont Plaza. The Leiter mansion was just one of many grand Dupont Circle buildings that would be lost to the wrecker's ball.

There were other things for the residents of the neighborhood to worry about as well, including the proposed Dupont Circle streetcar underpass, which local government officials believed was necessary to relieve the congestion on the Circle itself. From before the turn of the century, both northbound and southbound tracks of the Cabin John line had run side by side around the western rim of the Circle between Connecticut Avenue and P Street. In the mid-1930s the city considered decongesting the western side of the Circle by moving the northbound tracks to the east side. The change was not made, and thus one of Washington's most durable legends was born.

The story was that highway officials had not moved the tracks because of objections from Eleanor "Cissy" Patterson, the editor and publisher of the powerful *Washington Times Herald*. Legend has it that Patterson didn't want the noisy streetcars running in front of her mansion, which faced the Circle at P Street. Later she was to tell a reporter that she was flattered at the suggestion that she could wield so much influence, but she denied the story, as did highway officials.

Mrs. Joseph Leiter was hostess to many lavish parties in her mansion on Dupont Circle, as well as to the "Dancing Class" where Washington's elite young people learned the latest steps. Courtesy, Library of Congress, Prints and Photographs Division

Right: The building of the Connecticut Avenue underpass beneath Dupont Circle required the temporary removal of the center fountain and created this tangle of tracks, trucks, and trenches. The rerouted trolley was to see its last run a few years later. Courtesy, D.C. Public Library, Washingtoniana Division

Facing page: Crowds gathered near the steps of St. Matthew's Cathedral on Rhode Island Avenue, near Connecticut Avenue, N.W., on Easter Sunday, 1943. One of the city's most urban neighborhoods, Dupont Circle is a mixture of houses and apartments, office buildings, and businesses. Courtesy, Library of Congress, Prints and Photographs Division

When the underpass was first proposed in the early 1940s, little opposition was expressed by neighborhood residents. The projected cost was $500,000. But by 1947 when the digging began, the cost was projected as more than $3 million. A citizens' group protested the project, citing the cost and anticipated disruption of their neighborhood. Their fears were confirmed when construction left the park "a morass of mud and clay, surrounded by detours and dotted with concrete mixers, steam shovels, scaffolding and piles of assorted unattractive materials" for more than three years. It also meant the destruction of numerous trees and the temporary relocation of the Dupont fountain.

Patterson, who at one time had supported the underpass in the editorial pages of her newspaper, changed her mind and called the project a "blunderpass" and commented, "If it is ever finished, it will be the worst white elephant of them all."

She was right. In 1961, 11 years after it was completed, the streetcars were phased out in favor of buses. The semicircular trolley tunnels were closed, leaving the underpass as just another road for cars.

The park in the Circle was disrupted in other ways as well. Long thought of as a pleasant urban patch of green where children could splash in the fountain and adults could sit quietly and read the daily newspaper, the park began to attract the young would-be revolutionaries of the 1960s and the 1970s. By the mid-1960s Dupont Circle was known nationwide as the place to go to find hippies, cultists, black-power advocates, and other members of the counterculture of the time. It was also the staging area for many of the anti-war demonstrations that seemed to become a daily event during the last years of the Vietnam War.

In the blocks surrounding the park, students and other young people moved into rowhouses that had been converted to rooming houses, tiny apartments, or group homes. Grocery stores featuring organic produce and vegetarian restaurants popped up next to old neighborhood bars and staid clothing stores. The vitality of the neighborhood was contagious, and the mix of old and new seemed to bring yet more people to the area.

Not everyone was happy about the newcomers. The Dupont Circle Citizens' Association called on the Interior Department and the police department in 1966 to oust the "misfits, hoodlums, vagrants and perverts which . . . gather in large numbers" in the park. Some even called for the entire park to be fenced so it could be closed after nightfall.

The verbal war between the old-timers of the neighborhood who fought to retain the exclusivity that had characterized the neighborhood in its prime and those who wanted a more casual, counterculture life-style seems to have ended with the passing of time. Gone are the free spirits of the sixties and seventies and the rooming houses and other living arrangements that so disturbed the longtime residents. Today Dupont Circle is once again an expensive neighborhood where rowhouses sell for upwards of $300,000 and condominium apartments for about $100,000.

The upward spiral of real estate prices started from an all-time low following the riots of 1968, when many of the remaining middle-class families in the area fled downtown Washington for what they considered safer suburbs. Eventually the low-priced rowhouses attracted a whole new wave of middle-class owners who once again recognized what the neighborhood had offered 80 years before—substantial housing and a convenient location. Many of these new homeowners teamed up with the old-timers who had refused to give up on the neighborhood, and together they pushed to improve the area.

A coalition of community groups petitioned the city in 1976 to grant the neighborhood the status of a historic district. Encroaching commercial development had already destroyed many of the grand houses situated on and south of the Circle. They hoped to preserve the historic and residential character of the neighborhood with the protection of a historic district designation.

The application listed more than 100 notable buildings and included the black neighborhood north of T street. The primarily black Midway Civic Association and the mostly white Dupont Circle Citizens' Association agreed, the application noted, that although the groups had overlapping boundaries, "the proposed [historic district] boundaries are correct, and that for many years, as far back as recollection goes, anyone living in the proposed district was said to live 'in Dupont Circle.'"

When Dupont Circle won its historic-district designation in 1978, however, the northeastern area surrounding the 1700 blocks of T and U streets historically associated with the black community was left out. It was not until 1985 that this part of Dupont Circle was recognized as a separate historic district designated as the Strivers Section.

Today many of the rowhouses of Strivers Section as well as other parts of the Dupont Circle neighborhood have been restored or renovated by longtime residents as well as newcomers. There are still dozens of examples of fine family homes built as showplaces between 1890 and 1910 that survived the wrecker's ball and became private clubs or embassies. Others were converted to office space or condominiums.

The notable mansions that remain to serve new uses include the Walsh-McLean house (1903), at 2020 Massachusetts Avenue, now the Indonesian Embassy; the Heurich mansion (1892-1894), at 1307 New Hampshire Avenue, now the headquarters of the Columbia Historical Society; and the Boardman house (1893), at 1801 P Street, now the Embassy of Iraq. The Patterson house (1901-1903), at 15 Dupont Circle, is the last mansion with a Circle address; it is now the home of a private women's organization called the Washington Club.

Today Dupont Circle is perhaps the most completely urban of Washington's neighborhoods, its old buildings being used in varied but integrated ways. Some residents are able to live and work in the same area, much as residents did in the nineteenth-century walking city. It has preserved its heritage of grand houses and attractive rowhouses but has allowed space for the new as well. Dupont Circle has survived the stresses of a century of existence and is today one of the city's most livable neighborhoods.

10
SHAW
HEART OF BLACK WASHINGTON

Marcia M. Greenlee

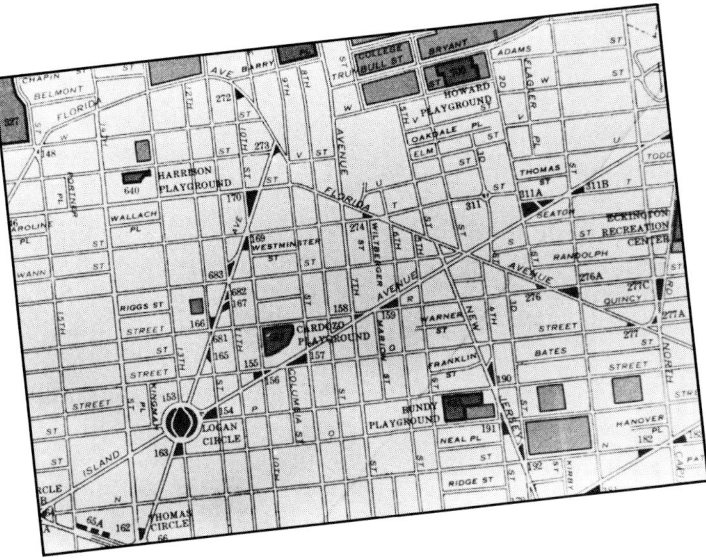

Photographer Addison N. Scurlock used the flash-powder technique to capture this formal dance at the Whitelaw Hotel in the early 1920s. It was a technical challenge that had to be accomplished on the first try, for the hall afterward filled with smoke. Courtesy, Scurlock Studio, Washington, D.C.

Map: Park System of the National Capitol and Environs. National Park Service 1962. Courtesy, D.C. Public Library, Washingtoniana Division

The central section of Washington, D.C., known today as Shaw, has no historic identity as a neighborhood of that name. Designation of the area as Shaw occurred in May 1966 when the National Capital Planning Commission and the city government, using the attendance boundaries of the Shaw Junior High School, established the perimeters of a Northwest urban renewal area between North Capitol and 15th streets on the east and west, and Florida Avenue and M Street on the north and south. This action joined a large and generally heterogenous region into a supposed unity for the purpose of urban renewal.

Shaw is, then, not one neighborhood but many, including communities of people who identify with such places as Logan Circle, Bates Street, U Street, or just their own residential block. The various parts of this large north-central section of old Washington City have something in common historically. While its population was racially and economically mixed for much of its history, its black businesses, churches, and institutions evolved in the late nineteenth and early twentieth centuries as among the strongest and most influential in Washington's Afro-American community. The experiences of black residents in this area reflect in some ways the experiences of black Washington as a whole.

Shaw contains more than 105 city squares. It was owned by only five men at the time the federal city was established in 1791; the most locally prominent among them were Samuel Blodgett, a real estate developer, and Robert Peter, a Georgetown tobacco merchant. Within a decade following the founding of the capital, the area, despite its division into squares, still had virtually no construction within.

The heart of black enterprise in segregated Washington, U Street, N.W., remained the black community's major business and entertainment street when this view of the Republic Theater and its adjacent shops in the 1300 block was photographed circa 1950. Courtesy, Columbia Historical Society

At the beginning of the nineteenth century, housing and businesses in the center of Washington City were concentrated south of K Street. Portions of the region that would become known as Shaw, especially between 13th and 7th streets and between M and S streets, were still forested. Tributaries of the Tiber Creek snaked through the northeastern part of the section, but because of its elevation, flooding does not seem to have been a problem, as it was farther south. With the exception of 7th Street, which was noted on early maps as "The Road to Rockville," none of the major streets ran beyond the City of Washington's Boundary Street (now Florida Avenue). Over the next half-century, there was little change in the area. The only construction shown on Albert Boschke's map of the city in 1857 was concentrated south of O Street between 5th and 13th streets. There were, however, five cemeteries on the 1857 map, one of them designated African.

It was during the Civil War era that Shaw began to grow and develop, due to improved transportation and an increased demand for housing. In 1862 streetcars began to travel along both 7th and 14th streets, making it easier for people to live farther from the city's core. This new accessibility, coupled with the presence of growing numbers of military men, civilian government employees, black refugees from slave states, entrepreneurs, and others, led Shaw property owners to believe that the time for the development of their land had come. Many of these landowners were connected with the building trades or real estate concerns. For example, on 11th Street between R and U streets a brick manufacturer, a builder, a carpenter, a contractor, a real estate broker, and a clerk in the Land Office were among the property owners who subdivided their land for the first time between 1859 and the early 1870s.

The region that would become Shaw developed from south to north. John P. Coffin described the northern part in 1870 as still being "in the woods." The District's territorial government between 1871 and 1874 made many physical improvements in Shaw, particularly in the southern section. Several roads were surfaced; some streets were included on the city's sweeping schedule; shade trees were planted; gas lamps, water mains, fire plugs, and sewers were installed, and telegraph lines were erected to enable the use of telephones.

Black and white, rich and poor, upper-, middle-, and lower-class persons all made their homes in the area in its early years. It appears that most of these families came to the District of Columbia before, during, or shortly after the Civil War, judging by the birthdates of their children listed in the census. Many were government employees, particularly the white resi-

Left: Civil War encampments such as this one near Campbell Hospital on Boundary Street between 5th and 6th streets, N.W., represented safety for black war refugees and were a magnet for a growing black population in the near-Northwest area that would become today's Shaw. Courtesy, Library of Congress, Prints and Photographs Division

dents, and this fact plus their presence in a newly developing area makes it likely they were attracted by the business and employment opportunities created by the war.

Shaw residents bought lots and built homes, or purchased or rented houses already built. They were civil servants, small-businessmen, skilled and unskilled laborers, and a few professionals. Some new residents were housed, at least temporarily, by social welfare agencies such as the Freedmen's Bureau, which was charged with the assistance of those displaced by the Civil War. The black churches of Shaw, in a role they have continued to fill to the present day, also helped in providing housing for the needy. Black and white people of all economic levels moved into Shaw simultaneously in this early period.

Until 1900 and as late as World War I in some sections, Shaw was a preferred neighborhood for middle-class white residents. The Logan Circle area near 13th Street at Vermont Avenue was considered particularly desirable. Its solid rowhouses of Victorian design, some embellished with fine ornamental ironwork, were built in the 1870s and 1880s after street paving and other improvements carried out by the territorial government encouraged development of what was still pastureland as the Civil War ended. The circle at its center was called Iowa Circle until 1930, when its name was changed to Logan Circle. These houses sheltered middle-class blacks and whites who worked as civil servants, business people, and professionals. There were also, by the 1890s, some foreign legations established on the circle.

Although middle-class blacks remained, Iowa Circle began to lose its cachet as a prestigious address for whites when residential areas to the west and northwest of the circle became available and streetcar lines made commuting attractive. Increasing racial segregation in the late nineteenth century was another factor; many whites throughout the city sought to distance themselves from their black neighbors.

Not all of the area's white residents moved at the same time. Some remained in various parts of Shaw at

Below: In 1956 a young resident of the Bates Street houses, one of many communities that are now considered part of Shaw, uses a makeshift sandbox. The Washington Sanitary Housing Commission built these row houses for low-income white families at the turn of the century, one of the first results of the housing reform movement in the city. Courtesy, D.C. Public Library, Washingtoniana Division, c. Washington Post

Students gathered on the steps of Minor Hall at Howard University in 1893. Courtesy, Howard University, Moorland-Spingarn Research Center

least until the 1930s and even longer. In fact, when most middle-class whites were leaving the area at the turn of the century, a large group of working-class whites was moving into 300 rowhouses built for whites by the Washington Sanitary Housing Commission on Bates Street, a section of former swampland near North Capitol Street. Bates Street remained mostly white until the World War II era, when speculators purchased the properties from whites and rented, rather than sold, them to blacks.

After the exodus of most of the whites from Shaw, black people were able to gain a bit more housing space but not enough for their needs. Barred from residence in many other parts of the city by restrictive covenants until 1948 and by continuing racism afterward, they did not have as many options in selecting a neighborhood as white Washingtonians did.

A number of factors had originally attracted blacks to Shaw. For those already living near the center of town in the mid-nineteenth century, a move northward may have come about simply as a part of the general residential expansion as population increased and public transportation improved. For others, especially black war refugees, Civil War encampments at the Wisewell Barracks at 7th and P streets, at Campbell Hospital on Boundary

Street between 5th and 6th streets, and at Camp Barker with its Freedmen's Hospital near 13th and R streets were the initial drawing points. The establishment of Howard University in 1867, just beyond Boundary along 7th Street, served as an additional magnet for black residents.

In 1879 the first mass migration of blacks from the South set in motion thousands who sought escape from white oppression and hoped to gain the employment and educational opportunities that oppression denied them. Some of these migrants found their way to the nation's capital and its central black community in Shaw. Not only were they drawn by Washington's established black population and black institutions; here they were able to purchase property without the impediments they faced from whites in many other parts of the city.

By the mid-1880s blacks in Shaw had formed building associations, such as the Industrial Building and Savings Company; realty companies, such as Oak Park Realty Company; and in 1888 the Capital Savings Bank of Washington, which was the first black bank in the United States. These businesses actively promoted home building and purchase among blacks in Shaw and elsewhere in the city. Property ownership was viewed as a positive social accomplishment and one that allowed a significant degree of control over the type of neighborhood one lived in. Many other blacks in the area, through preference or necessity, rented their homes.

Some of the poorest found shelter in alleyways. These alleys, intended to provide service access for the houses facing the main streets, were more than commodious for that function. As housing pressures increased, however, particularly for the poor, certain entrepreneurs recognized the economic potential of constructing small dwellings in these alleys. Many of the alleys were orderly and well maintained. Others, especially those built later, were cramped and unsanitary.

As Shaw began to become predominantly black, at about the turn of the century, the number of black businesses and institutions within it increased. As black businessmen were forced out of the downtown area by increasing segregation, many joined their fellows already settled just to the north. A bank, a printing company, a drugstore, and many other black-owned enterprises flourished between 7th and 15th streets. Edward E. Cooper, editor of the *Colored American,* operated his business from within the area, as did the architect William Lankford. In 1892 Andrew Hilyer established the Union League, an organization through which black businesses could work cooperatively. There were also at least a dozen black churches in the area, as well as black public schools, and private schools such as the Frelinghuysen University and the Washington Conservatory of Music and Expression. The black Twelfth Street YMCA, later renamed for Anthony Bowen; the Phyllis Wheatley YWCA, the first YWCA in Washington; Howard University's first dental infirmary; and the True Reformers Hall all were established in Shaw during this period.

The World War I era saw important changes for blacks nationally as well as within Washington, D.C. Having survived the turn of the century, the period of time the historian Rayford W. Logan has called "the Nadir" for blacks in American society, Washington's black population hoped for improved conditions during Woodrow Wilson's presidency. Although Wilson was an eloquent spokesman for the Progressive Movement and for the democratic advances it espoused, blacks soon discovered that neither the president nor the Progressives had any interest in improving the political, economic, or social life of black Americans. Wilson, who described himself as a "Southern man," extended and sanctioned racial segregation throughout the federal government. With this official endorsement, other discriminatory activities ensued, both nationally and locally.

In the summer of 1919, following the end of World War I, 20 or more white riots against blacks occurred throughout the nation. During this period, known as the Red Summer because of the amount of blood shed, a race riot broke out in Washington on the 19th of July and continued through the 23rd. A white mob composed mostly of soldiers, sailors, and Marines attacked blacks in several locations throughout the city. One of the areas supposedly targeted was the so-called "Colored Boulevard" of U Street, the principal commercial and entertainment corridor in Shaw. It was estimated that more than 2,000 armed black Shaw residents, some of them veterans of the same war in which the white military personnel had fought, assembled along U Street determined to fight for democracy on the homefront. They stood ready to protect their families and property from attack, and the rioting whites stayed away.

The Ku Klux Klan, after experiencing a revival in 1915, was strong enough by 1925 to stage a march in full regalia down Pennsylvania Avenue, N.W., with government sanction. White lynchings of blacks went on unchecked throughout the 1920s and beyond. Washington, D.C., was spared this most virulent expression of racism.

A young Billy Eckstine fronts the Tommy Myles orchestra, a favorite Washington dance band of the 1930s and 1940s, at the Lincoln Colonnade on U Street, N.W., in the mid-1930s. Courtesy, Scurlock Studio, Washington, D.C.

Most of the racial legislation considered by Congress in the early twentieth century was introduced during Wilson's administration and was specifically addressed to abrogating the civil rights of black Washingtonians. Laws were considered that would have legally segregated the civil service —despite the fact that it was already segregated in practice—segregated the streetcars, and prohibited racial intermarriage.

The response of black Washingtonians to these developments included protest, public education, and the establishment of organizations fostering civic pride. One such organization, the National Association for the Advancement of Colored People (NAACP), served all three purposes and received widespread black support. Although not originally organized in Washington, by 1916 the Washington branch of the NAACP had become the largest in the country. Shaw residents were prominent among its branch officers and many supporters, including Archibald Grimke, perhaps the best known of the NAACP's early Washington presidents. His brother, Francis J. Grimke, was the pastor of the Fifteenth Street Presbyterian Church.

Despite the obstacles white racism placed in their paths, black residents of Shaw continued to struggle to achieve. Black businesses increased along 7th, 9th, and 14th streets, and particularly along U Street, where blacks went for services, where their organizational headquarters were located, and where the most entertainment was available. Blacks gathered on U Street in spontaneous celebration of Joe Louis' victory as the heavyweight champion of the world in 1938. It was on U Street that District of Columbia native Edward "Duke" Ellington, then a young man known as "Eddie," worked as a soda jerk and played the piano at such spots as Jack's Place and the Poodledog Cabaret. Fraternal groups met in the True Reformers Hall, as did the black D.C. National Guard. Clubs, church groups, and others used the hall's auditorium and ballroom. U Street was the heart of black Washington enterprise.

Above: The Reverend Robert Brooks presided at the cornerstone-laying ceremonies for the new Lincoln Memorial Temple Congregational Church at 1701 11th street, N.W., in 1927. The temple was a center of community life, sponsoring sport teams, a drama group, and other activities. Courtesy, Scurlock Studio, Washington, D.C.

Right: Addison N. Scurlock, seen here in the late 1940s with his wife, Mamie, began recording the life of his community in photographs in 1905 from a home studio. The pair opened this commercial studio in 1911 at 9th and Florida Avenue, N.W. Courtesy, Scurlock Studio, Washington, D.C.

This baseball team, at Griffith Stadium in the late 1930s, was composed entirely of Washington dentists associated with Howard University, most of whom lived and practiced in Shaw and LeDroit Park. The team included Dean Russell Dixon of the Howard University Dental School, front row, second from right. Courtesy, Scurlock Studio, Washington, D.C.

Black social and cultural life in Shaw generally centered around family, church, and school, although there were, as has been noted, some commercial sources of entertainment as well. The Phyllis Wheatley YWCA and the Twelfth Street YMCA continued to provide recreation—everything from hikes in Rock Creek Park to games of indoor golf—but they could not meet the needs of the entire black community. Segregated from public facilities, blacks in Shaw used schools and school yards as community and recreational centers. Shaw-area churches also offered a variety of activities. The Lincoln Memorial Temple Congregational Church, for example, sponsored basketball, baseball, and tennis games as well as track meets in 1927. A drama group, the Lincoln Temple Players, presented plays attended by the public. Masonic groups met at the black-owned Scottish Rite Temple on 11th Street in Shaw. Patrons of the Hiawatha Theater could watch the *Perils of Pauline* to piano accompaniment. The S.H. Dudley (formerly the Minnehaha), Howard, Dunbar, and Lincoln were some of the other popular theaters where parents, depending upon the film and theater's reputation, might bring their children.

The Industrial Savings Bank of Washington opened on U Street in 1913 and was a great source of pride among blacks. It provided black business training that segregated white financial concerns prohibited. Harrison's Cafe on Florida Avenue was an attractive and popular local restaurant. The McGuire Funeral Home, the Hamilton Brothers Printing Company (which joined the earlier established Murray Brothers Printing Company), the Ware Department Store, Scurlock's Photo Studio, the Whitelaw Hotel, and the Dunbar Hotel were only a few of the black businesses established in the World War I and postwar era.

Two friends finish a day's work at a 1970 community cleanup campaign in Shaw. Courtesy, D.C. Public Library, Washingtoniana Division, c. Washington Post

Even though black people were successful, despite segregation, in the creation and maintenance of their own community institutions, there were some problems that were beyond their capacity to solve. Adequate housing was one of these. Exacerbated by the segregation that was enforced by restrictive covenants, the housing shortage for blacks in Washington was many times worse than any shortage experienced by whites. Crowding grew so severe in Shaw, and in other parts of the city where white bankers, real estate agents, and others allowed blacks to live, that by World War II the black community had almost reached the breaking point.

When Washington began to desegregate following World War II, especially after restrictive covenants were overturned by the Supreme Court in 1948, many blacks, particularly middle-class blacks, left for neighborhoods where they were able to find larger, newer properties in less crowded surroundings. Many single-family properties in Shaw then were converted to multiple-family use—often by renters—increasing the density of the neighborhood even further. As the relative poverty of the community grew, the attendant social problems multiplied. By the early 1960s Shaw was unquestionably in an economic depression, and the city mounted plans for a massive redevelopment of the region.

City planners met an organized community voice in Shaw in the form of the Model Inner City Community Organization (MICCO), led by the Reverend Walter M. Fauntroy. The members of MICCO, with the clear memory of the debacle of the city's "redevelopment" of the Southwest neighborhood, were determined to shape city efforts in Shaw and prevent the wholesale destruction of its physical fabric.

After the boundaries of the Shaw Urban Renewal Area were determined in 1966, the region was officially recognized by the Department of Housing and Urban Development in 1968 and made eligible for federal redevelopment funding. Since that time redevelopment in Shaw has combined new construction with the rehabilitation of existing properties. Condominiums and apartment buildings continue to exist alongside single-family homes. The old Shaw Junior High School was converted into apartments for the elderly, and a new school was built at 10th and Rhode Island Avenue. In 1980 a black developer, James Adkins, reopened the O Street Market at 7th and O streets. The public market, a landmark built in 1886, had been closed since the 1968 riots following the assassination of Dr. Martin Luther King, Jr. Both private and public funds have been used in these and many other projects. Efforts have been made to preserve space for low-income residents, but whether or not this aspect of renewal will persist is yet to be seen.

Most recently the construction of a major government office facility, the Frank Reeves Center, at 14th and U streets, has both pleased and alarmed residents, some concerned it might begin a cycle of gentrification which could result in a loss of the neighborhood's historic identity. The introduction of the city's subway system into Shaw is also likely to have far-reaching consequences. Whether the area will become an extension of the downtown commercial district, continue to provide housing for mixed-income residents, or turn into an exclusive preserve of the affluent is unclear. Today the future of Shaw is uncertain as competing forces seek to shape this historic area according to their particular political and economic visions.

Recess at Immaculate Conception School provides an opportunity for football on N Street, near 7th, N.W., which has been closed off for the purpose. The church, left, and school, center, are among many religious institutions that have been central to community life in Shaw. Photo by Emily Medvec

11

Mount Pleasant

COMMUNITY IN AN URBAN SETTING

Linda Low and Howard Gillette, Jr.

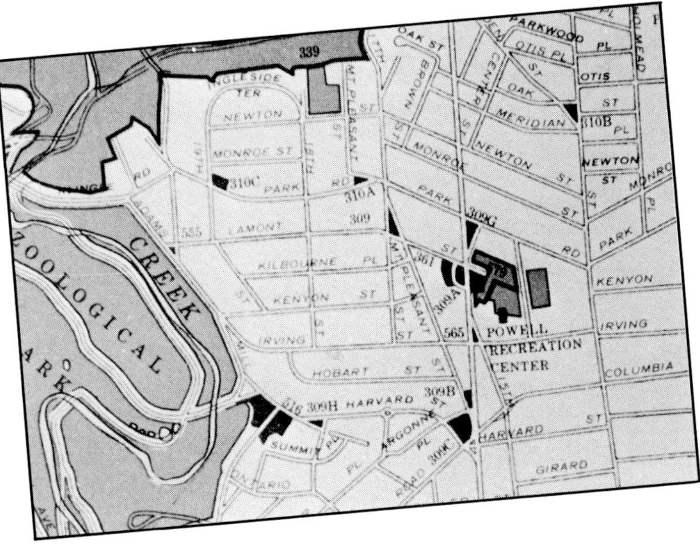

This row of pillared porches is typical of Mount Pleasant's early twentieth-century architecture, strongly influenced by the Classical Revival style popular at the time. Photo by Emily Medvec

Map: Park System of the National Capitol and Environs. National Park Service 1962. Courtesy, D.C. Public Library, Washingtoniana Division

Mount Pleasant began as a small village of New Englanders who came to work for the federal government just after the Civil War and settled in a new development near the 14th Street horsecar route, a group so homogeneous that the place developed strong New England village institutions and was referred to as "clerksville." By contrast, the Mount Pleasant of today, its center somewhat to the west of the original village, is one of the most economically, racially, and ethnically diverse neighborhoods in the city.

Today's Mount Pleasant is tucked into a bend in Rock Creek Park just north of the National Zoo and west of 16th Street. Its boundaries—Piney Branch Park on the north and Rock Creek Park on the west—give Mount Pleasant a strong sense of place, as does its cohesive architecture: rowhouses and some single-family dwellings strongly influenced by the Colonial Revival style popular at the turn of the century. Since about the 1930s an increasingly diverse population has chosen its convenient location near the central city, so that in the 1980s it is home to a mixture of people of various incomes, black and white, Asian and Latino. Its commercial core along Mount Pleasant Street is lined with a variety of shops, including Heller's German Bakery, the nearby African Room, and a host of small Latino grocery stores.

Mount Pleasant's hilly site was once part of a large eighteenth-century estate known as Pleasant Plains, belonging to Robert Peter and later to Anthony Holmead and his descendants. Running from today's 7th Street west to Georgetown, overlapping the boundaries of Washington City to the south, and extending northward across the Maryland line, it included all the streams and valleys of Rock Creek and Piney Branch.

The area north of the L'Enfant city remained largely

Above: Streetcars gather at the Mount Pleasant and Lamont streets, N.W., terminal on a November day in 1950. Heller's Bakery dominated the commercial strip at right; today it shares the street with a variety of multiethnic businesses. Courtesy, D.C. Public Library, Washingtoniana Division, c. Washington Post

Below right: This small triangular park at the juncture of Mount Pleasant Street and Park Road, N.W., offers a quiet refuge for three young residents on a June day in 1927. Courtesy, Columbia Historical Society

countryside before the Civil War, and the hill that would become the village of Mount Pleasant provided an ideal location for the Washington Jockey Club's racetrack in the early 1800s. Until the Civil War this hilly area above the city was occupied by a series of gentlemen's estates. Anthony Holmead's son John owned 46 acres west of 14th Street that stretched from Boundary Street (now Florida Avenue) on the south to today's Columbia Road on the north. His mansion was known as Meridian Hill, a name that would later be applied to a neighborhood along 16th Street. The site of his home near 14th Street would become the location of Columbian College, and its surroundings would later develop into a neighborhood known as Columbia Heights.

In 1850 U.S. Treasurer William Seldon bought a section of the old Pleasant Plains estate to the west of Meridian Hill near Rock Creek. He built on the land and lived there 10 years, but as a Southerner loyal to his native Virginia, he fled the city during the Civil War. His property passed to Samuel P. Brown, a Maine native who came to Washington in 1861 to serve as an Army contractor and was able to buy Seldon's land at a low price. Brown enlarged the Seldon house, near present-day Mount Pleasant Street and

Park Road, to a 30-room mansion. One other grand house stood nearby, Ingleside, the home of General Hiram Wallbridge, built on the former estate of John Ingle, a friend of George Washington. The estates of Brown and Wallbridge approximately comprised the area known as Mount Pleasant today.

During the war soldiers camped along 14th Street, one of the few roads that led up the hill beyond the boundary of Washington City. The Mount Pleasant Army Hospital was situated where the Tivoli Theater now stands at the intersection of 14th Street and Park Road. President and Mrs. Lincoln liked to take rides into the countryside along Piney Branch Road (now Mount Pleasant Street) when the weather was good enough for carriages to make it up the hillside. On one occasion during the Civil War, the First Lady was thrown from her carriage while on her way to review the troops and was taken to the Mount Pleasant Hospital, where the staff was proud of the chance to treat her.

Taking advantage of the depressed real estate prices that reflected the uncertainties attending the war, Brown invested in surrounding properties; with the war's conclusion he laid out several one-acre lots in a modified grid system, named the development Mount Pleasant, and sought investors. Demand was initially very low; Brown sold only five lots to four buyers in 1865. A group of government workers finally spurred development, pooling their money to buy a tract of land to divide. In the process, new streets named Howard (now Newton), Meridian, Brown, and Oak were created. These first streets of the original Mount Pleasant stand out today, straddling 16th Street in an angular pattern very different from the later street grid that surrounds them. Most of the early detached frame houses that remain in the area today are north of Park Road, concentrated in this corner of the neighborhood. By 1870 land that was worth only $650 an acre in 1866 had climbed to between $2,000 and $4,000.

The Mount Pleasant Army Hospital during the Civil War was on 14th Street N.W. near present-day Park Road. The hospital staff once treated Mary Todd Lincoln after she was thrown from her carriage while riding out to review the troops. Courtesy, Columbia Historical Society

Brown used his position as president of the Metropolitan Street Railway, founded in 1863, and as a presidential appointee to the District's board of public works under the territorial government to bring improvements to the area. Still, Mount Pleasant's relative isolation from the city left it very much in the country. Its location had advantages. A commentator in the early 1870s claimed, "It is perhaps the most healthy suburb of Washington, proved by its exemption from chills and autumnal fevers of malarial districts which frequently prevail in the city." In the winters of 1867 and 1868, however, the area's isolation turned to disadvantage when the weather was so harsh and the roads down to Washington so steep and muddy that the village was virtually cut off from the city.

Because of its isolation and the fact that so many New Englanders made Mount Pleasant their home, the area acquired many aspects of a New England village. Following the tradition of town meetings, residents

Picnickers pose on the rocks at one of several fords across Rock Creek in the National Zoo adjacent to Mount Pleasant around the turn of the century. Mount Pleasant is bordered on two sides by the park that was created along the creek and its tributaries in the 1890s. Courtesy, Columbia Historical Society

formed the Mount Pleasant Assembly in 1870, which "fearlessly discussed all questions grave or gay." They built Union Hall, which functioned as a church on Sunday and a hall for theater and dances during the week. The strong separate identity residents felt was clear in their response to President Grant's call for community histories during the 1876 American Centennial. The community produced the "Annals of Mount Pleasant" and gathered to hear it read in Union Hall on July 4, 1876. The Annals provide further evidence of a lively community in the 1870s, describing a continual round of festivities during the winter that included minstrel entertainments, balls, weekly debates on the issues of the day sponsored by the Mount Pleasant Lyceum, and meetings of the literary organization. No "spiritous liquor" was sold in the village.

The village was served first by an omnibus line that ran from 14th Street and Park Road down to the Treasury and Center Market and later by a horse-drawn streetcar. But as late as 1890, 14th Street was an unpaved road, dusty when dry and full of mudholes when wet. Children living west of St. Stephen and the Incarnation Church near present-day 16th and Newton streets often could not make it to services. Fifteenth Street was a curved footpath into the city, and despite the Highway Act of 1898 that created a standard street plan for the entire District, this curve was never eliminated. Fifteenth Street still leads right back to 16th Street at the top of the hill near where Mount Pleasant begins. Transportation was so bad that one resident claimed in an 1898 letter to Senate District Committee Chairman James McMillan that it took more time to commute downtown than it did to travel to Baltimore.

The village of Mount Pleasant was not to remain isolated into the twentieth century. As new electrified streetcar lines made feasible a relatively quick commute into the hills surrounding the downtown, population spilled out of the L'Enfant city into Washington County. This population growth, combined with the growing civic awareness that sought to restore the L'Enfant Plan and to expand the city's national and international image at the turn of the century, brought dramatic change to the city and to Mount Pleasant.

Responding to the efforts of Mary Henderson, wife of Senator John Henderson of Missouri, to turn 16th Street into a monumental "Avenue of the Presidents," as she would have had it called, this highway into the city was widened and straightened to the Maryland line. Coincidentally, Samuel Brown managed to secure electric rail service up old 16th Street, first called Piney Branch and now known as Mount Pleasant Street, right to his home on Park Road. With such improved transportation, land to the west of Mount Pleasant village, which had been virtually undeveloped except for a few frame houses and the old Ingleside estate, suddenly became ripe for subdivision. Within a few years in the early part of the century, a new Mount Pleasant emerged between the new 16th Street and Rock Creek Park.

Echoing the classicism embraced by the McMillan Commission's 1901-1902 plan for the city's monumental core, the first homes were given classical features, epitomized by the large home at 1801 Park Road designed by Frederick Pyle in 1903 for the owner of a Washington printing firm, Bryon Adams. The neighborhood attracted the best talents of Washington's budding architectural profession, and other distinguished homes followed. Rowhouses, some built as early as 1899, also carried classical details in dormer windows, columned porches, and patterned rooflines. Demand was sufficient to support speculative buildings in this style covering good portions of whole blocks. The neighborhood thus attained a unified physical character to match the largely homogeneous character of its residents, who were drawn primarily from the upper ranks of business and government.

This new group of people was as civic-minded as its predecessors. Residents founded the Mount Pleasant Citizens' Association in 1910 and secured, as a first project, a small park at the end of the streetcar line. Subsequently they worked for the construction of community buildings, most notably a library and a school, both of which were completed in 1924 on Lamont and Newton streets, respectively. The library, only the third neighborhood branch in the city, quickly became a center of community activities. It was the only one funded for its construction by a double gift of $200,000 rather than $100,000 from the Carnegie Foundation, possibly reflecting the influence of *Evening Star* editor Frank B. Noyes, who had lived at Ingleside at the turn of the century and had been instrumental in financing branch libraries in Washington.

The area west of 16th Street became increasingly self-sufficient in the 1920s, leaving the old Mount Pleasant largely behind. As if to signify where the attraction came to lie, a house that had to make way for the widening of 16th Street was moved, not to the east but rather into the relatively undeveloped area on what is today the corner of 19th and Newton streets. Some new businesses went up in the old Mount Pleasant, most notably a new branch of the Riggs bank and Crandall's Tivoli theater, both completed in 1924 at the intersection of 14th Street and Park Road. But the Mount Pleasant Citizens' Association seems to have sealed the identity of its neighborhood when in 1923 it named 16th Street as the eastern boundary. Concurrently, Columbia Heights, which had developed just to the east in the 1880s, claimed 16th Street as its western boundary.

The 1930s and 1940s brought changes to the neighborhood. Apartment buildings went up along 16th Street, bringing traffic and a greater number of short-term residents to the neighborhood. The early row houses of Mount Pleasant were exceptionally large, with as many as five to seven bedrooms, and many owners started subdividing them into several residences, especially during the housing crisis of World War II. After the war, suburban housing in attractive locations farther from the city lured many white residents away from older suburbs like Mount Pleasant. The neighborhood became racially mixed at this time as the 1948 Supreme Court ruling declaring

This early twentieth-century house on Park Road, N.W., reflects the preference for Classical Revival architecture in Washington at the turn of the century, a style also adopted by the 1902 McMillan Plan for the buildings in the city's monumental core. Courtesy, Columbia Historical Society

housing covenants unconstitutional opened up new housing opportunities for black people.

It was not until the 1960s, however, that the demographic change became dramatic, and the riots of 1968 were no doubt a factor in accelerating the pattern of white movement away from this close-in urban neighborhood. The 1960 census reported that of 11,554 residents, 8,445, or 73 percent, were white. By 1970 the white population had dropped to 3,332, or 32 percent of the total. While the area had formerly been dominated by the homeowners, 80 percent of Mount Pleasant's housing was rental by 1970.

During the 1960s the all-white Citizens' Association became a minority voice in a neighborhood with a black majority, leaving it often on the defensive. To fill the gap, some progressive residents, black and white, joined to form a new biracial citizens' association, Mount Pleasant Neighbors, to address common problems. This group was very active in planning neighborhood events that strengthened the area's sense of identity and emphasized the positive values of a racially and economically integrated neighborhood. Among other things, the Neighbors sponsored an annual fair on Mount Pleasant Street, which engaged the energies of most of the neighborhood for one weekend each year.

As in many other close-in neighborhoods, the change in neighborhood demographics brought a decline in housing prices relative to other parts of the city, and so it was only a matter of time before the area, with its excellent housing stock close to downtown, would be rediscovered. While conversions from single-family to multiple-unit dwellings and from private to institutional use were the norm of the 1960s and early 1970s, in the mid-1970s the pattern began to reverse. Young professionals, many not yet with families, saw a bargain in Mount Pleasant and began moving in. By the late 1970s, house renovations and demographic change were increasingly evident. According to a study done by Dennis Gale in 1976, these newcomers were largely white (77 percent), childless, professional (56 percent with graduate degrees), and migrants from rental housing in other parts of the city. Gale called these migrants part of the "stay-in-the-city movement" in contrast to the generation that had migrated to the suburbs earlier. Many actively sought an integrated urban neighborhood. By 1980 the population of 10,000 had shifted to 35 percent white and 49 percent black.

Of growing importance was another trend: the influx of Latino immigrants, who by 1980 made up 13 percent of the population. They congregated in apartment houses and group homes mostly between 16th and Mount Pleasant streets on the southeast side of the neighborhood, adjacent to Adams Morgan, where the Latino population was growing even more dramatically. In 1986 their presence in the neighborhood was revealed dramatically when 9 of the 16 Latino residents crowded into a group home died in the fire that tore through their Irving Street residence.

The Latino population was joined by a smaller group of Asians gathered at the head of Mount Pleasant Street in the Park Regent apartment building where Samuel Brown's home once stood. Little stores cropped up along Mount Pleasant Street to serve the neighborhood's new immigrants and others around the metropolitan area who were looking for beans and rice, tropical fruits, or unusual meats like goat and rabbit familiar to their national tastes. These new shops shared the street with black-owned businesses such as Logan Tailors and Cleaners and Scott's Barbeque as well as older neighborhood shops such as Heller's Bakery and Chin's Hand Laundry.

In 1978 the Mount Pleasant Neighbors became alarmed at the proposed demolition of the grand 1903 classical house at 1801 Park Road known as the Adams house. They saved it with a successful campaign to place the entire north side of the 1800 block of Park Road on the National Register of Historic Places. The Neighbors organization also worked to hold the neighborhood's diverse population together as the economic pressures that accompany gentrification began to threaten its less affluent residents. It spearheaded an effort to save the Kenesaw apartment building from conversion to condominiums. Once an elegant hotel for diplomats and others on short-term assignments to Washington, the Kenesaw, like the area around it, had fallen on hard times in the 1960s. The building was not kept up, pipes broke in winter, and the largely immigrant tenants held on because there was nothing else they could afford. When Antioch Law School as owner announced its intention to sell to developers, the neighborhood rallied to the defense of the tenants. A series of public and private meetings finally brought District government loans to the tenants, allowing for the building's conversion to cooperative apartments.

The Kenesaw project was the last major effort by Mount Pleasant Neighbors. A new neighborhood structure arose in the late 1970s that would overshadow it, the Advisory Neighborhood Commission, created by the Home

Rule Act of 1973. As in other neighborhoods across the city, the commission's official government status and small regular allotment of city funds gave it an edge over earlier totally voluntary organizations.

Citizen action on behalf of preservation intensified in the late 1970s. Stirred to action by the threat of demolition to the Adams house in 1977, a movement to retain the distinctive sense of place spread to other threatened buildings, most notably Ingleside at 1818 Newton Street, whose owner, the Stoddard Baptist Home, wanted to demolish it to make way for a nursing home. In doing research on the building, local activists found that the central portion of the complex could be attributed to Thomas U. Walter, the architect of the present dome and wings of the U.S. Capitol. And the grounds, they discovered, were laid out by Andrew Jackson Downing, America's first professional landscape architect and designer of the romantically inspired treatment for the Mall in 1851. As such, the building emerged as one of the most distinguished in the city, let alone the neighborhood.

Calls for preservation clashed, however, with the social objectives of the largely black Advisory Neighborhood Commission, and sides tended to divide along racial lines. A compromise was struck that seemed to work out well enough for all, whereby the new facility was built around the original home. Although the scale was out of line with the surrounding homes, architects made a point of designing the new buildings to relate to the houses nearby.

In the 1980s Mount Pleasant retains its strong sense of identity as a lively in-town neighborhood for those who prefer living in a diverse urban setting. It seems increasingly difficult, however, for neighborhood organizations to bridge the gaps between its varied populations. While many championed the recently successful movement to secure historic-district status in order to preserve the neighborhood's architectural character, others publicly opposed it, fearing designation would mean displacement and the end of ethnic and cultural diversity. Despite the disagreements, the neighborhood did become a historic district listed on the National Register of Historic Places, and Historic Mount Pleasant, Inc., the new group that shepherded it through the designation process, continues to be an active neighborhood organization. The neighborhood motto it has adopted, "Mount Pleasant: A Neighborhood in the City," represents its interest in fostering a sense of community in an urban setting. In an effort to deal with the fears of lower-income residents, it is working to establish a low-interest loan program for facade improvement for homeowners who might need assistance in making such repairs.

The Emanuel Baptist Church, now the National Baptist Memorial Church, anchors the corner of 16th Street where it is joined by Mount Pleasant Street in this 1925 view. Mount Pleasant Street was the original route of 16th Street, N.W., before it was straightened and paved to the District line at about the turn of the century. Courtesy, Columbia Historical Society

In some ways the neighborhood continues to function as a truly integrated community where mostly middle-class black and white homeowners of all ages share many city blocks, and participate together in the Friends of the Mount Pleasant Library and a recent effort to establish a neighborhood playground. However, the cultural and economic differences between these middle-class residents and the recently arrived Latinos to the southeast, some having fled their home countries with little education or means of support, have proved hard to bridge.

The line of whites and blacks still forms at Heller's Bakery, though ownership has now passed from Ludwig Heller, who died in 1987, to Pedro Lujan, a Peruvian. Black businessman John Saunders has left Scott's Barbeque for Alexandria, and the remaining carry-out is owned by Jae Young Cha, a Korean, as are other small businesses on the street. Although not the unified community of the past, Mount Pleasant remains a neighborhood with a strong sense of place and a vibrant social mix that encompasses the spirit of pluralistic America.

12

LeDroit Park

PREMIER BLACK COMMUNITY

Ronald M. Johnson

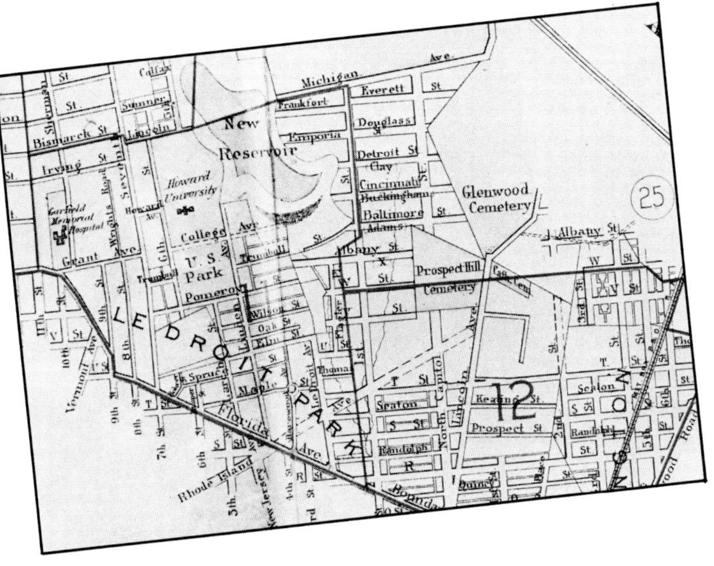

Educator Mary Church Terrell was a nationally known campaigner for equal rights and women's suffrage. She and her husband, a lawyer and the principal of M Street High School, were the second black family to move into LeDroit Park in 1894. Photo by Addison Scurlock. Courtesy, Howard University, Moorland-Spingarn Research Center

Map; 1894. Courtesy, Columbia Historical Society

LeDroit Park today still reflects an earlier generation's desire to live in a "beautiful little village," as one admirer fondly remembered it. Many of the original houses, constructed more than a hundred years ago, remain intact, as does the original street plan. A walk around the neighborhood conveys a strong impression of an earlier era in the city's development.

The neighborhood began in 1873 as a 55-acre triangular tract, situated just beyond the city's northern boundary line amid farms and fields. The project was the creation of Amzi Barber and Andrew Langdon, local land speculators, who had put together several parcels of property. Barber and Langdon conceived of their project as a planned community, a "romantic suburb," with the streets organized around a circular drive. To emphasize its separation from the city, the developers deliberately laid out the streets at an angle to the city's grid. They named the proposed development after LeDroit Langdon, the father of Andrew and himself a prominent Washington real estate agent.

To launch their plans, Barber and Langdon engaged James H. McGill, a local contractor and architect. In four years McGill designed and built 41 detached and semi-detached houses, adding 23 more over the following decade. The McGill designs incorporated the "picturesque" architectural styles that Andrew Jackson Downing had pioneered, such as Eastlake, Second Empire, and Italianate.

Location dictated LeDroit Park's desirability as a place of residence. Although outside the city limits, the subdivision was only a block from the terminal point of a recently built horse-drawn streetcar line, later electrified,

Dr. Anna J. Cooper graces the porch of her home at 2nd and T streets, N.W., in the 1930s. A highly respected educator in whose honor the area's central circle was recently named, she served as principal of M Street High School and as president of Frelinghuysen University, created to educate and uplift black working people. Courtesy, Scurlock Studio, Washington, D.C.

which allowed for rapid commuting to government agencies and businesses. The promoters of LeDroit Park also stressed that the "walking time," still the predominant way of getting around, was comparable to that for residents of Capitol Hill or Georgetown.

This closeness to the city, a major reason for LeDroit Park's immediate success, soon threatened the rural atmosphere of the neighborhood. Other residential and commercial development began to spread to the south, west, and even north of LeDroit Park. One such development was Howardtown, a black residential area founded in 1870 adjacent to Howard University on the north. Barber and Langdon had this section in mind when they encircled LeDroit Park with a combined cast-iron-and-wood fence. With no through traffic allowed and only the southern street entrances open, the neighborhood was insulated from its immediate surroundings. To close the street gates at night and keep out intruders, the developers hired a watchman. In addition, the developers carefully screened all applicants so that only whites were permitted. Le-

Droit Park was, recalled local historian John Clagett Proctor in 1928, as "exclusive a settlement as one might want or imagine," adding that "its residents were of the very highest type."

During the 1870s and early 1880s, government administrators and professionals, including doctors, lawyers, and teachers, bought homes in the neighborhood. Together they worked to maintain a climate of privacy. The physical setting was especially appealing, with abundant perennials and evergreens that helped to create a bucolic atmosphere. "LeDroit Park during that period," recalled former resident Charles Hamilton, "was the 'flower garden' of Washington. Every resident took pride in cultivation of all kinds, especially roses and chrysanthemums." Another observer noted that "the social life savored strongly of a village, and yet it was near to the city." In the late 1880s these unique attributes began to wane when, as the city spread northward, areas adjoining LeDroit Park became more densely developed, with extensive rowhousing, commercial activity, and street noise and traffic.

Picturesque architectural styles pioneered by Andrew Jackson Downing were the inspiration for many of the houses designed by James H. McGill for LeDroit Park, exemplified by this Gothic cottage that still stands on Anna Cooper Circle at U Street, N.W. Courtesy, Library of Congress, Prints and Photographs Division

LeDroit Park residents became especially concerned as Howardtown expanded in area and population. As more black families settled in Howardtown, they looked for a more direct route to downtown. Consequently, the numbers of individuals cutting through LeDroit Park and jumping the fence after the evening gate closings increased dramatically. In 1886, provoked by the enforcement of the ban against "intruders," a crowd of blacks shouted their complaints across the fence at LeDroit Park residents. Two years later, led by local land developers who owned lots in Howardtown and wanted greater accessibility, a large group of men attacked the fence and dismantled it. The LeDroit Park Citizens' Association replaced the fence with barbed wire, which also was torn down. Over the next three years the Washington newspapers reported on the "fence war," which raged until 1891. A final effort to restore the fence failed that year, leaving foot traffic to flow regularly through the subdivision. "With the opening of the streets," wrote one newspaper reporter, "the park soon lost its former characteristics and became a part of the city with all its advantages and disadvantages."

For a while advantages still outweighed disadvantages for those living to improve in LeDroit Park. The convenient location and handsome dwellings kept individuals like Patents Commissioner Benjamin Butterworth and geologist Henry Gannett firmly committed to the neighborhood. The conversion of LeDroit Park streets into thoroughfares did not lead to any sudden turnover among residents. In 1893, however, Octavius A. Williams became the first black homeowner in LeDroit Park, an event that reflected the new accessibility of the neighborhood. A barber in the Capitol, he brought a wife and young daughter to live in the McGill-designed house. The Williamses faced a distinctly hostile response from some LeDroit Park residents. The daughter later recalled when, "just after we moved in and were having dinner one night, someone fired a bullet through the window."

Civil War Medal of Honor winner Major Christian Fleetwood and his wife, Sarah, superintendent of the Training School for Nurses at Freedmen's Hospital, pose with their daughter outside their LeDroit Park home around the turn of the century. Courtesy, Library of Congress, Manuscript Division

She added that her father "left the bullet in the wall for years so his grandchildren could see it." After this incident the Williams family was for the most part left alone.

The following year a second black family purchased a house in LeDroit Park. They were Robert and Mary Church Terrell, a young couple only beginning careers that would eventually place them among the most respected black Washingtonians of their day. A graduate of Harvard University, trained as a lawyer, Robert Terrell was then the principal of the black M Street High School. His wife taught foreign languages at the school and was just initiating her work in the suffragette and civil rights movements, an involvement that would bring her an international reputation.

In her autobiography, *A Colored Woman in a White World,* Mary Church Terrell discussed her first effort to buy a house in the District of Columbia. She wrote of overcoming many difficulties, such as persuading real estate agents even to show her available houses. "Finally I selected one," she stated, "only one house removed from Howard Town" but "located in LeDroit Park." When the Terrells made a bid on the house, the owner refused to sell to them. A white real estate agent friend intervened to buy the house and transferred title to the Terrells. Four years later they moved to a larger home in LeDroit Park at 326 T Street (formerly Maple Street) and remained there for 15 years. By the time of their second move a growing number of black homeowners had come into LeDroit Park, including Robert L. Waring, Henrietta B. Turner, Clifton Hariston, Thomas Warrick, and Christian Fleetwood.

The earlier conflict between black Howardtown and white LeDroit

Park residents, followed by the gradual growth of black home ownership in LeDroit Park, reflected a major shift in the District's residential patterns. Once racially mixed, with residential segregation limited to smaller areas, such as alleys or blocks on one side of a street, the city's whites and blacks began to regroup into larger concentrations of population along racial lines. As more whites moved into newer suburban communities, older neighborhoods like LeDroit Park experienced a steady turnover from white to black. In fact, LeDroit Park became part of a larger black area in the Northwest quadrant. Other black residential neighborhoods, social and cultural institutions, businesses, and shops slowly formed around LeDroit Park. As a result, a new focus for black Washington emerged, centered around the meeting of U Street, 7th Street, Boundary (now Florida) Avenue, and Georgia Avenue.

This intersection was just a block west of LeDroit Park. In the general proximity, black-owned shops and retail stores joined seven movie theaters, a YMCA, two newspaper and publishing firms, and restaurants and dining clubs to form a separate black business section in the area known today as Shaw. Also here were numerous Baptist and Methodist churches, elementary schools, Miner Normal School, and Howard University. The latter, founded in 1867, occupied a site overlooking LeDroit Park and by 1900 had become the nation's most important black institution of higher learning. In time the District school board located Armstrong Technical School and Dunbar High School in this area. A growing black elite took up residence in the Northwest quadrant. They included members of old District families, such as the Syphaxes and Wormleys, but most were more recently arrived law-

Nationally acclaimed poet Paul Laurence Dunbar came to LeDroit Park from Ohio in 1897 and enthusiastically wrote his mother asking her to "come at once . . . my house is very beautiful, and my parlor is swell." Courtesy, Howard University, Moorland-Spingarn Research Center

yers, clergy, business people, teachers, and school administrators. Along with these individuals came even larger numbers of government clerks and skilled federal workers. To affirm their rising status and realize the fruits of hard work, they sought to buy houses in established neighborhoods such as LeDroit Park.

The most famous resident in the neighborhood during these years was Paul Laurence Dunbar, who was neither a homeowner nor a member of the black middle class. He was instead a young writer from Ohio, already acclaimed by William Dean Howells in *Harper's Weekly* as the best black poet in the country. Dunbar, then 25 years old, arrived in the District of Columbia in the fall of 1897 just after the publication of his *Lyrics of the Lowly Life* and a successful speaking tour in England. Offered a position on the circulation desk in the Library of Congress, Dunbar decided to settle in the city. Initially he stayed with Howard University professor Kelly Miller and family, spending his free time on his first novel, *The Uncalled*. With help from Miller, the founder of black sociology and a celebrated teacher, and Robert and Mary Terrell, Dunbar found a rooming house in LeDroit Park. By Thanksgiving he had written his mother: "Come at once to 1934 Fourth St., N.W. My house is very beautiful and my parlor suite is swell." He described his rooms in detail, alluding to "dark green plush and cherry-colored inlaid wood . . . polished floors . . . fine big Morris chair," and "a study off the parlor."

Even while his reputation soared, Dunbar experienced moments of depression over his battle with tuberculosis, a struggle that he would eventually lose. His job at the Library of Congress as a clerk, along with the heavily political atmosphere in the city, distressed him. In a letter written in 1898 he lashed out: "I still stagnate here among books in medicine and natural sciences, in what I have come to believe the most God-forsaken and unliterary town in America. I hate Washington very cordially and evidently it returns the compliment, for my health is continually poor here." Yet the record shows he was not always so critical. "I am afraid the climate of Washington does not suit me," he later commented, "but there is much to hold me here. The best Negroes in the country find their way to the capital, and I have a very congenial and delightful circle of friends."

Among them was Mary Terrell, who became an especially close acquaintance. He affectionately called her "Molly," and the two often discussed literature and art. In 1899 Dunbar and his new wife, the writer Alice Moore, moved into an old McGill house at 321 Spruce Street. There Mary Terrell came to know the famous poet well. "Precious memories rush over me like a flood," she later wrote, "every time I pass that house. I can see Paul Dunbar beckoning me, as I walked by, when he wanted to read a poem which he had just written or when he wished to discuss a word or a subject on which he had not fully decided." Indeed, Dunbar was happy in LeDroit Park, as seen in his rendering in *Lyrics of the Hearthside* of evening walks along Spruce Street: "Summah nights and sighin' breeze / 'Long de lovah's lane."

While in the city, Dunbar commented extensively on black Washington. In his essay "Negro Society in Washington," published in the December 14, 1901, issue of the *Saturday Evening Post,* he spoke of the black middle-class experience in the city. "Here exists a society," he wrote, "which is sufficient unto itself—a society which is satisfied with its own condition, and which is not asking for social intercourse with whites." Thinking specifically of LeDroit Park, he spoke of "homes finely, beautifully and tastefully furnished. Here comes together the flower of colored citizenship from all parts of the country." The next year, in failing health, Dunbar left LeDroit Park, returning to Dayton and eventually succumbing to tuberculosis in 1906.

Near the center of black Washington, LeDroit Park thrived as a socially elite, black middle-class neighborhood. By 1920, T Street was home to Anna J. Cooper, educator and pioneer in black adult education; Fountain Peyton, prominent lawyer; and Ernest E. Just and Alonzo H. Brown, respected members of the Howard University faculty. All worked hard to maintain the original setting of the neighborhood. When former resident Charles Hamilton revisited LeDroit Park, he found nothing changed except "the tint of the complexions of the inhabitants." He concluded that "the darker race" had "now made LeDroit Park the most orderly and attractive 'colored section' of Washington."

While LeDroit Park's physical setting remained largely unchanged during the early decades of the twentieth century, considerable change affected its perimeter: even more rowhousing, stores, and businesses. The largest development had come in 1919 when Clark C. Griffith constructed a 34,000-seat ballpark, complete with bleacher seats and a center field fence abutting the backyards of dwellings on U Street. Until 1956 LeDroit Park residents made the annual adjustment to the crowds and noise emanating from Griffith Stadium, home of the Ameri-

can League's Washington Senators. Also attracting the public to the neighborhood was the Howard Theater, just east of 7th on T Street. Here Edward "Duke" Ellington and Bessie Smith, among others, performed before enthusiastic audiences. The Howard ranked along with the Apollo in New York and the Pearl in Philadelphia as one of the nation's premier Afro-American theaters.

During the 1920s and 1930s LeDroit Park continued to house prominent individuals and families. Living in the neighborhood at different times were Anita J. Turner and Hattie Riggs, well-known Dunbar High School teachers; Emmet J. Scott, one-time personal secretary to Booker T. Washington and secretary-treasurer of Howard University; Oscar de Priest, the first black congressman since Reconstruction; Garnet Wilkinson, highest-ranking administrator for the city's black schools; and Langston Hughes, who lived briefly with a relative before moving into the Anthony Bowen YMCA. The fame of these individuals, and others, brought black Washington and LeDroit Park a national reputation, as documented in *Crisis,* the official magazine of the NAACP, edited by W.E.B. DuBois. In 1926 Kelly Miller published "Where Is the Negro's Heaven?" and six years later "The Secret City: An Impression of Colored Washington" appeared. Both favorably depicted life in the District of Columbia, a claim that some writers, including Langston Hughes and Jean Toomer, rejected in light of contemporary segregation laws and practices.

The impact of the Depression was felt in LeDroit Park when the National Capital Housing Authority (NCHA), using New Deal funding, placed public housing units on its northern boundary. When the Williston Apartments opened on W Street, all 30 units were immediately filled. The NCHA also opened the V Street Homes and the Kelly Miller Dwellings, totaling 169 rental apartments. The V Street complex was built on the site of

One of architect James H. McGill's grandest designs, this double house still presides over Anna Cooper Circle in LeDroit Park. Courtesy, D.C. Public Library, Washingtoniana Division, c. Washington Post

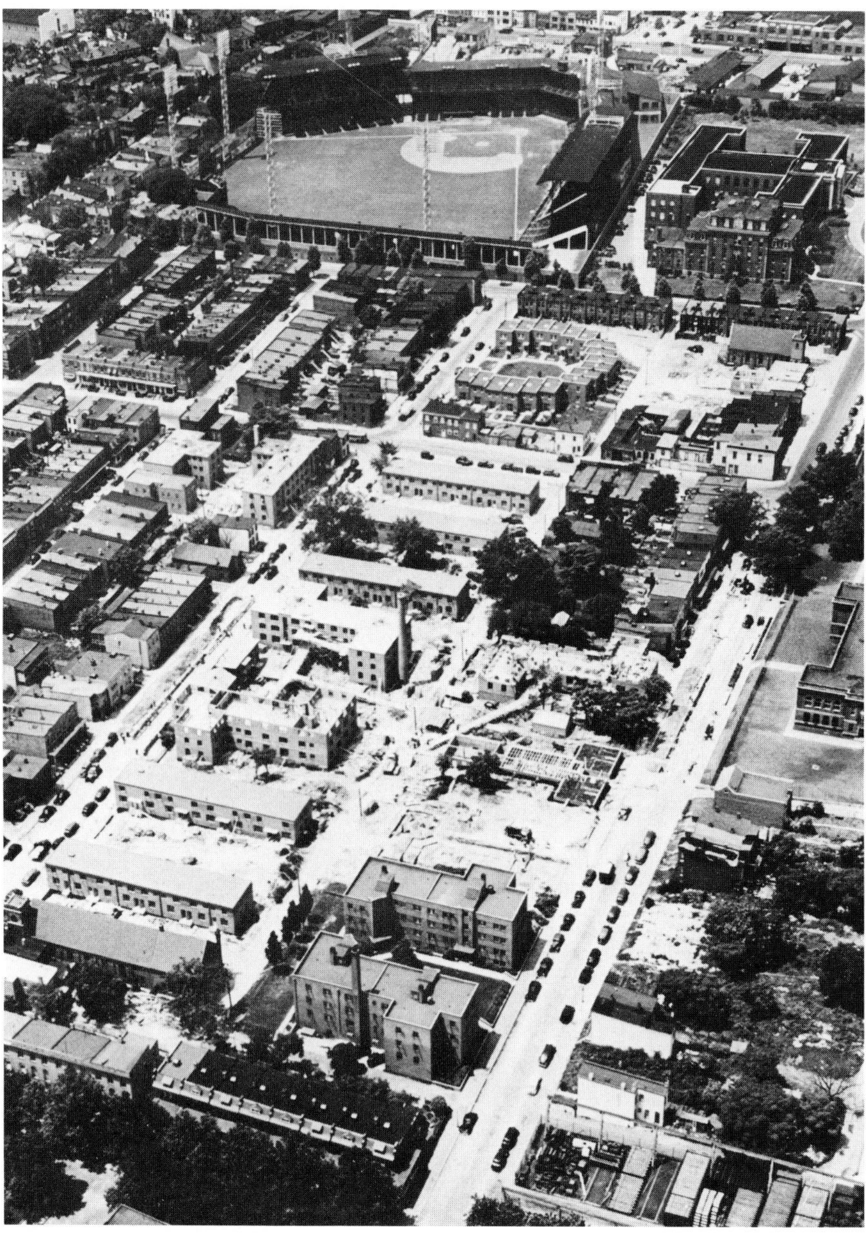

The sounds of major league baseball wafted over LeDroit Park from Griffith Stadium on its northern edge. This 1941 aerial of the stadium also shows the public housing developments built north of the neighborhood in the 1930s and 1940s. Courtesy, D.C. Public Library, Washingtoniana Division

Bland's Court, an old alley community that Paul Dunbar had frequented during his years in LeDroit Park. But the outbreak of World War II ended all development.

In the spring of 1951, *Evening Star* reporter George Kennedy visited LeDroit Park and noted that the residents had carefully maintained the "gingerbread gables, spiral pillars, stained glass windows and other romantic designs." Kennedy concluded that "Queen Victoria still reigns there." At the same time he sensed a growing change in LeDroit Park. During the 1950s and 1960s many whites fled the District of Columbia for the suburbs, placing houses on the market that formerly had not been available for blacks to purchase. With the Supreme Court decision to abolish racial covenants in 1948, large areas of the District, particularly in the Northwest and Northeast quadrants, opened to black middle-class migration. At the same time the NCHA began the urban renewal of Southwest, forcing thousands of low-income black families to seek housing elsewhere in the city. The combined result for LeDroit Park was a substantial loss of older, middle-class families and an equally large influx of low-income residents. By 1970 the neighborhood was in the throes of population turnover and dislocation. Physical decline of the older structures, as well as overcrowded conditions in the Kelly Miller complex, had increased in the postwar years. Vandalism and fire took their toll; many vacant lots were left where homes had once stood.

In response to these conditions, which had also bred extensive social problems and an increase in crime, the LeDroit Park Civic Association mobilized. Under the leadership of Walter E. Washington and his wife, Bennetta Bullock Washington, whose family had resided in LeDroit since 1918, the Civic Association worked for increased police protection, better government services, and youth programs. The organization also attempted to involve Howard University in the neighborhood. Living in the old family home on T Street, the Washingtons, with other LeDroit Park residents, became deeply involved in reviving the community. In time, because of his work in LeDroit Park, Washington became head of the NCHA and in 1967 was appointed by President Lyndon Johnson to be the city's first black mayor.

Beginning in the 1960s, the LeDroit Park Civic Association also encouraged individual homeowners to restore their properties, particularly the original McGill houses. Some residents successfully competed for city preservation awards, and soon restoration spread throughout the neighborhood. Concern over Howard University's projected expansion into the area led the Civic Association in 1972 to organize the LeDroit Park Historic District Project, which gained official designation by the Department of Interior two years later.

In the years since, progress has proved difficult, but restoration efforts continue and many of the McGill structures are now preserved. The early history of the neighborhood has been researched and made available to the general public. The LeDroit Park Preservation Society, headed by its founder and president Theresa Brown, stands guard over the neighborhood. Anna Cooper Circle, restored and landscaped, honors the memory of the original black residents who transformed LeDroit Park into a nationally recognized address. Today LeDroit Park is well known among preservationists, black and white, as an important historic site.

Walter Washington, who in 1974 became Washington's first elected mayor since 1871, posed with his wife, educator Bennetta Bullock Washington, in front of their LeDroit Park home in 1971. At the time he was "mayor-commissioner," appointed by the president. The house was Bennetta Washington's childhood home. Courtesy, D.C. Public Library, Washingtoniana Division, c. Washington Post

13

DEANWOOD

SELF-RELIANCE AT THE EASTERN POINT

Ruth Ann Overbeck

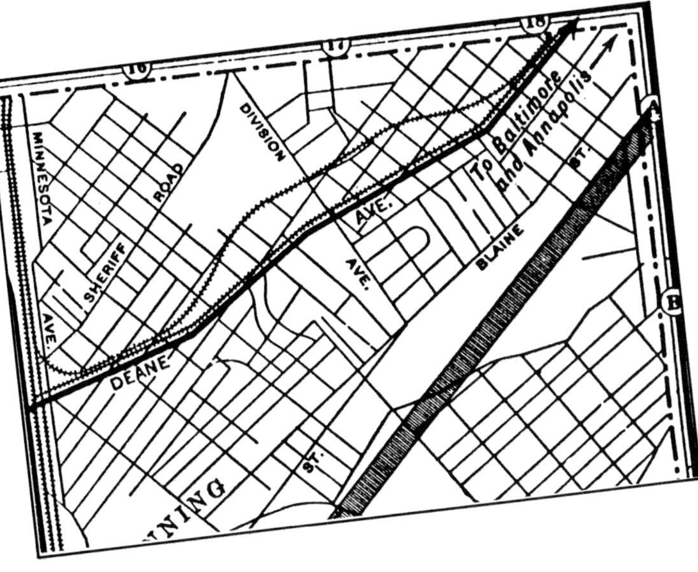

Tom Bowles, the caretaker at the Sheriff-Lowrie-Dean house after the last family members had moved out, stands amid the scattered tombstones in the families' cemetery in 1917. Courtesy, Columbia Historical Society

Map: 1924. District transportation routes. Courtesy, Robert Truax

Most Washingtonians know Deanwood only as a name on Metro bus and subway routes. Tucked just inside the city's eastern border, the triangular area is bounded by Eastern Avenue on the northeast, Kenilworth Avenue on the northwest, and East Capitol Street on the south. It encompasses three nineteenth-century suburbs platted from farmland in 1871 when the Southern Maryland Railroad cut through the area.

Today Deanwood is a solidly black community. It was born, however, when three white women, the daughters of Levi Sheriff, divided part of the farm they had inherited from their father. A series of subdivisions resulted: some black, some white, and some mixed, all loosely tied after 1888 by the name Deanwood. By 1910 Deanwood had a stable nucleus of blue- and white-collar black families with a network of laborers and skilled craftsmen working in the building trades. This network enhanced the strong sense of economic independence and self-reliance of Deanwood's black community.

The Benning-Sheriff-Lowrie-Dean and Fowler farms, both carved from Ninian Beall's 1703 land grant, undergird Deanwood's history. The Piney and Watts branches of the Eastern Branch (now the Anacostia River) crossed their land from east to west. The broad valleys they created left a high ridge, which provided a natural house site near springs; the meadows that flanked the streams proved ideal for agriculture. During the mid-1700s a north-south road cut across the branches to link Bladensburg, Maryland, on the Eastern Branch to Piscataway, the nearest important Potomac River port. The portion of Minnesota Avenue that is in Deanwood today follows approximately the same route.

The late eighteenth-century house that sat on the

Above: Deanwood's main street, Sheriff Road, N.E., still had a small-town appearance in 1948, when a mixture of houses and businesses shared this block west of 44th Street. The F.L. Watkins Co. was a Deanwood landmark for many years. Courtesy, Columbia Historical Society

Below right: Built on a high ridge in rolling farmland about 1790, this farmhouse was home to all the early families of Deanwood, including William Benning, who helped establish the first Benning Bridge, and several generations of the Sheriff-Lowrie-Dean family. It was photographed in 1917, six years after the last family member had moved out. Courtesy, Private Collection

ridge's best site for some 125 years was built for William Benning about 1790, soon after he acquired 330 acres of Beall farmland. Benning, a slave owner, moved from Virginia to the new federal district and helped establish the first Benning Bridge in 1797. Benning's nephew Anthony purchased the land after his uncle's death and in turn sold the farm in 1833 to Levi Sheriff, a white Maryland merchant.

Sheriff, twice a widower, amassed 524 acres and retired to the farm. In 1838 James H. Fowler, another white farmer, bought 83 1/4 acres that lay between the District of Columbia's eastern boundary and Sheriff's farm. Like Sheriff, Fowler depended on slave labor, although his operation was more modest. Both raised hogs and cattle, had fruit orchards and fields of corn, rye, hay, and vegetables. Sheriff also grew tobacco.

In 1850 Levi Sheriff had 19 slaves. According to family records in private hands, he supplied his white overseer, hired by the year to supervise the field hands, with a house and the privilege of keeping one cow, some pigs, and hens. The workday for the overseer and field hands, men and women, began at sunrise. The workers "came in" for breakfast and midday dinner, then "went out" again. Their workday ended at sunset. A cook, a "house woman," and a man to cut wood, bring water, care for the riding horse and the horse and carriage worked at the main house. The cook prepared her family's food at the same time that she prepared the Sheriffs' and fed the two families the same menu. Slave children stayed in or near the house. Boys went to the fields when they were about 14, the girls when they were somewhat older.

Slave families had "quarters" on the farm, distant from one another as well as from the main house. They

Post-World War II housing lines Sheriff Road, N.E., west of 51st Street in 1948. The city's wartime population boom reached into the still-open spaces of the District across the Anacostia River and brought city services to some older sections of Deanwood. Courtesy, Columbia Historical Society

maintained gardens with raspberries and fruit trees and raised chickens and pigs for their own use. Some owned guns and hunted to supplement their produce. Sheriff provided allowances of meal, bacon, and fish and gave each hand "cash money" at the end of harvest.

Sheriff died in 1853 and left the farm to his three daughters, who already lived there in separate houses. Spinster Emmeline suffered from tuberculosis; Margaret Lowrie, a widow, headed a household of two sons and two invalid daughters; and Mary Cornelia lived with her husband, John T.W. Dean, and son Julian.

The Civil War marked the beginning of the farm's decline. The military established checkpoints at the Benning and Navy Yard bridges, and soldiers stopped everyone entering the city for identification. They searched all wagons for contraband. Soldiers cleared the woodlands to provide nearby forts with unobstructed views of the area, a process described in a nineteenth-century history of the New York 10th Heavy Artillery. Once they selected a hill, choppers formed a line perhaps a mile long at the hill's foot. They cut partway through the first tree, went up the hill to the next, and cut partway through it. They continued on their way in this fashion to the crest, where the last tree in each row was cut to the point where it would topple with a single final stroke of the soldiers' axes. Then the bugler signaled; every soldier swung his ax one last time and brought down his top tree. Row after descending row crashed like thunder until the woods were no more.

The tree removal proved a boon to nearby black Methodists. Selby Scaggs, the slave-owning minister in whose Benning Road building they worshiped, overheard their pro-Union prayers and locked them out. Hoping to establish their own place of worship, the blacks turned to John Dean. With Dean's agreement, they built their new chapel with Sheriff farm trees, felled by the Union soldiers.

In June 1862, six months before President Abraham Lincoln's Emancipation Proclamation, Congress provided for the emancipation of all remaining slaves in the District of Columbia, then about 30 percent of the black population. Slave owners received up to $300 per slave as compensation. Harriet Watkins, Sheriff's cook, was among those freed. Sheriff's grandson, Randolph Lowrie, described her: "A woman of great dignity," tall, gaunt, with a man's hat, a very tall cane in her hand, and a corn pipe in her mouth. Her cooking repertoire included cabbage-stalk, pork-skin, and skillet bread, and "better persimmon beer than anyone else could make." She could find the earliest poke leaves and the last chestnuts. Harriet Watkins' life in freedom was short. In 1864 she was buried on the farm, with Margaret Lowrie and her son in attendance.

The Sheriff farm never recovered after the Civil War. The health of Emmeline and the Lowrie daughters deteriorated; two Sheriff grandsons chose medicine over farming; and Randolph Lowrie entered the Episcopal priesthood. With their slaves freed and the next generation unlikely to be farmers, Sheriff's daughters must have welcomed the Southern Maryland Railroad Company's arrival. In 1871 the company laid its track close to the old Bladensburg-Piscataway Road and built a station near the farm. Almost immediately Margaret Lowrie, Emmeline Sheriff, and Mary Cornelia Dean initiated three subdivisions. Whittingham, a triangular parcel, was bounded by railroad tracks on the west, Sheriff Road on the south, and present-day 45th Street on the east. A subdivision named Lincoln, apparently meant from the outset to be black owned, was platted near the farm's south edge. Burrville, just east of the ridge, completed the trio.

Land sales did not go well. Home buyers in the 1870s could choose from new suburbs as far from downtown Washington as Falls Church, Virginia, or as close in as LeDroit Park, near Boundary Street (now Florida Avenue) in the District. Major civic improvements were under way in central Wash ington across the Eastern Branch. Whittingham, Lincoln, and Burrville had only the railroad. One lone purchaser paid $50 for two Whittingham lots in 1873. No other buyer appeared until 1874, when the Sheriff heirs traded all of Whittingham for two lots in Washington City with frame houses on them. A black minister, the Reverend John H.W. Burley, acquired Whittingham and renamed it "Burley's Subdivision" but kept the original subdivision's street names. Burley lived in Northwest Washington from 1873 to 1879, while he served as the national secretary for the African Methodist Episcopal Church.

By 1880 a handful of nonfarmers lived in what would become Deanwood. According to the federal census of that year, three of them lived with their families on the Sheriff farm: Dr. Julian Dean, a physician and Levi Sheriff's grandson; Charles Diggs, a black laborer at a brickyard; and Jerry Smallwood, a mulatto brickmolder.

Around 1888 Dr. Dean added an *e* to his name and initiated the place name "Deanewood." The *e* in the community's name would later be dropped by common usage. He mortgaged real estate to fund his project and built about 20 houses. At the same time he poured money into Benjamin Charles Pole's "energizer," a "perpetual motion machine" that supposedly could use momentum as a source of power. Pole moved his family into one of Deane's houses and his experiments into a shop that Deane built for him. Pole's experiment failed, and Deane went bankrupt.

In 1895 Deane's real estate was sold at public auction. A Baltimore purchaser bought 57 acres and about 30 buildings for $18,000, including three Sheriff-Lowrie-Deane family dwellings. Margaret E. Lowrie and her son Randolph retained the rest of the estate and the 1790s farmhouse.

Deane and his family moved away but in about 1904 returned to his birthplace, the old farmhouse. He died there in 1905 and was buried in the family cemetery. Six years later his second wife and their children moved to Capitol Hill. In 1913 Randolph Lowrie's death signaled the end of the farm as well.

Deanwood grew slowly throughout this period. By 1893 a few houses dotted each subdivision and the lots along Sheriff Road. Five families lived in Burley's Subdivision, where all the lots had changed hands since 1874. Two men named William Saunders headed households within two houses of each other. Tax, census, and building records reveal that one was white, one was black. Their buildings were similar in size, material, and cost.

As the living arrangements of the two Saunders families suggest, blacks and whites lived as neighbors in Deanwood, a Southern residential pattern that persisted to a diminishing degree in the area until the 1930s, long after housing in most of the District of Columbia had become tightly segregated. From the beginning, however, there was clustering by race in the Deanwood subdivisions; some blocks were

The founder of the National Trade and Professional School for Women, Nannie Helen Burroughs, first row, right, with the faculty on the school grounds in the Lincoln subdivision shortly after the school opened in 1909. Courtesy, Library of Congress

white, some black, some mixed. By 1900 Deanwood's population consisted of the old farm families as well as new arrivals, homeowners as well as renters. Residents worked as clerks, railroad and Navy Yard employees, and members of the building trades, among other occupations.

By 1909 Deanwood's black community was large enough to require its own public school. A city architect, Snowden Ashford, designed Deanwood Elementary School, now George Washington Carver School. His four-room schoolhouse was built of frame and stucco rather than more expensive brick, reflecting the neighborhood's semirural character as well as the fact that its students were black. Black children from nearby Maryland had no school and crossed the District line to attend Deanwood School.

Another educational institution came to Deanwood in 1909 when the National Trade and Professional School for Women and Girls opened in the Lincoln section. Nannie Helen Burroughs, a black woman born in Virginia and educated in Washington, founded the school on behalf of the National Baptist Convention. Her program emphasized professional skills in housework, gardening, and interior decorating, as well as vocational skills, including weaving. By June 1910 the school had eight teachers, and its students had come from as far away as Louisiana. The school has survived dramatic social changes and continues today as Nannie Helen Burroughs School.

Most Deanwood adults of the 1910 era were U.S. citizens but not native Washingtonians. Their white- and blue-collar working-class jobs encompassed a diversity of status, skill, and income levels. Some occupations, such as Pullman porter, were racially segregated. However, one sizable trade represented in Deanwood had both black and white members—the unskilled laborers and skilled craftsmen who built Deanwood's houses. Black members of this pool passed their skills on to family members or to their black neighbors. They also helped one another locate jobs, build their own houses or additions to them, and make repairs.

Thomas H. Stokes became part of this network. He was described in the federal census as a mulatto from Virginia who worked at the Government Printing Office and lived in Northwest. In 1907 Stokes put together an unusual team: he bought a Deanwood lot, then hired architect W. Sidney Pittman to design his home and Owen H. Fowler to build it. Pittman, the black son-in-law of Booker T. Washington, had a degree from the

A solitary pedestrian crosses 49th Street, at Sheriff Road, N.E., in September 1948, a setting more reminiscent of a small rural town than the nation's capital after World War II. Many of these early wooden houses were built by Deanwood craftsmen. Courtesy, Columbia Historical Society

Drexel Institute and was one of the earliest academically trained architects to design a Deanwood building. Fowler, a white attorney and real estate broker as well as a builder, was a descendant of the old Fowler farm family.

When Stokes moved to Deanwood, Fowler returned the favor, engaging Stokes as the builder for about half of the projects Fowler undertook between 1907 and 1915. Other white Washington investors such as Gusack & Cohen and Joseph L. Tepper also employed Stokes as their builder.

Two black Deanwood brothers, Jacob and Randolph Dodd, followed in Thomas Stokes' footsteps. Between 1921 and 1930 the Dodds built more than 50 houses, with Jacob serving as builder on about a third of them and Randolph on the rest. Randolph Dodd often worked for Howard S. Gott, a white investor, sometimes as both architect and builder. Dodd, in turn, hired as many local black craftsmen and laborers as he could and provided on-the-job training as needed. His insistence on performance earned him a lasting reputation as the man who did more for Deanwood's building craftsmen than anyone else.

Randolph Dodd and his crews organized their work using the skills and production methods handed down by tradition rather than learned academically. They took pride in producing one house a week at very low cost despite the fact that their approach was labor-intensive. They avoided the price of ready-to-install window frames and sashes by buying bundles of framing and sash pieces they could put together themselves. They also installed windows on front and rear facades only: purchasers could add side windows later. The results are still visible. Some Deanwood buildings have no side windows at all; some have side windows that show they were placed after the fact; the rest have side windows that were part of the original design.

In 1924 the District of Columbia accepted the premise of the American Institute of Architects that only people who had passed a rigorous licensing process had the right to use the title "architect." Men such as Randolph Dodd had become recognized as architects in their communities but didn't have the academic background to pass the licensing exam. The law applied equally to black and white but hit black architects practicing under the old system far harder, as so few of them had had access to formal training.

Some of Washington's licensed black architects designed buildings for Deanwood: Lewis Giles, Sr.; H.D. Woodson; and George A. Ferguson. Woodson was also a principal in the firm of Woodson, Vaughn and Johnson. Giles lived in Deanwood for several years and designed more than two dozen of its houses, including the significant "craftsman" style of duplex he used as both home and architecture office.

There were opportunities for black home ownership in Washington, but home loans were hard to obtain, and the rates were often very high. The Deanwood market was largely defined and controlled by the major white investors, such as Owen H. Fowler, Joseph L. Tepper, and Howard S. Gott. Gott, who began investing in Deanwood in 1911 through the Municipal Improvement Company, controlled large sections by 1920, including 44 acres of the old Fowler farm and its subdivisions of Hampton Park and Hampton Heights. He defined Hampton Park as a black neighborhood, advertising it as "A PLACE TO LIVE: HOMES FOR COLORED PEOPLE," with "Lots and Homes sold on Monthly Payment." Even after they had completed all payments in a timely manner, some purchasers had to threaten Gott with lawsuits to get him to release their deeds.

Black community life revolved around the churches and schools. Residents were self-reliant, making up for what they lacked by turning to self-help projects. For example, mothers furnished the city's nursery-school classroom from bake-sale proceeds. The streetcar ran only on Deane Avenue, so Deanwood resident Bernie Chapman provided a shuttle service for the area. Many of today's residents remember his "B.C. Bus #1," so reliable that children used its last run of the day as a signal that it was time to stop playing and get home. Chapman's enterprise also turned his fleet of dump trucks into a business that made him one of Deanwood's wealthiest men.

Suburban Gardens amusement park, opened in 1921, was the major recreational attraction, drawing black Washingtonians throughout the region. It stood under the ridge of the old farmhouse site, facing Nannie Helen Burroughs School across Deane Avenue (now Nannie Helen Burroughs Avenue). It had a swimming pool, refreshment stands, a merry-go-round, and a roller coaster known as "the Dip." The big-band sounds of Cab Calloway and Duke Ellington regularly wafted on the summer air; women in their full-length evening dresses added to the fairy-tale-like quality of the dance pavilion, which was decked out in a thousand lights.

Deanwood was accessible from downtown Washington by streetcar year-round, but an hour-long ride in one of the open-sided "summer cars" that connected Connecticut Avenue to Deanwood added a sense of adventure for those taking a summertime trip to Suburban Gardens. Passengers boarded anywhere along the side, and the conductor swung along the outside of the car on the "running board" platform to collect their fares.

Its distance from the central city kept Deanwood a semirural area until after World War II. It was not until the 1950s that the city government provided services taken for granted in other areas—paved streets, sewers, and some sidewalks. And after 20 years of citizen lobbying, the city finally planted street trees in Deanwood. Its isolation, however, has taken its toll, and some of its residents now must struggle with the social problems that have struck lower-income neighborhoods across the city in recent years.

The recent historical survey that provided the basis for this chapter has revealed, however, that many longtime residents continue to feel a strong commitment to their neighborhood and a renewed interest in its past. The neighborhood today retains many physical reminders of its history, in the houses built by its own craftsmen, in the open spaces, and in the overall low scale of its structures. The community's location in the city's far eastern corner continues to give it a sense of a place set apart, a place where people still take great pride in their community's tradition of self-reliance.

All ages responded to the call for Citizen Air Raid Wardens in Deanwood during World War II. Courtesy, private collection

City council member Willie Hardy, facing the camera at center, and other city officials and area residents celebrate the prospects of a Metro subway stop in Deanwood in April 1975, a station that would connect the city's remote, far northeastern corner with the central city. Photo by Paul Myatt. Courtesy, Washington Metropolitan Area Transit Authority

Rock Cr. Ch. & Cem.
Cath. University
Brookland
Montello
Petworth
Brightwood Ave.
SOLDIERS HOME PARK
Glenwood Cem.
MICHIGAN AVE.
Kendall Green
Eckington
FLORIDA
Mount Pleasant
Rock Creek
National Zoological Park
Woodley
WESTERN UNION TELEGRAPH
U.S. Government Reservation
Arlington National
Ft. Meyer
Heights

PART FOUR

THE CITY LEAPS ITS BOUNDS

The 1880s witnessed a real estate boom in the capital. Federal employment tripled in the decade, reflecting the government's enlarged role in American life. As the population grew, new electrically powered streetcars carried development into the countryside and rendered the old District boundaries obsolete.

About 100 real estate firms operated in the city, representing then, as now, a major segment of the city's business community. Even Mrs. Susan Grigsby, a new $900-a-year clerk in the government Land Office, saw the potential. "There are still big fortunes to be made in this city on very small real estate investments," she wrote to her sister, "and I hope you and I will be amongst the fortunate ones." An 1890s wit claimed Washington was divided into two classes—those who were real estate agents and those who were not.

Improved transportation continued to be the catalyst. The new Metropolitan line of the Baltimore and Ohio Railroad, laid in 1873, inspired the development of Takoma Park (1883) and Brookland (1887) along its route. In 1888, the city's first electric streetcar ran on the Eckington and Soldiers' Home Railroad Company line, and by the 1890s electric lines, much faster than the earlier horse-drawn cars, were running in all directions from old Washington City and Georgetown to the District's boundaries and beyond.

The suburban movement blossomed as developers laid out new subdivisions throughout the District along the streetcar lines: for example, Kalorama, Cleveland Park, and Chevy Chase along Connecticut Avenue. Elaborate real estate brochures and decorated maps promoted the virtues of a residence on the heights beyond old Washington City—clean water, fresh breezes, beautiful views, and new homes with modern conveniences, some of them individually designed by noted architects. A 1903 *Washington Times* article rhapsodized over Cleveland Park, where "the breeze from the hills makes life one sweet song."

While the suburbs offered advantages to some, at the same time economic realities and discrimination, institutionalized in restrictive housing covenants in many places, increasingly separated people by class and by race. In Washington, as in other large American cities, neighborhoods became distinguished not only by their architecture and general physical character, but also by the kind of people who made their homes there.

Horse-drawn cabs await fares outside the old Baltimore and Ohio Railroad station at New Jersey Avenue and C Street, N.W., in the late nineteenth century. It was replaced by Union Station in 1908. Courtesy, National Archives

Map; streetcar routes, 1900. Courtesy, Robert A. Truax

House of Musical Traditions
BALI BLINDS
PAINTING
PAINT

14

Takoma Park

Early Railroad Suburb

Robert M. Bachman

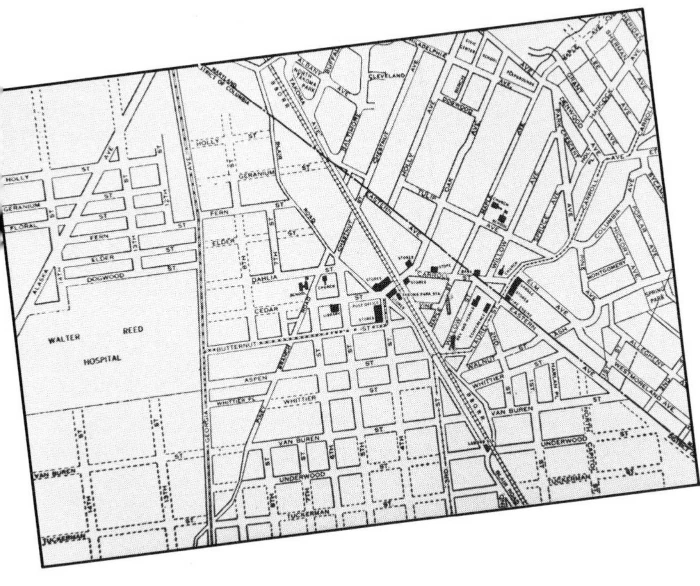

An old-fashioned lamppost, a brick sidewalk, and public benches complement the nineteenth-century buildings along Carroll Street in Takoma Park, Maryland, creating the atmosphere of a small town. Photo by Paul Jaffe

Map; 1922. Courtesy, Takoma Park Historical Society

Takoma Park, a railroad commuter suburb, arose more than a century ago from the vision of a real estate promoter who saw opportunity in the construction of a new Baltimore and Ohio Railroad line into the capital in 1873. Made possible by the commuter railroad, the neighborhood was improved, changed, and sometimes threatened by each new transportation technology—the electric streetcar, the automobile, and most recently the city's new subway system. From the earliest days to the present, residents of Takoma Park have taken an exceptionally active role in meeting the challenges posed by change, and in shaping their once very rural and now very urban residential community.

Benjamin Franklin Gilbert arrived in Washington from New York State in 1862 to pursue the many opportunities brought about by the sudden growth of population during the Civil War. He began a career as a real estate promoter and developer in Washington City in 1867, and his years in the business convinced him that the city would grow to the north and northwest. Acting on this belief, Gilbert determined to build a suburb, combining the advantages of nineteenth-century urban and rural life. On November 24, 1883, he invested $6,500 in a 90-acre parcel situated in both the District and Montgomery County, Maryland, at the uppermost edge of the District of Columbia.

Gilbert's site was practical and appealing. The Metropolitan Branch of the B&O, completed in 1873 from downtown Washington north to Point of Rocks, Maryland, provided reliable transportation to jobs, shopping, and cultural attractions in the city. The elevation, 300 to 400 feet above the Potomac River, kept it free of the malarial airs that plagued Washington in summer. He named it

Early residents of Takoma Park thought of themselves as pioneers, living seven miles from downtown and at first having no paved roads or sidewalks, no electricity or running water. A pioneer and her daughter pose here at the corner of Montgomery and Pine avenues about 1900. Courtesy, Takoma Park Historical Society

Takoma, an Indian word meaning "high up, near heaven," changing the *c* to *k* to avoid confusion with Tacoma in Washington State and later adding the word "Park" to emphasize its rural charms. Two natural springs guaranteed an adequate supply of excellent water, and the abundance of trees kept the "Park" 10 degrees cooler than the city. In contrast, the center of the city was crowded, with an unreliable water supply and a shortage of housing.

Gilbert disregarded jurisdictional lines when he made his original land purchase, believing that the District of Columbia and the Maryland sections would always be part of Takoma Park. Although the Maryland part of the neighborhood was incorporated as a Maryland municipality in 1890 and the District side remained a subdivision without any local power, the difference was not a barrier to cooperation. Marylanders and Washingtonians worked together to persuade the various governments—District, county, and state—to meet the community's needs.

Gilbert sought prospective buyers from the swelling ranks of government workers arriving in the city as the federal government grew in the late nineteenth century. His 1886 real estate brochure, *The Villa Lots of Takoma Park: A Suburb of Washington City,* advertised lots for 1.5 cents to 5 cents per square foot, compared to 48 cents per square foot in Washington City. Appealing to government workers, he pointed out that "all you need is a moderate income. Many department clerks are paying out sums as monthly rentals that would buy a home in Takoma Park if applied to purchase money." If one took into account "the keeping of a cow, the raising of chickens, and a garden spot," living expenses would be even further reduced.

Early Takoma Park houses cost between $1,000 and $5,000, with some of the architect-designed villas costing $10,000 to $15,000. These houses were "sub-urban," reflecting a reaction to the spatial and social constraints of downtown Washington and a nostalgia for small-town, rural living. They gloried in their space. Wide porches wrapped around the fronts and sides. Builders created individual designs, using multistoried wood-frame-and-shingle construction. The houses had distinctive exteriors and family-oriented interiors.

The suburban home was, according to architectural historian Vincent Scully, "one of the major vehicles of American architectural invention in the nineteenth century." Scattered throughout the earliest Takoma Park subdivisions are such styles as Queen Anne, Stick, Shingle, and Colonial Revival. Still, Takoma Park's mostly builder-designed homes can be best described as "Victorian-eclectic," reflecting a mixture of the housing styles of the period. Early efforts to preserve trees maintained the wooded character of the area and contributed to its country-like atmosphere.

The Metropolitan Branch of the B&O Railroad was the suburb's lifeline. With as many as 15 trains a day running between Washington and Takoma Park, being "on the railroad" was one of Takoma Park's chief attractions. The first streets, homes, and businesses clustered around the railroad station on Cedar Street within the District of Columbia. Here were the drugstore, livery stable, blacksmith shop, coal merchant, grocer, general stores, and Takoma Hall with its library, meeting rooms, billiards, and bowling. The most elaborate homes were built close to the tracks, advertising the "affordable elegance" of this "sylvan suburb."

Above: Houses in the open, wooded acres of early Takoma Park gloried in their space, with wide porches and varied shapes providing family-oriented interior spaces. This picture of the daughter of Arthur Colburn in front of the Colburn house that once stood on Carroll Avenue illustrates why the 1901 Takoma Park Citizens Association brochure was titled "Takoma Park, The Sylvan Suburb of the National Capital." Courtesy, Takoma Park Historical Society

Left: As many as 15 trains a day stopped at this 1886 Baltimore and Ohio station on Cedar Street in Takoma Park in the late nineteenth century, making this rural suburb very convenient for residents who worked in the city. Courtesy, Columbia Historical Society

As a matter of policy the B&O aided and encouraged developing communities on its right-of-way. In 1886 the railroad built a new station house on Cedar Street, N.W. (near the present Takoma Metro station), sufficient for 5,000-8,000 residents and complete with freight depot and side tracks. It also made concessions in fares and freight rates for builders and residents.

Gilbert had a grand design for his residential suburb. He continued to purchase land and lay out subdivisions. By 1888 he had land for a 1,000-acre community, which gave him the space to accommodate long-term growth and all the trappings of a successful suburb: grand homes, a business district, and a resort hotel, plus a potential hospital. He constructed the 140-room North Takoma Hotel in 1892, with its own railroad depot. He then persuaded Boston physician R.C.

Right: The nationwide Panic of 1893 hit B.F. Gilbert just as he had invested in this hotel, which he built despite the warnings from his real estate friends that it was a risky undertaking. He never fully recovered from the financial blow and lost control of the future development of the suburb he had created. Courtesy, Takoma Park Historical Society

Above: The lobby of B.F. Gilbert's new 140-room North Takoma Hotel welcomed guests with grand spaces and elegant furnishings in 1893. Courtesy, Takoma Park Historical Society

Flower, after whom the present Flower Avenue is named, to purchase land above Sligo Creek at the northeastern corner of the suburb for a sanitarium. Flower never realized his plans; it would be the Seventh-day Adventists who would later build a hospital there.

A special spirit developed in the suburb as residents shared the challenges of establishing a new town. Here was a cluster of homes, seven miles from downtown, with no electricity, no piped-in water, no paved roads or sidewalks, and surrounded by acres of tangled vines and trees. Takoma Park's "pioneers," as they liked to call themselves, were aggressive, cooperative, and public spirited.

Forced by circumstances to make their own selections of those elements of city life that could be transplanted outside the city, early residents gave priority to the essentials and pieced together their suburban environment. They tutored their children in one another's homes until 1887, when the Montgomery County Board of Education responded to their petitions and built the four-room frame schoolhouse on Tulip Avenue in the Maryland portion. The Takoma Park Citizens' Association of Maryland and D.C. was organized in 1889. One of their major accomplishments was to persuade the District government to build the classical-style Takoma Park Elementary School at Cedar Street and Piney Branch Road, N.W., in 1901. Both District and Maryland children attended this school until the 1950s. They worshiped in each other's homes until 1888, when the Union Chapel Association built a cooperative chapel on land donated by Gilbert. Soon Episcopalian, Presbyterian, Baptist, and other denominations attracted congregations and built churches.

Dependence on private wells and the town's two natural springs ended in 1900 when a $30,000 filtration plant and pump station were built on Sligo Creek, and water flowed to mains throughout the town. In 1903 Gilbert persuaded Elder Ellen G. White and other Seventh-day Adventist Church leaders to relocate the Church's headquarters from Battle Creek, Michigan, to rural, family-oriented Takoma Park. The Adventists bought land near the town center for their General Conference headquarters building and the *Review and Herald* publishing building. They also purchased a 50-acre portion of Dr. Flower's undeveloped land overlooking Sligo Creek for the Washington Training College and the Washington Sanitarium, now known as the Washington Adventist Hospital. Soon, in 1907, electric power lines were strung to serve the hospital. Gas mains and telephone lines followed shortly thereafter, and residents also acquired these "modern" conveniences.

The suburb attracted some well-to-do residents who built elaborate houses, but for the most part middle-income people made their homes there. There were numerous government professionals, including many Department of Agriculture scientists. A group of these men conducted experiments with azaleas in the neighborhood, carrying out extensive plantings throughout Takoma Park, leading to the designation of the community by the mayor as "azalea city."

Meanwhile, Takoma Park, D.C., acquired two new transportation

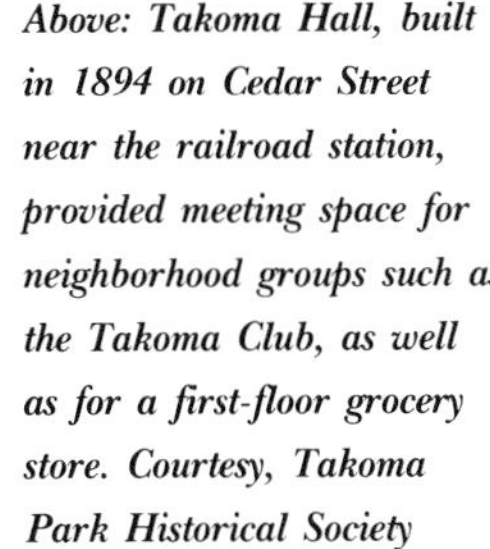

Above: Takoma Hall, built in 1894 on Cedar Street near the railroad station, provided meeting space for neighborhood groups such as the Takoma Club, as well as for a first-floor grocery store. Courtesy, Takoma Park Historical Society

Left: A Brightwood Railway Company electric streetcar at the turn of the century takes passengers right to the front door of the Takoma Novelty Store and Post Office. Service on the Brightwood line began in 1893, adding another transportation link to the central city. Courtesy, Takoma Park Historical Society

routes to the central city. In 1893 the Brightwood Railway Company ran a streetcar spur from its Georgia Avenue main line to 4th and Butternut streets. Soon after, Capital Traction extended its 14th Street line to Kennedy Street, where a spur ran east on Kennedy to 3rd Street, up to Aspen Street, and over to a terminal at Laurel Street and Eastern Avenue, in the heart of Takoma Park's business district. Wherever the streetcars went, homes, businesses, and people soon followed.

The Montgomery County side of Takoma Park even boasted its own private streetcar line, the Baltimore and Washington Transit Company, organized in 1897, which began at the terminal at Laurel and Eastern and headed for the Glen Sligo Hotel and the Wildwood Amusement Park, near present-day Heather and Elm avenues. Amusement parks were a common promotional feature of early suburbs, designed to lure potential buyers as well as generate off-hour revenues for the streetcar companies. Chevy Chase had its Chevy Chase Lake and Takoma Park had its Wildwood, which opened in May 1900 on the banks of Sligo Creek. It offered overnight accommodations at the Glen Sligo Hotel and dancing, gambling, bowling, and, once the dam was in place, boating on the creek. Unfortunately flash flooding and management problems closed the Wildwood Amusement Park within a few years and the Glen Sligo Hotel not long after. But the "Dinky" line, as residents called it, continued to provide streetcar transportation until 1907.

Takoma Park's emergence as a middle- to upper-middle-class residential suburb was significantly slowed by the economic panic of 1893. While the Washington real estate industry was only temporarily affected by this major national economic fluctuation, the fortunes of B.F. Gilbert declined dramatically. He was overextended, and his widespread holdings in Takoma Park could not be converted into cash to pay debts acquired in land purchases and in the construction of the North Takoma Hotel. To repay recalled notes, Gilbert sold his Takoma Park mansion and moved into the North Takoma Hotel to oversee its management personally. Gilbert's diminished role as principal developer and promoter soon proved permanent. No resident or subsequent land developer stepped in to fill the void.

Gilbert's experience and its impact on the future development of Takoma Park contrasts sharply with that of Francis Newlands, whose extensive capital allowed him to ride out the 1893 depression and keep control of his grand vision for Chevy Chase as a neighborhood of fine large residences. But in Takoma Park the changes in the nation's economy, excellent access to downtown via streetcar lines,

This turn-of-the century path through the woods was the first incarnation of Sligo Creek Parkway, now an automobile parkway that connects New Hampshire Avenue and University Boulevard and cuts across the eastern side of Takoma Park. Courtesy, Takoma Park Historical Society

A contingent of the Takoma Park Fourth of July parade in 1920 marches down Cedar Street at Blair Road. The buildings in the background stand today. Courtesy, Columbia Historical Society

and the arrival of the Seventh-day Adventists produced smaller subdivisions over which no single developer had control. These new subdivisions had smaller lots that accommodated smaller, less expensive bungalows. At the same time, more spacious lots in the earlier subdivisions continued to attract more affluent families, who built larger, more expensive homes. For the first time there was socioeconomic diversity among residents.

The bungalow was small, simple, and economical. It was single story with a low-pitched gable roof and attic space made usable by a dormer window in the roof or the gable. A few true bungalows were built in Takoma Park in 1900-1920; however a large number of houses were built along bungalow lines but with a second story, earning the name "bungaloid." The bungalow and bungaloid homes built in Takoma Park fit reduced lot sizes so well that despite the doubling of house density per acre, the spacious residential environment established by the early houses was not disrupted.

In 1908 Dr. Louis Denton Bliss, an associate of Thomas Edison, purchased the debt-ridden North Takoma Hotel and moved his Bliss Electrical School from downtown Washington to the Maryland side of the Park. Almost immediately after the hotel was remodeled into classrooms and dormitories, a fire destroyed the structure. Bliss promptly rebuilt his campus with three modern fireproof buildings and operated his school until after World War II, when Montgomery County bought the campus as the site of Montgomery Junior College in 1950.

In 1911 citizens from both sides of the Park successfully lobbied for a branch of the D.C. Public Library. Built at 5th and Cedar streets, N.W., it was the first branch library in the city. Citizens raised the money to buy the site; Andrew Carnegie, benefactor of the D.C. Public Library, donated $40,000 to construct the building; and Congress appropriated funds for maintenance and operation.

Between 1920 and 1940, Takoma Park's population nearly tripled, spurred in part by the advent of the affordable automobile. New roads were built and old ones were widened and extended, connecting previously separate subdivisions and neighborhoods. The East-West Highway threaded formerly unconnected roads together in Takoma Park and joined a necklace of suburbs north of Washington that ran from Hyattsville and Riverdale in the east through Takoma Park and Silver Spring to Chevy Chase and Bethesda to the west. Less than three years after the New Hampshire Avenue "super" highway opened from the District line to what is now University Boulevard, nine subdivisions were platted on the Prince George's County side of town as the pattern of development shifted from the town center in the District to the eastern edge bordering the new highway.

Growth demanded additional school, fire, recreational, and library services. Takoma Park again depended upon its "pioneers" to meet these needs. But a gradual change was occurring. The District line was becoming significant. The municipality of Takoma Park, Maryland, was becoming one of the largest cities in the state, and it wanted new services situated within its jurisdiction to avoid increasing dependence on the District and the Montgomery and Prince George's County governments. While people on the District and Maryland sides continued to cooperate in some ways, they were now more inclined to seek services of their own.

This preference produced new organizations in the Maryland and District sections of the Park. In 1922 the Community League of Maryland formed to improve the schools and, over the next six years, shepherded approval for the Philadelphia Avenue Elementary School and the Takoma Park-Silver Spring High School in Montgomery County and the Ray Elementary School in Prince George's County. In a similar fashion the District side formed a citizens' association of its own in 1924, naming it "Takoma, D.C." to distinguish it from the earlier Takoma Park Citizens' Association. It campaigned for an addition to the Takoma Park Elementary School and construction of Paul Junior High School. The two sides did join in persuading the District to build, and the National Park Service to maintain, the swimming and playing field complex at 4th and Whittier Street.

Takoma Park celebrated its 50th birthday in 1933. The late 1930s saw an upswing in business and civic development highlighted by the arrival of an F.W. Woolworth's, the dedication in 1938 of the New Hampshire Avenue "super" highway, and the completion of the 10-room Takoma Park Junior High School on Piney Branch Road in the Montgomery County section of town.

The World War II years brought population pressures to Takoma Park. The practice of dividing up homes into apartments, which began in the 1930s as a cost-cutting measure during the Depression, increased to meet the housing needs of a war-swollen capital. After the war the Maryland municipality changed its name to the City of Takoma Park and closed its "big" spring to control pollution. It also reactivated the chamber of commerce, created in 1927, to hold onto community patronage in the aging business district, which had long since spread from its center on Cedar Street in the District onto adjacent Maryland streets.

A building boom in the 1950s brought traffic and zoning problems, as well as some further deterioration of old buildings. The Washington Sanitarium built a multimillion-dollar addition, and apartment complexes sprang up on land once occupied by single-family homes. Many of the older homes, once showplaces, were now overcrowded and run-down, causing problems for residents and city officials. On the Maryland side, ordinances were passed establishing standards for single-family housing and requiring licensing of rooming and apartment houses.

Transportation patterns again had a strong impact. Takoma Park's business district, which had supplied the daily needs of the community, slowly withered as residents on both sides of the District line preferred to use their cars to drive out Georgia and New Hampshire avenues to enticing new stores in Silver Spring and Langley Park, Maryland.

In the 1960s changes occurred on both sides of the line that severely threatened the social as well as the physical fabric of the community. As black people began to move into the neighborhood, some real estate dealers tried to panic white residents into selling their homes, a process referred to as "block busting." Takoma Park, D.C., joined with the adjacent neighborhoods of Manor Park and Shepherd Park in a new organization, Neighbors, Inc., through which they worked to create a neighborhood where blacks and whites could live together in an orderly, small-town atmosphere. The District portion of Takoma Park gradually shifted from a predominantly white to an integrated neighborhood. To reflect this new identity, some residents made a point of calling the neighborhood "Takoma, D.C.," a preference that prevailed when the neighborhood's new subway stop was labeled the "Takoma" station.

Meanwhile the completion of a circular beltway around Washington in 1964 spurred plans for a series of 10-lane highways that would move large volumes of automobile traffic in and out of the center city. One such highway, the North Central Freeway, threatened to displace hundreds of homes and thousands of residents in

Takoma Park, Brookland, and Michigan Park.

The Save Takoma Park Committee was immediately organized under the leadership of community activist Sam Abbott and others. They created a coalition of residents of the neighborhoods, schools, and colleges in the projected freeway's path and attracted the support of representatives of the Metropolitan Citizens' Council for Rapid Transit, the American Institute of Architects, the Sierra Club, and the National Audubon Society.

The coalition vigorously opposed the North Central Freeway, calling it "White Men's Roads Through Black Men's Homes," and argued for a rapid transit system instead of highway construction as a cure for Washington's traffic congestion. After a long fight, during which Takoma Park's future as a residential community was in doubt, the community defeated the freeway proposal.

Subsequent planning for a rapid rail system also threatened the residents of Takoma Park. In addition to constructing a station on Takoma Park, D.C., land, the Maryland National Capital Park and Planning Commission, in cooperation with the Takoma Park, Maryland, mayor and city council, proposed in 1971 to rezone 42 acres of older residential and low-density commercial property to accommodate increased density development, a 500-car parking lot, and the widening of major residential streets for the anticipated heavy traffic.

The Save Takoma Park Committee was reactivated, and by 1974 the planning board had rescinded its recommendations. Residential zoning and low-density commercial zoning were reconfirmed; the parking lot was restricted to 100 non-rush-hour spaces; and the side streets were left unwidened.

Another challenge to the neighborhood came in the 1970s in the form of the Montgomery College plan to rebuild and expand its campus in a residential section on the Maryland side. A blunt letter from the college board of directors informed 21 residents that the college intended to buy and raze their homes in order to provide more parking and to construct new school buildings. The North Takoma Citizens' Association began an eight-year fight and was joined by a new neighborhood organization called CURE (Citizens United for Responsible Expansion). Before the dust settled, some homes had been razed and a few college buildings were constructed on Block 69.

Finally, after years of protest, the federal government recognized the historic value of B.F. Gilbert's earliest subdivisions. They were placed on the National Register of Historic Places in 1976, and Montgomery College backed down. The District side also sought to preserve its historic character and succeeded in placing its section on the National Register of Historic Places in 1983, this time acknowledging historical connections to its Maryland counterpart by once again calling itself Takoma Park, D.C.

These community protection campaigns saved Takoma Park from irreparable damage to its physical design and residential housing stock, the essential artifacts of the community envisioned by B.F. Gilbert. They also spurred continuing efforts to preserve and improve the community. Neighborhood energies are now channeled toward converting multiunit residences into single-family dwellings, revitalizing the business district, maintaining and improving the community schools, and encouraging citizen participation.

The faces of children at the Takoma Park Elementary School in Takoma Park, Maryland, reflect the multi-ethnic character of today's Takoma Park. Courtesy, Montgomery County Public Schools

The arrival of Metro and the efforts of Takoma Park's diverse citizenry brought Takoma Park full circle in time to celebrate its 100th anniversary in 1983. Once again Takoma Park "pioneers" are actively involved in shaping their own community, and once again commuters glimpse the affordable elegance of this old railroad suburb from Metro trains arriving at Takoma station.

NEWTON

15

BROOKLAND

SOMETHING IN THE AIR

John N. Pearce

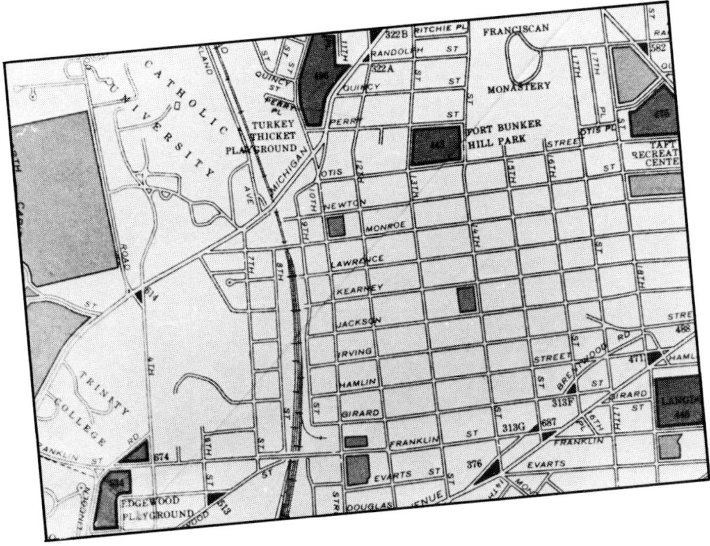

The Art Moderne Newton Theater, designed by noted theater architect John J. Zink of Baltimore, opened on 12th Street, N.E., to great fanfare in 1938. Photo by Howard Berger. Courtesy, Center for Washington Area Studies, the George Washington University

Map: Park System of the National Capitol and Environs. National Park Service 1962. Courtesy, D.C. Public Library Washingtoniana Division

Perhaps the air *was* different. At Brookland's heart, known as the old Brooks farm, Jehiel and Anne Brooks built in 1840 the handsome mansion they called Bellair—"beautiful air." Nearly 150 years later John Facchina would recall the reason his father, an immigrant Italian mosaicist, gave for settling there in the early 1900s: "It was for better air." And in 1938, as Thea Reachmack recently recounted, her doctor advised the Reachmacks to move from Dupont Circle "to the country" so that her asthmatic son would have better air to breathe—and Brookland's air was known as "pure and clean, healthy."

The mansion, almost as patriarchal as Brooks in his old photographs, is the first Brookland image seen from nearly every approach. Some of the Brooks descendants still live in Brookland and nearby, and one of Brookland's buildings, a once-decaying, turn-of-the-century pickle works, has been revitalized as Colonel Brooks' Tavern, where a photograph of Brooks welcomes visitors.

Although the name of Jehiel's wife, Anne Queen Brooks, is not marked on any present place, she is the connection to the eighteenth- and early nineteenth-century families who farmed this acreage. Anne received from her father, Nicholas Queen, the 150 acres, part of 1,500 colonial-Maryland acres Nicholas' ancestor, Richard Marsham, had owned. Nicholas Queen was proprietor of the Queen's Hotel, a Washington hostelry, where many congressmen and other notables stayed, and Jehiel and Anne Queen Brooks were to have many Washington connections. It is not surprising that the Brookses chose the Greek Revival style for the house of brick and granite they built in 1840 near the northwest corner of Bellair; it echoed the Greek Revival character of Arlington House, the White House porticoes, and the Treasury in the grand style of

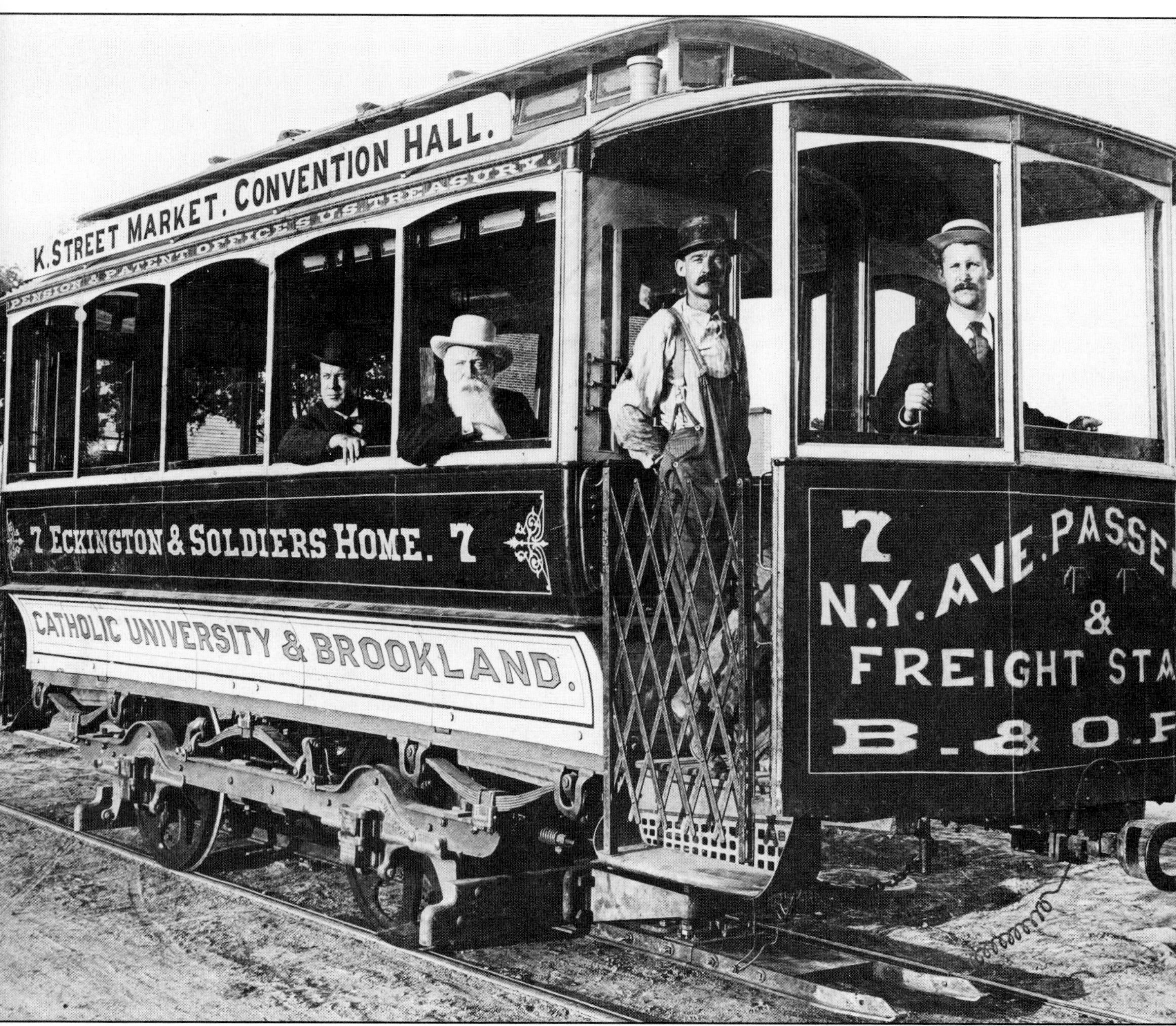

In 1889 the Eckington and Soldiers Home Railway began to run electric streetcars between Mt. Vernon Square in central Washington to Catholic University, boosting interest in the new Brookland development carved from the Brooks' farm just two years earlier. Courtesy, Library of Congress, Prints and Photographs Division

the federal city to the south.

Not long after the Brooks Mansion was built, the needs of the growing city brought new public facilities to the very borders of the farm. First, in the 1850s, the racially integrated Columbia-Harmony cemetery was moved from the city to a large tract south of the Brooks farm boundary, old Brentwood Road, near the present line of Rhode Island Avenue.

Then, in 1873, the Baltimore and Ohio Railroad built its western branch along the western edge of the farm, with a stop at the Brooks Station below the mansion where farmers loaded their vegetables for shipment to the city's markets. The stop also served a few Brookland commuters.

In 1885 Catholic University of America, a suburban campus of national importance, was established just beyond Brookland's western edge northwest of Brooks Station. In the hundred years in which the university and Brookland have existed side by side, the two have been intertwined both physically and culturally, as sug-

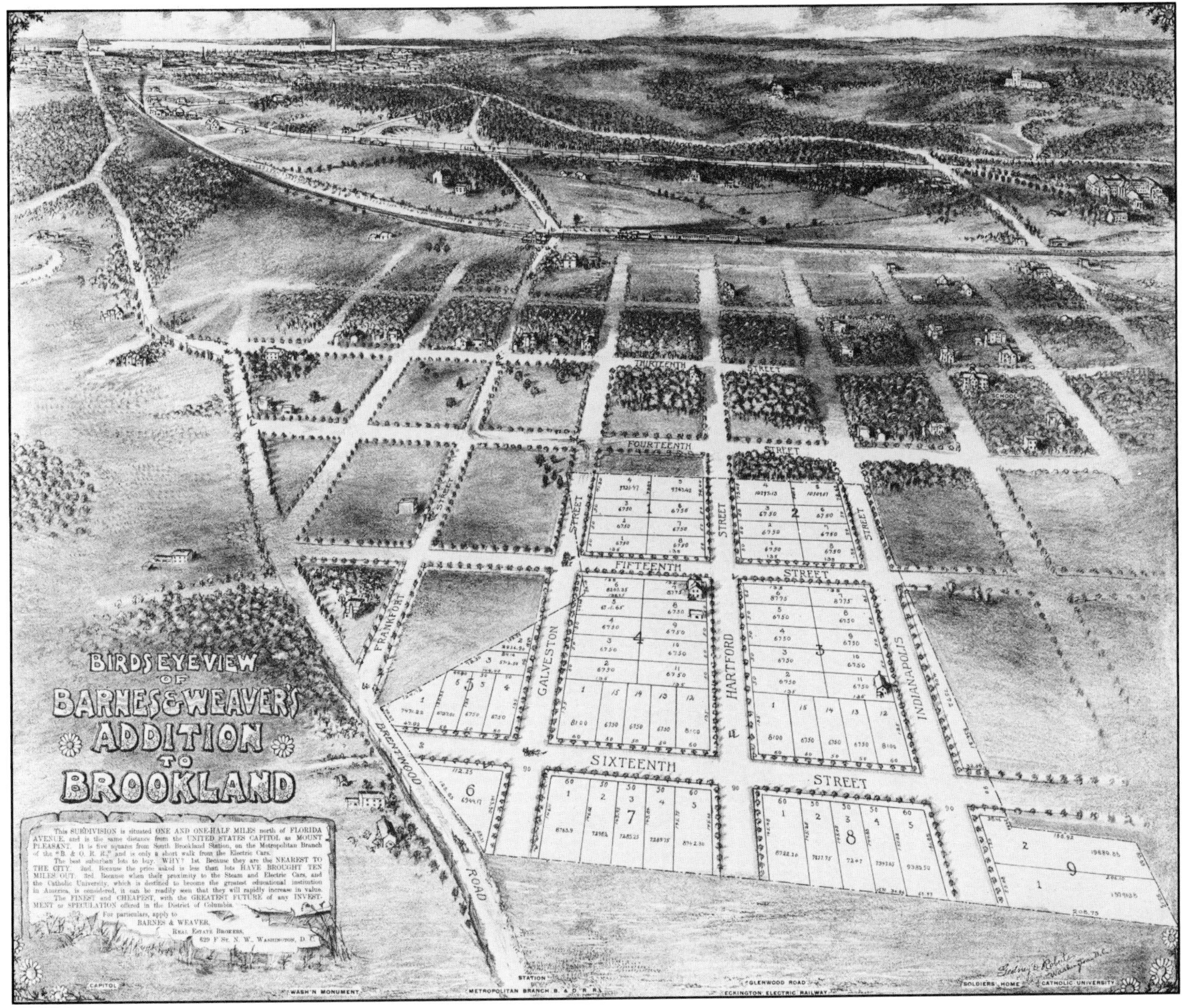

The developers of this addition to Brookland emphasized its combined virtues of a semirural location and easy access to the city, upper left, by train. Courtesy, Library of Congress, Map Division

gested in the name of the current Metro stop, "Brookland-CUA."

The arrival of cemetery, train, and university set the stage for eventual subdivision of the Brooks farm. After Colonel Brooks' death, in 1886, his heirs sold the property, and in 1887 the new owners recorded a plat of subdivision of 140 acres into narrow, deep lots—then the standard of suburban development. This was apparently the first recorded use of the name "Brookland." In 1889 the first streetcar line of the Eckington & Soldiers' Home Railway opened, linking Mount Vernon Square to Catholic University and vastly increasing interest in the development of the area. When the streetcars finally came into Brookland proper, longtime resident Helen Brosnan recalled, her mother was so delighted at this new convenience that she called the trolley bells "the sweetest sound I've ever heard."

Shortly after the original subdivision Brookland was proving both attractive and successful, as reflected in the additional subdivisions recorded with the Surveyor's Office of the District of Columbia. These additions extended the suburb east from the Brooks Farm to the line of 18th Street. All of these subdivisions, though bearing names of their own, were perceived then and now as one place called "Brookland."

Brookland's population reached about 700 by 1891. A map of 1894 shows that on most of the blocks at least one house had been built. By then the community had a post office, the stylish, brick Romanesque Brookland School (1891), and a Baptist church, and more than 50 oil lamps had been installed on the streets of the first subdivision. In 1892 the real estate firm of McLachlen & Batchelder ("Telephone 432") summed up Brookland's virtues:

Brookland . . . has an elevation of two hundred feet above THE POTOMAC RIVER AT HIGH TIDE. The Metropolitan Branch of the B. & O. R. R. and the Eckington and Soldiers' Home Road furnish rapid transit to the business part of the city. A charter has been granted the Suburban Street Railway Company to build an electric road from the Centre Market to Brookland . . . The District have built a Brick Schoolhouse erected Street Lights, and, LAID PLANK SIDEWALKS on a part of the streets . . .

In 1896 the Brookland School doubled in size. In 1903 it was enlarged again, this time in the newly stylish Georgian Revival mode. Also by 1903 Brookland boasted a firehouse and Catholic church. Many of the streets along the 12th Street corridor had been paved with gravel, and most of Newton Street and parts of 12th, Irving, and Evarts streets had macadam sur-

Residents of early Brookland built modest frame houses that took advantage of precut materials in creating simplified versions of many architectural styles, such as this Queen Anne cottage at 3425 14th Street, N.E. Photo by George McDaniel. Courtesy, Center for Washington Area Studies, The George Washington University

faces. In 1904 the street names and numbers were changed to conform to the pattern of the rest of the city.

By the 1880s the building regulations for Washington City, inside present-day Florida Avenue, no longer permitted the construction of wooden dwellings, but that was not the case outside the boundary in old Washington County. The middle-class suburbanites and speculators of Brookland built mostly wooden simplified versions in the Victorian, Queen Anne, Colonial Revival, and Craftsman styles. The ready availability of precut wood framing and cladding, and of machine-made nails of every type, made it possible to build almost any shape or decoration. There were a few high-style, architect-designed houses and some highly individual ones, such as builder John Louthan's Round House and suffragette/botanist Carrie Harrison's "Spanish Villa" of 1909, built of concrete piers infilled with terra cotta blocks.

A number of employees of the Smithsonian Institution and the Government Printing Office gave a scientific, intellectual, and engineering cast to parts of the community. The great Smithsonian ornithologist, Robert Ridgeway, built Rose Terrace at 3413 13th Street, and botanist Theodore Holm built a house for himself and another for Joseph Krause at 1432 and 1440 Newton Street. Several immigrant artisans and mechanics were among Brookland's early residents, including the Italian mosaicist Charles Facchina. Facchina's proudest achievement was the great mosaic panel of Minerva (after the drawing by Elihu Vedder) visible at the top of the stairway to the visitors gallery of the Library of Congress' main reading room. Facchina, recognizing that the edges of Brookland near Michigan Avenue would develop more densely, built the first apartment building in Brookland, the Brookland Courts Apartments, in 1924.

Brookland's eclectic architecture includes at least three houses ordered from mail-order catalogs, including this model, "the Rodessa," advertised for $998 in the Sears Roebuck catalog in 1920 and still standing at 1518 Hamlin Street, N.E. Courtesy, The George Washington University, Center for Washington Area Studies

A permanent home to many imaginative people, Brookland also nurtured bright and creative children, including novelist Marjorie Kinnan Rawlings, who grew up at 1221 Newton Street. Brookland provided temporary quarters for creative people on the rise as well, such as Pearl Bailey, who lived briefly at 1428 Irving Street in the 1930s. Yet notwithstanding these notable residents, Brookland has always been a middle-class community offering everyday families a secure, neighborly home. This was remembered with pride and humor by one of Brookland's early developers, James L. Sherwood. "For a time we thought we were going to have a nabob neighborhood. We had about eight families of social prominence. But they discovered their mistake about 1910 and moved elsewhere."

Although early Brookland was mostly white—and mostly segregated in work, play, and society—it always had black residents. Among the most prominent was Robert Weaver, the first black Cabinet member as secretary of Housing and Urban Development under President John F. Kennedy. Racial differences affected daily life, but outright conflict was rare.

From the 1920s through the 1940s the neighborhood's density increased, marked by brick rowhouses with Colonial Revival details, precut, mail-order houses of a mainly Craftsman architectural character, and the simplified, streamlined architecture of the brick commercial strip along 12th Street.

In 1927 Brooklanders paraded in the street to celebrate the paving of 12th Street from Rhode Island Avenue to Monroe Street. In 1931, 12th Street was paved as far as Otis Street, although its village-like character was maintained throughout the decade with vendors' carts hawking everything from ice to produce to rabbits.

The stores on 12th Street were built from the late teens to the early 1930s by a few developers who lived in the community. Among them were James L. Sherwood, manager of the Brookland branch of the Hamilton National Bank; his son, Jesse R. Sherwood; Dr. R.R. Hottel, a local physician; and George C. Heider, who owned and operated the grocery store at 3507 12th Street.

Stores along 12th Street reflected the vital mixture of both continuity and change in Brookland. For example, 3515 12th Street began as a bakery owned by John H. Haske in 1921; in 1939 it was purchased by Robert J. Baldwin, baker; and today it is still in operation as Baldwin's Bake Shop. In 1923, 3506 12th Street was Gaetano Valenti's barbershop; today it still houses a barbershop and retains the original mosaic tiles and cabinets that Valenti imported from Italy. Perhaps more typical of the variety of uses over time is the store at 3502 12th Street: 1922, tailor; 1923, dry goods; 1928, notions; 1935, Brookland Pharmacy; 1942, men's furnishings; 1962, men's clothing; 1970, University Record and Appliance; 1973, Psychedelic Haven; and 1979, World of Music.

The business people along 12th Street reflected the ethnic diversity of Brookland. Their names in the city directories over the years suggest their diverse origins: George C. Heider, grocer, 3507 12th Street; Salvatore Chisari, shoe repair, 3508; Paul F. Moore, hardware, 3509; Hong Lee, laundry, 3512; John Kotsanas, restaurant, 3513; Frederick Klotz, billiards, 3533; Marion F. Cord, beauty shop, 3523; James J. Hannon and Michael J. McGettigan, hardware, 3524.

The strong Catholic presence in the neighborhood enhanced its ethnic diversity; many Brooklanders of that faith were of Irish or Italian extraction. Catholic University had begun to influence the neighborhood as early as 1889, when the Brooks Mansion was converted to a Catholic school later operated by St. Anthony's Church. The foreign-born Smithsonian naturalists and the Europeans among those associated with Catholic University also contributed to the old-world atmosphere.

In addition, many Brookland houses were rented or bought by international Catholic orders. In the years between the world wars more than 50 religious orders were represented, and their members, walking from home to church or university in their habits, helped Brookland earn its nickname: "Little Rome." The building of the Franciscan Monastery on the northern edge of Brookland and the towering Shrine of the Immaculate Conception just across the railroad tracks gave further Catholic architectural presence to the area. The 1979 visit of Pope John Paul II to the university is remembered fondly by the people of St. Anthony's as "the Pope in our Parish."

In the 1920s and 1930s Brookland retained much of its small-town character. Its streets were lively with children and adult neighbors passing the time of day. The value of friendly relations among residents influenced the design and use of houses. Helen Krause Caruso recalled the house she and her husband built in the 1930s:

[When I was a girl in Brookland] we used to live out on the front porch. And when my husband built this house [1437 Otis Street], I told him there were three things I wanted and one of them was a front porch. So he had one built, and I still sit out there. Not too many people do that today but a few do. I love it. I knit and read.

For children the highlight of the winter season came after heavy snowfalls. Local police closed Newton Street between 15th and 18th streets and built bonfires at each end of the hill. "The sledding was great on Newton Street," former resident Harry Tansill recalled. "It was a mysterious phenomenon how the snow and ice lingered there long after it had melted away on other streets. Quite a break for me and my Flexi Flyer!" Ice skaters flocked to the pond near the Slowe School.

Teenage boys and girls met at chaperoned dances at St. Anthony's and the Masonic Hall and attended parties at one another's homes. There, young people cranked up the Victrola, and, recalled Leo Stock and his sister, Betty Stock Hardy (great-grandchildren of Jehiel and Anne Queen Brooks), they listened to popular hits

The Franciscan Monastery on the northern edge of Brookland at 14th and Quincy streets, N.E., is one of many local institutions, including Catholic University and the Shrine of the Immaculate Conception, that have contributed to the area's strong Catholic character. Courtesy, Columbia Historical Society

such as "The Sheik," and danced the Turkey Trot or the Paul Jones. Dates were treated to the movies or maybe an afternoon soda at the fountain in Baldwin's Bakery or Peoples Drug Store.

Beginning in the 1920s silent movies were regularly shown at St. Anthony's Church. In the mid-1930s commercial movie houses opened: the Jessie Theater at 18th and Irving streets and later, in 1938, the Newton Theater on the site of the old Brookland Baptist Church. The Newton's design by a noted theater architect and its formal opening ceremony underscored the important status given to movie theaters in this era. In attendance were not only the owner, Louis Bernheimer, but also civic leaders such as Marvin M. McLean, president of the Brookland Citizens' Association, and politicians, including Melvin J. Hazen, district commissioner.

Family and friends were often also neighbors in Brookland. Helen Krause Caruso grew up in the neighborhood and returned after starting her married life in Southwest Washington. When she came back with her own family in 1938, she found herself sharing her Brookland block with the close friends and next-door neighbors of her childhood, the Theodore Holmses as well as with her father, her father-in-law, her uncle, and her husband's aunt. Such strong kinship networks

Michigan Avenue, N.E., was still unpaved and lined with modest buildings when this 1926 photograph was taken, looking west toward the railroad crossing. Courtesy, Columbia Historical Society

were typical of the neighborhood.

Although still village-like, Brookland was nonetheless part of the changing metropolitan scene. The influence of the automobile was reflected in the number of garages added to existing Brookland houses in the 1920s and 1930s. In-town houses with car accommodations could not compete, however, with the new automobile-oriented suburbs to which rising young professionals aspired. As a result, many of the earlier railroad and streetcar suburbs such as Brookland were bypassed by young home buyers.

After World War II Brookland was one of many older suburbs that witnessed the accelerated transition from a predominantly white population to a predominantly black one. Residents of Brookland have mixed remembrances of the effects of the racial integration that began in the southern portion and moved northward. Some white residents have said fuller integration was not an event that substantially changed their world. Although the community became more mixed racially, it was still their community, to which they were loyal. In Helen Brosnan's words, "We didn't intend to move. It was home. That was all."

Others recall strong resistance to integration by some white residents. Until they were declared unconstitutional, racially restrictive covenants allowed some property owners to exclude blacks. Sometimes block busting tactics were used: a white blockbuster would purchase a home and immediately re-sell it to a black family, causing other white families in the neighborhood to feel they must sell their houses. Poet and Howard University professor Sterling Brown was not a blockbuster, but he remembers that when he moved to

Brookland in 1935, "For Sale" signs in the neighborhood seemed to sprout overnight.

By 1945 the desire for a neighborhood Sunday school for children of the black community had led to the founding of the Brookland Union Baptist Church, the first black church in Brookland. After the desegregation of the public school system in 1954, the schools became predominantly black, reflecting both the number of young black families moving to the area and the exodus of many white families to the new Prince George's County, Maryland, suburbs. Many of the black families found Brookland appealing for the same reasons that attracted the original residents, white and black. Helen Brooke, mother of former Massachusetts senator Edward Brooke, recalled that her family chose Brookland because it was "a nice, quiet neighborhood, and my friends lived there. It was a pretty place to live, and we loved it very much."

In the 1960s and 1970s Brookland went through a period of struggle over the shape of its future and emerged stronger and more self-aware. Part of the struggle for racial integration in the 1940s and 1950s focused on the Brookland Citizens' Association's refusal to admit blacks and its resistance to open housing and recreation. By the 1960s the black residents had formed the Brookland Neighborhood Civic Association; in the 1970s and 1980s, theirs became the organization that integrated and has since outlived its rival, the all-white Citizens' Association. The neighborhood of the 1980s, although predominantly black, still attracts new residents of both races. As in similar communities, most business and neighborhood or civic functions are fully integrated, while socializing typically divides among self-segregated and integrated activities.

Also unifying the neighborhood in the 1950s and 1960s was the protracted struggle against the city's plan to sacrifice a block-wide swath of Brookland in order to build Interstate Highway 95 next to the railroad right-of-way. As in other neighborhoods the plan called for an "Inner Loop" freeway within the city and freeways connecting the loop to the interstate highway system. The highway threat spurred an outpouring of individual and collective civic energy, and the Brookland leaders, black and white, helped focus and lead the entire city on this issue. Consequently the interstate highway was blocked, and in the process citizens from all parts of the city found themselves unified for the good of their neighborhoods. In addition to the revitalization of the Brookland Neighborhood Civic Association, the highway battles led to the creation of the Upper Northeast Coordinating Council, an umbrella organization for regional civic concerns. And from these battles emerged individual leaders and families—for instance, the John Kelleys and the Bernard Pryors—who fought in other ways to sustain Brookland in the 1970s and beyond.

In what must be seen as a victory for Brookland activists, the "highway houses," which had been acquired for the highway right-of-way, were finally rehabilitated and returned to the market after years of neglect. But when plans were made for sites for Metrorail lines and stations, the Brooks Mansion itself was threatened. A decline in the school-age population led St. Anthony's Parish, the mansion owner, to sell the property to the Washington Metropolitan Area Transit Authority (WMATA) in 1970. The WMATA planned to demolish this historic structure, the central symbol of Brookland's identity, to provide more parking space at its Brookland-CUA Station. But once again citizens and local political leaders managed to secure the preservation and reuse of the Brooks Mansion as a University of the District of Columbia neighborhood education center.

The introduction of Advisory Neighborhood Commissions to city affairs in 1977 added another vehicle for integrated community leadership, as did the private Brookland Corporation, formed by black and white residents. This group has taken direct action—including putting its members' own money on the line—to preserve and upgrade the area.

As Brookland enters its second century, the virtues apparent to its builders a century ago are still attracting new life among the old. The community's commitment to its future is evident everywhere in the rehabilitation, preservation, and reuse of its historic buildings, the growing economic revitalization of the stores on 12th Street, the rise in maintenance and rehabilitation of properties, and the vitality of the neighborhood and its organizations.

Brookland's people in the 1980s include those who have moved homes or businesses there only in the past few years and those who have lived there for 80 years, with memories reaching back to the days of unpaved streets and rural vistas. In Brookland, as in other neighborhoods of Washington, much remains to be done in order to pass on, intact and enhanced, those places that connect neighbor to neighbor and the present to the many-layered past. But for Brooklanders, new and old, something beautiful still lingers in the air.

SHERIDAN

16

KALORAMA

TWO CENTURIES OF BEAUTIFUL VIEWS

Emily Hotaling Eig

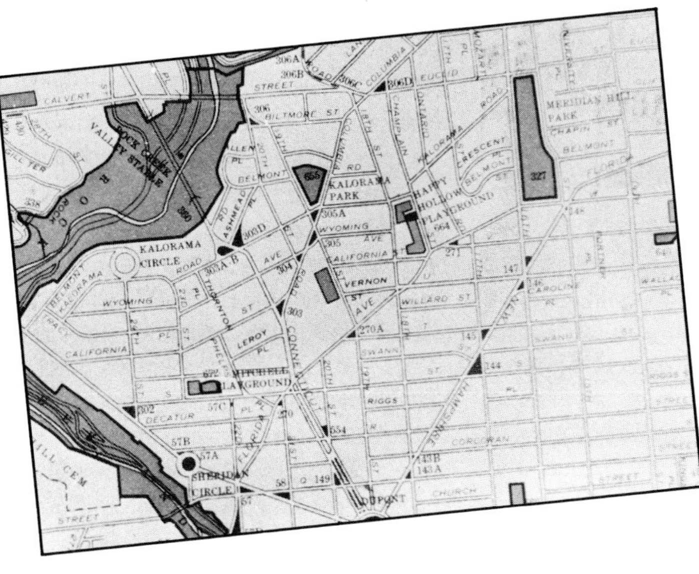

General Philip H. Sheridan, leader of the Union Cavalry during the Civil War and commander of the Army of the Shenandoah, presides over the circle that bears his name. The sculpture was designed by Gutzon Borglum, the sculptor of Mount Rushmore. Photo by Emily Medvec

Map: Park System of the National Capitol and Environs. National Park Service 1962. Courtesy, D.C. Public Library, Washingtoniana Division

Kalorama is an urban neighborhood that maintains a strong association with its rural beginning. Known well into the nineteenth century for its idyllic setting, it underwent urbanization in the early twentieth century as the growing population moved away from the old city's center in its quest for the suburban ideal. The curvilinear streets of this almost exclusively residential area, which straddles Connecticut Avenue just north of Florida Avenue, are filled with fine examples of the dwellings of this period. To the east, in Kalorama Triangle, undulating rows of attached three- and four-story houses are sited along treelined streets punctuated by triangular pockets of green space. To the west, known as Sheridan-Kalorama, elegant freestanding houses stand guard over this in-town enclave. Through the center runs the broad route of Connecticut Avenue, where stately apartment buildings hold court for the busy travelers passing to the north or south. The effect is that of an architectural quilt, a cohesive design harmoniously patched, carefully bordered, and skillfully stitched together.

The Kalorama area is historically associated with the large estate named Kalorama. Its beautiful natural setting and the elegant rural life-style of its owners earned Kalorama a romantic reputation. Documentation for the land reaches back to the time of Charles II of England and his 600-acre land grant to John Langworth. In the latter part of the eighteenth century, Anthony Holmead took possession of the part of Langworth's estate contiguous with Rock Creek. Holmead called his land Widow's Mite and in 1750 passed it on to his young English nephew. The younger Anthony Holmead built a three-story, brick house known as Rock Hill at the present-day intersection of 23rd and S streets. In 1795 the younger Holmead divested himself

Sheridan Circle was a fashionable choice of residence for Washington's social, industrial, and political elite, including the widow of General Philip Sheridan, who built a townhouse nearby on Massachusetts Avenue to be close to her husband's statue, erected circa 1910. Courtesy, D.C. Public Library, Washingtoniana Division

of excessive landholdings, selling his house and 30 prime acres to Gustavus Scott, a Maryland native. This acreage would become the heart of modern-day Kalorama.

Scott, who served as a commissioner for the District of Columbia in 1794, constructed a new, more grandly scaled house called Belair on the site of Holmead's Rock Hill. Feeling the financial pressure of his expensive investment, he sold off the gristmill and paper mill at the western edge of his property along Rock Creek. Despite his action Scott's financial situation worsened, leading to rumors of an impending sale of the estate. President Thomas Jefferson, in one of his many efforts to encourage persons of note to settle in the new capital city, attempted to lure Joel Barlow, an internationally recognized pamphleteer and poet, to Washington with the idea of living at Belair. However, Barlow and his wife, Ruth Baldwin, were not yet inclined to leave their Parisian home. When Scott died, in 1803, his destitute widow sold the property for $16,000 to William Augustine Washington, nephew of the president.

Within five years, however, the estate was again on the market. This time Joel Barlow responded to the offer, and in 1807, the same year he published his widely acclaimed epic poem, *The Columbiad,* he returned to the United States and settled in the District of Columbia. He and his wife counted presidents, congressmen, leading scientists, and military figures among their friends and acquaintances; they soon established their home as a political, literary, and social center. Barlow renamed the estate Kalorama after the Greek word "fine view," because of its location on a high hill overlooking the Potomac River.

Barlow spent only three years at his grand estate. He left in 1811, sent to negotiate a commercial treaty with the French Empire, and died the following year while en route to Poland to an official meeting with Napoleon I. His widow returned to Kalorama, continuing to live there with her sister and brother-in-law, Clara and George Bomford, until her own death, in 1818. The estate was passed on to a number of other owners, but the name Kalorama prevailed, even when the estate and adjacent acreage were subdivided in the 1880s by new and old owners alike for small urban lots.

The late nineteenth century found Washington City bursting its boundaries. Washington County, politically joined with the city in 1871, was undergoing subdivision throughout the outer regions of the District of Columbia. The pressures of a burgeoning population and the promise of new utility and transportation systems found landowners and new developers eagerly anticipating vast profits. Real estate agents were particularly interested in the Kalorama area because of its fine location on the heights just north of the old Washington City boundary. By 1887 it was platted into a number of subdivisions: Belair Heights to the far west, Kalorama as the center strip, Truesdell's Addition to Washington Heights to the northeast, Tuttle's Subdivision just east of the Kalorama estate, and Presbury & Goddard's Subdivision to its west.

An article in the June 17, 1882, issue of the *National Republic* addressed the issue of "Suburban Residences":

The city has extended so far to the north and west that the heights of the Holmead estate are now becoming the most attractive portion of the city for residences. The summer temperature is at least five degrees lower than in the city, and refreshing breezes sweep over from the valley of Rock Creek. There is no city in the land that has been so lavishly supplied by nature with locations for rural homes. Within a few months some of our leading citizens have taken steps to utilize and beautify these elevations overlooking the city. The lands on the Washington Heights, a part of the old Holmead estate, have been platted, streets have been opened, trees set, and building lots put into market . . . These lots lying close and overlooking the city . . . are the choicest investment offered to the public.

Kalorama may have appeared ripe for development, but the anticipated construction did not immediately materialize. The reluctance of some of Kalorama's owners to sell, the panic of 1893, the uncertainty created by the local Highway Act of 1893—all were factors in the delay.

In response to the rampant and uncoordinated subdivision of land in what had been Washington County, the U.S. Congress in 1893 ordered the preparation of a street plan that would extend L'Enfant's design of old Washington City into the rest of the District. Confusion surrounded the Highway Act of 1893 because it was not clear whether older suburbs already laid out would have to comply by redesigning existing roads, and because the city government was slow to produce the required maps. Land transfers and construction were virtually halted for fear of the condemnation of expensive property for street rights-of-way.

The only surviving photograph of the Kalorama Mansion, built by Gustavus Scott in about 1795, was taken after its use as a Civil War smallpox hospital. It had been heavily damaged by fire in May 1865. Courtesy, Library of Congress, Prints and Photographs Division

An amended act passed in 1898 produced a map that exempted subdivisions prior to 1893, relieving developers' uncertainties. Coupled with major improvements in public services and transportation, this act was a catalyst for the surge of building activity around the city after 1898. It also explains particularly well the development of Kalorama.

As Kalorama stood on the brink of urbanization, its landscape remained undeniably rural. The estate house at Kalorama stood on its ridge overlooking the city, as did a few large wood-frame houses, such as George Truesdell's Managassett, in the present-day nook of 20th Street and Columbia Road. The first house to be constructed after Kalorama was subdivided was a small house on Connecticut Avenue Extended (a meandering lane connecting the prominent avenue with the District's far-northwest area). Built in 1893 on Truesdell's Addition to Washington Heights, this freestanding, single-family house responded not to an intended urban setting but rather to its extant rural setting. The house is an early and important representation of the influence of the English Arts and Crafts movement on residential architecture in the United States. It was designed by its owner, Thomas Fuller, a young architect, and served as his home until his death. This portion of Connecticut Avenue Extended was later named Ashmead Place, in honor of Mrs. Fuller's family. Fuller was responsible for the design of a number of large Sheridan-Kalorama residences, but this was his first and most significant contribution. It remains today as a tangible reminder of the area's earlier times.

Although expanding population was the major force behind the urbanization of Kalorama, turn-of-the-century transportation systems shaped its physical growth. Two avenues played particularly important roles in the way the area developed. The first was Massachusetts Avenue. In 1886 the District commissioners held public hearings on plans to extend Massachusetts Avenue north of Boundary Street (now Florida Avenue) and to construct along its route a circle to be named in honor of naval hero Stephen Decatur. In *Washington on Foot,* Perry Fisher recounts the story of the protests made by Emmaline Lovett, the last private owner of the Kalorama estate, about the effect these public improvements would have on her property. Indeed, her fears were realized. In 1887 the last 60 acres of the Kalorama estate were sold for subdivision at a price of $354,000—$5,900 an acre—and Massachusetts Avenue was extended through the property.

An iron bridge was constructed to carry Massachusetts Avenue over the gully at Rock Creek. A more substantial stone bridge was put up in 1901; the current bridge dates from the 1940s. The circle originally intended for Decatur was reassigned in 1890 to General Philip Sheridan, who had died in 1888. By 1909 the circle and equestrian statue—designed by Gutzon Borglum, sculptor of Mount Rushmore—were in place. The statue has received more than its fair share of criticism, but, according to Fisher, "Mrs. Sheridan, of course, loved it instantly." It is believed that she had Waddy Wood design a town house for her at 2211 Massachusetts Avenue, simply to be close to the statue. Others may not have shared her reason, but they did share her choice of Massachusetts Avenue. Even before the street was completed, it became the fashionable choice of many of the American industrial, social, and political elite who had begun to view the nation's capital as an attractive seasonal residence. Soon it was lined with grand Beaux Arts-style houses that still make the street the finest avenue in the city.

The other critical event for the future growth of the area was the extension of Connecticut Avenue directly over Rock Creek. Initially, Kalorama was linked to the upper northwest quadrant by way of Calvert Street, then known as Cincinnati Street. The first bridge to connect this street on opposite sides of Rock Creek was a steel trestle built in 1891 for the Rock Creek Railroad Company. Public streetcar service began the following year. The first line ran north on 18th Street, then west on Calvert Street, across the bridge, and north on Connecticut Avenue to Chevy Chase Lake. In 1895 the Rock Creek Railroad Company merged with the Capitol Traction Company. Another streetcar line began to serve the area in 1897, running north on Columbia Road as far as 18th Street.

However, no bridge directly connected both sides of Connecticut Avenue. Throughout the nineteenth century, lower Connecticut Avenue held a major place in the traffic pattern of the city, but as it reached the northern boundaries, its importance dwindled. Above Boundary Street within Kalorama, it became a winding road that terminated abruptly at Woodley Lane (now Belmont Road), south of Rock Creek. To complete this route required the building of a new bridge that could support modern vehicles. A competition for the present Taft Bridge was won by George S. Morrison, a renowned railroad-bridge designer. Construction began in 1897, and by 1907 Washington possessed the first and largest unreinforced concrete bridge in the world.

The improvement of highways

Renowned railroad bridge architect George S. Morrison designed the massive concrete arches of the Taft Bridge, constructed in 1907 to carry Connecticut Avenue across Rock Creek. When built, it was the largest unreinforced concrete bridge in the world. Courtesy, Library of Congress, Prints and Photographs Division

The Mendota, built in 1901 at 2220 20th Street, N.W., was the first apartment building in Kalorama. Courtesy, Traceries, Inc.

and public transportation helped support the subdivision of the land for new housing development; however, the new and improved Connecticut Avenue physically bisected an area previously viewed as a single expanse. Private property was confiscated to make way for the new route, halting or demonstrably altering subdivision plans. Two neighborhoods, Kalorama Triangle to the east and Sheridan-Kalorama to the west, each distinctive in its social and physical composition, would evolve. Kalorama Triangle became a working middle-class neighborhood with well-designed, spacious, speculative housing located conveniently near the streetcars. Sheridan-Kalorama would develop with large lots and a wealth of individually commissioned, freestanding houses that provided homes for some of Washington's most prestigious citizens.

The earliest years of Kalorama Triangle's development followed the specific expansion of the streetcar lines. In 1892, when streetcar service was limited to one line running north on 18th Street and west on Calvert, Kalorama Triangle was undeveloped. It was in 1897, when a second streetcar line began to serve the area, running north on Columbia Road and connecting with the first line at 18th Street, that construction began. By 1903 the area was completely subdivided and many buildings had been constructed.

The first type of urban building in this neighborhood was the semidetached dwelling constructed along the 2000 block of Kalorama Road. Designed by a prolific but uncelebrated architect, Edward Woltz, it consisted of two units attached by a central party wall, small enough to permit front, rear, and side yards. Developer Harry Wardman later popularized this type of construction throughout Washington. The following year several prominent architects were commissioned to design large private residences on or near the Columbia Road corridor. These residences included freestanding town houses, such as the Lothrop Mansion at Columbia Road and Connecticut Avenue, and double houses, sometimes repeated in rows. Development continued in 1899 and 1900 when the most common urban type, the rowhouse, was introduced to 19th Street, Calvert Street, Columbia Road, Kalorama Road, and Mintwood Place. From 1900 on, almost without exception, construction on the east side of Connecticut Avenue produced specifically urban architectural forms. The architectural styles popular in Kalorama Triangle include the English Arts and Crafts, Georgian Revival, and Mediterranean (both Italian and Spanish derivatives) and beautifully illustrate the diffusion of high-style architecture to the middle class.

The lions guarding the entrance to the Taft Bridge, which takes Connecticut Avenue north from Kalorama across Rock Creek, survey a placid street in the 1920s. Courtesy, Columbia Historical Society

By 1901 Kalorama's first apartment building, the Mendota, was constructed at 2220 20th Street in the Triangle. Grandly executed by James Owen Hill, and epitomizing the latest in middle-class living, the building offered a fashionable and practical alternative to the problems of acquiring and maintaining a single-family dwelling. Apartment living suited Washington, as so many of its residents were part-timers seeking short-term living quarters. The Mendota was the first of nearly 50 apartment buildings to be constructed throughout Kalorama over the next 25 years.

By 1930 Kalorama Triangle was built up almost entirely with a myriad of rowhouses, town houses, apartment buildings of large and small scale, and only a few freestanding dwellings. Having been built rapidly in the same period, this assemblage of buildings is cohesive in scale, size, material, and use. The developers had accurately assessed their market and built buildings of good design and fine craftsmanship that attracted an upwardly mobile middle class. Though dependent on public transportation to jobs in the city, the new residents were attracted to a neighborhood that matched their high aspirations. The people who chose Kalorama Triangle were primarily government clerks for the many federal and District agencies, salesmen, lawyers, real estate agents, artists, physicians, butlers, waiters, and teachers. There were also a few higher officials including Harry M. Clabaugh, chief justice of the D.C. supreme court, Edward Stellwagen, president of Union Trust Company, and Senator Thomas P. Gore of Oklahoma.

The first development west of Connecticut Avenue in Sheridan-Kalorama was influenced by the nearby urban areas: rowhouses appeared in small clusters near Dupont Circle and along Connecticut Avenue, again because of convenient access to transportation. Large apartment buildings were introduced to the west of Connecticut Avenue along California Street. Such fine edifices as the Westmoreland, designed by E.S. Kennedy and Harry Blake in 1905; Florence Courts, the work of T. Franklin Schneider in 1905; and Albert Beers' Brighton and Lonsdale of 1909 contributed to the high quality of residential living possible in Sheridan-Kalorama. The stars of the neighborhood, though, were the large, single-family residences that continue to be built until the present day. Sheridan-Kalorama's stylistic preferences continue to focus on the revival styles: Georgian, Mediterranean, and Italian Renaissance. The dates of each style's early twentieth-century appearance in the neighborhood were remarkably timely, illustrating the rapid assimilation of nationally recognized trends in fashionable architecture.

The people attracted to Sheridan-Kalorama included some of Washington's most interesting and influential citizens. Such luminaries as Conrad Miller, noted lecturer and publisher; Charles Walcott, secretary of the Smithsonian Institution; Perle Mesta, the "Hostess with the Mostest"; and Frances Perkins, first female secretary of labor sought out this neighborhood. Among the first residents were the developers who had orchestrated the subdivision of the Kalorama estate. Thomas Gales, son-in-law of Thomas Fisher, was an executive in the Thos. J. Fisher Real Estate Co., and with his brother-in-law, Edward Stellwagen, turned the small business into a major financial force in the expanding city.

Gales built a large Colonial Revival house to the design of Appleton P. Clark at 2300 S Street. Later this house gained fame as the residence of Herbert Hoover during his appointment as secretary of commerce under Harding and Coolidge, and for a short time after his term of office. In fact, Sheridan-Kalorama has been the home of five presidents: Hoover (2300 S Street), 1921-1928 and 1933-1934; Franklin D. Roosevelt (2131 R Street), while he was assistant secretary of the Navy, 1917-1921; Warren G. Harding (2314 Wyoming Avenue), during his term as U.S. senator from Ohio until becoming president, 1917-1921; William Howard Taft (2215 Wyoming Avenue), from his return to Washington as chief justice of the Supreme Court until his death, 1921-1930; and most significantly, Woodrow Wilson (2340 S Street), upon leaving the presidency until his death, 1921-1924.

Wilson has been the only president to choose Washington for his permanent residence. A fine Georgian Revival house, designed by Waddy Wood in 1915 for Boston businessman Henry Fairbanks, it was purchased by the Wilsons with the help of "some good friends" who wished to ensure the former president's well-being. Hundreds of supporters waited along the edge of S Street to welcome him to his new home. Wilson was in deteriorating health and died in 1924. Edith Bolling Wilson, the president's second wife, drew public attention for her role as the "first woman president" during Wilson's first stroke while in office. Edith Wilson resided in the house until her death, in 1961. Two years later the house was opened by the National Trust for Historic Preservation as a historic house museum.

Among the most special of the Sheridan-Kalorama houses is its oldest—the Lindens. This fine 1754 Georgian house at 2401 Kalorama Road, however, was not constructed in Washington at all. The Lindens was moved here by its owner, George Maurice Morris, from Danvers, Massachusetts, in 1936 because, explained his wife, she was unable to find a house in Washington that was quite historic enough to meet her requirements.

Throughout the twentieth century the neighborhood has attracted many embassies. One of its finest houses, at 2221 Kalorama Road, was purchased by the French government in 1936 to house the ambassador. Jules Henri de Sibour designed this Tudor Revival mansion in 1911 for the mining magnate W.W. Lawrence. Massachusetts Avenue is now known as Embassy Row as, one by one, the various Beaux Arts mansions decorating its boulevard have become hosts to embassy chanceries and residences.

Kalorama Triangle and Sheridan-Kalorama are known in the 1980s as fine in-town, residential neighborhoods, each with its distinct character. While they attracted different residential groups, both are particularly important illustrations of the fashionable aesthetics of the early twentieth century. Sheridan-Kalorama is a showcase of some of the city's finest privately commissioned single-family residential architecture; Kalorama Triangle provides testimony to the value of good design in middle-class speculative housing. Together, the neighborhoods provide a representative sampling of Washington's middle- and upper-class twentieth-century ideals.

Both neighborhoods have grown in harmony with the wooded and hilly topography. Their cohesive design—in architecture and landscape—illustrates a continuing respect for the pastoral character that prompted Joel Barlow to christen the land "Kalorama."

The portrait of President Woodrow Wilson commands the library of the Sheridan-Kalorama house to which he retired in 1920, now a house museum maintained for the public by the National Trust for Historic Preservation. Five presidents have had homes in the neighborhood. Courtesy, Woodrow Wilson House

17
CHEVY CHASE
A BOLD IDEA, A COMPREHENSIVE PLAN

Judith Helm Robinson

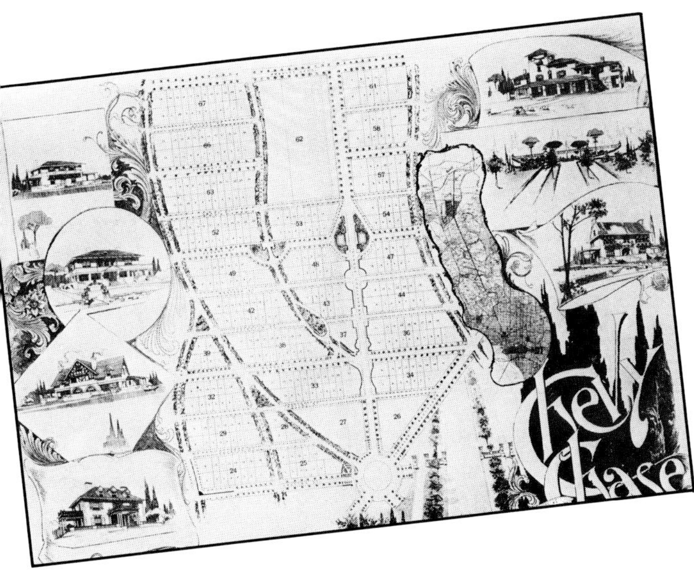

Senator Francis Newlands of Nevada was the driving force behind the development of Chevy Chase. His vision and his great wealth allowed him to plan on a grand scale. Courtesy, Library of Congress, Prints and Photographs Division

Thos. J. Fisher & Co., agents for Chevy Chase, featured some of its fine houses and landscaped streets and parks in this 1890s map. Courtesy, Library of Congress, Map Division

From the beginning, the development of Chevy Chase was a bold scheme. It required the initial purchase of more than 1,700 acres of farmland; the formation of the Chevy Chase Land Company with a capital stock of one million dollars; the construction of Connecticut Avenue's broad reach of more than five miles above Calvert Street; the creation of an electric railway line; and the establishment of clubs, churches, and schools to fill the new residents' needs. And it was intent on the highest-quality standards.

These grand plans of the 1890s took decades to realize, but they were the foundation of the quiet, picturesque community of Chevy Chase that even today bears the indelible stamp of its founders' ideals. Above all it is the "home suburb," the neighborhood of homes they envisioned. Broad verandas, patterned shingles and half-timbering, sleeping porches, decorative cornices, pergolas, and a variety of rooflines define a wide range of residential architectural styles. The urban profile its founders sought to prevent—crowded alleys, rowhouses, industrial and commercial intrusions—is still absent. Quality of life today is defined by stately trees, broad streets, green lawns, comfortable houses, porch swings, and swing sets.

Chevy Chase sits directly on the line between Maryland and the District of Columbia, with sections of development spilling into both jurisdictions and onto both sides of Connecticut Avenue. The hub of Chevy Chase Circle establishes a strong sense of place—along with the churches that line its circumference, the Chevy Chase Village Hall, two quietly elegant clubs, and a few carefully defined shopping areas.

In 1890 the area that was to become the new subdivision of Chevy Chase was well-settled farmland, crossed by several country roads. Brookeville Road ran from

The morning sun lit up these Chevy Chase houses as a jogger made her way down Irving Street near Magnolia Parkway. Photo by Lori Jesnek

Tennallytown to Brookeville, Maryland. Broad Branch Road, Jones Mill Road, and Milk House Ford Road wound through the farms, and the only crossroad leading from Brookeville Road to Old Georgetown Road was Jackson Road, now Bradley Boulevard. J.H. Bradley's large tract, later to form the key purchase of the Chevy Chase Land Company, straddled the line between Maryland and the District of Columbia, and a handful of other farms and houses dotted the countryside.

The transformation of this farmland into suburbs was initiated by the Chevy Chase Land Company. It was incorporated on June 5, 1890, by Francis G. Newlands and Senator William M. Stewart, two of the powerful and wealthy Westerners known to residents of the District of Columbia as the "California Syndicate," and Colonel George Augustus Armes, a retired Army colonel involved in real estate. Their long-range vision was extraordinary, for the site they chose to develop began about five miles northwest of the settled bounds of the city and was to become the first big development west of Rock Creek. The bridge they built across Rock Creek at Calvert Street opened the entire northwest section to new real estate ventures.

At the time of incorporation, Francis G. Newlands (1848-1917) was a young San Francisco lawyer. Early in his practice he had become attorney for William Sharon, the senator from Nevada from 1875 to 1882 who made a tremendous fortune revitalizing and managing the rich Nevada Comstock Lode. In 1874 Newlands married Sharon's daughter. Following her death, in 1882, and William Sharon's death, in 1885, Newlands became trustee of Sharon's huge estate, was himself one of the heirs, and managed major land holdings in California and Nevada. Newlands quickly moved his share of the assets to Washington. In 1892 he was elected to Congress, where he was a great proponent of irrigation and land reclamation in the West. He served as congressman from Nevada for 10 years and then as senator for 14 years.

William M. Stewart (1827-1909), lawyer and two-time senator from Nevada (1862-1875, 1887-1905), made his fortune prospecting for gold in California and representing the legal interests of the original miners of the Comstock Lode. He was a leading political figure in the West, among other things carving out the Nevada Territory and representing Western mining interests and railroads in Congress over a 29-year period.

Newlands and Stewart had experience with large-scale real estate ventures and a shared confidence in the future growth of Washington. They had been involved in other speculative land ventures in the city—at Dupont Circle, for example—albeit on a smaller scale than Chevy Chase.

Newlands is most often credited with being the primary catalyst for the development of Chevy Chase, although some sources credit Colonel Armes with the original concept. Whether or not Newlands first thought of the idea, it was he who was the driving force behind Chevy Chase in its formative years. He attracted a powerful and talented group of men to his new Chevy Chase Land Company. Stewart was a partner, purchasing $300,000 of the first issue of Land Company stock. Perhaps more important, he was its strong legislative supporter in Congress, backing both the creation of Rock Creek Park and the charter of the streetcar line.

In the years just preceding 1890 Newlands had launched an ambitious campaign of land purchases. His goal was to buy any parcel that touched on his projected length of Connecticut Avenue. Through straw purchases made secretly by his agents under a variety of names, he quietly bought up farmland amounting to more than 1,700 acres along the entire proposed length of Connecticut Avenue from Boundary Street (now Florida Avenue) to what is now Jones Bridge Road. Edward J. Stellwagen and Armes acted as principal agents and/or brokers for the acquisitions, and all holdings of the agents and trustees were transferred to the new Chevy Chase Land Company in 1890.

Newlands' key early purchase was Chevy Chase, a 305-acre plot of land straddling the line between Maryland and the District of Columbia. The name, which he subsequently adopted for the entire new subdivision, can be traced to the larger tract of land called "Cheivy Chace" that was patented to Colonel Joseph Belt from Lord Baltimore on July 10, 1725. It has historic associations to a 1388 battle between Lord Percy of England and Earl Douglas of Scotland. At issue in this "chevauchee" (a Scottish word describing a border raid) were hunting grounds or a "chace" in the Cheviot Hills of Northumberland and Otterburn. Part of the land patented in 1725 to Colonel Belt was sold in 1815 to Assistant Postmaster General Abraham Bradley. It was later acquired by businessmen and speculators, and then sold to the Chevy Chase Land Company.

Newlands was a farsighted businessman, intent on the finest quality of development. His goals are captured by a 1916 brochure, titled "Chevy Chase for Homes," which was produced by the Land Company's exclusive leasing agent, Thos. J. Fisher & Co.:

In the ordinary real estate development too frequently everything is sacrificed for quick financial returns, but this has not been done in Chevy Chase. Back of the development, so far as it has progressed today, is a big, comprehensive plan, and the men who formulated that plan believed that the best results could be obtained only where things were done right . . . Instead of developing one small tract without regard to the surroundings, the owners acquired more than two thousand acres of land and have spent hundreds of thousands of dollars in street improvements and the installation of every municipal convenience. The fixed purpose of The Chevy Chase Land Company was to provide for the National Capital a home suburb, a community where each home would bear a touch of the individuality of the owner, where each home would possess an added value by virtue of the beauty and charm of the surrounding homes.

Roderick S. French in his study of Chevy Chase in the *Records of the Columbia Historical Society* (1973-1974) points out that Newlands succeeded in keeping control and holding to quality standards in a way few other developers in the nation were able to do. "Newlands had the utmost interest in shaping the form and quality of the development," French explained. "In order to achieve that control, he was willing to forgo profit for himself and his investors for thirty years. He had, or had at his disposal, the capital necessary to such a comprehensive, long-term undertaking."

His vast share of his father-in-law's estate was the cornerstone of the plan. Two other important financial and real estate alliances were also crucial. The Union Trust Company, organized in 1899, was integral to the long-term financing necessary for large-scale development. The real estate mortgage investment banking firm, Thos. J. Fisher & Co., organized in 1872, became the real estate department of the Union Trust Company and the exclusive leasing agent for the Land Company. For a number of years the Fisher Company also handled all of the Land Company business from their offices. Stellwagen, vice president of the Land Company, was a link to both organizations—as president of Union Trust and president of Thos. J. Fisher & Co.

The Land Company's first task was to connect the new subdivision with Washington. Newlands privately launched the construction of Connecticut Avenue far beyond the improved streets of the city into the rugged countryside to the north, following the route of land Newlands had purchased. Workers excavated more than five miles of roadbed, bridged ravines, and constructed a series of deep cuts and fills. Much of this was done using pick-and-shovel and horse-drawn carts. Trestle bridges were constructed over Rock Creek at Calvert Street and at Klingle Valley (Klingle Street) in

A barrel-chested conductor poses on muddy Connecticut Avenue in 1913. Behind him lay Chevy Chase Circle and five miles farther, the city of Washington. The Chevy Chase Land Company's bold development plan depended on the purchase of over 1,700 acres of farmland through which Connecticut Avenue was extended and a streetcar line built. Courtesy, Montgomery County Historical Society

1891. The expense of the entire project was borne by the Land Company.

At the same time the company constructed an electric railway at an initial cost of $1.5 million. The Chevy Chase Land Company allied itself with the fledgling Rock Creek Railway Company, with Newlands as its president and principal stockholder. Officers of this new corporation were identical to those of the Land Company. The first segment of the line opened in 1892 and the rest soon thereafter. On May 31, 1903, the *Washington Post* reported that streetcars made the six-mile run from the Treasury at 15th Street and Pennsylvania Avenue to Chevy Chase in exactly 35 minutes, leaving every 15 minutes.

At the northern terminus of the line, two miles beyond Chevy Chase Circle, the Land Company built a small lake and an amusement park to lure prospective buyers. Pleasure-seekers flocked to Chevy Chase Lake on the trolley for concerts at the bandstand, which was a giant blue seashell covered with hundreds of twinkling lights. They rowed on the lake for five cents a half hour, bowled, rode the carousel and live ponies, tested their skills at the shooting gallery, and danced the two-step at the dance pavilion.

The first section of the new suburb to be laid out was just north of Chevy Chase Circle in Maryland, a section that is known today as Chevy Chase Village. Plans included broad streets, large lots, and parkland. Strict building regulations and covenants governed what future residents could build. Houses fronting upon Connecticut Avenue were to cost not less than $5,000 each, and on other streets not less than $3,000. Houses constructed on Connecticut required a setback of 35 feet; and on side streets, 25 feet. No lot could be less than 60 feet wide. Alleys, apartments, and rowhouses were forbidden, and no business was to be conducted in the section; other areas were set apart for that purpose. Stables and carriage houses were not to be erected within 25 feet of the front line of any lot. Similar restrictions were enacted in other sections developed later by the Land Company.

Research to date suggests that the first houses in the Village were built by or for officers of the Chevy Chase Land Company. An article in the November 1920 issue of the *Chevy Chase News,* written by Chevy Chase's first school mistress, Ella Given, names the first houses and their residents. According to her account, the four original homes—all in the vicinity of Connecticut Avenue and Irving Street—were designed by Lindley Johnson of Philadelphia, with Washington architect Leon E. Dessez as his associate.

Maryland commuters await the departure of the electric railroad to Chevy Chase. By 1903 streetcars ran from the Treasury Department to Chevy Chase in exactly 35 minutes, leaving every 35 minutes. Early residents ordered groceries, coal, and medicine for delivery via the cars. Courtesy, Chevy Chase Historical Society

Dessez himself was the first resident, moving into the house known today as the Lodge, just northwest of the Circle, in May 1893. Senator Newlands was the resident of a grand house (originally built for Senator Stewart) on the northeast side of the Circle; this house later became known as the Corby mansion for its owner, William S. Corby, who patented the first dough-molding machine. Howard Nyman, secretary of the Land Company, moved into the residence at the northeast corner of Connecticut and Irving, and Herbert Claude moved into the house at the northwest corner of Connecticut and Irving. As described in Ella Given's article, "These four houses, artistic and homelike, struck the keynote for the community which was to grow up around them."

Newlands and the Land Company provided every comfort and convenience within their control, including water from artesian wells and attractive surroundings. Under landscape architect Nathan Barrett's direction, a gracious landscape plan, with shade trees and ornamental shrubbery, was devised and partially executed. In addition to native trees such as tulip, poplar, oak, and locust, he specified many imports such as English elms, Japanese boxwood, pin oak, linden, and sycamore. Distinctive double rows of trees lined major streets.

The belief that "the best suburban section is always surrounding or adjacent to the leading suburban clubs" was expressed by Thos. J. Fisher & Co.'s 1916 real estate brochure. Land Company officers organized the Chevy Chase Club in 1890 soon after the formation of the company itself, with Newlands as its first president. It was a country club devoted mainly to riding and the hunt, in the days when it was the custom to ride to the hounds two or three times a week in season. The club adopted golf when that sport became popular. The old Bradley farmhouse on Connecticut Avenue served as the first clubhouse and was later remodeled into a guest house, incorporating portions of the old farmhouse.

The Land Company donated land for the first public school. Opening its doors in 1898, it was a small, four-room building surrounded by an expanse of mud, with a plank for a front stairway. In 1901 the Land Company also gave land on Chevy Chase Circle for the first church in the Village, the All Saints Episcopal Church (organized in 1897), whose first rector, the Reverend Thomas S. Childs, owned a house in the village. The post office building, now the Chevy Chase Village Hall at 5906 Connecticut Avenue, was a small, pebble-dashed structure that also accommodated the public library (an "artistically decorated room" with a collection of 1,000 books) and the fire apparatus (which included a fire engine, hose cart, and hook-and-ladder, as well as a fire bell located just south of the building).

The first residential section, Section II or Chevy Chase Village, located between Chevy Chase Circle and Bradley Lane, opened in 1893. The Land Company subsequently planned additional sections in both Maryland and the District of Columbia, which opened in the following order: Section III, east of Connecticut Avenue and north of Bradley Lane; Chevy Chase, D.C., located immediately southeast of the Circle; Section IV, west of Connecticut between the Chevy Chase and Columbia country clubs; Chevy Chase Heights, west of Connecticut about a half mile south of the Circle; and Section V, east of Connecticut above Section III. Curiously, there was originally no section one; although a portion of land added to Section II took this title on maps, it never gained widespread use.

The Chevy Chase Land Company was not solely responsible for developing the land. At times other developers were responsible for entire communities of homes. Otterborne, Martin's Additions, and additional lands were folded into Chevy Chase's boundaries on all sides as time passed. M. and R.B. Warren planned and engineered Leland, a tract of 57 acres that was later added to Section IV. More often, however, the Land Company sold lots singly to individuals, or in small groups for development. Evidently, in a few cases—perhaps to open a new section for development—they built houses themselves, but this was the exception.

Despite all of the amenities, the sale of land in Chevy Chase went slowly. The first section, the Village, opened in the panic year of 1893. Only 27 houses were occupied by 1897, and it required all the long-term financial solidarity of Newlands and his company to withstand the collapse of the boom of the previous decade. In fact, disbursements exceeded receipts for years. The Land Company would pay no dividends to stockholders until 1922. Accounts of growth patterns in Chevy Chase are varied; however, one source states that Chevy Chase Village had only 49 families in 1903.

The Land Company was perfectly situated, however, to benefit from the expansionary period that followed World War I. Between 1918 and 1931 sales totaled more than $7.5 million. By 1916 Thos. J. Fisher & Co. had reported that Section II, Section III, and Chevy Chase, D.C., were practically sold out, with sites still available in Section IV and Chevy Chase Heights.

This delivery truck advertised Sonnemann's store, one of the few commercial enterprises in Chevy Chase, where covenants and restrictions strictly limited commercial development. The store was on Brookeville Road at Quincy Street. Courtesy, Chevy Chase Historical Society

Right: By the 1920s Senator Francis B. Newlands' dream of a quiet residential suburb of individualized homes had become a reality, as seen in this east view looking down Rosemary Street from its intersection with Spruce, toward Connecticut Avenue. Young trees and empty lots still mark it as a new community. Courtesy, Robert A. Truax

Below right: These houses pictured in the 1914 Chevy Chase Land Company brochure, Chevy Chase for Homes, *demonstrated the company's intention to provide a residential suburb for the national capital, where each house would bear the owner's individual touch. Today's Chevy Chase gives testimony to the company's original vision. Courtesy, Chevy Chase Historical Society*

Because Chevy Chase's commercial development was strictly limited and controlled, the Land Company arranged for goods to be delivered to early residents. The *Chevy Chase News* of November 1920 described the system:

Coal was ordered through the Land Company, and during the summer months a wagon was sent into the city for ice several times a week. If medicine were needed it could be telephoned for and delivered to a car conductor at Fifteenth Street and New York Avenue, or anywhere along the route . . . The conductor would get off the car at Connecticut Avenue and Irving Street and put the medicine into a small box erected for that purpose.

Newlands did, however, plan for a small shopping area south of Chevy Chase Circle on the west side of Connecticut Avenue. Among the earliest stores to open there were W.B. Follmer's grocery store at 5630 Connecticut Avenue and Doc Armstrong's drugstore, adjacent to it. Sonnemann's store flourished on Brookeville Road.

The Land Company's early goal was a "home suburb where every home would reflect the individuality of its owner." Houses of all sizes were erected, and Thomas J. Fisher & Co. advertised them in the 1916 promotional brochure "Chevy Chase for Homes" as "each marked by the individuality of its owner." Although Chevy Chase was planned to "meet the requirements of discriminating people . . . that does not necessarily mean, in our opinion, people of great wealth. Scores of those of moderate means make their homes there." Residents have always maintained a range of occupations, from judge, senator, and physician to teacher, bookkeeper, and accountant.

From the outset Chevy Chase attracted the best of residential design. The Land Company engaged the talents of nationally known Philadelphia architect Lindley Johnson and New York landscape architect Nathan Barrett. Johnson, a successful and sophisticated Beaux Arts architect known for his large country houses and resort structures, received several key commissions in 1892, including six "cottages," a Connecticut Avenue office building, and homes for Stewart and Stellwagen. Barrett, who had been associated with Johnson at Winter Harbor, Tuxedo Park, Ponce de Leon, and other developments, devised the landscape plan in Chevy Chase. Along with local architect Leon E. Dessez, who is perhaps best known in Washington for his design of the Admiral's House (now the vice presidential residence), they set a tone of gentility with a few late Shingle Style houses and "Colonial style" houses in vogue in the 1890s. Newlands made Dessez a director of the Land Company in 1893 and gave him the responsibility of preparing strict building regulations, as well as building two houses for sale.

Construction slowed after the panic of 1893 and did not pick up until after World War I. Then one style of architecture tumbled out on the heels of the preceding one. Virtually all of the late nineteenth- and early twentieth-century styles are represented today, including the Shingle, Colonial Revival, Tudor, French Eclectic, Spanish Eclectic, Mission, Neoclassical, Italian Renaissance, Prairie, and Craftsman styles. Only modernistic and international-style houses are largely missing. Bungalows mix with grand Colonial Revival mansions, and designs range from formal architect-designed houses to Sears prefabricated structures. An extraordinary mix of talented local designers is represented, including Arthur B. Heaton, George S. Cooper, Thomas J.D. Fuller, Edward W. Donn, Waddy Wood, Clarence Harding, A.M. Sonnemann, Porter & Lockie, and Dan Kirkhuff, as well as prominent builders or developers such as Harry Wardman, Weaver Brothers, and M. and R.B. Warren.

Today the basic character of Chevy Chase as planned by the Chevy Chase Land Company in the 1890s has not changed, a powerful indication of the uniqueness of Newlands' enterprise. The large majority of the houses built over the years are extant. Of what were apparently the original four Chevy Chase houses, three remain: Newlands' home on Chevy Chase Circle, Stellwagen's house standing in midblock directly opposite the Corby Mansion, and Herbert Claude's house at 5900 Connecticut Avenue. Although there have been additions to the boundaries of the earliest land developed by the Land Company, the original sections still exist, each with its own distinctive character and identity. The Maryland sections each have an elected neighborhood government, headed by a section council or board of managers, that can contract for street improvements, police and fire protection, and the like.

Commercial incursions have continued to be strictly controlled. Newlands apparently planned for the Connecticut Avenue shopping district south of Chevy Chase Circle, and in general alignment with those plans, a low-rise shopping strip offers a first-run movie theater, the Chevy Chase Community Center, specialty book shops, a variety of small restaurants, and basic food and service businesses. However, the thrust of commercial development bordering on Chevy Chase was shifted in 1928 to the neighborhood's western edge, on Wisconsin Avenue, and the Land Company's construction there of Chevy Chase Center in the 1950s brought additional shops and offices to that area.

The Chevy Chase Land Company still exists, largely owned by descendants of Senator Newlands and collateral heirs. After Newlands' death, in 1917, Stellwagen became president, followed in turn by Edward L. Hillyer. Until the mid-1930s the company sold land and liquidated assets for distribution to shareholders. In 1946 William Sharon Farr assumed the presidency, and the company strategy changed as it began to develop its holdings into long-term, income-producing properties. Farr's son, Gavin, now serves as president. A recent Land Company undertaking is an apartment building at 8101 Connecticut Avenue, occupying the original site of Chevy Chase Lake and fittingly advertised as "built by the Chevy Chase Land Co. on land they selected and acquired in 1890."

Despite the passing of several characteristic features—Chevy Chase Lake was filled in during the 1930s, the electric railroad service was discontinued on Connecticut Avenue in 1935, and the bridges at Klingle Valley and Calvert Street have long since been replaced—Chevy Chase itself stands as Newlands envisioned it, a residential neighborhood, stable, comfortable, and quiet. Ninety years later it is a tribute to his long-range planning and high standards.

The Chevy Chase trolley rounds the treeless Chevy Chase Circle and passes Western Avenue on its route south to Washington in this 1913 postcard. Grafton Street is in the right center of the picture which looks northwest over a pastoral landscape. Courtesy, Montgomery County Historical Society

DAVIES
GABLE
NOW SHOWING
CAIN AND MABEL
MARION DAVIES
SOLD OUT

18

CLEVELAND PARK
COUNTRY LIVING IN THE CITY

Kathleen Sinclair Wood

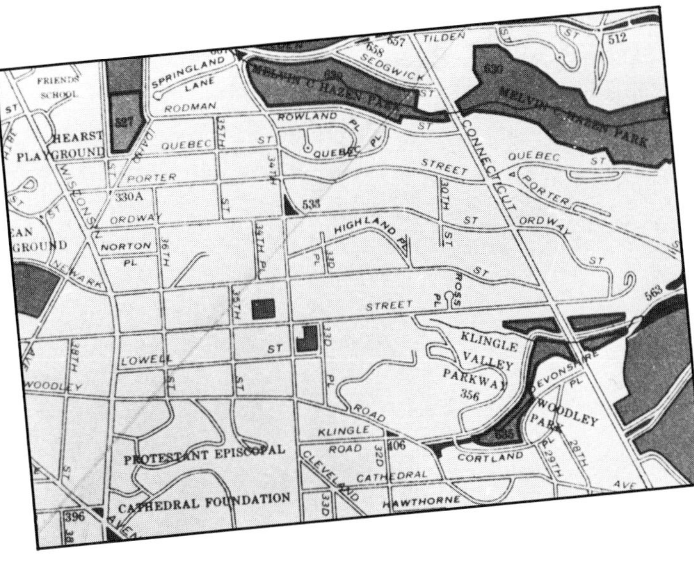

"Cain and Mabel," featuring Marion Davies and Clark Gable, drew crowds to the grand opening of the Uptown Theater on Connecticut Avenue in Cleveland Park in 1936. Courtesy, D.C. Public Library, Washingtoniana Division

Map: Park System of the National Capitol and Environs. National Park Service 1962. Courtesy, D.C. Public Library, Washingtoniana Division

The tree-shaded streets of Cleveland Park are dominated by turn-of-the-century frame houses, many with wraparound porches reminiscent of small-town America. Cleveland Park is thought of by many of its residents as a true community and a good place to raise children. It is a livable, in-town neighborhood with a mix of single-family homes, apartment buildings, shops, a multiplicity of schools, and a Metro stop, all within minutes of central Washington.

The neighborhood has been undisturbed by redevelopment and retains physical reminders of all phases of its growth. In the eighteenth century it was farmland, and one farmhouse remains. In the nineteenth century its hilly location above Georgetown made it a popular site for country estates and summer homes, and several of these have survived. By 1900 developers had laid out the streets of a new suburb on the site and were extolling the virtues of its individually designed homes, almost all of which stand today.

When the capital came to the Potomac, Cleveland Park was rolling farmland in rural Maryland, part of a large land grant patented in 1723 by George Beall. It was adjacent to the road to Frederick Town, an old Indian trail used by tobacco farmers taking their produce to the port of Georgetown. In the early 1790s part of this land grant was purchased by General Uriah Forrest, a former mayor of Georgetown and George Washington's aide-de-camp and friend. Forrest and his two partners, successful tobacco merchants and land speculators, amassed about 1,282 acres, which they patented as Pretty Prospects. By 1794 Forrest and his wife had tired of city living in Georgetown, built a simple frame farmhouse on part of Pretty Prospects, named their expansive estate Rosedale, and became the

Rosedale, revealed here through the leafless trees of winter, is the oldest house in Cleveland Park. It was built in the 1790s by General Uriah Forrest, one of George Washington's friends, as the new federal city was being established just to the south on the banks of the Potomac. Photo by Kathleen Sinclair Wood

first documented inhabitants of the area known today as Cleveland Park.

During the first half of the nineteenth century Pretty Prospects was gradually divided into smaller parcels of land sold for country estates on the outskirts of the growing capital city. Philip Barton Key built Woodley (now Maret School) in 1800, Major Charles J. Nourse built The Highlands (now Sidwell Friends School) in the 1820s, and H.H. Dent built Springland (still a private residence) in the 1840s. As English author Frances Trollope described it in 1830: "The country rises into a beautiful line of hills behind Washington, which form a sort of undulating terrace on to Georgetown; this terrace is almost entirely occupied by a succession of Gentlemen's Seats."

In 1865 Ann Forrest Green, daughter of Uriah Forrest, gave 23.5 acres to her son, George Forrest Green, and his family, who wanted to move to the country. In 1869 the Greens erected Forrest Hill: ". . . a roomy stone dwelling, built of native stone found on an adjacent field. It was a quiet home for a gentleman of moderate means and refined taste . . . on a hill commanding an extensive prospect, looking upon nothing but beauty and breathing nothing but health." It was this house that President Grover Cleveland purchased in 1885 on the eve of his marriage to his beautiful young ward, Frances R. Folsom. Extensive remodeling designed by W.M. Poindexter transformed the simple stone farmhouse into a fanciful Victorian summer house with a turret overlooking the city of Washington. Oak View, as he renamed it, served as the summer White House during Cleveland's first term in office.

Another summer resident was Gardiner Greene Hubbard, a Bostonian living at Dupont Circle. In the mid-1880s he purchased 50 acres on Woodley Lane and hired Boston architect Francis R. Allen to design a frame Colonial Revival summer house. Situated on a hilltop overlooking a rolling lawn, Twin Oaks, as Hubbard named his estate, was the center of family activities. The family included Alexander Graham Bell, an innovative educator of the deaf hired by Hubbard to teach his daughter, Mabel. A romance blossomed between teacher and student; Bell became Hubbard's son-in-law; and Hubbard became one of Bell's staunchest supporters and the financial backer of the nation's first telephone company. Twin Oaks remains as the only extant summer house in Cleveland Park; it is owned today by Taiwan.

Tregaron was built in 1912 as a year-round country estate on 20 acres originally belonging to Twin Oaks.

Members of the fledgling National Geographic Society gather on the ample porch of society founder Gardiner Greene Hubbard's 50-acre summer retreat off Woodley Road, N.W. Known as Twin Oaks, the Colonial Revival-style house was designed by Boston architect Francis R. Allen in 1888. Courtesy, Library of Congress, Prints and Photographs Division

Gardiner Greene Hubbard and his wife, Gertrude, enjoy afternoon tea on the porch of Twin Oaks, the only surviving summer house in Cleveland Park. The Hubbards left their residence at Dupont Circle to spend summers in the cooler, higher region outside the city center. Courtesy, Library of Congress, Prints and Photographs Division

Charles Adams Platt, a nationally known designer of country houses, was chosen by James Parmelee to design the Georgian Revival house and landscape the 20 acres of grounds with rustic stone bridges and bridle paths. Ambassador Joseph Davies and his wife, Marjorie Merriweather Post, settled here in the 1940s upon their return from the Soviet Union.

After Cleveland lost his bid for reelection, he sold his estate, but the president's brief presence was celebrated in the names chosen for three new subdivisions carved from his land and neighboring properties. Oak View, Cleveland Heights, and Cleveland Park were surveyed and platted by 1894. Of the three, Cleveland Park was the most successful and over time absorbed the other two. Cleveland's house remained a summer residence for Colonel Robert I. Fleming, a successful Washington entrepreneur, but by 1927 it had deteriorated and was razed.

Cleveland Park was one of many late nineteenth-century residential communities outside the old city boundary designed to lure city dwellers with the advantages of country living close to the city. The *Washington Times* in 1903 hailed Cleveland Park as "Queen of Washington Suburbs" and described its rural charms:

The park is a cool and pleasant resort. The breeze from the hills makes life one grand sweet song, and the music of the birds stirs the soul . . . It is within the District limits, and consequently enjoys every advantage which a downtown resident can claim, and in addition, it is as beautiful a spot and as free from annoyance of the city as if it were in the heart of the Adirondacks . . . there is every blessing of fresh country air, plenty of elbow room, woods and fields, peacefulness, coolness in summer and comfort in winter.

The development and settlement of Cleveland Park was made possible by Senator Francis Newlands of Nevada, who created the suburb of Chevy Chase, Maryland. In the process, the Chevy Chase Land Company laid out Connecticut Avenue, built a bridge across Rock Creek at Calvert Street and a second bridge across Klingle Valley, and constructed the tracks for the electric streetcar, creating development opportunities all along its route. The opening of streetcar service in 1890 on Wisconsin Avenue and in 1892 on Connecticut Avenue connected the land that would become Cleveland Park with the city center, and real estate entrepreneurs soon recognized its potential.

In 1894-1895 Thomas Waggaman and John Sherman formed the Cleveland Park Company and began

Cleveland Park takes its name from the Summer White House of President Grover Cleveland and his bride, Frances Folsom. The "Victorianized" 1868 stone farmhouse, seen here in a popular 1887 souvenir view, was known as Oak View. Courtesy, Library of Congress, Prints and Photographs Division

Robert Thompson Head, a carpenter's son from Leesburg, Virginia, designed this Queen Anne-style house with porches, varied gables and windows, a turret, and a strikingly tall central chimney for the Cleveland Park Company in 1898. Between 1897 and 1901, Head designed at least 17 houses for the Cleveland Park Company, far more than any other architect. Photo by Kathleen Sinclair Wood

constructing houses. It appears that Waggaman was the principal landowner and financier; Sherman, as president, was responsible for the design, construction, and sale of houses from 1895 to 1909. Ella Bennett Sherman, his wife, was a New York-trained artist and active in the Cleveland Park Company from its inception. Records indicate that she probably designed most of the houses constructed between 1902 and 1909.

John Sherman had a vision for Cleveland Park that exceeded the usual speculative development pattern of buying cheap rural land, platting it in standard lot sizes, and selling the lots to homeowners who built their own houses. He took great pride in hiring fine architects to prepare individual designs for all the houses in his streetcar suburb. Sherman also provided amenities for the residents. In 1898 he built an architect-designed stone lodge, which served as a community center providing comfortable heated space for neighbors attending meetings or waiting for the streetcar. The Cleveland Park Library occupies this spot today, marking the traditional entrance to Cleveland Park with a similar community-oriented facility. Sherman also provided a stable for residents' horses and carriages as well as a combined fire-engine house and police station.

Many notable local architects designed one-of-a-kind houses for the Cleveland Park Company. Between 1895 and 1901 Sherman employed Paul Pelz, one of the architects of the Library of Congress; Waddy Wood, who later designed the Woodrow Wilson house; Frederick Bennett Pyle, a prolific commercial and residential architect; and Robert Thompson Head, whose numerous houses give the neighborhood an appearance of great architectural variety. The houses designed by these architects set the tone for the neighborhood and established its architectural character and distinctiveness.

A 1904 promotional brochure advertising the virtues of living in Cleveland Park emphasized its architectural variety:

Among the sixty houses of the Park, with a single exception there is no repetition of design . . . The houses have been built in the last six years and planned by architects who combined in them beauty, durability and economy . . . They are recognized as the most beautiful and artistic homes in the District. In fact, they are known and spoken of far beyond the limits of the District for their beauty and originality.

The earliest houses were large frame structures resembling rambling summer cottages, with expansive porches and numerous Queen Anne and Shingle Style details. They were built with turrets, towers, steep gables, tall pilastered chimneys, and windows of all shapes and sizes, including bays, oriels, and numerous Palladian windows. Summer houses for the wealthy and suburban houses for the middle class were the two fastest-growing areas of housing design for architects during the last two decades of the nineteenth century, and their designs were published in the architectural journals and popular magazines. Consequently it is not surprising that there was some overlap and that many of the suburban homes have features reminiscent of summer homes built at the shore. In both cases the architects were designing for people who were looking for an escape from the crowded and unsanitary city centers.

The developers of this area of Northwest Washington sought to interest potential residents not only by featuring fine country-style houses in a healthful and beautiful setting but also by calling attention to nearby amenities. As a real estate brochure promoting Connecticut Avenue Highlands published in 1903 by Fulton R. Gordon pointed out, Rock Creek Park, 2,500 acres of beautiful woods purchased by Congress for public enjoyment in the 1890s, lay just to the east. New opportunities for employment were opening up nearby: the National Bureau of Standards was providing 300 jobs; the Geophysical Laboratory of the Carnegie Institute and the U.S. Geological Survey were locating just north of Cleveland Park in the early 1900s. The Naval Observatory had moved from Foggy Bottom to a hilltop just south of Cleveland Park in the 1890s and the Cathedral of Saint Peter and Saint Paul (Washington Cathedral) was rising on Mount Saint Alban at the neighborhood's southwest corner, with its affiliated schools. In addition, adjacent estates of the city's elite, such as Admiral George Dewey's Beauvoir, Friendship (McLean Gardens), owned by publisher John R. McLean, and Woodley, belonging to Senator Newlands of Nevada, added prestige to the area.

The occupations of the early residents of Cleveland Park suggest some were attracted to the neighborhood because of the nearby employment. For example, 20 scientists lived on Highland Place, and Macomb and Newark streets, in 1918, including Lyman Briggs, later director of the Bureau of Standards, and Arthur L. Day, director of the Geophysical Laboratory. The Cleveland Park homes were expensive by standards of the day, ranging between $5,000 and $8,000, and most of the early residents of the neighborhood were in professional and management positions. A significant number headed their own businesses.

Prominent early residents included Judge Walter Cox of the District's supreme court, his Highland Place neighbor T.L. Holbrook, president of the Washington Brick Company, and O.T. Crosby, founder of the Potomac Electric Power Co. Admiral Robert Peary, the Arctic explorer, lived in Cleveland Park briefly as did actress Helen Hayes as a child. Architects and developers such as Arthur B. Heaton and Frederick Bennett Pyle, both of whom designed houses in the neighborhood, also settled in Cleveland Park. W.C. and A.N. Miller, the influential developers of Wesley Heights and Spring Valley, operated their first real estate office in their home on Highland Place and built their first houses down the street.

The first residents were dependent upon the city for all their needs, from groceries to doctors, and many patronized the stores at the opposite end of the Calvert Street bridge in today's Adams Morgan. "In 1918 there was a Flu epidemic [and] my father had to go all the way down to the nearest drug store, at 18th and Columbia Road, to get medicine for us," one former resident remembered. It was

Right: The arrival of the Art Deco Uptown Theater in 1936, seen here as it looked in about 1950, brought Hollywood entertainment to the neighborhood and enhanced this stretch of Connecticut Avenue as Cleveland Park's "village" center. Noted theater architect John Jacob Zink designed the building, which then also housed the Cinema Hot Shop to the left of its streamlined awning. Courtesy, Columbia Historical Society

Below right: Connecticut Avenue's "Park and Shop," as it appeared in the 1930s, was an early prototype for today's ubiquitous shopping centers. Designed by Arthur B. Heaton in 1930 in a patriotic Colonial Revival style, it was situated between woods and the grand Broadmoor apartments at Connecticut Avenue and Ordway Street, N.W. Courtesy, Kathleen Sinclair Wood

not until the 1920s that the neighborhood began to get its own stores and services, first on Wisconsin and immediately thereafter on Connecticut Avenue. The Taft Bridge across Rock Creek, built in 1907, allowed passage directly north from lower to middle Connecticut Avenue for the first time. The bridge did not immediately bring commerce to Cleveland Park but did help spur residential development near this grand avenue. In 1920 the city's first zoning law controlled the development of the avenue itself with a novel approach that reflected the city's strong lobby for planned growth. Four specifically limited areas along Connecticut Avenue were designated neighborhood shopping districts, and all others were to remain residential. One such district was in Cleveland Park. The 1916 firehouse designed by Snowden Ashford heralded the imminent growth of the commercial area. The Monterey Pharmacy opened in 1923 on the ground floor of the Monterey Apartments, followed in 1925 by the Great A&P Tea Company and Piggly Wiggly Groceries, thus bringing basic needs within easy access of Cleveland Park residents for the first time.

The competition among grocery stores along the avenue and the increasing use of the personal automobile led to an innovative concept in marketing, the introduction of a prototype shopping center, which proved to be a turning point in the history of local and national commercial de velopment. The "Park and Shop" at the corner of Connecticut Avenue and Ordway Street was planned and developed by Shannon and Luchs, with Arthur B. Heaton as the architect. Opened in 1931, the complex introduced the idea of one-stop shopping—groceries to auto care—with a large off-street parking lot in front. It was a prototype for similar automobile-oriented shopping complexes across the country.

The Art Deco Uptown Theater opened in 1936 as a specifically neighborhood theater in a residential community, a forerunner of the 1950s' suburban theaters. Ironically, the Uptown Theater is now the one large undivided theater remaining in Washington and is the site of many openings and exclusive runs. The post office of 1940 and the library of 1952 completed the provision of essential services to Cleveland Park residents. The opening of the Cleveland Park Metro stop in 1981 encouraged new businesses such as ice cream parlors, delicatessens, small ethnic restaurants, and pubs, but the small-scale friendly village atmosphere of the shopping district has remained.

As residential Cleveland Park continued to grow and expand in the 1920s and 1930s, John Sherman was replaced by other developers: Charles and Louise Taylor, W.C. and A.N. Miller, and W.D. Sterrett completed the greatest number of houses. The Millers followed the example set by the Cleveland Park Company, varying the styles of their architect-designed houses and respecting the natural topography in the siting and landscaping. Sterrett developed the land that had belonged to his family's country estate, Springland. Throughout the years architects of local and national prominence designed new houses in a variety of styles for individual clients, including Appleton P. Clark, Marsh and Peter, Ayman Embury II, Hornblower and Marshall, Waldron and Winthrop Faulkner, William Lescaze, and I.M. Pei. Pei summed up the architectural character of the neighborhood in the early 1960s when he came to inspect the site for one of his few residential designs: "This neighborhood interests me. I don't feel the heavy hand of conformity . . ."

Many early residents of Cleveland Park remained in the neighborhood for the rest of their lives; in a few cases the next generation still lives in the same house or nearby. However, beginning with the Depression and into the 1950s, the old houses and the neighborhood came to be considered less fashionable. Some houses stood empty in the 1930s; others were divided up during the housing shortage of World War II. Miriam and Elliott Moyer described their difficulties in getting financing to build a house in Cleveland Park. "As an indication of the status of Cleveland Park in 1941, the finance and real estate institutions regarded this as a neighborhood that was potentially to be blighted . . . The interest rate was a point and a half higher than the usual rate because of the questionable future of this neighborhood." The Moyers persisted in their efforts, built their house, and remain in it today.

While the neighborhood may have temporarily ceased to be as desirable as it had been in the early 1900s, it continued throughout its history to have a strong sense of community. When John Eaton School opened in 1911, it immediately provided a focal point for the neighborhood. The elementary school's consistently high quality of education, ethnic diversity, parental involvement, and special programs continue to draw families to the neighborhood. In the 1920s a group of neighbors founded the Cleveland Park Club, acquiring one of the oldest houses in the heart of the neighborhood as a gathering spot for members. Until the 1950s the club sponsored regular meetings and dinners attended by members in formal attire. The club

District Commissioner Melvin Hazen addressed the opening-night audience at the Uptown Theater in Cleveland Park in 1936. Openings of neighborhood theaters were major events in the 1930s, and Commissioner Hazen often attended, representing the city government. Courtesy, D.C. Public Library, Washingtoniana Division

continues to be active today, emphasizing family-oriented events centered around its swimming pool.

This strong sense of community emerged as an ongoing theme in an extensive set of oral interviews conducted as part of the Cleveland Park History Project of John Eaton School in 1984. When Hilda and Sturgis Warner moved into the neighborhood in 1951, for example, they were immediately impressed with the spirit of the community. Neighbors were running a scrap-metal drive to help raise money to buy land for a public library. "Neighbors emptied their cellars of junk, old pipes, and discarded metal toys and carted them down the hill in kids' wagons or cars and piled them on the lot," Hilda Warner remembered. Other longtime residents reminisced about initiating the Macomb Street playground, working for a renovation of John Eaton School, and starting an after-school program and an annual neighborhood "Block Party" on the playground to pay for it. "It's thrilling to see that playground fill up every year," said Sally Craig, a neighborhood activist who helped organize the event for many years.

An influx of politically active residents rediscovered Cleveland Park in the late 1950s and early 1960s. Many were journalists, politicians, and academics with large families and small budgets who found the somewhat worn, rambling old wooden houses appealing and affordable and the local public school acceptable. The newcomers joined with longtime residents in fighting the citywide development pressures that began in the late 1950s; their organizational skills and political connections made them successful where other neighborhoods failed. In 1960 the neighborhood defeated a proposed freeway through its northwestern portion. In the mid-1960s neighbors organized Citizens for City Living, and after 20 years of consistent work they managed to save from replacement by high-rise commercial development some of the World War II low-rise, low-rental McLean Gardens apartments just across Wisconsin Avenue to the west. In the early 1980s the Friends of Tregaron succeeded in convincing the zoning commission that the landmark estate should be protected from intensive overdevelopment. Most recently the entire neighborhood successfully pulled together to have Cleveland Park declared a historic district and listed on the National Register of Historic Places. The neighborhood continues its activism today, organizing to preserve the small shops and the architectural integrity of its two shopping corridors through the efforts of the recently formed Cleveland Park Historical Society.

The large old frame houses with rambling porches, expansive yards, and numerous Victorian decorative details create an atmosphere of a small town in the Midwest or a summer community in New England, calling to mind memories of more relaxed, easygoing living. Children on bicycles and skateboards share the streets with men and women in their jogging shoes hurrying to work with their briefcases. This atmosphere in a community 15 minutes by Metro from the heart of the capital of the United States makes country living within the city a reality and characterizes the appeal of the neighborhood of Cleveland Park.

Architects Frederick Bennett Pyle and Paul Pelz designed some of these varied houses on Newark Street, N.W. John Sherman, president of the Cleveland Park Company, prided himself on the creation of a streetcar suburb with individually designed homes. Photo by Kathleen Sinclair Wood

MICHIGAN PK.
MANOR PK.
BRIGHTWOOD
UNIVERSITY HTS.
BROOKLAND
BRIGHTWOOD PK.
SOLDIERS HOME
PETWORTH
EDGEWOOD
ROCK CREEK PARK
PARK VIEW
CHEVY CHASE
CRESTWOOD
MOUNT PLEASANT
LE DROIT PK.
FOREST HILLS
COLUMBIA HTS.
WESTMINSTER
N. CLEVELAND PK.
LANIER HTS.
CHILDREN'S HOSPITAL
SHAW
TENLEY TOWN
CLEVELAND PK.
LOGAN CIRCLE
THOMAS CIRCLE
FRANKLIN McPHERSON SQUARE
THE WHITE HOUSE GROUNDS
ELLIPSE
NORTHWEST RECTANGLE
LINCOLN MEMORIAL

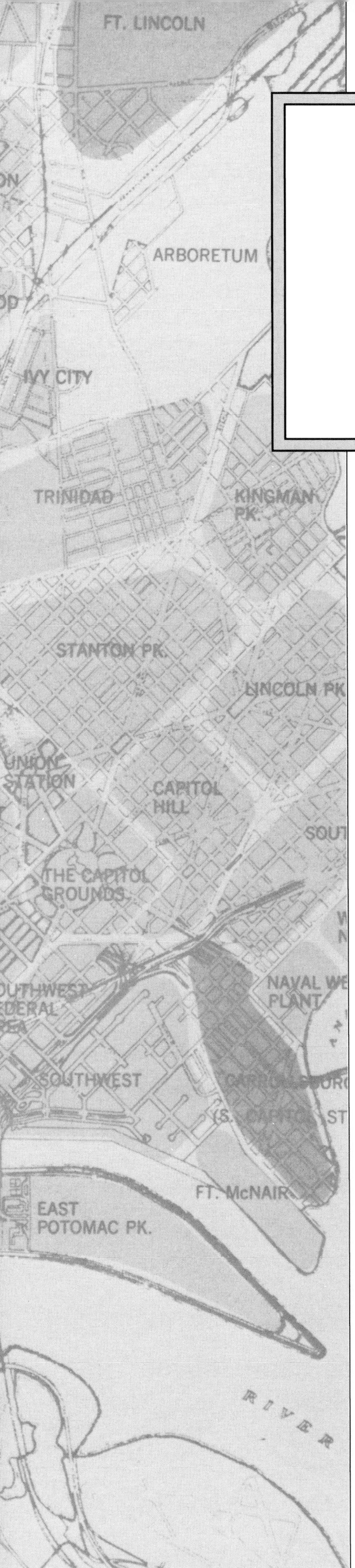

PART FIVE

TWENTIETH-CENTURY COMMUNITIES

The federal establishment mushroomed in the twentieth century as the nation fought two world wars and a depression. At the same time, the national capital became a world capital, and its population swelled and diversified. By the 1950s, the last large open spaces within the District of Columbia were developed, and suburbs proliferated far beyond the District's boundaries in Virginia and Maryland. The automobile was the transportation innovation this time, providing access to sections not convenient to the public transit lines. The last frontier in the District to be built up after World War II lay in far-Southeast, across the Anacostia River. Benning Heights represents these neighborhoods, most of which still remain to be researched.

The most recent period of neighborhood-building within the District represents not physical growth but rather a social phenomenon. As is the case nationwide, many city dwellers have been lured back to older neighborhoods by their convenience, interesting architecture, affordable prices, and more diverse populations. Such urbanites have in many places revived or restructured a sense of community that has reinforced the historical identity of Washington's varied neighborhoods.

This phenomenon is the particular focus of the Adams Morgan and Shepherd Park essays. Whereas some neighborhood stories in this book tell how the threat of unwanted development drew residents together, in Adams Morgan and Shepherd Park the significant ingredient has been changing demographics. Adams Morgan is today the center of the city's growing Latino population, which the city's Office of Latino Affairs estimated in 1987 as at least 85,000. There Spanish-speaking people from all over the area and the world come to find a sense of commonality in a shared language, even though their individual cultures differ.

Shepherd Park became more socially cohesive as it became racially more diverse. Joining with other neighborhoods such as Manor Park and Takoma Park, it took aggressive action to create a healthy, integrated neighborhood through a new organization named "Neighbors, Inc." It is a story that exemplifies the thesis that while neighborhoods are physical places, the people make and maintain them as living communities.

***Left:** Walter Reed Army Hospital, which today occupies more than 100 acres on the south side of Shepherd Park, was in its infancy when this photograph of its early hospital wards was taken. In 1911 Congress purchased the tract for the hospital in what was still an open, undeveloped area, and the subdivision of land nearby began soon after. Courtesy, Library of Congress, Prints and Photographs Division*

Map; 1967. Courtesy, National Capital Planning Commission

19

Benning Heights

A View from Another Hill

Maria Goodwin

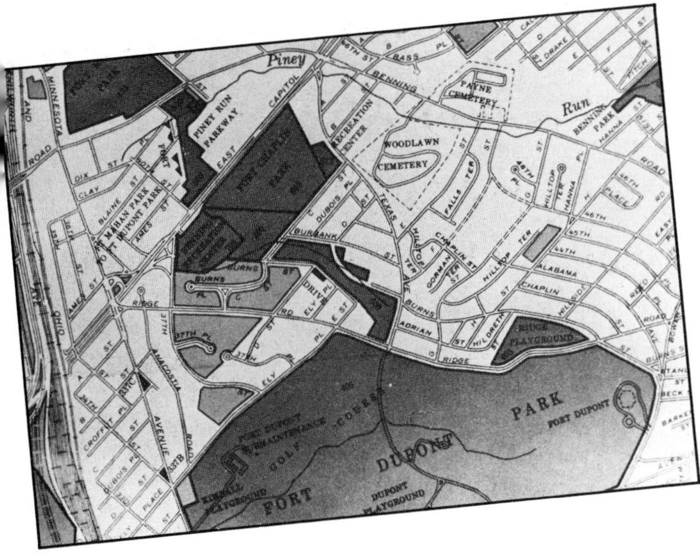

Early landowner William Benning was instrumental in the construction of the first version of the Benning Bridge in 1797 that linked the rural landscape across the Eastern Branch (Anacostia River) with central Washington. Courtesy, Library of Congress, Prints and Photographs Division

Map: Park System of the National Capitol and Environs. National Park Service 1962. Courtesy, D.C. Public Library, Washingtoniana Division

It is all a matter of perspective. The view of the Mall looking west from the Capitol down Capitol Hill, with its clean-line views and the near-perfect alignment of the Washington Monument and Lincoln Memorial, is one that is familiar to local residents and visitors alike.

But there are other hills in Washington, and other perspectives on the city: from Our Lady Queen of Peace Church at Ely Place and Ridge Road, for example, and from many other hilltop locations in the far-Southeast section of Washington—on the other side of the Anacostia River from that well-known view from Capitol Hill. The viewer here is keenly aware that central Washington is a place removed.

The Anacostia River has been a physical, economic, and even a psychological barrier between the neighborhoods of far-Southeast and far-Northeast and those on the west side of its course through the District. Most of the land to the east was still countryside until 1900, indeed some of it until World War II. Its lack of definition in the minds of people who do not live there is evident in the way they describe it—often simply referring to the entire area of the District across the river as Anacostia, when in fact local residents recognize at least two dozen communities in Southeast alone. Benning Heights near Fort Dupont in far-Southeast Washington is an example of such a community, cut off from central Washington not only by the Anacostia River, but by a string of parks named for Civil War forts that make it geographically more a part of Maryland than of the District itself. Until recently Maryland buses provided its only public transportation into central Washington. It is a post-World War II community that is representative of many such neighborhoods along the District's

Residents of far-Southeast Washington see the city from a different perspective, as in this view from the hill at the top of Morris Road, S.E. Photo by Linda Wheeler

eastern boundary with Maryland.

The name of the community is that of early nineteenth century landowner William Benning, who helped finance the wooden bridge built in 1797 by the Anacostia Bridge Company on the site of the present-day Benning Road Bridge. He later purchased and rebuilt the structure that would bear his name. There were three bridges across the Anacostia before the Civil War; the others were the 11th Street or Navy Yard Bridge and the Pennsylvania Avenue Bridge, all toll bridges chartered by the Maryland state legislature in the 1790s. These bridges connected Washington City with the plantations of Prince George's County and its county seat, Upper Marlboro, to the east.

Prominent men such as James Barry, who would become president of the first Washington City council, and William Marbury of the famous *Marbury v. Madison* case, began buying large tracts of land on the far side of the river early in the capital's history, speculating on future development along the Eastern Branch, as the Anacostia River was known in the nineteenth century. Hopes for the economic and residential development in that section of the District were raised in 1815 when the City Canal Company completed a canal through the city of Washington with branches to Buzzard's Point and the Navy Yard. When their hopes went unfulfilled, the speculators sold their large plantations in parcels of 200 to 500 acres that were then operated as small farms throughout the nineteenth century.

The only settlements on this side of the river by the time of the Civil War were the little crossroads community of Good Hope that sprang up in the 1820s and Uniontown, a speculative development laid out at the end of the Navy Yard Bridge in 1854. Barry's Farm was created nearby in 1867 by the Freedmen's Bureau. These are the oldest neighborhoods east of the Anacostia River. To think of these communities as representative of far-Southeast Washington, however, is no more accurate than considering Georgetown representative of all of Northwest. The more than two dozen communities of far-Southeast differ markedly from one to the next.

The definition of far-Southeast neighborhoods is made more difficult in that both old and current maps as well as current residents use a variety of names and boundaries. Current maps most often place the name Benning Heights in the area between Benning and Ridge roads on the east and west, East Capitol Street on the north, and Alabama and Southern avenues on the south. The frequently published city assessment maps, however, combine this area with Greenway across Ridge Road and label it all Fort Dupont. Some longtime residents use the name of early real estate developments and refer to the area as Hillcrest Heights or Bradbury Heights. In fact the neighborhood does not have strong community-wide organizations of the kind that reinforce consciousness of the place as a whole, and most people tend to identify with only the vicinity of their own home and city block and do not use a neighborhood name at all.

The 400-acre Fort Dupont Park on the community's western boundary is second only to Rock Creek Park in size. It is the site of one of 68 Civil War forts that provided a protective ring around the District of Columbia. The forts varied in size and manpower, from prominent structures to barebones defenses that were little more than hills protected by a handful of Union soldiers, most newly trained and pulling double duty constructing their forts as well as defending them. Fort

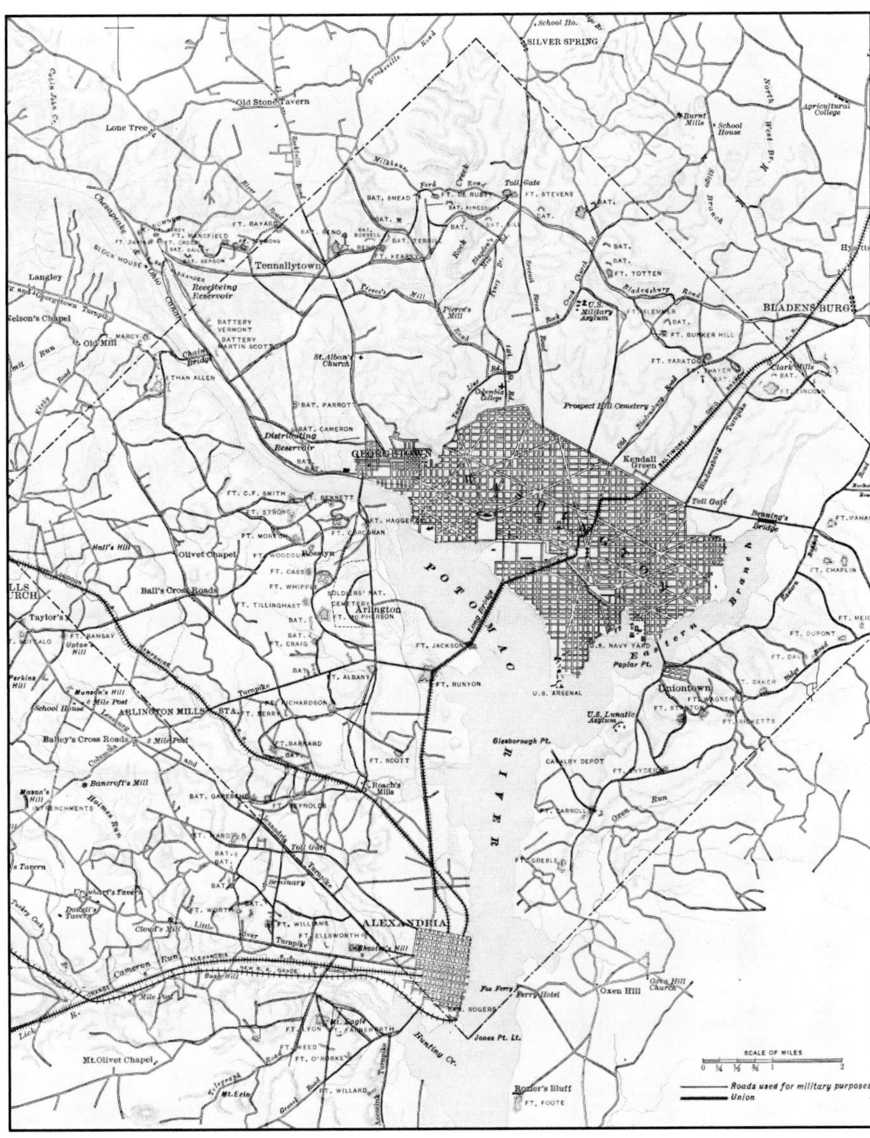

Fort Dupont, near the District line at far right center, was part of an extensive system of forts and batteries built to protect the capital during the Civil War. Like Fort Dupont, many are parks today. Courtesy, Library of Congress, Map Division

Blanche Kelso Bruce, Republican senator from Mississippi during Reconstruction, and many other black Washingtonians are buried in Woodlawn Cemetery in Benning Heights, a nineteenth-century burial ground that was suffering neglect when this photograph was taken in 1987. Photo by Linda Wheeler

Dupont consisted of five wooden structures, two buildings 16 feet by 24 feet for officers' quarters; barracks 100 feet by 20; a mess house 50 feet by 20; and a guardhouse 24 feet by 18. It had been obtained from a local landowner, Michael Caton, and was later returned to him along with its buildings, magazines, and stockyards. The fort never saw action, and today its remains are barely visible a short distance from the park's Alabama Avenue entrance. A plaque placed there in 1955 by the National Society of Colonial Dames notes that it had eight guns and one mortar and was named after Admiral Samuel F. Dupont, a commander of the South Atlantic Blockade Squadron.

The area around Fort Dupont, indeed most of Southeast Washington that lay east of Uniontown and Barry's Farm, remained countryside throughout the late nineteenth century and into the twentieth. An 1887 real estate atlas shows large segments of land still owned by a few landowners and only two roads, Benning and Ridge, cutting through the rural area.

In 1895 23 acres of land in the area were purchased from John and Mary Schultz for Woodlawn Cemetery. At that time very few of the approximately 40 cemeteries in the District would accept black burials. Woodlawn was created in the countryside to meet this need. Many of the most distinguished black residents of Washington, D.C., would be buried there. They include Blanche Kelso Bruce, Republican senator from Mississippi during Reconstruction, and his daughter-in-law, Clara Burrill Bruce, who in 1926 was the second black woman to be admitted to the Massachusetts Bar. Clara was the wife of Roscoe Conkling Bruce, assistant superintendent of the D.C. public schools. Also buried here are John Mercer Langston, prominent member of the District's territorial government and later Virginia's first black congressman, and Elnora Dickerson Davis, wife of Benjamin Oliver Davis—the first black general in the U.S. Army—and mother of Benjamin O. Davis, Jr., the first black Air Force general.

The cemetery and the remains of Fort Dupont stood isolated in the midst of woodland and fields. It was not until the 1920s that the first land development came to the large open areas of far-Southeast, developments made possible by the automobile, which had come within the price range of the middle class for the first time. Far-Southeast was not served by the extensive network of streetcars that sprang up in the 1890s on the other side of the Anacostia. In fact, as late as 1924 the only public transportation in far-Southeast was a trolley that ran to Old Anacostia and then down Nichols Avenue and a bus that crossed the Pennsylvania Avenue bridge to Randle Highlands just on the other side of the river.

A 1927 real estate atlas shows far-Southeast in transition from rural to suburban. The first major developments were along Alabama and Pennsylvania avenues: for example, the Parklands Apartments, off Alabama Avenue in the Garfield Section, and Fairfax Village, bounded by Suitland Road and Southern, Pennsylvania, and Alabama avenues. The first streets of Benning Heights appear on this map, but only about 25 structures had been built. Hundreds of acres surrounding it were still in the possession of about eight individuals. Indicative of the area's isolation from the rest of Washington, the new streets of Benning Heights were not the grid with diagonals inspired by L'Enfant and required by law west of the Anacostia. They were, rather, streets that curved

Above: A Benning Heights resident who was a mail carrier in the area in the late 1940s, when this picture of Ridge Road, S.E., was taken, remembers that "it was more like country out here . . . you could walk between houses and see nothing but woods." Courtesy, Columbia Historical Society

Left: Benning Heights was just beginning to develop in 1948 when this photograph was taken, just inside the District boundary with Maryland on 46th Street, S.E. Courtesy, Columbia Historical Society

and climbed with the hilly landscape, with dead ends and cul-de-sacs, a pattern more similar to twentieth-century suburban Maryland than to the planned District of Columbia. It was a pattern that would be typical of many of the twentieth-century developments of far-Southeast.

The Depression must have slowed developers' plans for the area. By 1936 there were still only about 50 structures on the streets of Benning Heights. This decade did see, however, the development of Fort Dupont as a public park—one of many created on sites that had served as Civil War fortifications, a citywide effort led by planners of the National Capital Park and Planning Commission. According to a 1927 real estate map, about 33 acres were donated for the park by Charles C. Glover, the prominent Washington banker and philanthropist who also gave the city large segments of what is now Glover-Archbold Park in Northwest Washington.

The Benning Heights community finally filled out in the 1940s, spurred by the return of prosperity, the new government jobs created by World War II, and the extreme housing shortage that resulted. The main burst of home building occurred between 1948 and 1952 and continued until 1960. In 1940, for example, there were no people at all living on 46th Place. By 1948 there were 34 occupied houses. Almost half of the owners listed in the city directory worked for the federal government; four were in the Army. The deeds of the new homes contained restrictive covenants excluding black residents; thus Benning Heights began as a totally white community.

The architecture of Benning Heights is typical of 1950s suburbs elsewhere: single-family, mostly one-story brick houses, often with garages or off-street parking and many of split-level design, with ample yards front and back. The homes on Easy Place and 46th Street, between Hilltop and Reed Terrace, are typical of the neighborhood. Twelve brick houses sat on these blocks amid vacant lots in the 1950s. James Ferguson, who grew up near the neighborhood and began delivering mail in Benning Heights in 1948, remembered there were still many open spaces at that time. "It was more like country out here . . . you could walk between houses and see nothing but woods." East Capitol Street had not yet been cut through. By 1960, however, most of the lots were filled.

Within about a decade of the construction of most of its houses, Benning Heights underwent a dramatic population shift, as racial barriers began to fall. In 1948 the Supreme Court ruled that restrictive housing covenants like those governing the first sale of Benning Heights houses were unconstitutional. The next year Cardinal Patrick O'Boyle called for the integration of all Catholic schools in the Washington Diocese, five years before the Supreme Court would hand down its historic ruling in *Brown v. Board of Education* in 1954. Benning Heights was not only immediately affected by these decisions; one of its schools, Sousa Junior High, played a significant national role in forcing the change.

On September 11, 1950, 12-year-old Spottswood T. Bolling, Jr., was one of 11 black children who were led by Gardner Bishop to the steps of the well-equipped and underenrolled new Sousa Junior High on the edge of Benning Heights and applied for admission to the all-white school. When they were denied entrance, Howard University law professor James M. Nabrit, Jr., filed a suit on Bolling's behalf against Melvin Sharpe, president of the D.C. board of education. In *Bolling v. Sharpe,* Nabrit argued that the burden was not on the plaintiff to show that schools were unequal, but rather on the District of Columbia to prove any reasonable purpose was served by the racial restrictions. Although a U.S. District judge threw the case out in 1951, the next year the Supreme Court invited Nabrit to bypass appeals in the lower courts and link his case with the *Brown v. Board of Education* suit of Topeka, Kansas. The May 17, 1954, unanimous decision of the Supreme Court that "separate educational facilities are inherently unequal" was thus a local as well as a national victory. Eight days later the D.C. board of education voted to integrate its schools the following fall, which, despite some protests from the Federation of Citizens' Associations and other groups, took place largely without incident.

The impact of these legal decisions on Benning Heights was swift. Interviews with residents who moved into the neighborhood in the 1950s indicate it was about 1956 that the dramatic change began to occur. One resident recalled she and her husband were unaware when they moved into the area, in January 1956, that they would be the only black family on the block. "When we saw the house, we liked it because it reminded me of home . . . I never thought about looking to see who the neighbors would be . . . As soon as we moved in, signs started sprouting . . . We still have one white neighbor . . . all the rest of the houses on the block, as far as I know, are black." Local residents remember that by 1960 the neighborhood had become almost a totally black community. The economic composition would remain the same, however—a mix of solid middle class, working class, and some very poor in the housing projects adjacent to the neighborhood on Ridge Road—except that after 1960 they were almost all black instead of all white.

The history of Our Lady Queen of Peace Parish, adjacent to Benning Heights at Ridge Road and Ely Place, reflects the growth and change of the community. It was one of many Southeast Catholic churches that sprang up as an offshoot of Saint Teresa of Avila Church, founded in 1878 in Old Anacostia. Between 1916 and 1960, Saint Teresa spawned nine churches, including Saint Francis Xavier in 1926, which in turn created the mission that would become Our Lady Queen of Peace in 1943.

The mission grew rapidly with the community in the 1940s, outgrowing temporary quarters in the City Bank building on Minnesota Avenue and moving to the Senator Theater for Sunday services to accommodate the large crowds. Father James H. Brooks became the church's first resident pastor in 1948 and built the mission into an independent parish. The church celebrated its first Mass in its unfinished new building on Christmas Eve in 1950 and dedicated the present finished structure in 1952. Its first confirmation class that year numbered 145 children. That same year the parish opened the doors of a new elementary school that enrolled 379 children; by 1957 enrollment had jumped to 604.

As the racial makeup of the community changed, so did that of the church and school, spurred by the desegregation of the Catholic schools in 1949. By the late 1950s the school was approximately 50 percent black. By the late 1980s school enrollment had reached 100 percent black; however, the congregation remains mixed, with a minority white membership of long-time local residents. The school draws its students from well beyond the neighborhood.

Benning Heights today is a stable middle-class community of homeowners. Many residents have lived there more than 15 years; some families, for two generations. For others, primarily young couples, the neighborhood has provided a first home; they tend to move on after 5 or 10 years. Though situated within blocks of streets that suffer from high crime rates and transient populations, Benning Heights has remained a quiet family neighborhood; "For Sale" signs are seldom seen, and property values have continued to rise.

Single-family houses dominate the neighborhood. Apartment buildings, however, cluster near its boundary lines along Benning Road, East Capitol Street, and Ridge Road. Made of brick and usually built as multiple low-rise structures with no more than five stories, they stretch for several blocks as large complexes, rather than

Young residents of the Benning Terrace housing project formed a club to pick up the litter around their apartment buildings in 1963. While single-family homes dominate Benning Heights, there are low-rise complexes of apartment buildings such as these, especially near the neighborhood's boundaries. Courtesy, Library of Congress, Prints and Photographs Division

Like millions of high-school seniors all over the country, the 1957 graduating class of Our Lady Queen of Peace School lined up for its official portrait. Father James H. Brooks, the priest to the left in the front row, became the first resident pastor in 1948 and built the mission into an independent parish with its own school. At Father Brooks' left is Father Twiddy. Courtesy, Our Lady Queen of Peace School

the single high-rise buildings found elsewhere in the city. Most were built without elevators. Unlike the trend in the rest of the city, only a few of these buildings have been converted to condominiums; almost all the residents are renters.

A few older homes dot the area as a reminder of its earlier, more rural days. For example, a rambling, mustard-yellow stucco house at the corner of Ridge Road and Alabama Avenue dates back to about 1915, when the very first few new homes were built in the area. It was then owned by E. Devine, a printer at the Government Printing Office.

Benning Heights in the 1980s is linked more closely to Maryland than to the District, due to transportation networks and the location of commercial areas. Indeed, until 1960 the orange/brown buses of Maryland's Department of Transportation, operating under the Washington Suburban Transit Commission, provided the only public transportation to central Washington. The Benning Metro stop, opened in 1980 on Benning Road, is well beyond easy walking distance for most residents. From the beginning the neighborhood has been oriented to the automobile and to shopping patterns that are more suburban than city. Except for a few clusters of stores on its Benning Road boundary, there are no shops and services in the Benning Heights neighborhood. On the other hand, Marlboro Pike in Prince George's County, just a five-minute ride away and in some places within only a several-minute walk across the District line, offers the closest grocery stores, gas stations, banks, and shopping malls. In addition, easy access to the 55-mile-per-hour section of Pennsylvania Avenue, called Pennsylvania Avenue Extended, or Route 4, by the locals, and to the Capital Beltway makes it possible to reach one of several enclosed Maryland shopping malls in less time than it takes to get downtown.

Activities in the neighborhood itself center on the family. There are no active neighborhood organizations, though a significant number of people in the area are associated with activities at Our Lady Queen of Peace church and school or at other churches nearby. Fort Dupont Park does function as a neighborhood center, often providing the setting for picnics and family reunions. The home, for most people, however, is the focus. As Benning Heights raises its third generation, it continues to strengthen as a stable residential community with a magnificent view of the capital and its monumental symbols across the river.

The atypical style and the location of this stucco house below street level mark it as one of the oldest dwellings in Benning Heights, built around 1915. It was occupied by an employee of the Government Printing Office at that time, long before the area was laid out in city streets. Photo by Maria Goodwin

BIENVENIDOS AL
III PROGRAMA DE
VERANO
CTRO. DE JUVENTUD/CTRO. DE ARTE

20

ADAMS MORGAN

NEW IDENTITY FOR AN OLD NEIGHBORHOOD

Olivia Cadaval

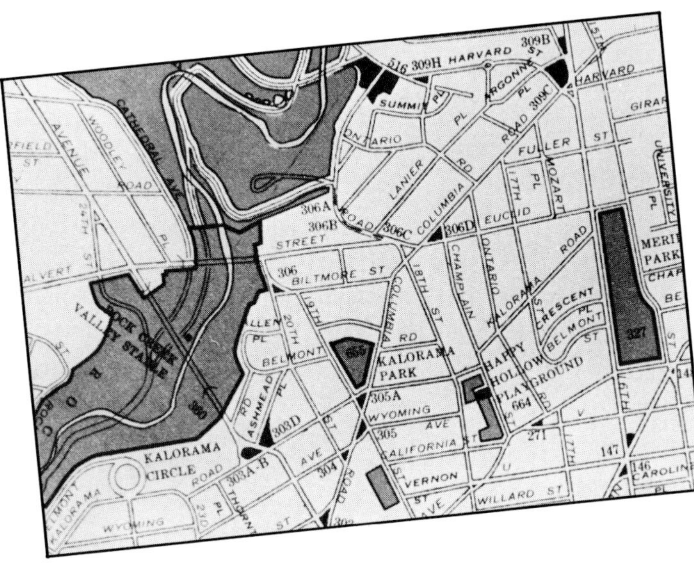

The annual Hispanic Festival in Adams Morgan began in 1970 with 21 makeshift booths and 15 floats. By the 1980s the parade and other festivities were drawing crowds of more than 150,000, the biggest community festival in the city. Photo by Rick Reinhard

Map: Park System of the National Capitol and Environs. National Park Service 1962. Courtesy, D.C. Public Library, Washingtoniana Division

Adams Morgan, today the capital's most multi-ethnic neighborhood, was one of the earliest desirable suburbs of Washington, D.C. Its attractions were country charm, the breeze from its location on the heights, and its proximity to the city. In the 1920s and 1930s it was considered an elite neighborhood. "It was a fine area. Fine people, fine houses. We had many friends who were prominent then or who became prominent later on," Joseph Rod, a resident for more than 35 years, remembered.

This image of homogeneous gentility prevails in the recollection of many of the neighborhood's older residents. In fact, it has always been a dynamic community populated by people of different backgrounds and aspirations. Today it is the most culturally and economically diverse neighborhood in Washington, a racially mixed community that is also the center of the city's growing Latino population. In 1984 the *Washington Post* described it as "a blend of rich and poor, black, brown and white, young and old—a vivid kaleidoscope of individuals and experiences constantly changing."

There are many stories to be told about this place. This chapter will focus, however, on the evolution of the Spanish-speaking community that has developed in the area since the 1960s. The term "Latino" rather than "Hispanic" is used throughout, as it is the name used by the community itself.

The hub of the neighborhood is the crossing of 18th Street and Columbia Road. On these two commercial streets Latino restaurants and stores, bearing the stamp of many Caribbean, Central American, and South American cultures, share the scene with African restaurants, fast-food stores, and a variety of other local shops and services. Though diverse, the place has a very strong identity and sense of community. In the 1960s and 1970s it had a reputation for being one of the most organized and community-conscious neighborhoods in the city. Today two of Washington's major street festivals are community-organized events in Adams Morgan—the Hispanic Heritage Festival, held annually in July, and Adams Morgan Day, held in September.

For a place with such a strong identity, it is remarkable that Adams Morgan's name and generally recognized boundaries are only 30 years old. They are products of a late 1950s community-organization effort to improve the area, and the boundaries overlay four nineteenth-century neighborhoods—Meridian Hill on the south, Lanier Heights on the north, and Washington Heights and Kalorama Heights. Geographically contiguous, these communities overlooked the city from the hills just above Boundary Street (now Florida Avenue). They were all considered fashionable neighborhoods in the nineteenth and early twentieth centuries due to their location on the heights, their proximity to elite Dupont Circle, and their fine houses and apartments. They all were served by the same genteel commercial area around 18th and Columbia Road. Their history has been briefly described in Jeffrey R. Henig's published study of the process of gentrification in today's Adams Morgan.

This young man makes his contribution to the scene on 18th Street near Columbia Road, N.W., the hub of neighborhood activity in Adams Morgan. Photo by Rick Reinhard

Perhaps the best-known resident of Meridian Hill, located west of 16th Street, was Mary Henderson, who spent decades promoting that street as the "Avenue of Presidents," as she preferred to call it. She and her husband, Senator John B. Henderson of Missouri, built a Victorian version of a medieval castle, known as Henderson Castle, at 16th and Boundary streets in 1888, where they held countless dinner parties and other social events. After her husband's death she built almost a dozen elaborate houses in the area between 1906 and 1910 and unsuccessfully offered one to the government as a home for Vice President Calvin Coolidge. There were people of poor and moderate incomes, black and white, in this area as well, but Mary Henderson's lavish life-style and bold plans for the area stamped it in the public perception as an elite place.

George Brown Goode, noted scientist and director of the National Museum of the Smithsonian, was central to the development of Lanier Heights, north of Columbia Road, as a fine residential neighborhood in the 1880s. He bought a large tract, had the first streets put in, and sold many lots to his friends who were part of his intellectual and social circle. Washington Heights, to the west of 18th Street, and Kalorama Heights, west of

Noted scientist George Brown Goode spurred the development of Lanier Heights just north of Columbia Road, N.W., where he built this elaborate house for his family and then sold adjacent lots to friends. Lanier Heights is now considered part of the Adams Morgan neighborhood. Courtesy, Smithsonian Institution

Above: Mary Henderson promoted 16th Street, N.W., as the "Avenue of the Presidents" from this elaborate medieval castle she built with her husband, Senator John B. Henderson of Missouri, at Florida Avenue and 16th Street at the foot of Meridan Hill. This photograph records the day of her funeral in 1931. Courtesy, D.C. Public Library, Washingtoniana Division

Columbia Road, were built up with substantial rowhouses in the early twentieth century. Some of the first prestige apartment buildings also began to rise in Washington Heights, Kalorama, and Lanier Heights in the first decades of the century, when this style of urban living began to be popular in the city. Fine examples of these buildings remain today, such as the Wyoming on Columbia Road and the Ontario on Ontario Place. Kalorama Heights is today known as Kalorama Triangle, and its history is included in the Kalorama chapter of this book, since that neighborhood, as well as Adams Morgan, claims the section as its own.

By the 1920s the entire area had entered into what Jeffrey Henig has termed its "white glove era." The elegant Knickerbocker Theater, which opened at 18th Street and Columbia Road in 1917, and the fashionable caterer Avignon Freres, which arrived on Columbia Road the next year, were both representative of this section's social elan.

The area began to change during World War II, when a citywide housing shortage caused many larger residences in Adams Morgan and elsewhere to be transformed into rooming houses. Henig has pointed out that in some neighborhoods in this period citizens sought zoning changes to prevent uncontrolled increases in density and commercial development, but in Adams Morgan existing zoning went unchallenged and actually encouraged change. Change accelerated in the late 1940s and early 1950s, when many white families chose to move from the city to new homes in the suburbs, a shift spurred by Supreme Court rulings striking down housing covenants in 1948 and segregated schools in 1954.

By the 1950s the prices and rents

of the elegant old apartments and rowhouses were within reach of a less affluent group. Good prices and the convenient location of these old neighborhoods began to attract a new and younger population. A mixture of working-class people and young middle-class intellectuals, some of whom came to be at the forefront of the political movements of the 1960s, moved into the area and changed its social character. City council member Frank Smith later remembered that Adams Morgan at that time was "the home of most of the communes and collectives and freedom houses in Washington."

These old neighborhoods did not consciously identify as one community until the late 1950s, when the general physical decline of the area, the new federal government interest in urban renewal, and the integration of schools stimulated community action and coalesced the several neighborhoods into what is now officially

Left: Crowds gather on Columbia Road, N.W., to view the wreckage of the Knickerbocker Theater at the right where the roof collapsed during a heavy snowstorm in January 1922, killing 96 people. Courtesy, Library of Congress

Below left: The elegance of the reclaimed lobby of the Ambassador Theater at 18th and Columbia Road, N.W., reflects the nature of its clientele in the 1920s. As the Knickerbocker Theater, it had been the scene of one of the city's greatest tragedies. Courtesy, D.C. Public Library, Washingtoniana Division

known as Adams Morgan. Local activists fought for community control of neighborhood schools, first in the black Morgan School and then in the predominantly white Adams School. In 1958 the principals of the two schools were instrumental in organizing the Adams Morgan Better Neighborhood Conference, which brought together residents and representatives of local organizations to plan neighborhood improvement. In the same year, the Adams Morgan Community Council was formed. It cut across previous racially and economically drawn boundaries by bringing together different neighborhood organizations. The Community Council boundaries extended to New Hampshire Avenue and R Street on the south, 16th Street on the east, Harvard Street on the north, and Connecticut Avenue and Rock Creek on the west, encompassing all or portions of the four nineteenth-century neighborhoods previously described, creating the generally accepted boundaries of today's Adams Morgan.

Meanwhile, the old businesses along Columbia Road that had catered to a more fashionable clientele in the 1920s and 1930s began to decline. The riot of 1968, when a number of local stores were looted and smashed, was the final blow for many, and such businesses as Gartenhouse Furs and Ridgewell Caterers that had once anchored the elite shopping streets moved away.

The 1960s also saw a further addition to the mosaic of races and cultures that is Adams Morgan today—the influx of thousands of Spanish-speaking people from Central America, South America, and the Caribbean. The increase had begun to be noticeable in the 1950s. Though an accurate census of this community has always been difficult, the 1970 federal census numbered the Latino population in the District of Columbia at 17,561. The Office of Latino Affairs estimates that there are at least 85,000 today. In the greater Washington area there are approximately 250,000 Latinos. The Spanish language is the common bond that links their diverse cultures into what has come to be known as the Latino community.

Washington always had a small Spanish-speaking population; it grew along with the rest of the city in the twentieth century as Washington increasingly became a world capital as well as a national one. Members of the Spanish-speaking embassies and world organizations, professional staff members as well as domestic workers, took up residence in Adams Morgan, which is convenient to many embassies situated around 16th Street and Massachusetts Avenue just to the west. Many of the domestic workers stayed after diplomatic tours of duty ended or after their host families left the city, settling in the area and encouraging family and friends from home to join them. Latin-American students in area universities were another significant segment of the growing Spanish-speaking population. White-collar Mexican Americans began to come to the area in great numbers following the increase of federal jobs that started with the New Deal and continued through World War II. In the main, however, the students and the Mexican American professionals maintained themselves separate from the nascent Latino community.

In the 1960s the Spanish-speaking population began to grow rapidly. The economic hardship and political turmoil in Latin America, combined with the attraction of an alluring image of the United States, created a flow of legal and illegal immigration to this country. Adams Morgan became a magnet, since an earlier Spanish-speaking population had already begun to settle there. As a 1968 article in the *Washingtonian* put it, "Once a nationality establishes a bridgehead in Washington, the community grows." In this article a Cuban lawyer, Luis Rumbaud, described the typical process. "The first person to arrive here from a given village sends his address back home, and he's the first stop when the next person arrives," Rumbaud wrote. "One shabby apartment building just north of Ontario and Columbia Roads is a de facto recreation of a small village in the Zacapa province of Guatemala."

Cubans came in the greatest number in the late fifties and early sixties, and between the sixties and seventies there was a sizable flow of South Americans. But the largest migrations have been in the eighties—a result of the growing Central American conflicts.

In the early 1960s there was no sense of community. Many Latinos were embassy employees, mainly women, who were discouraged from going out into the streets that were described to them as dangerous. Casilda Luna, a Dominican who came in 1961 as a domestic worker for a general, seldom went out during her first year in Washington. When she did, she managed to find a few people who spoke her language.

The only store . . . that sold Latino produce that I could find was an Italian store on Columbia Road . . . at the Sacred Heart of Jesus Church there was a Latino priest and he helped us with English there. The majority of the persons that went through there were women employees of the embassies. We would get together and speak the language. We were from different countries

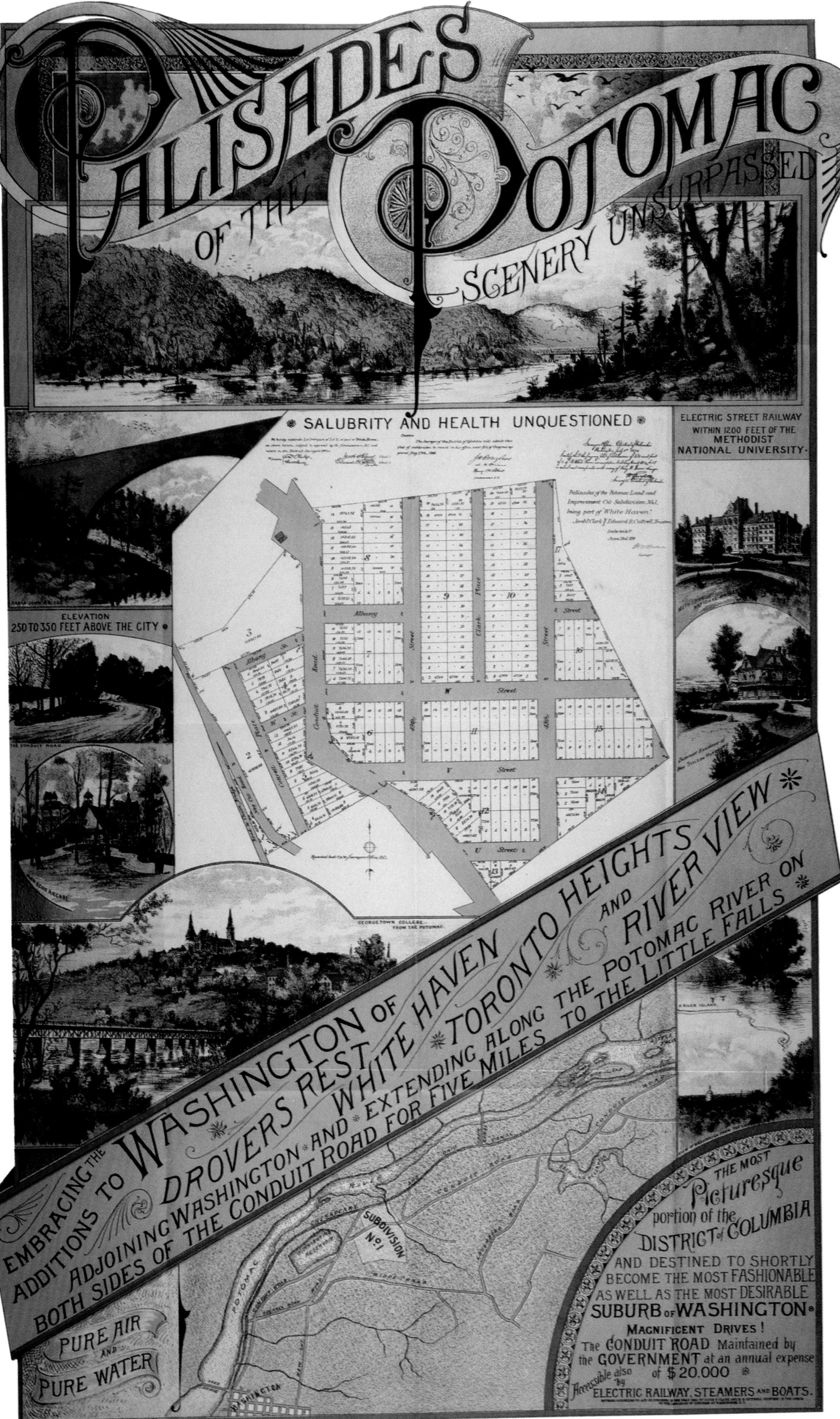
PALISADES OF THE POTOMAC
SCENERY UNSURPASSED
SALUBRITY AND HEALTH UNQUESTIONED
ELECTRIC STREET RAILWAY WITHIN 1200 FEET OF THE METHODIST NATIONAL UNIVERSITY
ELEVATION 250 TO 350 FEET ABOVE THE CITY
GEORGETOWN COLLEGE FROM THE POTOMAC
EMBRACING THE ADDITIONS TO WASHINGTON OF DROVERS REST WHITE HAVEN TORONTO HEIGHTS AND RIVER VIEW
ADJOINING WASHINGTON AND EXTENDING ALONG THE POTOMAC RIVER ON BOTH SIDES OF THE CONDUIT ROAD FOR FIVE MILES TO THE LITTLE FALLS
SUBDIVISION No 1
PURE AIR AND PURE WATER
THE MOST Picturesque portion of the DISTRICT of COLUMBIA
AND DESTINED TO SHORTLY BECOME THE MOST FASHIONABLE AS WELL AS THE MOST DESIRABLE SUBURB OF WASHINGTON
MAGNIFICENT DRIVES!
The CONDUIT ROAD Maintained by the GOVERNMENT at an annual expense of $20.000
Accessible also by ELECTRIC RAILWAY, STEAMERS AND BOATS.

Left: Lincoln Hospital, one of many military facilities built quickly throughout Washington during the Civil War, spread out on the broad flat top of Capitol Hill near present-day Lincoln Park. Courtesy, Columbia Historical Society

Previous page: All aspects of the nineteenth-century suburban ideal are summed up in this promotional piece. The development of the Palisades was made possible by the construction of Conduit Road (now MacArthur Boulevard, N.W.) along the route of the city's water main from Great Falls, as well as by an electric streetcar route along the Potomac that began in the 1890s. Courtesy, American Antiquarian Society

The benefits of suburban life in Washington's beautiful tree-shaded homes within easy reach of central Washington are celebrated in a 1910 promotional-booklet cover. This area is Cleveland Park today. Courtesy, D.C. Public Library, Washingtoniana Division

Georgetown, seen here in the 1840s, began as a tobacco trading port a century earlier. It was an established town of about 3,000 people when it was absorbed by the new District of Columbia in 1791. Courtesy, The Kiplinger Washington Collection

The elaborate entrance hall of the 1890s house of German brewer Christian Heurich exemplifies the grandeur of Dupont Circle's late nineteenth-century mansions. Heurich's home is now a house museum and the headquarters of the Columbia Historical Society, the local historical society of Washington, D.C. Courtesy, Columbia Historical Society

Above: The thriving Christian Heurich Brewery in Foggy Bottom produced this engaging advertising poster in 1890. Foggy Bottom was one of the capital's few industrial, working-class neighborhoods until new developments of the 1950s and 1960s changed its character. The Kennedy Center stands near this site today. Courtesy, The Olde Heurich Brewing Company

Left: The historic streetscapes of Georgetown are protected by the provisions of the Old Georgetown Act, passed by Congress in 1950 at the urging of local preservationists. Photo by Marvin Ickow

Above: Victorian brick row houses built just after the Civil War line this section of East Capitol Street on Capitol Hill. The restoration of old buildings on the Hill began shortly after World War II, making it one of the first Washington neighborhoods to recognize and protect its architectural heritage. Photo by Emily Medvec

Right: Abandoned rails in the old stone pavement of P Street, N.W., remind modern motorists of Georgetown's earlier days when it was the hub of a network of electric streetcar lines. Photo by Emily Medvec

Below: Logan Circle in Shaw is the only original L'Enfant Plan circle to survive as a residential area. Its Victorian town houses were built after Alexander "Boss" Shepherd brought city amenities to the circle in the 1870s. Photo by Marvin Ickow

In 1906 when this Cleveland Park house was built, the Classical Revival style of architecture, popular all over Washington at the time, had replaced the informal and romantic cottage style that marked the first houses in the neighborhood. Photo by Kathleen Sinclair Wood

Right: Shepherd Park's serenity shows in this autumnal scene as the school bus discharges its passengers. Situated near the northern point of the District, Shepherd Park is one of the city's most successfully intergrated neighborhoods. Photo by Emily Medvec.

Below: This panoramic view of the city from the hills of far Southeast offers a perspective not often seen by those who live west of the Anacostia river. Photo by Emily Medvec

Grande dame of Washington hostelries, the Willard Hotel at 14th and Pennsylvania Avenue, N.W., has been restored to its turn-of-the-century elegance. Designed by New York hotel architect Henry J. Hardenbergh in 1901, it stands on the site of a pre-Civil War Willard's Hotel, the scene of many important events in the nineteenth-century capital. Photo by Marvin Ickow

The Watergate Hotel dominates the Potomac River waterfront in the Foggy Bottom district of Washington, D.C. Photo by Emily Medvec

The fanciful Italianate Sumner School building at 17th and N streets, N.W., housed the first black high school in the city. Winner of several national preservation awards, the structure now serves as the archives of the D.C. Public Schools as well as a community center. Photo by Bill Rice

Above: *Georgetown is a social center of the city. Along Wisconsin Avenue, N.W., family businesses that existed for generations have given way to antique shops, clothing boutiques, restaurants and bars. Photo by Emily Medvec*

Right: Washington's local government, headquartered in the District Building at 14th and Pennsylvania Avenue, N.W., was appointed by the president of the United States until 1974, when Home Rule was reinstated after a hiatus of over 100 years. Photo by Bill Rice

Left: The commercial center of Brookland, 12th Street, N.E., retains much of its original architectural character. Most of its buildings were built between World War I and the early 1930s by developers who lived and worked in the neighborhood. Photo by Emily Medvec

Below: A gift of the People's Republic of China, this ornate arch across H Street, N.W., in Chinatown is a result of Washington, D.C.'s, new relationship with Beijing as its "sister city." Photo by Emily Medvec

Right: More than 100,000 water plants, including some of the most rare and colorful water lilies known, are on display in the Kenilworth Aquatic Gardens along the Anacostia River in far-Northeast Washington. W.B. Shaw, a government clerk, began the collection in the 1880s. Photo by Emily Medvec

Below: These aquatic plants thrive at the National Arboretum, which was established in 1927 on 444 rolling acres in Northeast Washington. The Department of Agriculture-managed retreat also includes the National Bonsai Collection, the National Herb Garden, and extensive species of trees and shrubs. Photo by Emily Medvec

Above: This fisherman tends two lines at Hains Point across the Washington Channel from Southwest, one of many popular spots for local anglers along the Potomac River. Photo by Emily Medvec

Left: The Georgetown waterfront was one of the city's few industrial areas until its redevelopment in the 1970s and 1980s. Photo by Emily Medvec

Right: *A fishmonger displays his fresh catch at the riverside fish market in Southwest. Photo by Marvin Ickow*

Below right: *Morgan's fish market on the Southwest waterfront sells the fresh harvest from Chesapeake Bay every day. Photo by Emily Medvec*

Arlington Memorial Bridge spans the Potomac from the Lincoln Memorial to Arlington National Cemetery. First proposed after the Civil War, this symbol of the unified North and South was not completed until 1932. Photos by Marvin Ickow

Right: D.C. Mayor Marion Barry celebrates the 1987 Hispanic Festival in Adams Morgan with the organizer of the festival parade, Vilma Williams. The annual event attracts over 150,000 Washingtonians. Courtesy, Eduardo Lopez, Office of Latino Affairs

Below: This 1920s watertower at Fort Reno in Tenleytown reflects the site's military role during the Civil War. Today a park adjacent to Alice Deal Junior High School, the area is the scene of contests of a friendlier kind. Photo by Emily Medvec

Above: The Capitol Hill Arts Workshop sponsored this pageant put on by neighborhood children outside the Marine Barracks on 8th Street, S.E. Founded in 1972, this neighborhood arts center offers dance, drama, art, and music classes for children and adults in a former elementary-school building at 7th and G streets, S.E. Courtesy, Capitol Hill Arts Workshop

Left: A float created by Guatemalans and a Panamanian stilt-walker parade down Mount Pleasant Street, N.W., during the 1985 Hispanic Festival. The annual event began in 1970 and now attracts crowds of more than 150,000, making it the oldest and biggest community festival in Washington. Photo by R.H. Quintanilla

Right: Dexter Manley of the Washington Redskins celebrates following the Superbowl XXII victory on January 31, 1988. Photo by Scott Cunningham. Courtesy, NFL Photos

Below: Redskins running back George Rogers (38) turns upfield behind the blocking of the Redskins offensive line, affectionately known as the Hogs. Redskins tickets consistently sell out. Courtesy, Washington Redskins

but we felt so happy because we could speak Spanish.

Language and food became basic organizing forces. In the heart of what was to become the Latino neighborhood of Adams Morgan and in neighboring Mount Pleasant, family stores began to open. The first to open in the 1950s was the Sevillana on 18th Street. In 1962 Casa Dilone opened on Mount Pleasant Street. Casa Lebrato, El Gavilan, and La Americana followed on Columbia Road. Traditionally the mom-and-pop grocery store has dealt with more than consumable products. As in many other communities, it also has been the hub of social interaction. As Gerald Suttles wrote in his study of Chicago communities, "Most business establishments are not just a way of making a living but also of enjoying an enduring set of social relations where money is only one of the tokens that change hands."

Within this setting the concept of "Latino" began acquiring a special meaning for the Spanish-speaking people coming together in this area. Into these stores a unique mix of people, sharing a common language yet representing different cultures of the Caribbean and later South America and Central America, would come seeking familiar foods. They would often find that they were all facing similar problems with language, housing, and employment. In these stores a sense of solidarity began to emerge.

Besides the stores, the churches and a movie theater were also meeting places for the Latinos. In the sixties the most significant events were the Saturday-night dances at Saint Stephen's and the Incarnation Church on Newton Street and films shown at the Colony Theater on Georgia Avenue.

Carlos Rosario, who became a key figure in the organization of a self-conscious community, established the first Latino theater program in 1962 at the Colony Theater. "I had visualized how the community was growing," he reminisced. He used the weekly theater programs to help people find jobs and housing. "I always announced: any person who is looking for a job call me, and I would help them. And there were people who wanted to bring others into the country but they had to have an assured place here and I'd help them . . . This is how the community began to grow, overnight it grew."

The Colony Theater became a source of companionship and information. Films in Spanish and announcements about events in the area, available jobs, and places to go for assistance drew crowds. These get-togethers and the dances at Saint Stephen's Church provided the basis for the later development of more-formal social and political leadership.

By the late 1960s community leaders had begun to use bureaucratic

Latino grocery stores provided the first social centers for the Spanish-speaking community. Typical was this Dominican store, La de Tedos, in Mount Pleasant. Photo by Rick Reinhard

mechanisms to obtain government funds for the community. While people from Puerto Rico were in the minority in the community, it was they who produced most of the leaders. Puerto Ricans were already American citizens and did not have to worry about the immigration officials, who at that time were busy raiding local businesses and restaurants in search of undocumented workers. In addition, they had steady jobs, were somewhat familiar with the American system, and spoke English. The new political awareness of the community coincided with and was encouraged by many new government programs, such as the United Planning Organization, created by the U.S. Office of Economic Opportunity. Help also began to come from the city government's Department of Human Resources.

The first funds for social services were received in 1966 through the Barney Community House, a black social service organization (originally founded as a settlement house in Southwest, it had been forced by urban renewal to relocate in 1960 to Mount Pleasant, just north of Adams Morgan). Then in 1968 a Presbyterian minister from Colombia, the Reverend Antonio Welty, established a Latino congregation, *La Iglesia Presbyteriana Buen Pastor,* in the education building of the Central Presbyterian Church at 15th and Irving streets. This was once a large Presbyterian congregation, which at one time counted President Woodrow Wilson among its members, but many had left as the neighborhood changed. Welty was sensitive to the tensions between the different national groups of Latinos that had settled in Adams Morgan, but he also recognized the potential for community collaboration. He organized eight o'clock breakfasts at the church so that people could discuss their problems and differences. Later, Welty founded a Latino social service agency at this site, calling it the Wilson Center. The center, although just beyond the Adams Morgan boundary, became a "lighthouse" for the Spanish-speaking community.

Carlos Rosario, often referred to as "the Old Man" or "the Godfather" in the community, was instrumental in the formation of the D.C. Office of Latino Affairs, which was first established in 1969 as the Office of Spanish-Speaking Affairs. Born in Ciales, Puerto Rico, Rosario served in the Army during World War II and came to the United States in 1950, going to work for the Department of Health, Education and Welfare in Montana. In 1957 he was transferred to Washington, D.C. Rosario was central in getting the local government to recognize the Latino community. In an interview in 1981 he recalled the way he and a group of other local residents began to "make noise" to let the city government know the needs and frustrations of the community. A letter in 1967 to the newly appointed mayor, Walter Washington, resulted in a telegram from him: "Rosario, I want to meet with you." Rosario's group decided to ask for an office of Latino affairs. "Well, promises as usual," Rosario remembered. "The only thing that came out of that was that he named me to the board of the Office of Human Rights."

The group continued to press the newly appointed city council. A meeting with senators Robert Kennedy, Joseph Tydings, and Maryland governor Marvin Mandel was pivotal. "Tremendous luck," Rosario recalled. "They asked us did we want them to write the mayor." The mayor responded again with a call and said he would talk with the council. "If that is what you want, you get it," he said.

As the newly political and culturally self-conscious community took shape, its presence became known to the city at large through the annual Hispanic Heritage Festival, which was first celebrated in 1970. Casilda Luna remembered that she and several others ran a dance and charged one dollar for admission to finance the first effort. The first event, including 21 makeshift booths and 15 floats, drew 10,000 people. By the mid-1980s the festival had become the biggest and oldest community festival in the city, drawing crowds of more than 150,000. The event is a recognized institution whose development has paralleled that of the community.

In the mid-1970s new styles of leadership and cultural differences surfaced with each wave of immigrants from South America and Central America, many of whom left their countries for political reasons. According to Arturo Griffiths, a Panamanian who came to the area in the 1960s, many of the South Americans came from middle-class backgrounds, which contrasted with the majority of the earlier immigrants. "South Americans are different," he said. "They are not the poor, the worker, but they want to organize the poor."

In 1975 several South Americans with other community members organized the first community cultural center, *El Centro del Arte.* This young group of artists began to depict the struggles and experiences of the Latino community in large murals on building walls in the neighborhood. They saw the murals as being for and about the people. Carlos Salazar, originally from Chile, designed one of the first murals on a wall behind a bank on Columbia Road. The mural includes a group of people presented almost as one figure, "trying to show people are one . . . trying to show unity," Salazar said. "It shows the cultural aspects of the Latino community—their music, their dances." The mural also depicts a group of developers, "playing with houses, playing with money. They are speculating with neighborhoods," he continued.

The threat to the community from growing real estate interest in Adams Morgan that Salazar saw in the 1970s has intensified in the 1980s. The cost of housing is rising as the well-to-do begin to consider the area desirable once again. As the Latino community has become larger and more established, it is concerned about its future in Adams Morgan.

The community has also become more complex. According to *Migration World* magazine, it has the second-largest Salvadoran immigrant population in the United States. The growing numbers and diversity of population present new challenges to the community. Nevertheless, Latinos have created their space within the neighborhood, and, although many move away to growing Latino neighborhoods in suburban Maryland and Virginia, they continue to identify with Adams Morgan and with Columbia Road, the heart of the community.

The fine nineteenth century brick row houses of 18th Street, N.W., provide the backdrop for the social activity at the playground of the Marie Reed Learning Center. Photo by Rick Reinhard

21

SHEPHERD PARK

CREATING AN INTEGRATED COMMUNITY

Marvin Caplan

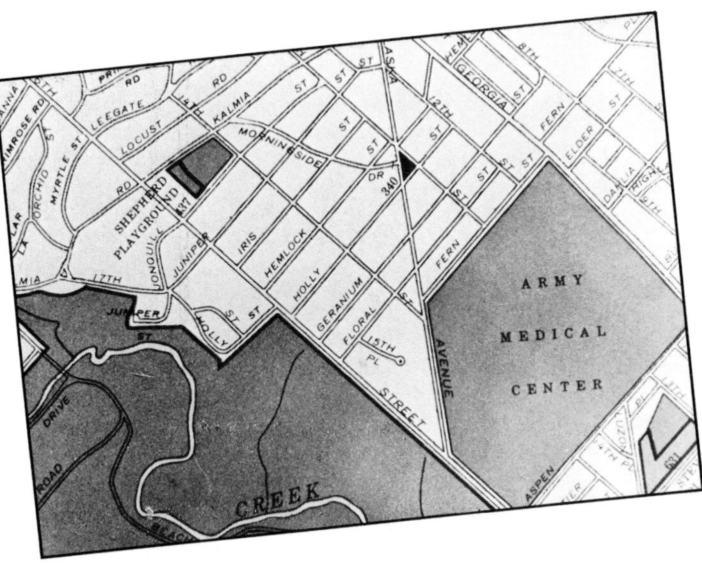

The Shepherd Park neighborhood takes its name from one of the most colorful figures in Washington history, Alexander Shepherd, territorial governor of the District in the early 1870s. His bearing in this portrait suggests the power that inspired his familiar nickname, "Boss" Shepherd. Courtesy, Columbia Historical Society

Map: Park System of the National Capitol and Environs. National Park Service 1962. Courtesy, D.C. Public Library, Washingtoniana Division

Shepherd Park, a serene and verdant neighborhood in the northernmost tip of the District, is notable in Washington's history as a battleground. In 1864, when it was woodland and rolling farm field, Confederate soldiers under Major General Jubal A. Early were engaged here as they mounted an attack on nearby Fort Stevens. Almost 100 years later residents of the area found themselves engaged in a civil war of their own. Confronted by the race-exploiting tactics of a troop of real estate speculators, they fought back with such success that the present-day head of the citizens' association, a black woman, says she moved in because she considered it as "the only integrated middle-class neighborhood in Washington."

The area derived its pastoral-sounding name from Alexander Robey Shepherd, governor of the Territory of the District of Columbia from 1873 to 1874 and one of the city's ablest and most powerful politicians. In 1868 he bought a tract of land off the 7th Street Turnpike (now Georgia Avenue) and built a large summer home that he and his wife called Bleak House, after the Dickens novel they were reading with great enthusiasm at the time.

A handsome, gleaming-white, three-story Victorian structure at 7714 13th Street is known to many Shepherd Park residents today as "the Shepherd Mansion." But that is a misnomer, since the Shepherd house that once stood near 14th and Geranium streets was torn down in 1916. The house on 13th Street is most likely Pomona, the pre-Civil War summer home of Darius Clagett, a prosperous dry goods merchant who operated "the largest and handsomest store on Pennsylvania Avenue," according to the November 3, 1837, *National Intelligencer.*

For many years the area was given over to large farms and the summer estates of wealthy Washingtonians who

Above: The fanciful summer home of Alexander Shepherd that once stood near 14th and Geranium streets, N.W., was incongruously called "Bleak House," after the Charles Dickens novel. Built in the late 1860s, the house stood in the rural area that would become Shepherd Park until it was razed in 1916. Courtesy, Columbia Historical Society

The pre-Civil War summer home of early Washington merchant Darius Clagett awaits these visitors on a Shepherd Park house tour in the 1960s. Courtesy, Neighbors, Inc.

sought its wooded hilltops to escape the muggy downtown heat. Then, in 1909 Shepherd Park acquired its first major institution when Congress appropriated $300,000 to enable the Army to purchase land and build the hospital that eventually became Walter Reed Army Medical Center at 16th Street and Alaska Avenue. It was named for the noted sanitarian and bacteriologist who discovered the cure for yellow fever.

About the same time Walter Reed was taking root, land developers discovered the neighborhood. A large part of the Shepherd estate was sold to an investment company in 1911. The contours of new streets appear on a real estate map for that year, many of them bearing the names of trees and flowers, one of Shepherd Park's distinctive features. Bleak House was razed in 1916 to make room for the construction of new houses in styles that set the pattern for the neighborhood we see today: spacious Colonial and Tudor houses of red brick, stone, or stucco, set among old shade trees and azalea bushes on broad sweeps of lawn. At the outset there was little mass development. The three builders most active in the area built to order or sold building lots.

The original Shepherd Park residents shared more than middle-class affluence. They were also white Anglo-Saxon and Protestant. And the builders, who were of that group themselves, meant to keep it that way. Almost all the deeds contained restrictive covenants designed to keep out "any negro or colored person or person of negro blood extraction," Jews, and other Semitic people.

Indicative of Shepherd Park's early character was its first church, Northminster Presbyterian, still the neighborhood's largest. The result of

a 1906 merger of two old central-city congregations, Assembly Presbyterian and North Presbyterian, Northminster followed its congregants from downtown to the suburbs. In 1926 the church established a chapel at the corner of Kalmia and Alaska, on land it bought from one of the neighborhood's largest builders, L.E. Breuninger and Sons. When its city church burned down in 1935, the congregation decided to rebuild on the chapel grounds. The citizens' association contributed to the church's building fund, and a door-to-door solicitation in the neighborhood produced sizable contributions from residents who weren't even members—perhaps further evidence of the community's homogeneity.

From the first the area was fortunate to have residents who were energetic, civic minded, and influential. In 1917 when there were more jackrabbits than homeowners, they formed a

Left: Shepherd Park's first church, Northminster Presbyterian, followed its congregation from downtown to the suburbs in 1926. Photo by Kathryn Smith

Below: Shepherd Park Elementary School children celebrated Flag Day on June 15, 1932, just six months after their new school opened at 14th Street and Kalmia Road. The neighborhood was only about 20 years old; residential construction can be seen in the background on Kalmia Road. Courtesy, Summer School Archives

Shepherd Park in the 1920s had the appearance of a new subdivision, with newly paved streets and young trees as seen in this view of 13th and Holly streets, N.W. The house at the center is on Alaska Avenue. Courtesy, Columbia Historical Society

citizens' association. High on the agenda were such projects as the extension and paving of 16th Street from Alaska Avenue to the District line and persuading the District to build an elementary school to educate neighborhood children as well as attract more families to Shepherd Park. After more than a decade of importunings, the school board responded to petitions from parents of 143 children and agreed to provide a school. But, school in 1928 consisted of two wooden, one-room portables parked near Kalmia Road on the farmland that the association had recommended for a building site. It took another four years, but finally the red-brick Alexander R. Shepherd Elementary School opened in January 1932. The descendants of Governor Shepherd—a daughter, a son, and a grandson—helped dedicate the school and unveiled a photographic portrait of its namesake. Shepherd continues to be one of the most highly regarded elementary schools in the District system.

By coincidence, the area's other major educational institution also opened in 1928: Marjorie Webster Junior College for women. Named for its founder, the college moved to 17th Street and Kalmia Road after outgrowing its rowhouse home on Thomas Circle where it had begun in 1920. The college's new complex of Spanish mission-style buildings spread dramatically across the highest ridge of 10 acres of farmland. Essentially a family enterprise involving Marjorie Webster, her brother, her sister-in-law, and two nephews, the school had begun with 23 students. In its new plant, which contained a gymnasium, swimming pool, and dormitory, the enrollment grew to slightly more than 500 by 1966, some three years after its founder's death. At that time and throughout its 51-year history, the school's upper-middle-class students came mostly from out of town. They were not, a teacher once observed, "the rebellious type." The

school closed in 1971. It is now the northwest campus of Gallaudet University, Washington's internationally known school for the deaf.

The Marjorie Webster Register for 1929-1930 gives the college's address as Rock Creek Park Estates, suggesting a confusion about Shepherd Park's boundaries that exists even today. During Shepherd Park's earliest phases, the "Estates" was one of the area's three major subdivisions. The other two were Shepherd Park (L.E. Breuninger's name for his development) and Sixteenth Street Heights. When they first organized, in 1917, the residents called themselves the Sixteenth Street Heights Citizens' Association. They did not become the Shepherd Park Citizens' Association until sometime in the 1940s, when one of their members, retired Superintendent of Police Ernest W. Brown, noted how easy it was to confuse them with Sixteenth Street Highlands, an area immediately to the south.

Today the citizens' association says Shepherd Park lies north of Aspen Street (Walter Reed's southern boundary) to the District line at Eastern Avenue and west of Georgia Avenue to Rock Creek Park. These are the boundaries of Shepherd Elementary School and Census Tract 16, a neighborhood of some 80 squares and, according to the 1980 census, 5,101 people. These boundaries, however, include two well-defined enclaves that lie west of 16th Street, Colonial Village and North Portal Estates. Most of the people living there insist they are not part of Shepherd Park.

Both enclaves were developed after much of Shepherd Park was al ready established. Begun in 1931, Colonial Village's theme was Colonial America. The 80 houses designed for the development included reproductions of such famous Colonial structures as Washington's boyhood home, his headquarters at Valley Forge, and the Yorktown house in which Lord Cornwallis signed the articles of surrender. The houses were expensive and the village exclusive: restrictive covenants barred "negroes . . . Armenians, Jews, Hebrews, Persians, and Syrians."

North Portal Estates was the work of Jewish developers who undertook most of their building in the wake of the 1948 Supreme Court decision invalidating racially restrictive covenants. The 220 houses that were eventually built there were larger, showier, and more contemporary than the older homes in Shepherd Park, and they became a haven for wealthy Jewish families.

In the early 1940s, before the development of North Portal Estates, and often despite restrictive covenants, Jews began to move into Shepherd Park. The wealthy German Jews of an earlier immigrant generation had tended to settle west of Rock Creek in Forest Hills, which was free of covenants, and in other pockets of open housing in that far-northwestern section of the city. The Jews of eastern European extraction followed a different pattern, beginning early in the century to move straight northward from Southwest and downtown along the 7th and 14th street corridors.

At first the shopkeepers among them frequently lived with their families over the store, as did shopkeepers of all kinds, including Yankee businessman Darius Clagett, who lived above his first emporium in Georgetown. As their wealth and standing improved, these Jews moved north into Petworth and Brightwood and conducted business elsewhere. With their strong familial and religious commitment, the Jews tended to move in communities so that synagogues, delicatessens, kosher butcher shops, and bakeries moved with them. Shepherd Park, located just north of Brightwood and boasting a newer housing stock, was a logical next step in this northward migration. As Jews moved in, non-Jews moved out. By 1964, according to the estimate of a pastor of Northminster Church, the Reverend Roland W. Anderson, the parish—largely Shepherd Park—had become about 80 percent Jewish.

Georgia Avenue, the area's one shopping district, began to reflect its new clientele. From 1947 to sometime in the late 1950s, four kosher meat markets, a Jewish bakery, and Posin's, the first Jewish supermarket, opened on the stretch of avenue that borders Brightwood and Shepherd Park. Hofberg's, one of the District's major delicatessens, established itself near the corner of Georgia and Eastern avenues. In 1957 a Conservative synagogue was dedicated on 16th Street and an Orthodox synagogue came to Eastern Avenue, and in 1960 another Orthodox synagogue moved to a corner of 16th Street, diagonally opposite the Conservative congregation. Soon Jews assumed positions of leadership in the citizens' association and the Shepherd Elementary PTA.

A few years later Shepherd Park underwent still another profound change: black families began moving into the neighborhood. The housing market for Washington's middle-class black families in the two decades following World War II was even more limited than it was for Jews. Notwithstanding the Supreme Court's 1948 nullification of discriminatory covenants, the practice of denying housing to blacks still prevailed. No fair-housing law protected their rights. The burgeoning subdivisions of the suburbs—

Levitt and Sons' huge Belair development in Bowie, Maryland, for instance—were explicitly shut to them. By tacit agreement most real estate agents sought to keep the neighborhoods west of Rock Creek Park exclusively for whites; black homeseekers were directed to areas east of the Park, where they were often the prey of real estate speculators who frequently overcharged them while at the same time placing them in hostile situations in unwelcoming neighborhoods. Such housing segregation was reinforced by the District's three newspapers, which permitted the use of racial designations in classified housing ads and thus facilitated the exclusion and "steering" of blacks. Civic-group protests and congressional pressure persuaded the papers to discontinue the practice in 1960.

Even so, the speculators were still able to exploit the situation. Their general tactic was to move a black family onto an all-white block and then harass the white homeowners into selling their homes, warning them that property values would fall now that blacks were moving in. In the ensuing panic, that warning became a self-fulfilling prophecy. The sudden dumping of a large number of houses onto the market did bring the prices down—at least for the frightened whites who sold and fled to the suburbs. The speculators then re-sold the houses at inflated prices to blacks long hungry for decent places to live. Petworth and Brightwood and Manor Park, neighborhoods of relatively modest homes south of Shepherd Park, underwent these agonizing upheavals.

In 1958 a group of black and white homeowners in Manor Park determined to take a stand. Unable to persuade the area's established citizens' association to amend its bylaws and accept black residents into membership, they formed a new, racially integrated organization, Neighbors, Incorporated. With a $10,000 grant from the Eugene and Agnes Meyer Foundation, they undertook a two-front program: to fight the speculators and to bring white and black families together in a genuinely integrated community. In 1959, warned by salesmen friendly to their efforts that the blockbusters' next targets were Shepherd Park and Takoma, D.C., Neighbors, Inc., quickly extended its operations into those neighborhoods.

Shepherd Park was generally cordial to the efforts of Neighbors, Inc. The blockbusters arrived, but a number of factors dampened the panic they sought to provoke. For one thing, the houses in Shepherd Park were considerably more expensive than those in the other neighborhoods. It was harder to scare their owners into selling and it took longer to re-sell them. And Neighbors, Inc., already was

An array of homemade cupcakes tempts these young customers at a Neighbors, Inc. Art and Book Festival in the 1960s, held at Coolidge High School. Courtesy, Neighbors, Inc.

there, holding block meetings in living rooms throughout the area, counseling home owners that property values would not fall if they didn't sell, introducing them to one another and to the people moving in, and encouraging all to make common cause against the speculators.

By then, too, Neighbors, Inc., had captured the attention and the imagination of many home seekers in the area. A Jewish broker active in Shepherd Park in the 1960s was struck by the kind of young whites who began moving in, "liberal, Kennedy-style families," already pre-sold on the neighborhood and favorably disposed toward an integrated community for themselves and their children. Many of the old-time residents were also ready to accept black neighbors. And the Shepherd Park Citizens' Association, which, unlike its fellow members in the citywide federation, had never specifically prohibited blacks in its bylaws, was receptive to black members. Most new families tended to join Neighbors, Inc., and often brought fresh ideas for projects. Dr. Robert Good, Neighbors' second president, who later became the first American ambassador to Zambia, organized a community reception on May 14, 1961, for diplomatic families of newly independent African nations that received nationwide attention.

On hand to open the first Neighbors, Inc., Art and Book Festival in June 1963 was U.S. Attorney General Robert Kennedy, who declared, "What is so impressive about what you have done here is that you have shown the way, that it can be done, that it is possible . . ." Annual home and garden tours, monthly open houses, a garden club, and a children's singing group were among the other means used to attract newcomers and bring residents together.

Yet though idealistic white and black families were drawn to Shepherd Park and helped build a genuine community spirit, the ongoing religious and racial changes made even the most committed wonder whether integration was an attainable goal. The Reverend Anderson of Northminster Church noted that by 1974 Jewish residents had joined their non-Jewish brethren in the move to the suburbs, and the Jewish population had shrunk to 17 percent. Since their homes had been sold to Christians—albeit black Christians—Anderson saw that turn of events as a boon to recruitment. Needless to say, the synagogues that had been attracted to Shepherd Park because of its large Jewish population viewed this development with alarm. Chaim Lauer, demographer for the United Jewish Appeal Federation, estimates that 160,000 Jews live in the Washington metropolitan area today, but he can locate only 218 Jewish households in postal zone 20012, which includes not only all of Shepherd Park, Colonial Village, and North Portal Estates but sizable portions of other neighborhoods as well.

At the beginning of the racial turnover, in 1960, the Census Bureau counted 93 blacks in a neighborhood of 5,458. By 1970 blacks constituted 48.3 percent of a population of 5,913; by 1980, 66 percent of 5,101. Like the Jewish families whom they had followed northward, the black householders proceeded to involve themselves in civic matters and assumed leading roles in the citizens' association, Neighbors, Inc., and the Shepherd PTA. Wealthy Jews had already moved into Colonial Village, and blacks of means followed them there. Many black community leaders and professionals were attracted to North

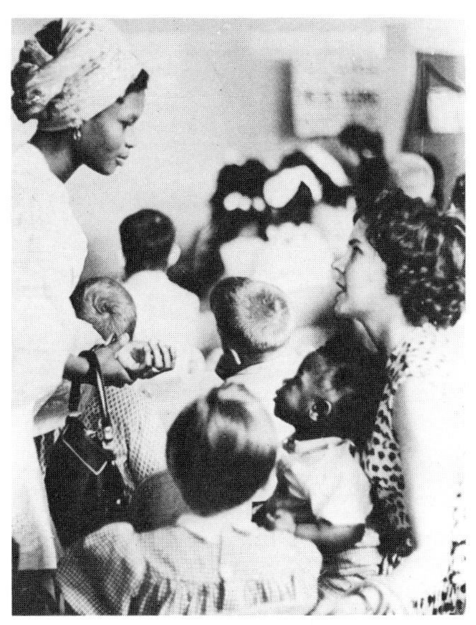

Women of two cultures meet at a community reception for diplomatic families of newly independent African nations, sponsored by Neighbors, Inc., in 1961. Courtesy, Neighbors, Inc.

Portal Estates; today they constitute two-thirds of its home owners. The convention of calling an affluent black neighborhood the "Gold Coast" is altered, in some black circles, to convey North Portal Estates' cachet: it is called the "Platinum Coast."

The changing religious and racial composition of Shepherd Park has strongly affected the fortunes of the churches and synagogues that chose to locate there, often in ways these institutions found disappointing. Northminster Church had prospered at first: by 1962 its congregation had 1,200 members, many of them within walking distance. But the growing Jewish and black populations, the move to the suburbs, and the attraction of newer churches have reduced its numbers so that today it has only about 300 members on its rolls.

Shepherd Park Christian Church, which had moved uptown from Park Road with about 400 members in 1947, today has about 140 active members, and very few live in Shepherd Park. St. James Lutheran Church, established in 1951, dissolved itself in 1972 and sold the building to St. Mary's Baptist Church, a black congregation, many of whose members live in Silver Spring, Maryland. The First Alliance Church of the Christian and Missionary Alliance moved from Brightwood to Shepherd Park in 1957 but by 1975 decided to follow its members into the suburbs. It sold its building to a black congregation, the First United Church of Jesus Christ Apostolic, whose membership of 400 includes only a dozen families that live in Shepherd Park.

The strongly Jewish character of Shepherd Park in the fifties and early sixties impelled three old Jewish congregations to relocate in the area. Some of the businessmen among their congregants warned that the neighborhood might change racially, but no heed was paid by the congregants, who were fiercely loyal to the city in which they had prospered. Today Beth Sholom at 13th Street and Eastern Avenue and Ohev Sholom Talmud Torah at 16th and Jonquil streets, the two Orthodox congregations, have dwindling, aging memberships. Although it is still maintaining its Eastern Avenue facility, Beth Sholom has opened a successful branch in Potomac, Maryland. Ohev Sholom has no such plans; says its rabbi, "We don't have the manpower for it."

The Conservative congregation, Tifereth Israel, has survived to a considerable extent because of its commitment to the neighborhood. Discouraged by the racial change, some of its most influential members, who had chosen to build the synagogue in Shepherd Park, proposed in the late sixties to sell the building to a black church and move to the suburbs. Those opposed found unexpected allies in young Jewish families recently attracted to the neighborhood by Neighbors, Inc.; the proposal to move was defeated. Because of Tifereth Israel's reputation for idealism and innovation, it has attracted members from throughout the metropolitan area. It has opened its facilities to many neighborhood events. One of its presidents was once also president of Neighbors, Inc.; its rabbi was on the board. Today it has about 370 members and is still growing, but only 14 or 15 families still live in Shepherd Park.

In the midst of the neighborhood's racial change, two new religious groups moved into the area. In 1961 Our Lady of Lebanon Maronite Seminary, which trains priests for this country's 300,000 Maronite Catholics, bought an old house on Alaska Avenue where its students—an average of 9 or 12 at any time—could study without distraction. The Washington Ethical Society wanted an integrated neighborhood for its meeting place and the small high school it established subsequently, so it chose to build in Shepherd Park in 1966, though its members do not live in the neighborhood.

In the 1970s Shepherd Park's pacific aura was shattered by two terrifying events involving the Hanafi Muslims, a small sect that moved into a large, fortress-like stone house on 16th Street in 1972. By an irony that subsequent events made even more pronounced, they shared the block with Ohev Sholom and opposite corners with Tifereth Israel. On January 18, 1973, assassins from a rival sect descended on the house and killed five children and two adults in what police said was the largest mass killing in Washington's history. The neighbors were shocked; but put off by appearances, by the barred windows and the guards who marched around the Hanafi compound all day armed with machetes, they made no attempt to convey their sympathy.

Many regretted that lapse when four years later 10 of the Hanafi Muslims forcibly occupied the national B'nai B'rith headquarters downtown, the Islamic Center on Massachusetts Avenue, and the D.C. city council chamber. Killing a young reporter and wounding others, they demanded among other things that the seven Black Muslims accused of the 1973 murder be turned over to them. They held more than 100 people hostage for 38 hours in the B'nai B'rith building before surrendering. It troubled consciences in Shepherd Park when the Hanafi leader expressed his conviction that the community had never

A small park on Alaska Avenue, N.W., provides the setting for the play of these Shepherd Park boys in the 1960s. Photo by Douglas Chevalier. Courtesy, Neighbors, Inc.

properly appreciated the tragedy that had befallen him. The terrorists were jailed soon after. And yet, a few years later, when a deranged man broke into Ohev Sholom in the middle of the night and began vandalizing the sanctuary, the Hanafi Muslims notified the police. And in 1982, on Yom Kippur Eve, when a young woman going to services at Tifereth Israel was struck by a car and lay in the street waiting for an ambulance, the Hanafi Muslims brought a blanket out to shield her from the rain.

Shepherd Park has changed little in physical appearance over the years. New homeowners are as ready with mowers, rakes, and paint brushes as the old ones were. Whatever changes there have been in faith and race, the character of the residents has remained the same: resolutely middle-class and cohesive.

The major civic concern today is the development of Georgia Avenue. The avenue was never known for elegant shopping. Most of its businesses were small family enterprises—places you went to for hardware, shoe repair, dry cleaning, liquor, a haircut, or a quart of milk. A few ethnic restaurants and groceries give it some exotic flavor, although of the Jewish markets only Posin's remains. In recent years, however, to the neighborhood's dismay, four "go-go joints," a massage parlor, five fast-food chain outlets, and a 7-Eleven opened in the nine commercial blocks that border Shepherd Park. The older citizens' groups, spearheaded by a new one, the Upper Georgia Avenue Planning Committee, have fought these encroachments: a public library is slated to be built on the site that yet another fast-food outlet had intended to occupy. And all but one of the go-go joints have folded.

The neighborhood is still integrated. Shepherd Elementary School has about 30 white children in a student body of 400, but the white population is larger than that proportion suggests. Although the school still enjoys a good reputation, many white parents—and many black ones—opt for private or parochial education. Real estate brokers say they have almost as many white buyers as black ones and that the trend among purchasers is toward young families and singles.

Residents are generally optimistic about the neighborhood's future. While some are wary, many foresee the rejuvenation of Georgia Avenue in the Gateway project, an ambitious plan to build a nine-story complex of apartments and fine shops at the District line, where Eastern, Alaska, and Georgia avenues come together.

Old garden apartments on the Maryland side of Eastern Avenue are being renovated into luxury units. The sales brochure invites you to enjoy "City Sophistication in Silver Spring" and to cross the street into "one of the Capital's most prestigious residential neighborhoods." Many Shepherd Park residents will tell you that isn't a sales pitch; it's no more, they feel, than the plain truth.

Takoma Park
Historic District
SPEED LIMIT 25
VOLKSWAG

PART 6

PARTNERS IN PROGRESS

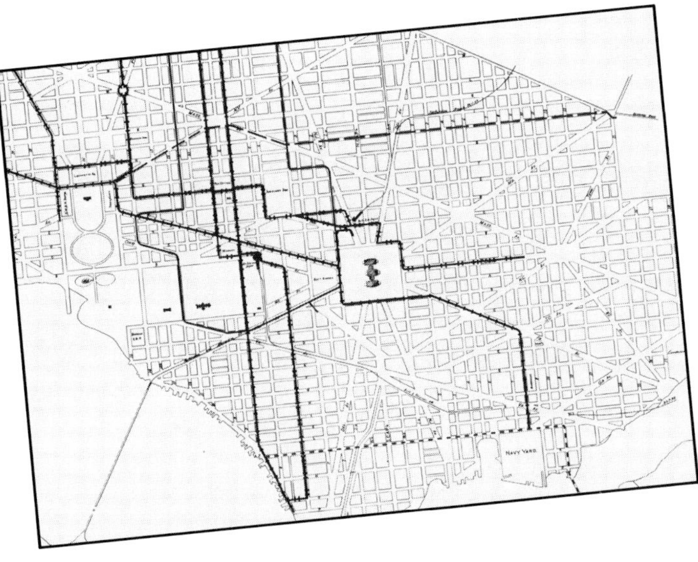

Takoma Park residents celebrate their historic district. Courtesy, Takoma Park Historical Society

Map; horsecar routes. Courtesy, LeRoy O. King, Jr.

Mark Twain wrote: "The Capital of the Great Republic gathered its people from the four winds of heaven, and so the manners, the faces, and the fashions there, presented variety that was infinite."

A popular cliche about Washington says that the local economy produces just three products: power, access to power, and the illusion of access to power. Like much that is repeated in Washington, the phrase prefers a pretense of cleverness to communicating an accurate perception. It is true, however, that its role as "America's Home Town" makes Washington unique—and occasionally peculiar. Only in Washington do the buildings talk.

Every evening reporters tell us that "The White House says . . ." The embassies of Massachusetts Avenue, the offices of the federal triangle, and the museums and monuments of the National Mall all mark the District of Columbia as the nerve center and soul of the nation. The Capitol, White House, and Supreme Court eloquently remind us that this is the headquarters town. So too do traffic circles and streets jammed with impatient bureaucrats, ostentatious limousines, and confused tourists.

When Washington became the national capital, local merchants and real estate speculators expected a major center of international commerce to blossom on the banks of the Potomac. Such was not to be—not for more than a century. The anticipated unlimited federal largesse never materialized, and without commercially attractive waterways or other geographical advantages, there was little early natural impetus for rapid commercial development.

Worse yet, after the British invaded the city, the federal government almost pulled out entirely. Only powerful southern politicians (and locally raised money) prevented the national capital from retreating to New York or Philadelphia. Even then fears and uncertainties about

Washington's future continued.

At first, competition from Georgetown and Alexandria and a complex patchwork of laws and administrative authorities produced a confusing commercial environment. Ever since, the distractions of glamorous national issues have made it all too easy for Congress to ignore local needs, while too many of the city's most powerful citizens and interest groups have been transients with primary loyalties elsewhere.

From its earliest days, taking potshots at Washington has been a popular pastime. Not that there was any shortage of legitimate material. Early construction along the river destroyed natural woodlands, fouled the delicate ecosystem, and produced unpleasant swamps. Building a compromised version of the Chesapeake and Ohio Canal when the rest of the nation was turning to railroads produced economic failure instead of boom.

For decades Congress postponed funding desperately needed water and sewage systems for Washington, while local residents refused to pay for amenities that would primarily service the federal bureaucracy. Congressional toleration of Washington's slave trade until 1850 and of slavery until 1862, the middle of the Civil War, remains an enduring shame.

After the war, while the nation debated how best to provide care for freed blacks, tens of thousands of them came to Washington to await federal action. It was not congressmen but Washingtonians who responded, and not just with political promises but with acutely needed philanthropic action. Many of Washington's proudest local institutions date from the Civil War and Reconstruction era.

The national and international crises of the twentieth century have been good to Washington. World War I, the New Deal, World War II, and the Johnson administration's War on Poverty all dramatically benefited the local economy. War and peace are critical issues in Washington, affecting not simply life and death, but jobs and careers. Yet even as the size of the federal government has grown, the proportion of the federal contribution to the local Washington area economy has decreased. The nongovernmental sector has been growing far more rapidly.

The real estate boom, anticipated by local speculators when L'Enfant first laid out his plan, finally arrived. Promises of cultural enrichment implicit in Corcoran's gift of his endowed collection have been realized. Airlines, railroads, and highways have brought the benefits of improved transportation facilities first advertised by builders of the C&O Canal. The rewards of improved communications—imagined by Samuel F.B. Morse when he strung his telegraph wires through Washington and by Alexander Graham Bell in his Dupont Circle laboratory—now outstrip fantasy.

Foreign diplomats no longer receive hardship pay for duty in Washington. The swamps are gone; in their place stand expensive riverfront developments and the cherry trees of the tidal basin.

Once criticized as a cultural desert, Washington is now home to world-class theaters, museums, and libraries. Often labeled as hopelessly provincial, Washington's retail market is now highly competitive and *au courant.* No trendy designer or upscale retailer can really consider itself world class without representation in Georgetown, Downtown, or Old Town.

Today's Washington eludes pigeonholes. Through the late 1950s its people reflected southern origins, mores, and inclinations. The current population reflects national diversity and international tastes. The aroma of fried chicken and collard greens is still part of Washington's atmosphere, but so too are curries, sushi, moussaka, paella, escargot, schnitzel, black beans with rice, and Szechuan delicacies.

The pages that follow document the intriguing histories of many local businesses and institutions. Some serve national markets, but most are more important for their role within the Washington community.

The organizations whose stories are told here have chosen to support this important literary and civic project. Not only do their own accounts illustrate the variety of ways in which individuals and businesses have contributed to the community's growth and development, but their decision to participate is itself evidence of the growing pride of Washington.

They have every right to that pride. Their work—in cooperation with the people of Washington—has made the District of Columbia much more than a center of government. They have taken an unpromising 10 square miles of real estate and—in spite of the presence of the national government—made it an outstanding and exciting place to live.

THE COLUMBIA HISTORICAL SOCIETY

ABOVE: The blue parlor and gold drawing room of the restored Christian Heurich Mansion, home and historic house museum of The Columbia Historical Society. Photographs courtesy of The Columbia Historical Society

LEFT: The Columbia Historical Society is headquartered in the Christian Heurich Mansion, a District of Columbia landmark built in 1894.

The Columbia Historical Society was founded in 1894 for the purposes of collecting, preserving, and teaching the history of the District of Columbia. It was created by 36 eminent Washington citizens—including historian Henry Adams, politician Henry Cabot Lodge, diplomat and poet John Hay, geologist and explorer John Wesley Powell, banker E. Francis Riggs, editor of the *Washington Star* Theodore W. Noyes, and journalist, author, lecturer, and actress "Kate" Field.

Today, with more than 1,100 individual and corporate members, the society continues this mission, working to preserve and share the documentary history of the capital city. Its Washingtoniana library contains approximately 100,000 items, including books, maps, early government documents, real estate atlases, prints, graphics, and collections of more than 70,000 photographs. The library is professionally staffed and open to the public Wednesdays, Fridays, and Saturdays. The society's Washingtoniana Book Store carries a wide selection of books, reprints, and maps relating to Washington's very special local history.

A dedicated board and talented staff, both professional and volunteer, has created a broad spectrum of educational offerings, including an innovative outreach program to schools throughout the Washington area, daytime and evening lectures for adults, tours, workshops, and seminars all related to Washington's history. The *Records of the Columbia Historical Society*, published continuously since 1897, is a highly respected historical journal.

The Columbia Historical Society's headquarters is in the Christian Heurich Mansion at 1307 New Hampshire Avenue, NW, an architectural oasis among the steel-and-glass edifices that rise south of Dupont Circle. Built in 1894, this Richardsonian Romanesque masterpiece was called by *The New York Times*, "a walk into the late nineteenth century; gold leaf parlor sets . . . intricately stenciled walls, mahogany woodwork . . . a historic house that reflects the grandeur of America's 'Gilded Age' . . ." Christian Heurich, a prominent Washington businessman, real estate investor, and philanthropist, was founder of the Heurich Brewing Company and an active member of The Columbia Historical Society. His family donated the mansion to the society in 1956.

Today the organization is carefully preserving and restoring the mansion, which is listed on the National Register of Historic Places. Wednesday through Saturday the society's trained docent staff leads tours of the historic house, interpreting its interior furnishings, remarkable technology, and significance to the growth of urban Washington. The charming and secluded Victorian garden is open to the public weekdays and is a favorite luncheon spot for nearby office workers.

The Columbia Historical Society is a member of the Dupont Kalorama Museums Consortium and has close links with local universities and research libraries. The society cosponsors the annual D.C. Historical Studies Conference with George Washington University and Martin Luther King Library.

HOWARD UNIVERSITY

Howard University was founded in 1867 in a single building. Today the main campus (shown here) encompasses 89 acres with 65 major buildings. Photo by Air Photographics, Inc.

Howard University traces its origins to a November 1866 prayer meeting of the First Congregational Society of Washington, D.C. At that meeting 10 society members recognized that an end to slavery was but the first step to real freedom and proposed the establishment of a theological seminary to train black ministers. They expanded this concept first to include teacher training, then to envision "a university for the education of youth in the liberal arts and sciences."

The charter of Howard University was enacted by Congress and signed by President Andrew Johnson on March 2, 1867. The new institution was named in honor of one of its key founders, a man who later served as an early president of the university, Major General Oliver Otis Howard. General Howard was a Civil War hero and commissioner of the Freedmen's Bureau (the federal agency responsible for the welfare of emancipated slaves).

When Howard University opened in May 1867, the campus consisted of a single building; the only members of its first student body were the four daughters of white trustees and faculty members. Today the campus' physical plant consists of 65 major buildings on the 89-acre main campus, the 22-acre West Campus housing the School of Law, a School of Divinity in northeast Washington, and a 108-acre tract in nearby Maryland. Total enrollment exceeds 12,000 full- and part-time students.

"Some institutions are trapped by tradition," says the university's president, Dr. James E. Cheek. "Howard University thrives on it. For more than a century Howard University has demonstrated a commitment to scholarship, to giving students the tools they need to be tomorrow's leaders."

The board of trustees of Howard University once included two great pioneers of black rights and education, Frederick Douglass and Booker T. Washington. Dr. Ralph J. Bunche, who in 1950 became the first black to win the Nobel Peace Prize, served as a professor and head of the political science department.

At Howard students are expected to become pacesetters when they graduate. And many of them have. The long list of distinguished alumni includes Supreme Court Justice Thurgood Marshall, Atlanta Mayor Andrew Young, former National Urban League executive director Vernon Jordan, former U.S. Secretary of Housing and Urban Development Patricia Harris, and Jessye Norman, the internationally acclaimed opera soprano.

Howard University is comprised of 18 schools and colleges and offers master's and doctorate degrees in its graduate programs, as well as degrees in professional areas such as law, medicine, and dentistry. Throughout most of the university's history its faculty has been and still is comprised of perhaps the largest concentration of black Ph.D.s in the United States.

"This university was founded to become one of the instruments through which our racial wounds would be cleansed and healed," says Cheek. "For this purpose we were created and toward this end we shall continue."

Frederick Douglass, black abolitionist and pioneer of black rights and education, was one of the early trustees of Howard University. This classroom building was named in his honor. Photo by Harlee Little

HOWARD UNIVERSITY HOSPITAL

The critical need for a hospital arrived with the flood of black refugees of the Civil War. The first primitive care facility grew out of the mud and swampland of an old cemetery and brickyard along 13th Street, NW. Originally known as Camp Barker, a combination asylum, convalescent center, and staging area for black refugees or "contrabands," the Washington area's first black hospital at times housed as many as 600 residents.

During one month in 1862 nearly half of the patients died. In the fall of 1863 Camp Barker experienced a death rate of 3.5 per day. Many more perished in a smallpox epidemic that winter. One year later the facility was relocated by the War Department to 14th and Vermont streets, NW, and in 1865—under the authority of the newly created Freedmen's Bureau—to LeDroit Park. Four years later Freedmen's Hospital and Asylum moved to buildings on land owned by Howard University at Fifth and W streets, NW.

The last move was largely the work of the chief commissioner of the Freedmen's Bureau, General Oliver Otis Howard. Hampered by congressional opposition, he used Freedmen's Bureau funds acquired by a wartime head tax on employed black refugees and by sales of crops raised by freed black workers on confiscated southern plantations. The hospital shared its new facilities with the new Howard University Medical School.

Throughout its history Freedmen's provided a base for distinguished black physicians who were frozen out of other regional hospitals and professional groups such as the American Medical Association. Several Washington hospitals cared for black patients, but the professional medical establishment remained segregated; Freedmen's Hospital was the only area institution where blacks could receive a medical education.

As recently as 1961 only 7 percent of black physicians in Washington could practice at hospitals other than Freedmen's. That year President John F. Kennedy signed legislation that transferred control of the hospital to Howard University (effective July 1, 1967), and authorized the new 500-bed hospital, which opened at 2041 Georgia Avenue, NW, on April 12, 1975.

Howard University Hospital has become a major national teaching facility, offering clinical postgraduate programs in a wide variety of specialties. The institution pioneered intraoperative radiation therapy.

Besides the full gamut of acute medical, surgical, pediatric, dental, and psychiatric services, Howard University Hospital hosts special centers for cancer, sickle cell disease, organ transplants, family health, substance abuse, vitiligo research, therapeutic child life, trauma, rehabilitation, and neonatal care. The radiological diagnostic and treatment facilities support tertiary care services, including heart catheterization, laser treatment and research, and noninvasive nuclear imaging.

From Camp Barker to Freedmen's to Howard University Hospital—this institution has come a long way in 125 years.

Freedmen's Hospital as it appeared in 1894 at the Fifth and W streets, NW, location.

President John F. Kennedy signed legislation transferring control of the hospital to Howard University in 1961, and this 500-bed health care facility was authorized. Located at 2041 Georgia Avenue, NW, the new hospital opened April 12, 1975.

WYNMARK DEVELOPMENT CORPORATION

Mark G. Griffin and Richard W. Naing have been working together successfully for more than 15 years. They began their relationship as lawyer and client, and gradually it evolved into a business partnership. In 1982 they formed Wynmark Development Corporation.

Wynmark's first historical renovation project was the Teddy Roosevelt house at 1215 Nineteenth Street, NW, which Wynmark restored and enlarged. It is now used as corporate offices. Another interesting project involved the restoration of Georgetown's old High Street School, located at 1640 Wisconsin Avenue, NW. This building is a wonderful example of Georgian revival architecture and now serves as the headquarters of a national corporation.

One of the most difficult yet interesting projects Wynmark has undertaken to date is the old Gaslight Club, located at 1020 Sixteenth Street, NW. Once one of the most prestigious private clubs in the city, the structure has been completely rebuilt and expanded while the existing historic facade has been maintained. The project has emerged from a two-year restoration process as professional offices and luxurious corporate suites, available for long-term lease.

The most recent historic restoration project undertaken by Wynmark is the Hillandale mansion in Georgetown. The mansion will be completely renovated and will serve as the centerpiece for a new luxury condominium/town house development.

"We like the details of the past," says Griffin. "We try to save it where we can and reproduce it where we can't." Griffin is also the president of The Columbia Historical Society.

Wynmark does not confine its work to historic preservation. With its affiliated companies, the organization is active in hotel construction and management, commercial development, and other venture capital activities. Its recent projects include hotels, office buildings, mixed-use developments, condominium projects, and apartment complexes.

"We always look for unique opportunities that we hope will be both profitable and interesting," says Naing. This included Wynmark Development Corporation's own corporate headquarters at 1521 New Hampshire Avenue, a completely renovated late-Victorian mansion. The facility features extraordinary moldings, woodwork, and other historic details. "We tried to maintain the historic nature of the building," says Naing. "We feel it is a perfect representation of our corporate image."

ABOVE: The Lafayette, at 1020 Sixteenth Street, NW, was one of Wynmark's most difficult but rewarding restorations. Once the prestigious Gaslight Club, it is now professional offices and luxurious private residences.

BELOW: Now the headquarters of a national corporation, Georgetown's old High Street School, at 1640 Wisconsin Avenue, NW, was renovated by the firm in keeping with its Georgian revival architecture.

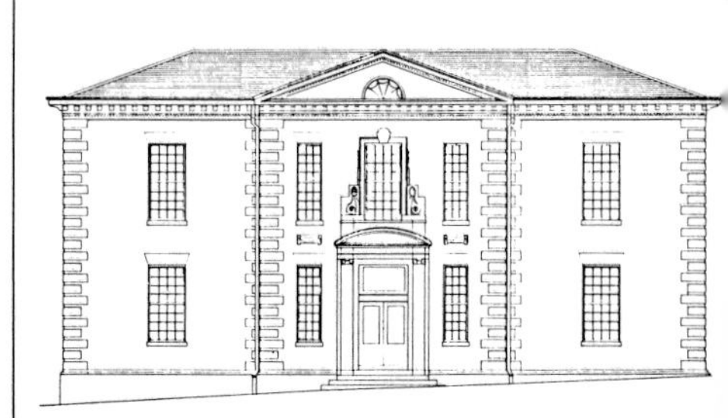

ARNOLD & PORTER

Once the Washington home of Chauncey Depew, this 19th Street mansion housed Arnold & Porter's offices until 1980.

Arnold & Porter, one of Washington's most prestigious and internationally respected law firms, was conceived in the era of the New Deal. In its maturity it has contributed several stars to government service, but it was created by three men who brought their extraordinary federal experience to the private sector.

Thurman Arnold brought the firm his experience as President Franklin Roosevelt's trust-busting assistant attorney general and judge on the United States Circuit Court of Appeals for the District of Columbia.

Abe Fortas served as counsel to the Security and Exchange Commission, general counsel of the Public Works Administration, head of the Office of Price Administration, and undersecretary of the Interior.

Paul Porter was a veteran of the New Deal's Agricultural Adjustment Administration and several other government agencies, closing his government career as head of the American economic mission to Greece that launched the Truman Doctrine.

The firm attracted national attention in the 1950s as champion of hundreds of government employees who had been charged with disloyalty.

Throughout its history it has helped to develop and expand important principles of American law, including the right of the indigent to competent counsel and a new definition of criminal insanity. In representing survivors of the 1972 Buffalo Creek mine disaster, the firm's attorneys successfully established the right of a group of West Virginia coal miners and their families to compensation for psychological as well as physical and economic damages.

Arnold & Porter currently employs more than 225 lawyers and 350 support staff, and occupies the top five floors of the office building at 1200 New Hampshire Avenue. It has branch offices in New York City and Denver.

The firm's clients include major domestic and foreign corporations, individuals, foreign governments and private entities, public and quasi-public agencies, public interest groups, universities, trade and professional associations, and other law firms. Its practice emphasizes litigation and administrative law, banking, securities, antitrust, taxation, international trade and finance, and a wide range of other fields of practice.

Recent pro bono actions at Arnold & Porter include representing death row inmates in Georgia and Virginia, and persons arrested for protesting apartheid at the South African Embassy in Washington. Other causes supported on a pro bono basis include support of American Indian land claims in Connecticut, New York, Nevada, New Mexico, and California, and representation of numerous and diverse charitable and non-profit organizations, indigent persons charged with crimes, and victims of child abuse.

Arnold & Porter remembers its roots.

THE GEORGE WASHINGTON UNIVERSITY

On March 30, 1981, a horrified nation watched as President Ronald Reagan was attacked by a would-be assassin. For the next several days people everywhere awaited news bulletins issued by the staff of The George Washington University Medical Center. The attempt to kill President Reagan brought national attention to a medical center and a university that has been bringing quality education to the nation's capital for more than 167 years.

The George Washington University, like the great European academic centers of the Renaissance, draws its strength from both the international community of scholars and from the surrounding urban society. From its inception the university has dedicated itself to fulfilling the finest promises of this synthesis.

During the past two decades, under the leadership of its president, Lloyd H. Elliott, The George Washington University has pursued a precise strategy for developing its physical and financial foundation as a basis for academic excellence.

On May 15, 1986, GW inaugurated the first comprehensive, university-wide fund-raising campaign in its history, a $75-million Campaign for George Washington. In announcing the campaign, Elliott noted that "now the time has come for GW to proclaim the academic quality that has been achieved in the past 25 years, to point to what is possible in the decades ahead, and to invite all its friends to join in making those possibilities reality."

President Elliott emphasized the goal of positioning the university "among the best" in the nation primarily by bringing the academic presence in line with the finest universities in the country. The moneys raised during this five-year effort will be distributed throughout the university departments, namely for university professorships, scholarships, teaching and research equipment, and libraries.

The George Washington University was founded in 1821 as The Columbian College in the District of Columbia. The charter, signed by President James Monroe, fulfilled "an ardent wish" of President George Washington, while still in office, for the establishment of a university in the nation's new capital city.

The Academic Center is the newest building on the university campus.

The Columbian College, founded in 1821, was the birthplace of The George Washington University.

Despite continual financial distress, the college continued to grow. The School of Medicine and Health Sciences was started in 1824. It opened the National Law Center in 1865. In 1873 the institution changed its name to Columbian University.

As the university distanced itself from the Baptist Church, it also found itself increasingly distanced from sources of financial support. Seeking to rebind itself to Baptist support in 1898, the trustees demanded and won a new charter from Congress, a charter that formally vested control of Columbian University in members of Baptist churches. Church leaders responded by giving the university their prayers, but not their money.

Once again the trustees sought a political solution for their still-growing financial woes; they petitioned Congress for still another new charter. The nondenominational charter of 1904 reconfirmed the concept of nonsectarian control. With the new charter came a new name: The George Washington University.

Conservative budgeting proved far more successful than new charters and new names in alleviating an ongoing financial crisis, and the university was able to purchase modest facilities at 2023 G Street, NW, in 1912 and greet its 1921 centennial year with optimism and its first major fund-raising campaign.

In his comprehensive history of The George Washington University, the late professor Elmer Kayser credits president Cloyd H. Marvin (1927-1959) with the vision and leadership that brought the university into the modern era. Marvin coordinated the three major structures on the north side of G Street between 20th and 21st streets, and then worked toward grouping additional facilities around this nucleus. Under his guidance, the amorphous collection of facilities gradually emerged as the University Triangle south and east of Washington Circle.

The campus now includes 74 buildings in a 23-block area. Three libraries house more than 1.5 million volumes and 15,000 periodicals. The faculty includes 1,100 scholars.

Marvin also reorganized the administration of the university and the board of trustees into its modern form and attracted substantial financial gifts—including a million-dollar endowment from the Scottish Rite (Masons), which made possible the establishment of the School of Government. The gift was among the first major contributions to the university endowment, which is now valued at more than $200 million.

Perhaps most critically, Marvin initiated policies that have tied The George Washington University closely to the city of Washington and to the nation—policies that have been enthusiastically continued by his successors.

The George Washington University brings 17,000 students from throughout the nation and the world to Washington, but that is just one facet of its contribution to the community. A major regional business with an annual budget exceeding $350 million, the university employs more than 10,000 metropolitan area residents.

Dr. Lloyd H. Elliott, the 14th president of The George Washington University, served from 1965 to 1988.

If the university has benefited from its unique location in the capital city, it has contributed to the city as well. The medical center admits 17,000 patients to its hospital each year, and sees 250,000 in emergency and ambulatory services. University departments, clinics, programs, and centers provide countless other benefits to residents, agencies, organizations, and institutions throughout the region.

The city and The George Washington University have been partners for 167 years. Both anticipate continued close cooperation as they go forward together to the future.

DISTRICT OF COLUMBIA CHAMBER OF COMMERCE

"The District of Columbia Chamber of Commerce is alive and well and vibrant and necessary," said Washington Mayor Marion Barry at the chamber's 49th Annual Awards Banquet in 1987. "Give yourselves a round of applause."

The leaders of the District of Columbia Chamber of Commerce deserve that applause. They have built the D.C. Chamber into one of Washington's proudest institutions, an organization that continues to play an increasing role in the economic health of the city.

The chamber was chartered June 20, 1938, as the Washington Chamber of Commerce by Thomas W. Parks, Sr., John R. Pinkett, and A.W. Scurlock. They founded the Washington Chamber of Commerce as an organization that could serve and defend the interests of black businesses in the city, a sad reflection on the racial segregation and discrimination that were then facts of political, commercial, and social life in Washington. In August 1946 the organization changed its name to the Negro Chamber of Commerce, reflecting its exclusively black membership and constituency.

The present name, District of Columbia Chamber of Commerce, was adopted on October 23, 1957. With the name came a new direction and sense of purpose for the organization. Not only would the chamber stimulate the economic development and growth of minority businesses, but it would now work for *all* businesses with a District of Columbia address.

Its mission: "To promote the economic, commercial, industrial, and civic welfare of the District of Columbia; to mobilize technical and management resources; to provide management training and technical assistance to small business entrepreneurs and aspirants desirous of going into business."

The District of Columbia Chamber of Commerce, founded in 1938, has become a strong and effective leader in the Washington, D.C., business community.

The road has not been easy and included such hazards as financial difficulties and problems recruiting members, but all those challenges have been overcome. The chamber has become a strong organization that effectively represents the entire Washington business community in the political decision-making process, conducts community economic development programs, promotes conventions and tourism, and functions as a vehicle for informational exchange.

Today its more than 875 members include manufacturers, hotels, associations, professional organizations, and individuals. The chamber remains primarily interested in serving the interests of small businesses.

The organization functions through three active departments: Business and Economic Development, Conventions and Tourism, and Membership. It operates a Business Resource Center that responds to more than 30,000 information requests annually, providing information on area demographics, marketing, and business relocation. It also provides technical assistance on business and business development, and offers seminars and workshops on a wide range of business topics.

Under progressive leadership, the District of Columbia Chamber of Commerce anticipates continued growth and a continued vitality as a Partner in Progress of the Washington business community.

THE AMERICAN UNIVERSITY

LEFT: Bishop John Fletcher Hurst, founder of The American University. Courtesy, The American University Archives

RIGHT: Richard Berendzen, president of The American University.

Bishop John Fletcher Hurst first saw the land for his long-envisioned Methodist postgraduate university at Washington on January 3, 1890. The site, known as Bellevue, comprised 90 acres in upper northwest Washington. It commanded a panoramic view of the District of Columbia, the Manassas Plains, and the mountains of western Maryland.

The new institution was incorporated by an act of Congress as The American University on February 24, 1893, but Bishop Hurst's work as university chancellor was just beginning. His university's official approval by the General Conference of the Methodist Episcopal Church required the trustees to raise $5 million before opening for instruction.

When Hurst resigned in 1902 due to poor health, the total assets of The American University totaled only $2 million, including the still-vacant colleges of history (Hurst Hall) and government (McKinley Memorial Building). The General Conference removed its disabling restriction in 1904, but opening day was delayed until May 27, 1914.

The university awarded its first degrees on June 2, 1916: two Ph.D.s and an M.A. It was an auspicious occasion, but one darkened by approaching thunderclouds of war.

Throughout its history The American University has taken advantage of its location in Washington, D.C., to build bridges between the academic world and the worlds of work: professional activities, international affairs, and public administration. However, twice in its history the university has lent grounds and facilities to the war effort, while classes continued uninterrupted. The return of peace has always brought a rededication at the institution to its primary mission.

Today The American University is comprised of the College of Arts and Sciences, the Kogod College of Business Administration, the School of International Service, the School of Public Affairs, and the Washington College of Law.

The American University is committed to attracting the best international and nontraditional students to join outstanding traditional undergraduates at an institution with a cohesive and exciting community. Its 11,000 students come from the District of Columbia, every state in the union, and 120 foreign nations. Its 1,000 full- and part-time faculty members provide an exceptional synthesis of academic theory and practical experience.

Academic excellence, institutional distinction, and a strong sense of community have been hallmarks of The American University since it was little more than a dream of Bishop Hurst. Under the leadership of president Richard Berendzen, they have become fundamental plans guiding the development of the university as it prepares for its centennial.

USAIR

USAir's newest aircraft—the Boeing 737-300—is the most advanced, quiet, and fuel-efficient aircraft of its size and range.

USAir has become one of the leading airlines serving Washington's three major airports. Long a leader in the Northeast, USAir's recent merger with California-based Pacific Southwest Airlines (PSA) and its planned merger with Piedmont Airlines will make it one of America's most popular and prominent airlines.

USAir and PSA operations were integrated in spring 1988, while Piedmont operations will be merged into USAir in January 1989. After that merger, USAir will rank as the nation's second-largest airline company in terms of passenger boardings.

USAir's current operations hubs are at Pittsburgh and Philadelphia. Over the next several years, as USAir expands to include the routes previously operated by Piedmont, its network of hubs will expand to Baltimore, Charlotte, Dayton, and Syracuse, as well.

The national headquarters of USAir is located in northern Virginia. Until this year the airline was headquartered at Washington's National Airport. Washington was among the first cities served by USAir when, under the name of All American Aviation, it began carrying passengers in 1949.

USAir first took to the skies carrying mail to small towns in the Allegheny Mountains region of western Pennsylvania, making use of a technological breakthrough created by Dr. Lytle S. Adams, a Chicago dentist. Adams developed a device that would enable an airplane to pick up and deliver mail sacks without having to land. He demonstrated his ingenious

The mail must go through! With its unique airmail pickup service, USAir (then All American Aviation) delivered the mail to remote locations in Pennsylvania, West Virginia, Delaware, and Ohio.

system at the Chicago World's Fair, where he met champion glider pilot and businessman Richard C. du Pont.

Du Pont was fascinated. He decided to start a company that would provide air-mail pickup and delivery service to isolated locations using Adams' device. He chartered All American Aviation, Inc., as a Delaware corporation. Then he filed bids on two experimental air-mail pickup routes advertised by the United States Post Office.

All American Aviation won both routes without contest. The bids established air mail routes 1001 and 1002, connecting cities in Pennsylvania, West Virginia, Delaware, and Ohio.

The largest sections of each route lay in the Allegheny Mountains and required flying over difficult terrain known for some of the worst possible weather and conditions. More exacting conditions for testing air-mail pickup would be hard to find, but All American Aviation went ahead.

The first air-mail pickup flight was on May 12, 1939. Norm Rintoul piloted the small plane that snatched a mail sack suspended between two steel masts in Latrobe, Pennsylvania. Flight mechanic Victor Yesulaites operated the winch that reeled in the bag.

All American Aviation carried the mail for 10 years with a team of pilots, flight mechanics, and ground employees who returned romance and adventure to aviation. The stories of those who flew the scarlet Stinson Reliants may remind listeners of the barnstorming days of the 1920s, but records show that it was also a serious and profitable business.

During the early years of air-mail pickup flights, du Pont headed the company. One of America's leading experts in gliders, du Pont left All American Aviation during World War II to help the U.S. Army Air Corps establish its glider program. All American Aviation engineers working under his direction redesigned pickup devices for gliders used to transport troops. Major Halsey R. Bazley succeeded du Pont as president in 1942.

With the introduction of the local-service airline era following World War II, All American Aviation decided that its best future lay with carrying passengers as well as the mail. It applied to become a local-service airline, part of the federally subsidized system of short-haul carriers.

All American Aviation received government approval to carry passengers early in 1949, moved its headquarters from Wilmington to Washington, D.C., changed its name to All American Airways, and on March 7 started in the passenger transportation business with a fleet of 11 DC-3s. The first major cities on the All American system were Washington, D.C., Baltimore, Philadelphia, New York, Pittsburgh, Buffalo, and Cincinnati—with service to many of the smaller cities between.

Robert M. Love guided All American through the transition from air-mail pickup to scheduled passenger service. Love remained active with the airline until 1975, when he was named director emeritus, after serving as president, chairman, and as a member of the board of directors.

By 1953, when the firm changed its name to Allegheny Airlines, Inc., the fleet consisted of 13 DC-3s, and the route network had expanded to Erie, Pennsylvania; Cleveland, Ohio; and to Parkersburg and Huntington, West Virginia.

Based in the populous East with its many important short-haul markets, Allegheny grew rapidly, developing new ticketing, reservations, and baggage-handling systems to meet the increasing demands of short-haul air transport.

All set for an on-time departure on USAir's (then All American Airways) first scheduled passenger flight on March 7, 1949.

In 1953 Leslie O. Barnes was named president and Henry A. Satterwhite joined the board of directors. Satterwhite served as chairman of the board from 1956 to 1978. He and Barnes piloted Allegheny through the "feeder-line" era, through mergers with Mohawk and Lake Central airlines, and into the jet age.

One of the nation's largest passenger-carrying airlines, USAir operates more than 1,600 flight departures per day and carries more than 30 million passengers per year.

In 1959 Allegheny expanded to several New England cities and became the first airline to put the Convair 540 turboprops into service. By 1963 the airline that had started with 11 DC-3s had a fleet of 38 aircraft—23 Convair 440 jetprops and 15 Martin Executives. The growing fleet required increasingly specialized facilities, so Allegheny moved its maintenance, engineering, flight operations, and flight control personnel from Washington to a new, multimillion-dollar facility at Greater Pittsburgh International Airport.

In 1966 Allegheny introduced its first pure jet, the DC-9. The company's last piston-engine aircraft, a Convair, was phased out of service in September 1977.

The Allegheny Commuter System, USAir's innovative network of independent airlines that provides efficient, convenient service to smaller localities, first took wing as a commuter airline assuming Allegheny's service between Hagerstown and Baltimore with four daily round-trip flights.

This Allegheny Commuter program enabled Allegheny to serve smaller markets without requiring federal subsidy payments. At the same time the communities gained by receiving more frequent service and the same benefits—joint fares, reservations, baggage checking—they had received from Allegheny itself.

The first Allegheny Commuter flight took off on November 15, 1967. Today a full network of Allegheny Commuter airlines contract with USAir to carry more than 2 million passengers per year between local and connecting hub airports.

Allegheny was ready for more, but in the era of federal regulation of air transportation, airlines could only grow through acquisition. By merging with Indianapolis-based Lake Central Airlines (effective July 1, 1968), the Allegheny system expanded to 77 airports serving an area in which more than 50 percent of the nation's population lived.

Allegheny stretched its regulated wings even farther in 1972, when it merged with Mohawk Airlines based in Utica, New York. That merger made Allegheny the nation's sixth-largest passenger-carrying airline.

With its expanded route system, its strong Allegheny Commuter network, and a fleet of 37 DC-9s, 31 BAC 1-11s, and 40 Convair 580s, Allegheny was positioned for continued growth. In 1974 Allegheny became the first local-service airline to make itself totally self-sufficient, allowing it to be removed from the federal subsidy program.

Barnes retired as president in 1975, and the board of directors elected Edwin I. Colodny to succeed him. Colodny had joined Allegheny in 1957 as assistant to the president; he held several other executive positions before being named chief executive officer. Colodny is now chairman of the board, president, and chief executive officer of the airline.

The modern age of American aviation began in 1978 with the passage of the Airline Deregulation Act, a law that radically altered the nature of the industry. It brought with it a rapid growth in passenger volume on all scheduled airlines in the United States. Allegheny was no exception. With both the business and vacation travel markets expanding rapidly, each month brought new records for numbers of passengers carried.

To meet new public demands, the airline modernized its equipment, phased out the last of the Convair 580s, and became an all-jet fleet. With both public interest and value growing, the company's stock was listed on the New York Stock Exchange.

Responding to the new competitive atmosphere, Allegheny adopted innovative pricing practices offering travelers a variety of discount fare plans. It also started service to Houston—followed by new service to Orlando, Tampa, and West Palm Beach. The following year Allegheny added flights to Birmingham, Phoenix, Tucson, New Orleans, and Raleigh-Durham.

Allegheny had become a major airline and was planning to expand its route network across the country. But market research revealed that much of the public still, incorrectly, perceived the company as a small, local-service carrier. Consultants suggested that Allegheny would not shake the "small and local" image without changing its name. Corporate executives sought a name that would reflect the airline's new size and scope. On October 28, 1979, Allegheny Airlines became USAir.

Taking advantage of newly won freedoms under deregulation, and despite intense competition in the airline industry, USAir continues to function profitably and to expand. Its system now stretches coast to coast and includes more than 100 cities in 30 states, the District of Columbia, and two Canadian provinces, and the airline is continuing to add new destinations.

Edwin I. Colodny, chairman of the board and president of USAir Group, Inc., and USAir, Inc.

In December 1986 USAir Group (the holding company for USAir), announced that it had agreed to purchase PSA. With the approval of the Department of Transportation, that purchase became final in late May 1987 and the operations were merged in spring 1988. With this acquisition, USAir is now a major carrier in the California market, one of the nation's busiest air travel corridors.

On March 6, 1987, USAir Group announced that it had agreed to purchase Piedmont Aviation, a North Carolina-based airline with a history and tradition remarkably similar to that of USAir. Department of Transportation approval was received on October 30, 1987, and the acquisition was completed on November 5. The acquisitions of Piedmont and PSA will give USAir a comprehensive network of service throughout both the East and West coasts, convenient connections to USAir cities throughout the nation, and international service to Canada, Mexico, and Great Britain.

With its modern fleet of comfortable, quiet, and efficient aircraft; its flexible operations hubs; and its strong balance sheet, USAir is one of the nation's most successful airlines. The company has flown through the storms of deregulation, emerging stronger than ever with both continuous profits and outstanding customer loyalty.

According to Colodny, USAir's net and operating margins continue to be among the best in the industry. "The company has reported a profit in every year since 1976," he says. "Our number-one objective is to remain financially strong. Over the years we have followed a policy of controlled growth. We will stay strong by continuing prudent financial planning and by continuing to serve our markets well. Our scheduling philosophy has been geared to serving the business traveler, and we will continue this emphasis."

In 1984 USAir introduced America to the latest aviation technology with a new aircraft type—the Boeing 737-300. This 138-seat twin-engine jet, which USAir helped design, is the most advanced, fuel-efficient, and quiet jet of its size and range. Its large on-board storage compartments brought new convenience to business travel. In late 1988 USAir will introduce an even newer aircraft, the 105-passenger Fokker 100.

USAir and Washington, D.C., have flown a long way together.

COLUMBIA HOSPITAL FOR WOMEN MEDICAL CENTER

Columbia Hospital for Women moved to its second home, the Maynard Mansion at 25th and M, streets, NW, in 1873. The mansion was once the site of the British Embassy and the center of Washington social life.

The Columbia Hospital for Women was conceived in crisis. At the end of the Civil War thousands of women came to Washington seeking help from the War Department, as well as information about relatives who had not returned. Anxiety, fatigue, sickness, and deprivation took a heavy toll. Many of the women had no means of support; they sought help from Washington charities and from congressional representatives of their home states. Existing resources could not meet the need.

In 1866 Secretary of War Edwin Stanton, responding to a proposal by Dr. J.E. Thompson and a group of wives of prominent Army and Navy officers, authorized the surgeon general to furnish 50 beds and to issue a "full supply of medicine and medical stores." Twenty of the beds would be for the exclusive use of wives and widows of soldiers and sailors. The hospital opened March 4, and was chartered by an Act of Congress on June 1.

The first home for the hospital was the Hill family mansion on the northwest side of Thomas Circle. In 1873 Congress purchased the Maynard Mansion at 25th Street and Pennsylvania Avenue, NW (once the site of the British Embassy). The four-acre estate cost only $25,000, but other prices were also lower in that era. Patients in the hospital's pay department were assessed only $6 to $10 per week, "in accordance with the room requested," including board, medicine, medical, and surgical attendance.

The dedication of the Columbia Hospital staff helped keep the institution's doors open during the years of struggle. For a three-month period employees worked without pay to keep the hospital from closing. Some Columbia nurses worked just for room and board.

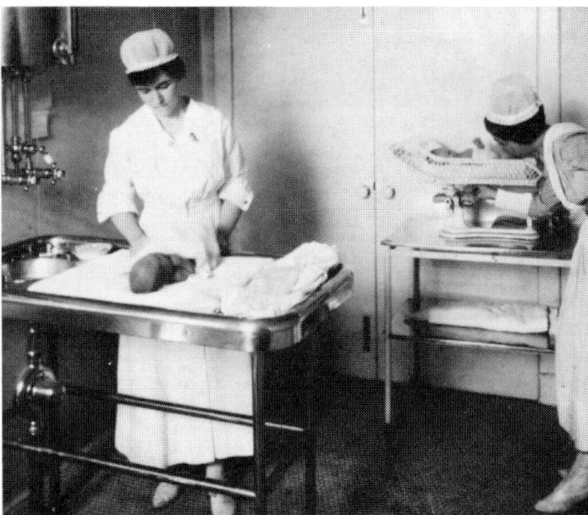

The early years of Columbia Hospital history witnessed continual political skirmishing for control of the institution and endless battles of the budget. The hospital was popular with Congress in the 1890s. That popularity—and financial support—allowed it to open a school of nursing and a pathology department, as well as expand the obstetrical facilities. That faith was repaid when the hospital was able to supply trained nurses to support troops in the Spanish American War.

Yet by 1910 waning congressional interest combined with opposition by the District of Columbia Board of Public Welfare almost forced the hospital to close. Then Congress changed its mind and provided a $300,000 authorization, which not only saved the institution but provided new facilities.

Demands that the hospital become a general care facility were another continuing problem. So too were attempts to have Columbia placed under the control of other District institutions. On the eve of the Great Depression—faced with declining occupancy, a deteriorating physical plant, and a lack of support from Congress—it appeared that Columbia might finally yield to these long-standing political and financial threats.

Instead, Washington's newly organized Community Chest came to the rescue with sufficient funding for institutional survival, and the hospital's fortunes changed for the better. In 1935 the District commissioners finally rejected long-standing efforts by the Board of Public Welfare to take over operations of Columbia. By 1938 Congress too was again supporting Columbia with new appropriations, making it possible for the hospital to improve facilities and provide a neonatal care facility—a nursery for premature infants—that won national acclaim.

The post-World War II era that

duced boom times at Columbia Hospital. Designed to accommodate 1,000 births per year, the institution's actual annual birth rate soared past 4,000. Plans for urgently needed physical expansion were derailed by Korean War priorities, but planned (and unplanned) family expansions continued unabated. Fifty-one pairs of twins were born at the hospital in 1951, and on February 11, 1955, 24 babies were born in one 24-hour period.

Despite such extraordinary demand, funding again became a major problem. Its quasi-federal status made Columbia ineligible for government aid programs, so in 1953 President Dwight D. Eisenhower signed legislation transferring title of the hospital land and buildings from the United States to the hospital's board of directors. The transfer qualified the facility for federal matching funds and helped attract private philanthropy. With donations from the public and a major gift from the Ford Foundation, Columbia was able to finance the Wilfred Goodwyn, Jr., wing that opened in 1958.

Columbia has often distinguished itself. In 1928 the institution was the first to establish a footprint identification system and, in the 1940s, the first to conduct classes for expectant fathers. A book by clinic executive director Linda McClure Woods, *Your New Baby,* became required reading for new parents throughout America. In 1976 Columbia became the first hospital on the East Coast to perform gynecologic laser surgery. The hospital's Reproductive Toxicology Center is the only one of its kind, and its Betty Ford Breast Diagnostic Center, providing early diagnosis of breast disease, is unique in the region.

In 1978 British gynecologist Dr. Patrick Steptoe lectured at Columbia Hospital. It was his first visit to an American medical institution following the birth of Louise Brown, the first baby born of *in vitro* fertilization. Columbia Hospital for Women established its own In Vitro Fertilization Program in 1983 as part of the Center for Fertility and Reproductive Endocrinology.

Over the years Columbia has evolved into a first-class teaching hospital and today enjoys a reputation as Washington's center for excellence in obstetrics, gynecology, and neonatology.

Columbia completed construction of the Columbia Hospital Professional Building at 25th and M streets, NW, in 1986. The new facility provides office space for physicians of all disciplines, and was designed with patient comfort and satisfaction as its highest priority. The professional building offers access to the hospital's laboratory and radiological facilities, and provides a full range of amenities such as parking, a pharmacy, and a coffee shop.

Over its 120-year history the institution has evolved from a federally supported charitable organization into a private, not-for-profit teaching hospital that continues to provide the most comprehensive scope of services available to women and infants in the metropolitan region. Its obstetrical/gynecological surgery and infertility services, as well as its Neonatal Intensive Care Unit, are among the most admired programs of their type in America.

Good thing, too. With nearly 5,000 babies born there each year, Columbia Hospital for Women is the cradle of the future of metropolitan Washington.

More than 5,000 infants are born at Columbia each year, more than at any other hospital in the District of Columbia. Columbia physicians continue to develop new surgical techniques, and the hospital's ongoing research has brought about vast improvements in the care of women and infants. Photo by Suzie Fitzhugh

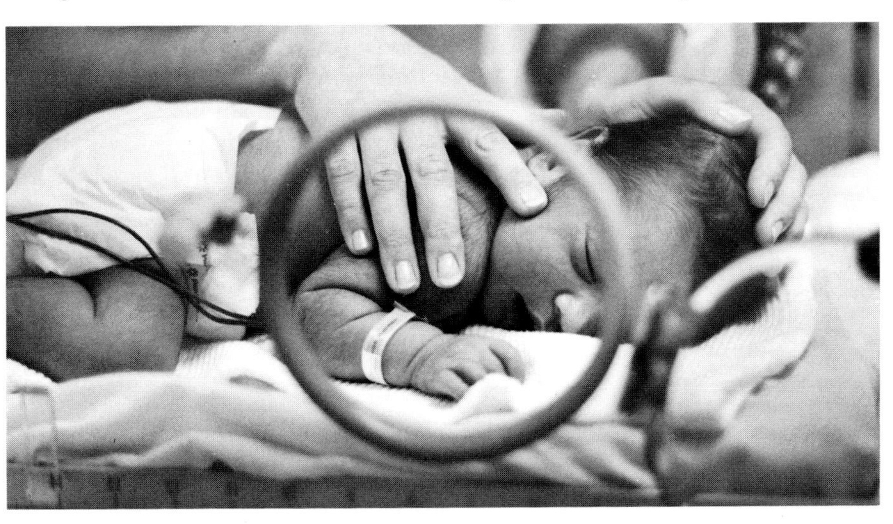

THE DONOHOE COMPANIES, INC.

Those burgundy and white "Donohoe" signs are everywhere! Traveling from Baltimore through Washington to Richmond, one sees projects being developed, built, sold, rented, or managed by The Donohoe Companies—external evidence of a great Washington business success story.

"In this business, you're not just saying you can do the job," says Clarence F. Donohoe, Jr., a grandson of the founder and chairman of the board of The Donohoe Companies. "Your product is there to say it for you. Reputation is a product of performance."

Back in 1884 Emily Donohoe believed that there was a good future in the real estate business. She and her husband—John F. Donohoe, a Washington grocer—had some investments in land, and neighbors often sought their advice or assistance in buying and selling properties. John F. took her advice, closed his grocery store, and opened a real estate office at 1001 New Jersey Avenue, SE.

When the firm became John F. Donohoe & Sons, it moved to 308 East Capitol Street. In 1909 the successful and expanding company moved to 314 Pennsylvania Avenue, SE, where it stayed until 1965, when it relocated to 2139 Wisconsin Avenue.

Crown jewel of Donohoe projects is Georgetown Park, the elegant Victorian shopping mall and condominium complex built within a preserved nineteenth-century warehouse along the C&O Canal. To build the modern structure within the historic district required the close cooperation of the National Park Service and the creation of a whole set of new construction techniques.

The foundations had to be set 17 feet below the canal water level. Because of preservation considerations—both for the warehouse exterior and the canal walls—no blasting or heavy equipment could be used. Much of the excavation had to be done by hand. Donohoe has a hard-won and highly respected reputation for bringing jobs in on time and on budget, but Georgetown Park proved to be the supreme test. The job took a year longer and $6 million more than expected. Engineers came from all over the nation to study the project, which had become widely known as the most complex construction job in the East.

John F. Donohoe, the Washington grocer who founded the real estate firm in 1884 that evolved into today's Donohoe Companies.

Other remarkable Donohoe projects that were recently completed—or are still under construction—include the Hechinger Mall, which anchors H Street renewal in the northeast corridor; Federal Center Plaza, with its two office buildings and the 529-room Capitol Holiday Inn; the Washington World Trade Center; the Jordanian Chancery; and several projects along the upper Wisconsin Avenue corridor and Maryland gateway.

Another highly visible Donohoe endeavor is the new Japanese Chancery at 2520 Massachusetts Avenue, NW, for which it imported tons of limestone blocks from Japan and built an indoor rock garden, complete with a two-story Japanese maple tree. Donohoe is also the general contractor for Washington's Ronald McDonald House.

With the end of World War II, Washington became a commercial boom town. The revitalized civilian business community wanted offices,

The John F. Donohoe & Sons staff and turn-of-the-century real estate brokerage firm on East Capitol Street.

warehouses, and parking facilities, and among the returning GIs was the third generation of Donohoes, eager and ready to meet the requirements of these new commercial clients. "Everyone had the same demands," recalls Clarence Donohoe, "but we didn't have the listings. We were really forced into the development business."

The family's first building, a $21,000 warehouse on Sumner Road, SE, was completed in 1954. Donohoe Construction Company was formally organized the following year.

In 1958 a complex series of zoning changes and financial deals brought the firm an option on land along Wisconsin Avenue. Page Communications had purchased the land in anticipation of building a new headquarters facility; unable to build, it was seeking to sell. The option ran out, and the deal appeared to be doomed to collapse. Then, while the deal was kept alive with a one-week extension on the option, Page was sold to Northrup Corporation, and Northrup agreed to lease a building for its new subsidiary.

The deal was saved, and the structure at 2001 Wisconsin with an extension to the rear at 3300 Whitehaven became Donohoe's first major project. When Page moved out, the building was leased to the National Oceanographic and Atmospheric Administration. It is currently under renovation and has been leased to the National Academy of Sciences.

The Donohoe Companies is a real estate supermarket, offering a full range of services from acquisition through management of apartment buildings, condominiums, office buildings, shopping centers, banks, mixed-use complexes, or whatever else is required. The firm works closely with owners, architects, engineers, and financiers. Donohoe's Complete Building Services provides computerized mechanical and energy management services as well as extensive consulting.

Donohoe has built 25 hotels, including the Georgetown Holiday Inn at 2101 Wisconsin Avenue, NW (which is owned by the corporation and houses its headquarters), two Embassy Suite Hotels, two Guest Quarters, and the Sheraton National in Arlington, Virginia. The firm also manages the Ballston Holiday Inn, which it recently completed building.

The Donohoe Companies, Inc., is a closely held corporation, with a majority of the stock owned by family and employees. Four grandsons of the founder are still active in the organization: Clarence F. Donohoe, Jr., is chairman of the board of directors; Richard J. Donohoe is chairman of the executive committee of the board; Francis X. Donohoe is vice-chairman of the board of directors; and James A. Donohoe, Jr., is secretary of the corporation and a director.

The next generation of Donohoes is working its way up through the ranks. James III and Robert are president and vice-president, respectively, of the Donohoe Development Company. Bert and Steve, sons of a Donohoe who left the family firm to become a physician, are both property managers.

Transformed from warehouses to a modern shopping, office, and residential complex, Donohoe's Georgetown Park is now a Capital City landmark. Built along the C&O Canal, it is a monument to design, engineering, and historic preservation.

GOVERNMENT EMPLOYEES INSURANCE COMPANY

In 1936 a brand-new Pontiac coupe could be purchased for $585, and gas cost 18 cents a gallon. America was in the depths of the Great Depression, and Leo Goodwin, an insurance company accountant in Fort Worth, Texas, believed that automobile insurance was too expensive. After all, a typical one-year policy might cost $30 or more.

He had an idea, a way to sell insurance at 20 to 30 percent below market rates. The concept: Limit sales to preferred-risk customers (government employees seemed to be sober, stable, and reliable sorts), and deal with them directly rather than through commissioned agents.

Leo and his wife, Lillian, put up $25,000 of their own capital and convinced Cleaves Rhea, a local Texas banker, to invest $75,000. The Government Employees Insurance Company was chartered on September 1, 1936.

GEICO Corporation assets now exceed $2 billion, with gross sales topping half that figure annually, but the business grew slowly at first. The first year Leo and Lillian Goodwin worked 365 twelve-hour days for a combined monthly salary of $250. Their system appeared to be working, but not as quickly as expected. So, having targeted government employees as their market, they decided to go where the New Deal action was. In November 1937 GEICO moved to Washington, leasing offices in the Investment Building at 15th and K streets, NW.

The Goodwins proceeded to endow their firm with a reputation for top-quality policyholder service. Company historians still tell about the 1941 hailstorm that damaged thousands of cars. Leo and Lillian Goodwin personally arranged to have several repair shops work around the clock under direct contract to GEICO. Expecting difficulties in finding parts because of wartime shortages, Leo brought in several truckloads of automobile glass. GEICO policyholders had their cars repaired in days; others waited weeks. The word spread through the federal bureaucracy.

World War II brought other difficulties to the young company. GEICO sold policies to customers through direct mail; its military and government employee clients were suddenly changing addresses frequently as they moved throughout the country. Rationing, shortages, and price freezes impacted the automotive industry severely. And while Leo Goodwin was 55, too old for military service, several talented young GEICO employees enlisted.

William B. Snyder, chairman of the board, chief executive officer, and president.

Leo and Lillian Goodwin, founders of GEICO. Their two-person operation, started in 1936, has grown into a multibillion-dollar corporation.

The owners assumed operational duties. The Goodwins worked to keep the office running. They were joined by a small but dedicated group of Washington women who took on new and increased responsibilities.

The end of World War II brought soaring success to GEICO. Returning veterans wanted new cars and new homes and needed new insurance policies to go with them. GEICO was perfectly positioned to meet their requirements and to participate in the exploding postwar economic boom. The $2.5 million in premiums written in 1946 marked a 50-percent increase over the previous year's business.

In 1948 the Rhea family sold its GEICO stock to a New York investment firm that distributed those shares to investors. GEICO became publicly owned, valued at more than $3 million. Its stock was traded over the counter, hovering briefly at $20 per share before starting to climb.

In 1952 GEICO expanded its definition of eligibility to include all state, county, and municipal employees, greatly increasing its marketing base and business. When Leo Goodwin retired in 1958 at age 71, stock that had been valued at $2,000 in 1948 was worth $95,000. Goodwin died in 1971.

GEICO Plaza, located in Chevy Chase, Maryland, is the home office for all of the GEICO companies. It was opened in 1959.

Rapid expansion of company business brought with it a continuous corporate housing crisis. By 1949 the organization needed additional space to house its rapidly expanding staff and purchased the GEICO Building at 14th and L streets, NW; four years later it relocated to the old Federal Housing Administration building at Vermont Avenue and K Street, NW. In 1959 GEICO moved to its own specially constructed Operations Building in Chevy Chase, Maryland.

In 1958 the firm expanded its policyholder base to include civilian professional, technical, and managerial occupational groups. It removed all occupational limits in 1973.

This expansion of GEICO's policyholder base into occupational groups with which the company was not familiar and the advent of no-fault insurance, led the firm to underprice its policies and brought GEICO to the brink of collapse. In May 1976 the board of directors elected John J. Byrne as chairman, president, and chief executive officer, charging him with returning the organization to its former robust financial good health.

Byrne's measures included increasing GEICO insurance rates, trimming its policyholder rolls to eliminate poor risks, shrinking the work force, and re-underwriting all GEICO policies. Byrne returned the organization to profitability in less than two years.

In October 1980, with GEICO restored to outstanding financial condition, a holding company, GEICO Corporation, was formed, and its stock was listed on the New York exchange. William B. Snyder was elected president of GEICO Corporation in 1982; Byrne continued as chief executive officer and chairman of the board.

GEICO Corporation today is a diverse enterprise consisting of 33 subsidiary companies. Although automobile and home owners' insurance remains by far the primary business, GEICO companies also handle life insurance, investment management, and industrial banking.

The new GEICO is quite different from the organization first envisaged by Leo Goodwin, but is still based on the founder's principles—disciplined operations and a fanatic dedication to customer service.

Byrne retired in 1985. In addition to his role as president, Snyder became chairman of the board and chief executive officer of GEICO Corporation.

WTOP NEWSRADIO 15

From studios located on upper Wisconsin Avenue in northwest Washington and from its 50,000-watt transmitter in Wheaton, Maryland, WTOP Newsradio 15 has long been a reliable source of news and information in the nation's capital.

WTOP Newsradio 15, the city's only all-news station, is a powerful component of Washington radio. Whether broadcasting debates between senators Robert Dole and Ted Kennedy; "Today on the Hill" with Dave McConnell; business reports by Bob Dalton; commentaries by Dan Rather, Charles Kuralt, and Charles Osgood; "The Larry King Show"; or any of its other popular features, WTOP Newsradio 15 consistently attracts a substantial portion of Washington's radio audience. And WTOP's is an influential audience, perhaps the most influential audience of any station in the world. It includes congressmen, senators, supreme court justices, and White House executives—decision makers from all three branches of government.

The history of WTOP makes up an important part of the golden age of broadcasting. One of its top "Morning Men" was Arthur Godfrey. "Godfrey would do two shows a day as Barbasol's 'Singing Sam,'" recalls Granville Klink, former chief engineer and now consultant, who often worked the control panel for Godfrey.

"Once for the East Coast, and then three hours later we'd do it all again for the West Coast stations." The station's technicians were responsible for broadcasting President Franklin D. Roosevelt's "Fireside Chats." And from hotels throughout the District, the station broadcast live performances by Benny Goodman and Glenn Miller as well as "Blond Bombshell" Ina Ray Hutton and her all-girl band.

WJSV Studio Three in the Earle Theater Building where Arthur Godfrey broadcast in the late 1930s. Photo by Reni Newsphoto Service

The 1942 WJSV mobile fleet used to record Arthur Godfrey's "Sundial" and other shows.

Technically and artisticallly, WTOP crews, producers, and talent helped create entire chapters of broadcasting lore in the early days of radio. On different occasions WTOP crews were called upon to transmit signals from a remote mountaintop, moving trains, and blimps; from baseball diamonds, football fields, and wrestling rings; and from various hotels, the Capitol, and the White House.

WTOP's signal always came through. In 1937 the station developed a new program called "Professor Quiz." It was one of the first quiz shows. It also produced "The Old Skipper," one of America's first children's programs.

"Report to the Nation," the radio forerunner to television's "Face the Nation," originated at WTOP. Orson Wells' "Mercury Theater of the Air" was occasionally produced at the National Theater, with WTOP originating the CBS network broadcast. In the 1940s "Janice Grey" was a locally produced soap opera that kept radio audiences waiting for the next episode. John Daly of "What's My Line" and Timex commercial fame was a WTOP announcer. Ross Martin went from WTOP microphones to "Mr. Lucky" and "Wild Wild West."

Washington Post "District Line" columnist Bill Gold was a WTOP performer. The brilliant news commentator Eric Sevareid headed the station's radio newsroom in the late 1930s and during World War II. Winston Burdett and Robert Trout worked at WTOP as part of Sevareid's distinguished staff of radio reporters. Sam Donaldson, Roger Mudd, and Connie Chung are among the other newspeople who worked at WTOP in the early days of their careers.

The venture began in 1926 as a small, 50-watt radio station in Brooklyn, New York, known as WTRC. Its first licensee was New York's 20th Assembly District Regular Republic Club. Less than a year later the license was transferred to James S. Vance, publisher of *Fellowship Forum*. (*Fellowship Forum* was a magazine published in support of the Ku Klux Klan.) The station was moved to Mount Vernon Hills, Virginia, and the call letters changed to WTFF. Later the call letters were changed to the initials of the new owner, WJSV, and moved to 1460 on the AM dial.

In June 1932 the Columbia Broadcasting System acquired the license and moved the station to an Alexandria, Virginia, site on Memorial Highway. Broadcasting journals took note of WJSV's new location, equipment, and place in the radio fraternity. "WJSV has just completed the installation of improvements which make it the last word in radio broadcasting transmission plants. With the newest approved Crystal Controlled Transmitter in operation under full power of 10,000 watts, WJSV is reaching out into all sections of the United States as well as into foreign countries with a strength and clarity of reception hitherto thought impossible."

CBS opened the station's first Washington studios in the Shoreham Building. It brought in Harry Butcher as general manager, and Butcher brought in an entirely new staff. The network viewed WJSV as a critical part of its system, its representative in the nation's capital. In 1933 the station changed its official city of license from Alexandria to Washington, and built new studios in the Earle Theater Building at 13th and E streets, NW.

It was a dynamic time for the station, for broadcasting, and for world events. When President Franklin D. Roosevelt wanted to speak to the nation, he had a whole new technology at his disposal. WJSV general manager Butcher coined a name for the president's informal radio speeches when he referred to them as "Fireside Chats." WTOP Newsradio 15 engineer-

Harry Reasoner (left) and former WJSV chief engineer Clyde Hunt during a presentation of WTOP equipment to the Smithsonian Roosevelt exhibit.

The WTOP transmitter building, erected in 1939, represents one of the finest examples of art-deco architecture in the Washington area. Photo by Reni Newsphoto Service

ing consultant Klink, then a young WJSV technician, handled presidential events for CBS.

"The Fireside Chats were broadcast from the oval room," recalls Klink. "At first there were only microphones for the three networks: CBS, NBC, and Mutual. Each of us had our own microphone and our own technical staff. We had the newsreel people around, of course, so we had to get over there early to get the best microphone positons.

"Those guys carried 150-pound cameras. There was no getting them out of the way. So we'd go over there early to get set up, and then we'd wait. FDR would make a grand entrance. Make no mistake of it, he was a real star."

In 1940 the station moved its transmitter from its location on the Potomac to Wheaton, Maryland, where its new transmitter fed an increased signal power of 50,000 watts to a three-tower directional antenna system. The Wheaton facilities were housed in a specially designed transmitter building. A showplace at the time, it had a full-time receptionist on duty who conducted tours for the public. Edward R. Murrow's reports from London were broadcast over WTOP via the CBS network.

While the news from World War II told of death and destruction in Europe and the Pacific, entertainers fought a battle to keep up morale on the home front. Celebrities from throughout the nation came to Washington to entertain government workers, and WJSV broadcast their performances through the CBS network.

Glenn Miller played at the Wardman Park Hotel in October 1940, and Eddy Duchin brought "Your Hit Parade" to Washington in January 1941. Mickey Rooney and Charlie Chaplin were featured guests on Christmas specials from Constitution Hall. Other remote broadcasts featured Benny Goodman and Fred Waring. WTOP crews traveled with singer Kate Smith to broadcast her concerts from military camps and other remote locations. In Washington, they helped with such local productions as the May 6, 1941, broadcast of "Amos 'n Andy," broadcasts of the National Symphony Orchestra, and an episode of "Inner Sanctum."

In March 1941 WJSV's frequency was changed from 1460 to 1500 kilocycles, then the top end of the AM commercial band. The station changed its call letters to WTOP in 1943. (The new call letters were obtained from a police radio station in Ohio where they stood for Tiffin, Ohio, Police.)

The Washington Post Company purchased 55 percent of WTOP from CBS in February 1949 and WOIC-TV from the Bamberger Company two years later. The television station soon carried the call letters WTOP-TV. It picked up the radio side's tradition of innovation as well: To cover President Dwight D. Eisenhower's 1952 inaugural, company technicians put a camera, generator, and small microwave transmitter in a rented Packard; joined the parade; and transmitted television pictures from a mobile camera via a receiving dish on the Capitol dome.

To house its new television station, the Washington Post Company built Broadcast House at Fortieth and Brandywine streets NW, surrounding and incorporating the existing WOIC transmitter and tower. The new building was completed in October 1953, just in time for Pick Temple to ride a pony into the new studios and start a national craze for local cowboy programming. WTOP moved its own studios from the Earle Building to the new facilities. In December 1954 the Washington Post Company purchased the remaining 45 percent of WTOP from CBS.

As AM radio lost ground to television and the new FM and FM stereophonic technology in the 1960s, WTOP moved to retain its popularity with several different formats. The station became an all-news broadcaster on March 9, 1969.

On June 26, 1978, Post Newsweek Stations sold WTOP radio to The Outlet Company (now Outlet Communications, Inc.). WTOP Newsradio 15 moved out of Broadcast House and into new studios in the Steuart Investment Company building next door, where it is housed today. Under Outlet management, WTOP Newsradio 15 has become an even more potent force in area broadcasting.

WTOP anchor Jamie Bragg writes news copy using the electronic newsroom computer system.

Today WTOP operates from a state-of-the-art computerized newsroom, which is virtually paperless.

In 1984 Outlet Communications merged with The Rockefeller Group, and on July 31, 1986, a group of Outlet executives repurchased the company. The new Outlet group owns four television stations and four radio stations, including WTOP Newsradio 15 and WASH-FM in Washington.

The company's other properties are WJAR-TV, Providence, Rhode Island; WCMH-TV, Columbus, Ohio; WATL-TV, Atlanta, Georgia; WXIN-TV, Indianapolis, Indiana; WIOQ-FM, Philadelphia, Pennsylvania; and KIQQ-FM, Los Angeles, California. Bruce Sundlun is chairman of the board of Outlet Communications, Inc.; David Henderson is president and chief operating officer; and Joseph T. Chairs is vice-president/Radio Group.

WTOP Newsradio 15 vice-president and general manager Michael L. Douglass is proud of the station's heritage and pleased that WTOP is among the few AM radio stations that are still growing.

Affiliated with the CBS radio network for the past 55 years, WTOP combines locally originated programming with network programming, Baltimore Orioles baseball games, and syndicated features. Since 1969 the station has emphasized the all-news aspect of its programming and, as they have since the 1930s, Washingtonians still love it.

BLUE CROSS AND BLUE SHIELD OF THE NATIONAL CAPITAL AREA

This old brownstone, on Vermont Avenue, NW, was the first home of Blue Cross and Blue Shield of the National Capital Area.

Blue Cross and Blue Shield Plans are a nationwide system of hospitalization and medical care. In Washington, D.C., the national Blue Cross and Blue Shield system is represented by Blue Cross and Blue Shield of the National Capital Area (BCBSNCA).

Today health and hospitalization insurance has become so much a part of our economic lives that it is hard to imagine an era when no such coverage was available—when people either paid the full costs of hospitalization and medical services themselves, became charity cases, or made do without care. But in fact, the origins of prepaid hospital and medical care are relatively recent.

The Blue Cross method of prepayment for hospital care originated in Baylor, Texas, where Dr. Justin Ford Kimball of Baylor University conceived the Plan in 1929. The concept—prepaid hospitalization for groups of employees—was originally adopted by individual hospitals, but the idea of communitywide agreements soon became a popular part of the Blue Cross system.

E.J. Henryson, secretary to the Health Committee of the District of Columbia, introduced the concept of prepaid hospitalization to Washington. He enlisted the help of Washington businessman and financier Joseph Hendrix Himes, then president of Columbia Hospital, who agreed to chair a blue-ribbon committee of local leaders of the health care community. When Group Hospitalization, Inc. (GHI), was formed late in 1933, Himes was elected as its first president.

E.J. Henryson, secretary to the Health Committee of the District of Columbia, introduced the concept of prepaid hospitalization to Washington, D.C., in 1933.

The initial Plan covered employees for only 21 days of hospital care and cost 75 cents per month. A contract that covered dependents was introduced in December 1937 at a cost of $1.75 per month, and the cost of individual coverage was cut to 65 cents.

By the end of its first year the Plan had 2,876 members. Further growth was threatened when the District's insurance department ordered GHI to reorganize into a stock or mutual insurance company, thus making it subject to department regulations and District taxes.

Arguing that the insurance department's orders were inappropriate to its mission and organization, GHI won a federal charter as a nonprofit, public service corporation. Signed by President Franklin Roosevelt on August 11, 1939, the charter authorized GHI to continue providing benefits for health care services, and to carry out other activities to safeguard and promote the public health.

By the end of World War II nearly 350,000 area residents were enrolled in GHI. In the 1950s GHI extended its coverage to individual non-group subscribers, agreed to participate in the national Inter-Plan Benefit Bank and transfer agreement, and adopted the Blue Cross symbol, a trademark that was gaining widespread national recognition. In 1962 the organization became Operations Center for the Blue Cross and Blue Shield Governmentwide Service Benefit Plan, in which 3 million federal employees and dependents are enrolled nationwide. By 1964, when GHI enrolled its one-millionth participant in the Washington region, the Plan had become a vital component of health care in the District of Columbia. In 1966 it became the fiscal intermediary for most hospitals in the region under Part A of the Medicare Program.

The Blue Shield system of prepaid medical care was born in the lumber and mining camps of the Pacific Northwest, where employers routinely sponsored and administered prepaid medical care plans. As early as 1917 physicians in Tacoma, Wash-

ington, organized a county medical service bureau that could contract with employers and provide care directly to employees.

From their inception, the Blue Shield Plans were nonprofit organizations. Participating physicians agreed to accept the Plan's reimbursements as full payment for services rendered in many instances and to receive payment directly from the Plan.

The modern Blue Shield concept was originally represented in Washington by Medical Service of the District of Columbia, which incorporated in 1946 and began operations two years later. Under the guidance of its first president, Dr. Frank D. Costenbader, it offered a simple and realistic program that could be readily understood by both subscribers and health care providers.

The Plan covered surgery, obstetrics, anesthesia, and in-hospital-related services. Member physicians agreed to accept Medical Service's schedule of fees as full payment for low-income subscribers ($2,500 for individuals, $4,500 for families). Despite early difficulties in establishing an acceptable schedule of payments to participating physicians, the new Plan was successful immediately. Within a year more than 111,000 subscribers had enrolled. Medical Service became a member of the national Blue Shield Association in 1952.

ABOVE: Today Blue Cross and Blue Shield of the National Capital Area is headquartered in this building at 550 Twelfth Street, SW.

RIGHT: Joseph Hendrix Himes, first president.

When it began operations Medical Service named GHI as its administrative agent, and offered its prepaid medical care plan to all GHI subscribers. In 1956 the two organizations began offering subscribers a comprehensive contract combining benefits of both programs, as well as a new major medical plan.

Over the past three decades plan benefits have grown and changed to conform with continually shifting regulations and expectations, but GHI and Medical Service continued cooperating with each other and with their national associations to provide area residents with the finest-possible program of benefits and care.

In 1985 GHI and Medical Service merged to form Blue Cross and Blue Shield of the National Capital Area. BCBSNCA employs more than 2,700 people at its corporate offices in southwest Washington, D.C. In 1986 BCBSNCA paid more than 6.8 million claims totaling $840 million in benefits. The organization is the national capital region's largest provider of health care coverage. The Plan is a leader in community health planning, health services and benefits research, and health care cost-containment activities. The organization has pioneered in introducing benefits for such services as outpatient surgery, home care, and hospice.

Charles P. Duvall, M.D., is currently chairman of the board of Blue Cross and Blue Shield of the National Capital Area. Joseph P. Gamble is president, executive division, and chief executive officer.

AT&T

AT&T, with $40.5 billion in assets and $34.9 billion in annual revenues, is among America's most important and successful corporations. In the short time since its federally mandated reorganization, AT&T has reaffirmed its position as a technological leader while maintaining its century-old tradition of outstanding customer service.

AT&T has about 9,000 employees at more than 30 locations in the Washington metropolitan area. There are major office centers in the city as well as in Silver Spring, Beltsville, and Rockville, Maryland, and throughout northern Virginia. The largest AT&T office and operations complex in the national capital region is on Chain Bridge Road in Oakton, Virginia.

AT&T engineers, builds, and manages a modern international telecommunications network supplying telephone, data, and image services. The company offers domestic and international telecommunications services that can be interconnected with a wide variety of information systems.

The company also designs, manufactures, markets, and services equipment for telecommunications networks; information systems, including computers and networks for offices and factories; telephone products for homes and businesses, and related electronic components for high-technology products.

The Washington area is headquarters for AT&T's Eastern Region Network organization. With responsibility for telecommunications services from Maine to Virginia, the AT&T network uses digital switching machines, lightwave communications systems, satellites, microwave radio towers, and coaxial cable to carry voice, data, and television signals to their destinations.

The federal government is AT&T's largest local customer. Headquartered in downtown Washington, AT&T Federal Systems provides the U.S. government with systems solutions to its unique information movement and management needs in both the civilian and defense sectors. More than 50 AT&T Federal Systems offices nationwide are supervised from Washington.

AT&T traces its corporate history directly to Alexander Graham Bell, inventor of the telephone. Established in 1885 as a subsidiary of Bell's original company, AT&T became the Bell System's parent company in 1889.

The city of Washington has played an important role throughout telephone company history. Bell was often in Washington, where he would meet with Joseph Henry of the Smithsonian Institution and other members of the local scientific community. On February 14, 1876, Bell visited Washington to file specifications and apply for his first patent on the telephone.

Alexander Graham Bell conducted many of his Photophone experiments in Washington and received a patent on the device in 1880. The precursor of today's lightwave communications system, Bell was able to transmit sound more than 1.25 miles with the device, but the system did not work well enough to be used commercially.

Bell moved to Washington in 1878. His home was on Connecticut Avenue, just off Dupont Circle. In 1880 he received the 50,000 francs (approximately $10,000) Volta Prize from the government of France, and

AT&T manager Chris Stelter discusses the installation of a new multimillion-dollar digital telecommunications system for the House of Representatives with Bill Kinter, assistant director for the House Office of Telephone Services. In 1986 AT&T was awarded a 10-year contract to install and maintain the system.

he used the money to establish the Volta Laboratory in Washington.

At the Volta Laboratory, Bell and a Washington optical instrument maker named Sumner Tainter experimented with the Photophone, which used light beams to transmit sound. The Photophone and its successor, the Spectrophone, were patented in 1880 but never caught on for popular uses. The optical reflectors, however, foreshadowed antennas used for microwave transmission, and the basic concept is now the foundation of fiber-optic technology.

For many years the history of AT&T in the national capital region was intertwined with that of the Chesapeake and Potomac Telephone Company (C&P). It is a story that starts with George C. Maynard, the owner of an electrical supply store at 1423 Sixth Street, NW. Maynard obtained an exclusive license to use and lease Bell telephones in the District of Columbia and suburban Maryland. He opened his first exchange, the National Telephonic Exchange, in 1878.

Early subscribers included the White House, the State Department, the Bell residence, the Willard Hotel, the Washington Gas Light Company, and E.M. Gallaudet, president of the Gallaudet Institute.

Late in 1879 the operations of Maynard's telephonic exchange were transferred to the National Capital Telephone Company, which was owned in part by Bell's father-in-law, Graham Hubbard, a Washington resident and a director of the National Bell Telephone Company. The new organization bought out the Washington telephone assets of Western Union at the same time. It purchased Maynard's interests in 1881 for $50,000.

National Capital Telephone merged with the Maryland Telephone Company in 1883 and reincorporated as the Chesapeake and Potomac Telephone Company. Among the first directors was Theodore N. Vail, a former Washingtonian and supervisor of the post office department's railway mail system. "Bell invented the telephone," says one bit of AT&T lore. "Watson constructed it, Sanders financed it, and Vail put it on a business basis."

AT&T introduced its public-address technology at the 1921 inauguration of President Warren G. Harding. For Calvin Coolidge's inaugural in 1925, long-distance telephone lines carried his address to 120 broadcasting stations in cities from coast to coast. When Herbert Hoover took the oath of office in 1929, Bell System Talking Pictures enabled four sound motion picture companies to record the event. AT&T Long Lines pioneered inaugural telecasts when it helped to transmit the 1949 opening ceremonies of Harry Truman's swearing in.

The 500,000th phone in Washington was installed on April 23, 1951, 75 years after Bell received his patent. The one-millionth telephone customer in Washington signed up for service in April 1976.

Today AT&T is embarked on an ambitious, multibillion-dollar program to expand the company's communications network to handle the increasing demand for a variety of data and voice services. Part of that expansion includes the installation of lightwave communications systems, both domestically and across the Atlantic and Pacific oceans.

In 1983 Washington became a central link in a major lightwave communications system stretching from Boston to Atlanta. AT&T's digital communications network links about 215 cities throughout the United States. By the end of 1989 AT&T will have advanced digital communications systems linking 350 major cities in the United States and key points in Europe, Japan, and other locations in the Far East and Caribbean.

AT&T communications technician Tony DeRosen prepares to install a new circuit pack on a lightwave-terminating module. This equipment converts light into electrical signals for distribution on the AT&T network. Washington is a central link in a major AT&T lightwave communications system stretching from Boston to Atlanta.

THE KIPLINGER WASHINGTON EDITORS

From left to right: Knight A. Kiplinger, vice-president/publications; Austin H. Kiplinger, president; and Todd L. Kiplinger, director of investments.

The Kiplinger Washington Letter *was launched September 29, 1923, and the* Tax Letter, *the* Agriculture Letter, *the* Florida Letter, *the* Texas Letter, *and the* California Letter *have been added since.*

A brief but sharp economic crisis brought distress to the national financial community late in 1920. One effect: A young Washington business writer had to seek new clients and move to a less expensive office. A theater marquee partially blocked the view from his new, low-rent quarters, but W.M. Kiplinger's vision remained clear. Soon his insights would be providing clients with unobscured Washington perspectives.

A former Associated Press reporter covering the Treasury Department, Federal Reserve Board, and Justice Department, Kiplinger had an insider's understanding of national affairs. Experience as Washington representative for the National Bank of Commerce had yielded an understanding of private-sector interests.

His new business, The Kiplinger Washington Agency, offered clients not only his counsel but also such personal research services as obtaining unpublished government reports and copies of congressional bills, expediting passport applications, and simplifying access to federal information and programs. One client even asked him to check out President Herbert Hoover's preference in gloves.

Kiplinger launched his *Washington Letter* September 29, 1923, but it did not become self-supporting for a decade. (The publication was priced at $18 for many years. A year's subscription now costs $58.) Gradually dropping other agency activities, he kept the operation afloat with freelance writing. His first book, *Inflation Ahead! What To Do About It,* appeared in 1935.

The economic gyrations of war and peace brought a nationwide hunger for business news from Washington. Kiplinger's semi-telegraphic sweep-line style with its underscored flag words, ellipses, and short sentences gave his newsletter a distinctive identity. By getting behind the news and publishing evaluations and predictions, he made the *Washington Letter* particularly useful.

LEFT: Four Kiplinger books, written over the years, are Washington Now, Washington Is Like That, Inflation Ahead, *and* The New American Boom.

BELOW: Changing Times *is the Kiplinger magazine of personal finance.*

"The Letters reflect our considered judgments," says W.M. Kiplinger's son and successor, Austin Kiplinger. "We look at options with objectivity. We appraise prospects for the future. We don't offer our opinions and seldom use words such as 'good' or 'bad'; our readers have their own points of view."

Austin Kiplinger brought his own broad experience to the Kiplinger organization. Following a stint as office boy with the *Washington Letter* and studies at Cornell and Harvard universities, he worked as a reporter with the *San Francisco Chronicle* before assisting his father in writing *Washington Is Like That* (1942).

After World War II service as a Navy carrier pilot, he helped create *Changing Times* magazine—but left Washington to work as a columnist and broadcaster in Chicago. He returned as executive vice-president of The Kiplinger Washington Editors in 1956 and has been president of the corporation since 1959. W.M. Kiplinger died in 1967. Under Austin Kiplinger's leadership, the organization remains responsive to audience needs. "We want our readers to be as well informed as possible. They need to plan for the future. We give them the information they need to make financial decisions. That's our only mission, and like Bauhaus design, the form of our letters just follows that function."

Kiplinger writers never quote sources directly. When speaking with them, government officials and business leaders know that they are speaking only for guidance, and are free to talk frankly and openly.

Judgments appearing in the letters usually reflect staff consensus, says Austin Kiplinger. "It's not a question of votes or conflict. Our conclusions surface through discussion and analysis. We work together assembling the pieces, and usually the picture reveals itself. But the final responsibility for all content is mine. That's why my signature appears at the bottom of the *Washington Letter.*"

Kiplinger's *Changing Times* magazine, which has a monthly circulation of 1.2 million today, was the first magazine to provide its readers with how-to guidance on personal-finance topics such as investing, taxes, insurance, and home buying. Now 41 years old, *Changing Times* has accepted advertising only since 1980.

"Advertising has no effect on editorial policy," says Austin Kiplinger. "We occasionally lose advertisers who wish we wouldn't tell our readers so much, but a good market only results when well-informed buyers meet well-informed sellers."

Besides *The Kiplinger Washington Letter* and *Changing Times,* the organization publishes the *Tax Letter* (created in 1925), the *Agriculture Letter* (started in 1929 as the *Farm Board Letter*), the *Florida Letter* (since 1956), the *California Letter* (since 1965), and the *Texas Letter* (originated in 1980).

The editorial offices and corporate headquarters have been located in the Editors Building at 1729 H Street NW since 1950. Editors Press of Hyattsville, Maryland, is a wholly owned subsidiary of Kiplinger Washington Editors. A commercial printer, it has handled most Kiplinger production and mailing (now exceeding 100 million pieces per year) since 1960.

The Kiplinger Washington Editors is one-third owned by the employees' profit-sharing fund, but control rests with Austin Kiplinger. He also heads the Kiplinger Foundation, a philanthropic organization that supports youth organizations, education, the arts, health, and civic affairs. An active member and former president of the National Symphony Orchestra Association, he is also a staunch supporter of public broadcasting, the Washington Journalism Center, the Columbia Historical Society, and Cornell University.

Two of Austin Kiplinger's sons are executives with the organization. Knight Kiplinger is vice-president/publications and editor-in-chief of *Changing Times.* Todd Kiplinger is vice-president/investments.

The Kiplinger Washington Editors remains primarily concerned with helping readers prepare for the future. The company published *The New American Boom,* in 1986. Its determination: "activity, vigor, and a strong resurgence of growth in this country over the next two decades." You have Austin Kiplinger's word on it.

COLUMBIA FIRST FEDERAL SAVINGS AND LOAN ASSOCIATION

Columbia First Federal Savings and Loan Association traces its roots to a small, part-time organization started in 1907 by John B. Harrell and two associates, Albert Denham and Albert White. Originally known as the Columbia Building Association, the company was organized as a sideline to Harrell's main business, the American Workman Insurance Company. The savings and loan association's assets totaled only $15,000. It occupied one desk in the insurance company's headquarters at 615 F Street, NW, and accepted customers only one night each week. Today Columbia First Federal Savings and Loan Association has 27 branches throughout the tri-state region of Washington, D.C., Maryland, and Virginia.

The economic shocks and financial disruptions of the Great Depression threatened an early end to the history of the Columbia Building Association, yet it emerged from the national crisis in outstanding health. The Federal Savings and Loan Insurance Corporation accepted Columbia for membership on August 31, 1935—without condition. It was the first savings and loan in the city to qualify for the federal insurance. In 1939 the association was issued a federal charter and a new name—Columbia Federal Savings and Loan.

In February 1957 Columbia Federal merged with Mutual Federal Savings and Loan. In May 1971 Columbia merged again, this time combining its assets with those of District Building and Loan Association. In October 1974 another merger combined the assets of Columbia Federal with those of Hamilton Federal Savings and Loan Association.

On March 1, 1981, Columbia Federal Savings and Loan Association merged with another Washington thrift institution boasting a distinguished history, First Federal Savings and Loan Association of Washington, D.C. Organized by 14 shareholders led by A.E. Giegengack and Edwin Jacobson, First Federal Savings and Loan Association received Federal Charter No. 1381 in April 1937, making it the first federally chartered savings and loan in Washington.

First Federal opened for business at 610 Thirteenth Street, NW, in headquarters originally occupied by the old Fidelity Building and Loan Association. Its first order of business was the purchase of Fidelity's assets. By November 1939 First Federal had doubled its assets, enlarged its quarters, and installed a new vault, a new bookkeeping system, and new central air conditioning.

First Federal came to national attention when in 1944 it became the first thrift institution in the nation to make a G.I. home mortgage loan, then newly authorized under the Servicemen's Readjustment Act. (The house, on Kennedy Street, NW, sold for $9,500. The interest rate on the $7,500 G.I. loan was 4 percent.) In 1953, when conditions forced an unacceptable freeze of new G.I. loans, First Federal cooperated with the Federal National Mortgage Association (FNMA) to thaw the system with a purchase of more than $4.7 million in G.I. loans from FNMA.

The combined institution, known as Columbia First, is one of Washington's largest savings and loan associations. Clarence E. Kefauver, Jr., chairman of Columbia Federal, became the first chairman of the board of the merged Columbia First Federal Savings and Loan. T. William Blumenauer, Jr., president and chief executive officer of Columbia Federal, became the first president of Columbia First. Dewitt T. Hartwell, president and chief executive officer of First Federal, became executive vice-president and chief administrative officer of the new organization.

Hartwell became president and chief executive officer of Columbia First Federal Savings and Loan in October 1982. When Kefauver retired as chairman of the board in 1983, Hartwell assumed the chairmanship in addition to his other responsibilities.

John B. Harrell, one of the organizers of Columbia First Federal Savings and Loan Association in 1907.

Bright-green MOST signs tell people throughout the Mid-Atlantic region that a MOST network automated teller machine (ATM) awaits their financial transaction needs. In 1982 Columbia First played a vital role in the emergence of Washington as a leader in electronic financial transactions. As an organizer and equity partner in Internet, Inc., Columbia First helped establish the Mid-Atlantic region's largest network of shared ATMs. Today the MOST system is the most successful ATM network in the national capital area

Columbia First launched its INVEST program in October 1983. INVEST, a service of ISFA Corporation, is a full-service brokerage operation offered through nearly 150 savings and loan associations nationwide. In September 1985 Columbia First acquired Family Federal Savings and Loan Association of Springfield, Virginia. This acquisition brought Columbia First a branch network serving customers in northern Virginia.

On November 27, 1985, Columbia First began a new era, with its public offering of 2,446,625 shares of common stock at $10 per share in connection with its conversion from mutual ownership to stock ownership. The offering resulted in approximately 1,800 stockholders and net proceeds of $22.5 million.

In 1986 Columbia First Federal Savings and Loan Association moved to take an active place in the international financial community with the issue of $150 million in 10-year Eurodollar notes. In March 1987 Columbia First expanded its Maryland franchise by a total of six branches with the acquisition of the insured deposits of First Federal of Maryland, FSA.

At September 30, 1987, Columbia First had assets of $1.86 billion, net worth of $83 million, and deposits of $1.05 billion, making it the largest savings and loan association headquartered in Washington, D.C.

RIGHT: Dewitt T. Hartwell, chairman of the board, president, and chief executive officer. Photo by Breton Littlehales

BELOW: Left to right: C. Gay Harrell, Jr., executive vice-president and secretary; William B. Swift, executive vice-president; Dewitt T. Hartwell, chairman of the board, president, and chief executive officer; Thomas P. FitzGibbon, Jr., executive vice-president, and C. Malcolm West, senior executive vice-president and chief financial officer. Photo by Breton Littlehales

THE NATIONAL BANK OF WASHINGTON

Washington had been the capital of the United States for only nine years when its oldest bank, then named the Bank of Washington, first opened for business. The city's streets were unpaved and unlighted. Cattle grazed along Pennsylvania Avenue. Most people lived and shopped in Alexandria and Georgetown, which were also the locations of the region's only banks.

From its founding to the present, The National Bank of Washington, as it became known, has consistently demonstrated an unparalleled commitment to the national capital city and region. However, when a group of citizens first decided to charter the bank in Washington, they met with unexpected obstacles. Neither Virginia nor Maryland had jurisdiction in the District, and Congress refused to consider chartering a bank other than the then-operative national bank—the First Bank of the United States.

Frustrated, the would-be founders agreed to adopt Articles of Association in lieu of a charter. Essentially, they entered the banking business without any real legal authority to do so.

The bank, nicknamed "the Little Bank on Capitol Hill," opened December 1, 1809, in a converted Carroll Row residence. Less than a year later it moved to New Jersey Avenue, SE. The first president of the bank was Washington landowner Daniel Carroll of Duddington. His holdings included the land that is now the site of the Capitol and the Library of Congress, as well as the original House and Senate office buildings.

Congress chartered the bank in 1811, yet more difficulties were immediately ahead. On August 14, 1812, British troops attacked the city. Cashier William A. Bradley loaded the records and holdings onto a wagon and raced to safety in Brookville, Maryland. According to bank folklore, Daniel Carroll spent the day assisting First Lady Dolley Madison in her efforts to save the furnishings of the White House. The Madisons were, after all, customers of the bank.

The British burned the Capitol, the White House, and other government buildings, but two weeks later the Bank of Washington was back in business at its New Jersey Avenue location. Shortly thereafter the bank subscribed a $50,000 loan to the United States, part of a half-million-dollar emergency program to revive the federal treasury. Only the success of local citizens in raising this loan persuaded Congress to resist powerful lobbies that sought to remove the national capital from Washington.

In 1828 the bank recognized that Washington's business center was moving from Capitol Hill toward the northwest quadrant. It followed, moving to Sixth Street and Pennsylvania Avenue NW, where it leased quarters on the first floor of the National Hotel. In 1831 the institution purchased its own building on Market Space at C Street and Louisiana Avenue. The three-story brick building served as the bank's headquarters for many years.

Federal controversy over the Second Bank of the United States reached crisis proportions in the 1830s, and in the early 1840s continued antibanking sentiment in Congress almost resulted in actions that would have forced the Bank of Washington to dissolve. But while its location in Washington sometimes brought undue political opposition, it also brought illustrious and powerful customers.

Davy Crockett was a customer of the Bank of Washington. Other early depositors included Chief Justices John Marshall and Roger Taney; poet Francis Scott Key, author of the national anthem; and Eli Whitney, inventor of the cotton gin.

The "buck" may have stopped on President Harry S. Truman's desk, but he kept his dollars in Washington's oldest bank. So did such national leaders as Secretary of State Daniel Webster and Speaker of the House Henry Clay. President Abraham Lincoln and his Secretary of War, Edwin Stanton, also were among its distinguished customers, as was Civil War photographer Matthew Brady.

On December 28, 1885, the Bank of Washington adopted a new charter under the National Bank Act. With the charter came a new name, The National Bank of Washington. Four years later the institution opened its new building at 14th and G streets NW.

On April 1, 1907, The National Bank of Washington purchased all assets of the Central National Bank, including its turreted, five-story brick headquarters on an adjoining corner. The merger, accomplished with the full support of both boards of directors, produced a significantly stronger National Bank of Washington.

At many times in its history national crisis brought extraordinary responses from the bank. When the United States entered World War I, the bank remained open until 9 p.m. to receive subscriptions to Liberty Loan bonds. After the Bank Holiday of 1933 the National Bank of Washington was among the few banks in the city that were able to reopen and meet all depositor demands from their own assets. It had no need to borrow from the Federal Reserve.

In 1954 The National Bank of Washington expanded through merger with Hamilton National Bank. Hamilton had been created in 1933 as a result of the consolidation of several Washington banks after the Bank Holiday. Following the merger the National Bank moved its headquarters to the building previously occupied by Hamilton. The National Bank merged with Liberty National Bank in 1957 and with Ana-

From 1831 to 1889 the home of The National Bank of Washington was in this building at Market Space, C Street, and Louisiana Avenue, NW.

costia National Bank three years later.

In 1949 the United Mine Workers of America acquired a controlling interest in The National Bank of Washington. Under UMW ownership, the institution continually demonstrated an active interest in community and social affairs. That interest continues, unaffected by the 1985 sale of majority ownership to Colson, Inc., a diverse investment group. Currently the National Bank of Washington is a subsidiary of Washington Bancorporation, a publicly traded company.

Luther H. Hodges, Jr., is chairman of the board of directors of Washington Bancorporation and of The National Bank of Washington. The executive office of the bank is located at 619 Fourteenth Street, NW, and there are 18 branch offices throughout the city and a loan production office in Baltimore, Maryland. In 1986 Washington Bancorporation purchased Enterprise Bank in Vienna, Virginia, giving the corporation a metropolitan banking presence.

MOUNT VERNON COLLEGE

ABOVE: Mount Vernon Seminary, 1901.

BELOW: The Charles Ellison Eckles and Anita Heurich Eckles Memorial Library, 1987.

Mount Vernon College is the oldest continuing educational institution for women in the nation's capital. A private, four-year college, Mount Vernon offers B.A. degrees combining liberal arts and career-oriented courses. Throughout its history Mount Vernon has remained committed to educating women for success —in their careers, community activities, and personal lives. As women's needs have changed over the years, Mount Vernon's educational programs and mission have also evolved.

Elizabeth J. Somers, a woman far ahead of her time, founded Mount Vernon Seminary in 1875 with a six-year program: four years of preparatory work and two years of college-level study. Formal study was supplemented by her "at homes," gatherings that were frequented by authors, poets, musicians, politicians, and diplomats. Evidence of the outstanding success of her program is seen in the fact that graduates of the junior college were automatically accepted to the junior year at four-year colleges.

In 1916 Mount Vernon was incorporated under a board of trustees as a nonprofit institution. The school's growth required construction of a new campus along Nebraska Avenue. In 1942, just as its exquisite chapel, dedicated to Elizabeth Somers, was completed, the U.S. Department of the Navy took possession of Mount Vernon's Nebraska Avenue campus in the interest of the World War II effort.

For the duration of the war Mount Vernon found temporary quarters in the Spring Valley area of Washington. Classes were held on the upper floor of the Garfinkel's store. After a long search Mount Vernon moved to its current 26-acre site on Foxhall Road in 1946.

Continuing the tradition of evolving to meet the changing needs of women, Mount Vernon phased out its preparatory school in 1969, when the institution formally changed its name to Mount Vernon College. In 1973 Mount Vernon College was licensed by the District of Columbia to offer the Bachelor of Arts degree and the degrees of Doctor of Humane Letters and Doctor of Laws.

The college's eight academic departments are Arts and Humanities, Business Administration, Communications, Human Development, Interior Design, Math and Science, Physical Education, and Political Science. The institution offers a total of 11 degree programs. Mount Vernon also offers evening certificate programs in Business Management and Human Resource Management.

The completion of the Florence Hollis Hand Chapel in 1969 and a new dormitory, Pelham Hall, in 1971 initiated an era of physical expansion to create facilities for a four-year college that is continuing under the leadership of president Jane Coutant Evans and Norman S. Portenoy, chairman of the board of trustees.

On September 18, 1987, Mount Vernon College opened the doors of its new library, a contemporary facility that will provide Mount Vernon students with ample study space and allow for a growing collection of scholarly material. The building has been totally financed by a private capital campaign, which also substantially enriched the college endowment. As it did in the days of Elizabeth Somers' "at homes," Mount Vernon College is still providing women with unique and personalized learning opportunities.

INGERSOLL AND BLOCH, CHARTERED

Where many attorneys see problems, William Ingersoll and Stuart Marshall Bloch see opportunities—for their clients, as well as themselves. Partners in the Washington, D.C., law firm that bears their name, Ingersoll and Bloch are known nationwide for their innovative resolution of real estate regulatory and related banking problems. Many of America's leading real estate investment and development firms and major financial institutions seek the firm's services, as do national corporations and government agencies.

The firm's headquarters building, constructed in 1888 by Samuel Edmonston, is an enduring symbol of the creativity and quality of its work, as well as the partners' long-standing commitment to historic preservation in Washington. Once a center of Washington political power and social gaiety, the building had been allowed to deteriorate until its restoration by Ingersoll and Bloch.

The building's past owners include Senator Russell A. Alger of Michigan and James Schoolcraft Sherman, vice-president under President William Howard Taft. After Sherman's death it found adaptive reuse as an opulent bordello, a dental hospital, and a boardinghouse. Today it has found creative new life as the home of an imaginative and dynamic law firm.

Ingersoll and Bloch is America's premier expert in the complex forest of federal and state laws and regulations surrounding real estate development.

The firm is widely respected for its work in preparing disclosure statements and other documents for the state and federal registration of subdivided land, condominiums, condo-hotels, cooperatives, timeshare projects, campgrounds, planned unit developments, and other real estate offerings. It has qualified real estate projects in most of the states, as well as in Canada and other countries where U.S. real estate is sold. This focus has taken the practice into such diverse areas as environmental affairs, taxation, securities transactions, advertising, licensure, and registration.

In the past few years the firm has responded to a changing industry by adding litigation and banking experts to its team, with a focus on workout negotiation and loan underwriting standards.

William Ingersoll is a nationally respected expert on state and federal regulation of real estate development. "Real estate is among America's most regulated industries," he says, "and that breeds opportunities for lawyers." His partner, Stu Bloch, is widely acknowledged as the creator of the asset-audit concept and regarded as the pioneer in examination of asset performance on a case-by-case basis. Their experience in real estate transactions of all types provides them—and their clients—with an insider's edge.

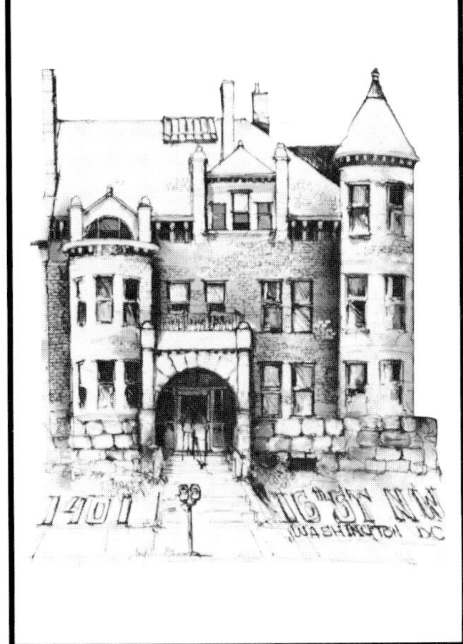

The Sherman House has been restored to its former grandeur by Ingersoll and Bloch and now serves as the law firm's headquarters.

Stuart Marshall Bloch (left) and William B. Ingersoll in front of the Sherman House.

The firm remains a moderately small organization. There are four other partners: Robert M. Chasnow, Larry Paul Ellsworth, Reuben B. Robertson, and Jeffry Blake Stern. The firm also owns and operates Land Development Institute, Ltd. (LDI), publisher of legal treatises, newsletters, and other resources for the real estate industry. As LDI's editor and coeditor in chief, respectively, Bloch and Ingersoll edit such publications as the *Land Development Law Reporter*, *Timesharing Law Reporter Briefs*, *Real Estate Opportunity Report*, and the *Digest of State Land Sales Regulations*.

M.S. GINN COMPANY

M.S. Ginn Company, whose history dates back more than 100 years, has retail stores in Washington, D.C.; Baltimore, Maryland; Philadelphia, Pennsylvania; and Richmond, Charlottesville, and (shown here) McLean, Virginia.

Ginn's fleet of delivery trucks in front of the Ager Road headquarters.

The M.S. Ginn Company traces its roots to the Stockett-Fiske Company, founded in 1886, more than 100 years ago. The enterprise, named M.S. Ginn, was started in the mid-1920s by five executives of The Washington School for Secretaries for the purpose of selling supplies to graduates of the school. Mildred S. Ginn was the school's secretary and provided the name for the new organization.

The M.S. Ginn Company has had several different owners over its century-long history. Hugh V. Kaiser purchased it from The WSS in 1932, and Marsh S. Marshall became owner in 1965. Ginn was publicly owned during the 1970s, its stock traded over the counter. In 1980 a Pittsburgh-based company bought the stock and took the firm back into private ownership. Presidents of the M.S. Ginn Company have included Marsh S. Marshall, 1965-1982; Dwight S. Sapp, 1982-1986; and Ronald E. Ruberti, 1986-.

Despite competition from approximately 200 other local suppliers, M.S. Ginn has become one of the largest office products dealers in the country. There are 5 marketing arms of the company, serving all segments of the market; 22 retail stores in metropolitan Washington, Baltimore, Philadelphia, Richmond, and Charlottesville (with 2 more scheduled to open each year); an outside sales staff of more than 100 salespeople selling commercial and government accounts; and a staff of 15 designer-salespeople operating from a 10,000-square-foot furniture showroom in the heart of Washington. The firm's 241,000-square-foot warehouse and executive office complex in Hyattsville, Maryland, distributes office products to more than 20,000 accounts from its extensive inventory of office supplies, furniture, and Smith Corona typewriters, utilizing a fleet of 40 distinctively decorated M.S. Ginn Company trucks.

During a recent 12-month period the M.S. Ginn Company delivered more than 2.5 million ballpoint pens, more than 5 million felt-tip markers, and .75 million typewriter ribbons to its customers. That is no mistake, although it also delivered 398,000 bottles of correction fluid. In addition, the company sold 153 million paper clips and 58 tons of staples. To keep all the paperwork orderly, the firm distributed more than 58 million file folders and 12,000-plus file cabinets, and, to keep its customers comfortable, more than 31,000 office chairs and enough carpet to cover 16 football fields. No one could have imagined those numbers 100 years ago.

RIGGS NATIONAL BANK

The history of Riggs National Bank begins when William Wilson Corcoran opened a note brokerage house in Georgetown in 1836. A year later he moved to Pennsylvania Avenue and began dealing with Elisha Riggs, an influential New York banker. In 1840 Corcoran formed a partnership with George Washington Riggs, Jr., Elisha's son, and the firm became Corcoran & Riggs.

John Tyler became the first of 20 presidents to bank with Riggs. In 1844, during the Tyler Administration, the institution became an official depository of the Treasury.

Four years later Corcoran successfully created a financial syndicate that sold millions of dollars in bonds to European financial houses. The sale helped finance war with Mexico and established Corcoran & Riggs as an international banker.

George Riggs retired in 1848, allowing his younger brother, Elisha Jr., to represent the family at the bank. As Corcoran's interests shifted toward his art collection and philanthropic activities, however, he withdrew from an active role in the operation.

In 1854 Corcoran retired to devote all his energies to his other interests, and George Riggs returned from New York to head the newly renamed Riggs & Company. Corcoran would claim a permanent place in the hearts of his city and nation with his support of Gallaudet and The George Washington universities, and the gift of his art collection and the Renwick Gallery to the nation.

At the outbreak of the Civil War Jefferson Davis closed his Riggs account, and Abraham Lincoln opened one. In 1867, shortly after the war, the institution headed the syndicate that obtained $7.2 million in gold bullion needed to pay for Alaska.

Charles Carroll Glover became cashier of Riggs in 1874. He headed the bank for nearly a half-century, and played a vital role in district affairs as the moving spirit behind construction of the National Cathedral and establishment of Rock Creek Park.

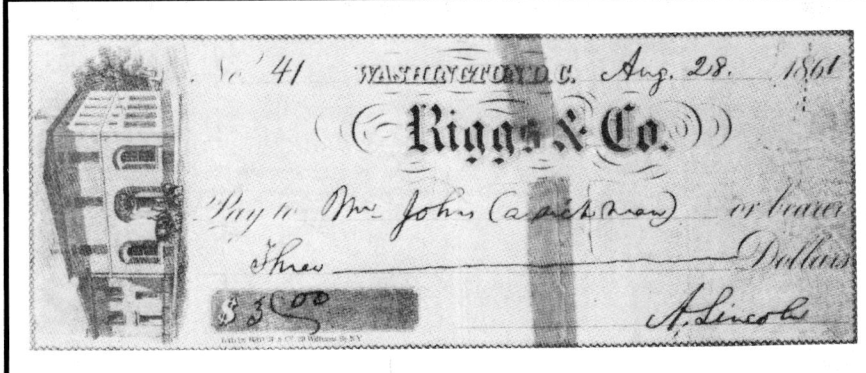

During Abraham Lincoln's presidency he wrote many memorable checks, among which is this one to Mr. Johns (a sick man). Legend has it that President Lincoln would often walk the streets of Washington alone and, coming across a sick or impoverished person, would write a check to the person on Lincoln's own account.

Riggs & Company joined the national banking system in 1896 and became Riggs National Bank. The last member of the Riggs family associated with the operation, Lawrason Riggs, retired from the board of directors in 1900.

Milton Ailes, a former Assistant Secretary of the Treasury, headed Riggs from 1921 to 1925 and brought the firm into the modern banking era. He introduced savings accounts in 1920, opened a trust department in 1921, and initiated Riggs' branch banking network with the acquisition of two other local banks.

Ailes was succeeded by Robert V. Fleming, who acquired the Farmers & Mechanics Bank at M Street and Wisconsin Avenue, NW, perhaps Riggs' most distinctive branch. Fleming led the institution successfully through the Great Depression, the New Deal, World War II, and the early 1960s. His successors included Lewellyn Jennings, John Christie, and Vincent Burke.

In 1981 Joe L. Allbritton purchased a controlling interest and created Riggs National Corporation as the parent company of Riggs National Bank. Five years later the organization reached an agreement with Guaranty Bank & Trust Company of Virginia to acquire the Virginia bank. This move will introduce Riggs as an interstate bank.

Riggs Bank was founded in 1836 and celebrated its 150th anniversary in 1986. Twenty presidents and first families have banked with Riggs, including Theodore Roosevelt.

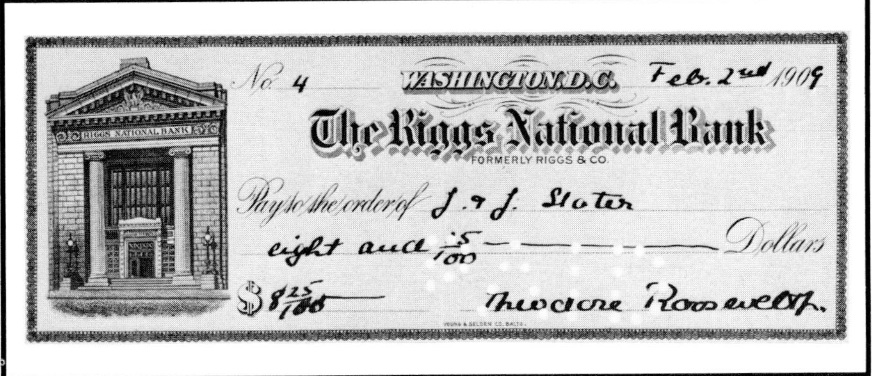

COVINGTON & BURLING

J. Harry Covington, raised in Talbot County on Maryland's Eastern Shore, had political ambitions. Barely 30 years old and an 1894 graduate of the University of Pennsylvania Law School, he ran unsuccessfully for the state senate in 1901 but was elected state's attorney of Talbot County in 1903. Five years later he was elected to Congress, where he became a leader of the Democratic caucus.

In June 1914 President Woodrow Wilson introduced Covington to his antitrust adviser, Louis D. Brandeis, and a young attorney, George Rublee. The two were working on a piece of legislation that would be part of Wilson's New Freedoms program. At President Wilson's request, Covington shepherded the measure through the House and through conference. It became the Federal Trade Commission Act.

Covington resigned from Congress to accept appointment as Chief Justice of the Supreme Court of the District of Columbia. He also became a professor at the Georgetown University Law School. After service on two presidential missions, he resigned from the court to open a private law practice in July 1918.

Edward B. Burling of Eldora, Iowa, graduated from Grinnell College and Harvard before entering Harvard Law School, where he became friends with George Rublee. Burling took his first post with a Chicago law firm, where he formed a partnership with his friend from Harvard. The association was short lived; Rublee moved to New York and Burling moved on to a more successful Chicago partnership. Burling came to Washington in 1917.

George Rublee was the son of Horace Rublee, chairman of the Wisconsin Republican Party, United States Minister to Switzerland in the Grant Administration, and editor of the *Milwaukee Sentinel*. George Rublee graduated from Harvard Law School in 1895 and spent the next few years teaching at Harvard, practicing law in Chicago and New York, and traveling through Europe.

Covington and Burling became friends, then associates, and then, shortly after the armistice ended World War I, partners, when Burling joined Covington at offices in Washington's Evans Building on January 1, 1919. On July 1, 1919, the new firm moved to the Union Trust Building at 15th and H streets, NW. With Rublee's arrival in November 1921, the firm became Covington, Burling & Rublee.

The firm's name changed several times during its early years. Rublee left the practice for government service, and others signed on. At various times the named partners included Dean Acheson (whose name was dropped when he became Secretary of State), John Lord O'Brian, and Paul Shorb. The firm decided to go back to its original name effective January 1, 1951.

The firm's founders sought to establish a national and international

Covington & Burling offices, at 1201 Pennsylvania Avenue, NW, are conveniently located for the firm's involvement in most major programs and agencies of the federal government.

legal practice, representing major corporations, trade associations, and foreign governments. At the same time they maintained a commitment to the District of Columbia community, representing D.C. citizens, businesses, and institutions. The object of the national practice was the growing federal involvement in the national economy through the federal income tax, antitrust laws, and food and drug laws.

The burgeoning growth of the federal government and the legal prowess of the firm's founders allowed their aspirations to be realized, possibly beyond their imagining. In the following decades the practice gained national prominence for its assistance to a wide variety of clients in federal legal matters. Some involved counseling of clients regarding compliance with new federal regulations. Others involved litigation of disputes between clients and the federal government. Prominent among these cases was the firm's successful defense of United States Steel on constitutional grounds when the compay was threatened with presidential seizure in 1952 to avoid a wartime labor strike.

At the end of 1987, with 236 lawyers and 600 supporting staff members, Covington & Burling was the largest law office in Washington, D.C. Consistent with the vision of its founders, the firm's representation includes major national and foreign corporations, trade associations, state governments, and others in widely diverse matters involving most major programs and agencies of the federal government. At the same time the firm has maintained strong roots in the D.C. community, representing local businesses, individuals, schools, churches, and foundations.

A significant portion of the firm's practice is *pro bono publico.* The firm provides three lawyers, two paralegals, and two secretaries on a full-time basis to the Neighborhood Legal Services Program. In addition, the firm encourages its lawyers to undertake other worthy projects without charge. Examples are representation of the residents of a tiny island near Puerto Rico in an action to stop the U.S. Navy from using their island for target practice, and aiding inmates in Lorton Penitentiary seeking protection from overcrowding and inhumane conditions.

Over the firm's history many of its partners, such as Dean Acheson, have carried on the public service tradition of its founders, Covington and Rublee. Present partners of the firm have served in high-level positions in numerous government agencies, including the Departments of State, Defense, Justice, Commerce, Energy, and the Navy; the White House; and the Food and Drug Administration. Still another served as United States Attorney for the District of Columbia.

In 1969 Covington & Burling moved to new offices at 888 Sixteenth Street, NW, and in 1981 to its current quarters at 1201 Pennsylvania Avenue, NW. This second move added significant impetus to the redevelopment of Washington's Pennsylvania Avenue corridor. In mid-1986 the firm opened an office in nearby Virginia to service high-technology businesses and other firms locating in the suburban areas north and west of Washington.

OMNI CONSTRUCTION, INC.

A rustic, two-story town house in historic Georgetown was the birthplace of OMNI Construction, Inc. Formed in 1977, the firm today builds $300 million of construction projects annually. In only 10 years it has grown into one of America's premier general contractors.

OMNI Construction's first project was the Four Seasons Hotel and Georgetown Plaza Office Building at 2800 Pennsylvania Avenue. The company's original offices were housed on the second floor of a neighboring town house. The new enterprise's philosophy: Provide quality merit shop construction on time and within budget. OMNI convincingly demonstrated that commitment with its work on the Four Seasons complex. Even before that endeavor was completed, OMNI had signed other contracts and was hard at work on other projects in downtown Washington, suburban Maryland, and northern Virginia. By the end of 1979, only its second full year in business, OMNI's volume had already grown to $100 million per year.

The young organization was demonstrating its capabilities in office buildings, hotels, condominiums, garden apartments, banks, corporate headquarters, and industrial projects. Executives at OMNI credit several key factors with responsibility for its rapid ascent to success. They give top billing to the company's strong management capability.

"Delivering quality construction projects on time takes precise scheduling and continual hands-on management," explains R.V. Caruso, chairman and chief executive officer of OMNI Construction, Inc. Caruso has spent more than 30 years in the construction industry. He attributes OMNI's management ability to constant training. "We continually work to keep both field and office personnel aware of ongoing changes in the industry. But even more important," he says, "is the experience they get on a day-to-day basis. We have some of the industry's most experienced professionals working side by side with our new employees. This daily exposure teaches our new people about our high standards and expectations, and gives them the most valuable training they can get." The firm's constant goal, according to its chairman, is to "build projects our clients can be proud of."

R.V. Caruso, chairman and chief executive officer.

OMNI's first project was the Four Seasons Hotel and Georgetown Plaza Office Building at 2800 Pennsylvania Avenue, NW.

OMNI has become a major contributor to the dynamic growth of Washington. In 10 years the corporation has built more than 5 million square feet of downtown Washington office space. In addition to helping build the new city, OMNI is working to preserve the remnants of Washington's historic buildings.

Historic restoration has become an important component of the OMNI portfolio. In early 1983 the company began work on a pioneering project, incorporating the restored facade of a historic landmark into new construction. The nineteenth-century Demonet building was completely restored and connected to a new 12-story office structure designed to complement its older companion.

OMNI began a similar effort a year later. On Pennsylvania Avenue, just six blocks west of the U.S. Capitol, the firm reconstructed the facade of the 1890 Atlantic Coastline Building on the structure of a new 364,000-square-foot office building. The delicate procedure required the careful dismantling, labeling, and storing of the nineteenth-century building. Then the entire old facade was integrated into the new complex.

OMNI has also restored several downtown office buildings in their entirety. Such work requires painstaking attention to detail and constant caution by workers. Because old blueprints have usually been lost, workers must gradually unravel old mysteries of technique, design, and method. The Washington Building, hailed as a landmark when it was built in 1927, was restored to its original beauty and renovated to accommodate modern tenants' needs. In the process an extra floor was added, making it an 11-story structure. Two blocks away OMNI has converted a 78-year-old building into a magnificent new home for the National Museum of Women in the Arts. The restored building features an elegant lobby and great hall which host receptions and exhibits.

Renovation takes many forms, from restoring structures in historic sections of town to the renaissance of an entire area. OMNI Construction, Inc., has significantly contributed to the rebirth of Washington. Its work is evident with such notable projects as the new flagship of the Hyatt Hotel chain, the Park Hyatt Washington at 24th and M streets in the West End, and several fine new office buildings in Washington's emerging East End.

In the decade since its founding, OMNI Construction, Inc., has built a construction company that responds to the diverse needs of the Washington building market. According to Caruso, "We have achieved this with the ability of skilled professionals who have dedicated much of their careers to the construction industry."

OMNI's flagship project is the Bethesda Metro Center. The entire complex covers 1.3 million square feet. Developed by the Alan I. Kay Companies of Bethesda, the three buildings are the new 384-room Hyatt Regency Hotel, a 17-story office building, and a retail arcade. In a style reminiscent of New York's classic Rockefeller Center, the pedestrian area features pathways, sculpture, fountains, seating areas, and a skating rink. A transportation hub, the complex houses Metrobus and Metrorail stations.

Whether preserving the heritage of the city or building solutions to twenty-first-century needs, OMNI Construction, Inc., has become a vital part of life in the nation's capital. The bold black letters of its distinctive white signs are seen on construction projects throughout the region. The corporation has made itself a symbol of the new Washington.

OMNI converted this 78-year-old building, at 13th Street and New York Avenue, NW, into the new home for the National Museum of Women in Arts.

The Bethesda Metro Center at Old Georgetown Road and Wisconsin Avenue in Bethesda, Maryland. Shown here, at left, is the 384-room Hyatt Regency Hotel and at right, the Bethesda Metro Center Office Building.

WOODWARD & LOTHROP

Woodward & Lothrop celebrated its centennial in 1980. On that occasion the employee magazine cited a memoir written 50 years before, quoting a rare and remarkable appreciation of the potential of provincial nineteenth-century Washington: "Mr. Woodward and Mr. Lothrop had an unwavering faith in Washington. In their vision they saw a city constantly enlarging its population, rebuilding its structures, and becoming more and more the center of the best life in the nation." The city has repaid their faith and the accuracy of their vision.

Washington's leading department store was founded by two natives of Maine who started their business in New England. Samuel Walter Woodward and Alvin Mason Lothrop established their first store in Chelsea, Massachusetts. When the entrepreneurs moved to Washington, they opened their doors as the Boston Dry Goods House. The shop was located at 705 Market Space in the old central market, a site now occupied by the National Archives.

The partners' innovative merchandising policy intrigued the public; a bold sign advertised "one price." There would be no special discounts for volume purchasers, cash customers, friends of the management, or highly skilled bargainers; all customers would be treated equally.

Its popularity burgeoning, Woodward and Lothrop decided to move their store to the popular F Street shopping district. The Carlisle Building, erected especially for the firm at F and 11th streets, cost approximately $100,000. It opened April 2, 1887. The proud proprietors soon found it necessary to begin purchasing and expanding into adjacent buildings.

The store featured only the finest, most popular, and most up-to-date merchandise. In 1893 the boys'

ABOVE: Edwin K. Hoffman, chairman of the board.

BELOW: Woodward & Lothrop as it appeared in 1913, with additions on each side of the original Carlisle Building.

department offered the Knockabout suit, "made for rough wear, but very dressy." The trousers were "double thick in the knees and seat" and, like the coat, treble sewed with silk, warranted nonripable, sizes 10 to 15 years, $5. Another department offered Haviland French china, flower pattern, blue dinner plates at $4.50 a dozen.

In 1901 Woodward & Lothrop acquired St. Vincent's Orphan Asylum at 11th and G streets, demolished the structure, and replaced it with another new building (a new home was found for the orphans). The addition gave the enterprise almost the entire square block. The real estate alone cost an unprecedented $500,000. However, female customers of the store could spend considerably less when making their own purchases: One excellent buy that year was the "Ladies Eton suit made of habit cloth in all the leading shades, large Empire revers, full sleeved, and skirt and jacket silk lined; sizes 32 to 48, $10."

Donald Woodward, son of the cofounder, became president of the company in 1917. He demolished the Carlisle Building in 1926, replacing it with a taller, more elaborate, more efficient store, and merging it into the establishment's other facilities. The resulting Woodward & Lothrop comprised 10 acres of floor space. The complex forms the core of today's Woodies Metro Center.

Expansion beyond the downtown location began in 1937 with the construction of warehousing and service facilities at 131 M Street, NE. The 1946 purchase of Palais Royal from the Kresge Foundation brought stores at the Pentagon and in Bethesda, Maryland, as well as the building on the north side of G Street, across from the downtown complex. Woodward & Lothrop recently sold the "North Building." The Pentagon store remains an active location. The Bethesda facility was destroyed by fire.

In 1947 the third generation of the founders' families assumed control of Woodies. Andrew Parker, a grandson of S.W. Woodward, became president, and A. Lothrop Luttrell, grandson of Alvin Mason Lothrop, became executive vice-president.

Woodward & Lothrop branched out to the Chevy Chase location at Friendship Heights in 1950, then to Alexandria in 1952. Woodies established its Seven Corners store in 1956. The pace of openings accelerated in the following decade: in Wheaton Plaza, 1960; Eastover, 1963 (it was sold in 1972); Annapolis, 1964; Landmark Mall, 1965; Prince George Plaza, 1966; Iverson Mall, 1967; and Tysons Corner, 1968. Continuous expansion has made the latter the largest of the suburban stores. Facilities opened more recently include the Woodward & Lothrop stores in Columbia Mall, 1971; Landover Mall, 1972; Montgomery Mall, 1976; Lakeforest Mall, 1978; Fair Oaks Mall, 1980; and White Marsh, near Baltimore, 1981.

Andrew Parker retired as president of the company in 1969. Edwin K. Hoffman was elected president and chief executive officer; in 1978 he was named chairman of the board and chief executive officer. Robert J. Mulligan is vice-chairman and chief administrative officer of Woodward & Lothrop, while Tom L. Roach serves as president.

"It's hard to describe the aura of this store, but shopping here is part of living here," says Hoffman. "Our customers have a personal, almost a proprietary interest in us. They're as much a part of Woodies as Woodies is part of Washington."

In 1984 A. Alfred Taubman purchased Woodward & Lothrop. A resident of Bloomfield Hills, Michigan, Taubman is an innovative real estate developer whose projects include Lakeforest and Fair Oaks malls. Other Taubman properties include Sothebys, the A&W chain, and numerous multiscreen movie theaters.

In October 1986 Woodward & Lothrop completed the $20-million remodeling of its downtown store, now known as Woodies Metro Center. It is a new store, designed for Washington in the 1980s, but its roots go back more than 100 years.

"The new owner appreciates and respects what this company stands for," states Hoffman, "the way we treat our people, and the way we participate in civic affairs. He's a man of tremendous principles. He understands and values Woodies' history and traditions. Nothing will change the image of Woodward & Lothrop."

Restored and remodeled, the new Woodies recreates the grandeur of the old.

SYSCON CORPORATION

Syscon Corporation was created in 1966 by Jose J. Yglesias, Edwin E. Tritch, Fred Israel, Nils Ericson, Ramon Novo, and Horace U. Pearce. Their challenge: help the defense community develop the ideas, requirements, and designs for the new, emerging electronics-based systems—a process known as Systems Engineering. The company and its approach to its mission were so new that the vocabulary to describe them is only now approaching widespread use, but Syscon has succeeded beyond even its founders' most extreme projections.

The organization began with a single government contract. Today it services more than 200 active contracts with government agencies, local municipalities, and commercial customers. It started with a single office in Washington, D.C. Now Syscon has 30 engineering offices, research centers, and production facilities across the United States. It became a public company in November 1981.

The firm's capabilities cover five basic areas: Systems Engineering, Computer Systems, Technical Services, Facilities Management, and Commercial Products. But the company is not segmented into isolated divisions. Instead, its corporate organization is open and flexible, allowing a single project to evolve, if necessary, through all five areas.

"That provides our people with the variety and challenge they thrive on," says Syscon chairman and chief executive officer Yglesias. "More important, it means our clients always get the best mix of talent and effort for each project."

Syscon is a creation of the era of the digital electronic computer. With the computer, the military adopted new devices and implemented a new technology. The founders of Syscon recognized a critical need for an organization that could facilitate the integration of new concepts. They believed a major opportunity existed for an organization that could take new concepts from the idea stage to product testing and verification, providing the ultimate validation of the original vision. "We seek to start with conceptualized requirements, and to end with a fully tested and verified product," Yglesias says.

Ideas are subject to alteration as they go through such processes. The intent behind Syscon was to form a cadre of about 25 experts who would define and establish their own new technology. Soon Syscon found that the U.S. Navy and other satisfied clients were pressuring the firm to expand. By 1970 profits were doubling annually, it had created a national presence, and the originally envisioned tasks were accounting for a decreasing proportion of Syscon contracts. Today instead of 25 employees the firm has nearly 1,600, the vast majority with outstanding high-technology skills.

Activities that have been added include computerized financial planning and tracking systems, and facilities management systems originally developed as part of the testing program for the company's own software. Similarly, Syscon has developed a major reputation for simulation and certification projects, functions that originated as part of the firm's own internal activities. "It all evolves," says Yglesias, "from computer people and engineers, from talented experts talking together and working together."

Systems Engineering is the first step in new system development. Currently Syscon is testing concepts for the multiservice IFFN (Identification-Friend, Foe, or Neutral) program, which will lead to the development of advanced systems that will identify hostile aircraft in a dense air traffic and combat environment.

Working with Control Data Corporation in the development of the Navy's Ada Language System/Navy (ALS/N), Syscon is providing the certification and validation testing. Syscon has also developed communications software and signal-processing software for the Integrated Underwater Surveillance System (IUSS) now in use by the Navy. For the Air Force, Syscon provides the Automated Technical Orders System (ATOS), which permits the Air Force to maintain total documentation of its weapons systems in computer format.

Computer Training Systems has created NAVTAG, a computer game designed by Syscon and the Navy to give surface officers tactical experience through the use of simulation. The ULQ-13 is a computer-controlled threat simulator developed by Syscon for the Fleet Electronic Warfare Support Group (FEWSG). The company has also developed a comprehensive Automated Instructional Management System (AIMS) for the Army and ATSS for the Navy that keep track of personnel through the entire training process.

Technical Services is working with the Navy's Space and Warfare Command (SPAWAR) to provide engineering, maintenance, and logistic support for shore-, sea-, and submarine-based communications facilities.

Facilities Management is involved with the environmental test facility for the NASA Ames Research Center, where equipment used in space shuttle missions and other space operations is thoroughly tested. The Software Certification facility, located at the Naval Underwater System Center (NUSC) in Newport, Rhode Island, also is managed by Syscon. So are four major computer centers owned by Syscon—centers that support the firm's engineering, design, and software development activities.

Commercial Applications has been responsible for the Programmable Interface Peripheral Equipment (PIPE) program, a system enabling otherwise incompatible military computers to communicate with each other and with civilian computers. Meter Reader and VersaTerm devices bring Syscon's high-tech approach to everyday problems. They are used by utilities to gather a variety of field data, including reading utility meters and helping to compute customer bills. To help market Syscon products and train personnel in their use, Syscon has created Syscon Video Productions.

Syscon Corporation sees itself as a company with a short but impressive history, and with an unlimited future. "We're working to facilitate adoption of a technology that is still evolving," says Yglesias. "This is the new Washington."

Jose J. Yglesias, one of the original founders and now chairman of the board and chief executive officer.

JOHNSON & HIGGINS OF WASHINGTON, D.C.

The history of Johnson & Higgins of Washington, D.C., Inc., is closely intertwined with the history of business insurance in the United States. As the country's oldest insurance brokerage firm, dating from the clipper ship days of 1845, J&H has participated in and helped guide the scope and character of the entire insurance industry.

The company was founded by a pair of young men who started in business as marine average adjusters and insurance brokers on New York's Wall Street. Because insurance companies in those days preferred to deal directly with their clients, the brokerage business was slow to develop.

But the young partners were exceptional marine adjusters. Their role was to decide how losses were to be shared when more than one party was involved in a marine incident, such as a collision, a need to jettison cargo, or piracy. As their reputation for arranging equitable settlements grew, shippers began using them as brokers to negotiate insurance terms as well.

At the time of the Civil War J&H had become so well established that it was commissioned by the Secretary of the Navy to survey the wreck of the Union gunboat *Varuna* off New Orleans. Two decades later, in 1883, the firm opened its first branch office in San Francisco, followed two years later by a second East Coast office in Philadelphia. And by 1899—when the partnership was restructured as a corporation—Johnson & Higgins had established offices in seven U.S. cities, including Baltimore, Boston, Buffalo, Chicago, and New Orleans. Concurrently, the J&H brokerage business was expanding to include fire, casualty, and other kinds of insurance.

By the turn of the century Johnson & Higgins had established a branch office network stretching from the Atlantic to the Pacific. It had also, by then, formed an international connection with the leading English brokerage firm Willis Faber & Co., Ltd., now known as Willis Faber & Dumas, Ltd.

The Johnson & Higgins reputation for professionalism was greatly enhanced early in the new century by the dispatch and efficiency with which it settled claims resulting from two world-famous disasters: the San Francisco earthquake and fire of 1906 and the sinking of the *Titanic* in 1912. And when World War I imperiled the nation's shipping, a senior J&H executive was named to the three-man advisory board of the Federal Bureau of War Risk Insurance.

Perhaps the company's severest test occurred during the Great Depression of the 1930s, when insurance activity was severely curtailed by business stagnation. Johnson & Higgins weathered the crisis by stressing ingenuity in finding and providing insurance services. Equally remarkable, J&H kept its entire staff intact at a time when countless Americans were thrown out of work.

During World War II, when the federal government began to import strategic raw materials, leading marine brokers were appointed as an insurance committee to provide the necessary coverages. Out of this group, Johnson & Higgins was selected to act as the servicing broker. The firm's business expanded further during this period as employee group insurance and pensions—hitherto a small percentage of the nation's business payroll—took hold in the workplace and developed quickly into the elaborate employee benefits programs that we know today.

The postwar business climate of acquisitions, conglomerates, and multinationals led to a period of unprecedented growth for Johnson & Higgins. During the 1950s and 1960s J&H opened a number of new offices in North America and created a network of offices and exclusive correspondent firms throughout the world.

J&H soon became identified as the preeminent international insurance broker, a reputation that continues undiminished to the present. Today Johnson & Higgins and the worldwide UNISON network of which it is a charter member employ some 13,000 people based in more than 200 cities and 50 countries worldwide. Moreover, J&H acts as insurance broker or employee benefit consultant for 75 of the 100 largest U.S. multinational corporations.

Johnson & Higgins of Washington, D.C., Inc., was opened in January 1982. As is characteristic of most J&H offices, the operation was started from scratch with employees from Johnson & Higgins of New York and Wilmington. The office is managed by William C. Bauman, formerly with J&H New York, and now has a staff of more than 40 employees.

From its inception the Washington office has been a full-service component of the J&H system, offering brokerage and consulting services in all areas of risk and insurance: property, casualty, international, marine, aviation, space, risk management services, self-insurance, captive insurance companies, pensions, and employee benefit plans.

Johnson & Higgins of Washington, D.C., has a client base made up of many of the largest public, private, international, municipal, institutional, and association risks in the metropolitan area. The office's greatest strength and its major emphasis lie in its ability to serve these large accounts locally. While it has concentrated over the past five years on the largest and most complex risks located in Washington, the office is now also applying that knowledge and ability to the relatively large number of medium-size "middle-market" companies located in the metropolitan area. Though their risks may differ in scale from those of a multinational, these businesses have exposures that can be just as complicated. Further, because middle-market companies rarely employ risk management personnel, they rely heavily on insurance professionals who can understand their business and their problems.

In 1983 Johnson & Higgins acquired Edward H. Friend & Co., a well-established privately held firm in Washington, D.C. With a superb reputation in pension, casualty actuarial, and employee benefit group consulting work, Edward H. Friend & Co. also is nationally known for its consulting work for municipalities and state and local governments. J&H of Washington merged its employee benefit operations with those of EHF & Co. in 1983. Then EHF & Co. continued operations as the benefit consulting arm of Johnson & Higgins of Washington, D.C. Effective January 1, 1988, J&H restructured its employee benefit operations nationally by establishing a subsidiary, A. Foster Higgins & Co. , Inc. , to provide the full spectrum of employee benefit consulting services on a fee basis. What was formerly the EHF & Co. division is now a major part of the Washington region of A. Foster Higgins & Co., Inc. The Washington region, which now has a staff of more than 70, is headed by Robert L. Bein.

Johnson & Higgins has grown with the times. While its headquarters is still at the southern tip of Manhattan, the firm has expanded to a worldwide network of consultants and insurance brokers. Today the global network of Johnson & Higgins consists of 48 offices in major cities in the United States, 11 offices coast to coast in Canada, 40 of its own offices overseas, and a 107-office worldwide network of exclusive correspondents in 35 countries—a total of 206 offices around the world.

The chairman and chief executive officer of Johnson & Higgins is Robert V. Hatcher, Jr., who previously had headed Johnson & Higgins of Virginia, based in Richmond.

GALLAUDET UNIVERSITY

The cafeteria at Gallaudet University is quieter than similar facilities at most schools, but the conversations are just as intense, and often more animated. At Gallaudet, American Sign Language (ASL), Pidgin Sign English (PSE), fingerspelling, and lipreading take the place of more conventional methods of communication.

The world's premier liberal arts institution of higher education for deaf students, Gallaudet serves not only the hearing impaired community but also parents, professionals in the field of deafness, and the general public. As schoolteachers and administrators, authors, inventors, businessmen, entertainers, academicians, members of the clergy, publishers, scientists, and leaders in numerous other fields, the university's alumni have made major contributions to America and the world.

Gallaudet has almost 400 deaf individuals on its faculty and staff, the largest concentration of deaf employees in the world. The National Information Center on Deafness, the National Center for Law and the Deaf, and the International Center on Deafness all share the campus with the university. So too does the Hall of Fame, honoring individuals who have made significant contributions to the lives of deaf people, and a museum.

Amos Kendall—a journalist and politician who found wealth as a partner of Samuel Morse in the telegraph business and served as postmaster general under presidents Andrew Jackson and Martin Van Buren—donated land and helped found the Columbia Institution for the Instruction of the Deaf and Dumb and the Blind in 1857. The main campus in northeast Washington is still known as Kendall Green, the name it bore while part of the donor's estate.

Kendall hired Edward Miner Gallaudet as superintendent of the institution. Edward's father, the Reverend Thomas Hopkins Gallaudet, founded the first permanent school for deaf children in the United States. Thomas Hopkins Gallaudet and his first student, Alice Cogswell, are memorialized in the famous statue that stands at the front of the campus. There is also a statue of Edward Gallaudet on Kendall Green—possibly the only father and son on the same campus in the world.

In 1864 President Abraham Lincoln signed congressional legislation authorizing Columbia Institution to grant college degrees, enabling the school to form the National Deaf Mute College. Lincoln became the first president of the United States to be designated as patron of the institution.

The following year it was determined that the Columbia Institution could better serve its students with a more distinct mission. Blind students attending the school were transferred to the Maryland School for the Blind, and the words "for the blind" were dropped from the institution's name. The Columbia Institution was later renamed Kendall School, and in 1970 Congress made it a national demonstration elementary school. In 1969 the Model Secondary School for the Deaf was started on campus.

The college graduated its first students in 1869. As patron, President Ulysses S. Grant signed diplomas of all three distinguished graduates and started a tradition. Since then presidents of the United States have signed all Gallaudet diplomas.

Women were first admitted to the college in 1887; four years later a graduate department was added in order to prepare hearing graduates of other colleges to become teachers of deaf children.

In 1894, at the request of the alumni, the board of directors renamed the college in honor of Thomas Hopkins Gallaudet. The supervisory corporation continued to be known as the Columbia Institution until 1954, when Congress changed the name of the entire institution to Gallaudet College.

At the same time Congress strengthened the federal financial commitment to Gallaudet, which made it possible to enrich the curriculum and improve facilities. In 1957 the institution achieved full academic accreditation.

Congress accorded university status to Gallaudet as part of the Education of the Deaf Act of 1986. The same federal act established a federal matching program for endowment gifts to the school.

"All this well-deserved recognition of Gallaudet as a national and international center of scholarship could not overshadow its standing as a Washington institution—as part of life in the capital city as well as a provider of community services," editorialized *The Washington Post,* when the school officially became Gallaudet University on October 24.

The university offers all academic and extracurricular activities usually associated with student life. The Gallaudet Dance Company has performed worldwide, and several drama department productions have placed among the nation's 10 best at the American College Theatre Festival. Gallaudet alumni were intimately involved in founding the National Theatre of the Deaf.

The university's athletic program is also active and well rounded. In the 1950s the college wrestling team won 36 straight conference victories and three championships. The basketball and women's volleyball teams have also known years of glory.

Gallaudet's most enduring contribution to American sports history was made by the football team in the late nineteenth century. Faced with opponents stealing plays called by all too visible hand signals, the team gathered around its quarterback to conceal his signs with a "huddle." The technique has been widely imitated since. In 1987 the football team had its best season ever, ending the year with nine wins and one loss. There are two athletic halls of fame at Gallaudet: one honoring university athletes, the other post-college deaf athletes.

Gallaudet currently enrolls 2,200 students in a full range of university programs, offering degrees from the associate of arts to the Ph.D. The university has more than 9,500 deaf and hearing alumni. Two-thirds of all college graduates in the United States who were deaf as undergraduate students today hold Gallaudet degrees. In 1987 Gallaudet University was named the best small college in the East by *U.S. News & World Report.* Jerry C. Lee is the current president, only the sixth president in the institution's long and distinguished history.

There are two Gallaudet University campuses. Kendall Green, the school's original location, is at Florida Avenue between West Virginia Avenue and Sixth Street, NE. It houses the undergraduate and graduate programs, the Kendall Demonstration Elementary School, the Model Secondary School for the Deaf, and the College for Continuing Education. The School of Preparatory Studies is located along Kalmia Road, at 17th Street, NW.

The clock tower of Chapel Hall at Gallaudet University and the United States Capitol symbolize the long and close relationship between Washington and this unique educational institution.

THE BEGG COMPANIES

On July 5, 1950, J.F. Begg Incorporated opened its doors at 1620 Twentieth Street, NW. Its first sale was the handsome eighteenth-century estate, "His Lordship's Kindness," in Prince Georges County. This was the forerunner of a number of great estates and famous houses that have been the hallmark of Begg Incorporated's tradition. In 1953 Begg Incorporated bought its own building at 1714 Connecticut Avenue, NW, where the offices remained for some 30 years.

Often called the "Grande Dame of Washington Real Estate," Jeanne Begg, through her organization, Begg Incorporated, brings a special meaning to the word "service," in what is one of the world's most unusual and sophisticated real estate markets. Specializing in marketing fine residential properties from cosmopolitan town houses to country estates, Begg Incorporated also serves the international market, both U.S. clients seeking real estate overseas and those from abroad wishing to invest in commercial and residential properties here in the D.C. area. To round out its services, out-of-town and overseas clientele will find that Begg Incorporated offers a most professional property management group.

Jeanne Begg's personal background offers some insight into why she has been able to serve the Washington real estate market so well. Born in the Netherlands, she took a B.A. honors degree and an M.A. in modern languages from Oxford University. Mrs. Begg speaks five languages fluently. She was captain of the Oxford tennis team and played in the Forest Hills U.S. Championship. Her first job was as assistant editor of the former *New York Daily Mirror,* and later she became the first female feature photographer to be hired by the Hearst International News Photo organization. Her service in the OSS earned her a Knighthood of Orange and Nassau from Queen Wilhelmina after World War II.

Georgetown Court, the first mixed-use development in Georgetown. Photography by Amr Mounib

Notable transactions are the Bodisco House, the Todd-Lincoln House, the Carriage House, Prospect House, the Lindens, and "The Rocks" in Washington, D.C.; and in Virginia, Hickory Hill, the Ballantrae estate, and Annefield. Begg Incorporated is also proud of the sale of the smallest house in Georgetown on P Street, NW.

Over the years Begg Incorporated has handled the sale of many ambassadorial residences and diplomatic properties. Recently it has negotiated the sale of the land for the Japanese Ambassador's residence on Nebraska Avenue, the site for the Korean Ambassador's residence on Glenbrook Road, and a built-to-order, 70,000-square-foot office building for the Taiwanese Chancery and Cultural Center. The firm has also represented a Middle Eastern country in the disposition of its property on Woodland Drive.

Jeanne F. Begg, president and founder of Begg Incorporated. Photography by Amr Mounib

Jeanne Begg's business philosophy is simple and direct: to give service and make a friend. Thus, from its inception in 1950, her agency has grown to four offices in the Washington metropolitan area, staffed by more than 100 agents. Indeed, she was a pioneer of the women's movement into business. A founding member and former president of the Women's Council of D.C. and founder of the D.C. Chapter of FIABCI,

LEFT: An elegant Georgian residence. Photography by Amr Mounib

RIGHT: The Bodisco House was built by the Imperial Russian Minister to the United States, Baron Alexander de Bodisco. Photography by Amr Mounib

she is the first and only woman who is a Certified International Property Specialist (CIPS), among a total of seven, designated by FIABCI, the International Real Estate Federation.

With more than 20 years' experience in international real estate, Mrs. Begg has been involved in many syndications in the Caribbean and the marketing of properties in Europe, especially Spain, France, England, and Italy. Islands Investment Corporation, one of her early international corporations, now Begg International, represented the Aga Kahn's project Costa Smeralda in Sardinia.

Among her other accomplishments she was invited to do the interior of the historic Governor's Mansion in the Panama Canal Zone by the Panama Canal Company because of her reputation as an interior designer.

In 1970 Jeanne Begg opened the commercial division and developed Georgetown Court with the Kraft Corporation, the first multi-use building approved and built in Georgetown with the truly unique feature of a rooftop pool. She has also served as director of NS&T Bank and the District Realty Title Company, and is on the advisory board of Ferris and Company, a leading Washington, D.C., stockbroker. She is active in the National Trust for Historic Preservation.

Widely known and respected in Washington social circles, Mrs. Begg has her primary residence at Roedown in Davidsonville, Maryland, an eighteenth-century estate where she raises Thoroughbred horses. She also maintains a house in the Virgin Islands that she uses as a base of operations for buying and selling properties in the Caribbean.

Jeanne Begg is proudest of the people in her organization and the service they give to an ever-growing list of influential clients. They believe, as she does, "that nothing is too small or too big for Begg Incorporated's attention."

Article coordinated by John A. Vardas

Kalorama Villa. Photography by Amr Mounib

THE ALAN I. KAY COMPANIES

The Alan I. Kay Companies, based in Bethesda, Maryland, is an industry leader in the Washington region. The proof is in its projects, which fill the skylines.

The business was founded by Alan I. Kay and Allan "Buddy" Rozansky, close friends since their days together in junior high school. After graduation from college they sold residential real estate with a local brokerage company. A year later, having saved enough money to paint their names on a door, the two men started their own brokerage. In 1958 they went into construction and development.

Today The Alan I. Kay Companies develops more than 1.25 million square feet of office space annually. Since 1960 the firm has put its mark on Washington and other communities by building more than 14,000 apartments and 4.5 million square feet of office space. In 1986 *Building Design and Construction Magazine* listed the company as the 16th-largest diversified developer in the United States.

The business knew difficult days in its early history, however. "Sometimes we didn't sleep too well," recalls Kay. Once their venture had to fend off threatened bankruptcies and foreclosures.

In 1968 Kay and Rozansky found themselves holding thousands of acres of mortgaged land when the market suddenly went slack. "We couldn't sell it, and we couldn't eat it. We lost a lot of money."

Over the past decade the firm's business has grown and prospered at a remarkable rate. In 1971 it did a total volume of $22 million. By 1980 it had become a $90-million operation, and by 1985 its remarkable growth had taken Rozansky and Kay to the $215-million level. In 1983 the District of Columbia Subcontractors Association named the firm the outstanding owner-developer of the year.

Located in San Diego's Golden Triangle area, this $50-million project, adjacent to the new Marriott Hotel, provides 225,000 square feet of office space in its first phase, scheduled for completion in 1988.

Alan I. Kay, president.

On January 1, 1985, Kay purchased Rozansky's interest in the business and renamed the organization The Alan I. Kay Companies. Alan's sons, Michael and Bryan, are working at the firm on a full-time basis. Alan is hopeful that daughter Donna will join the company in the future, promising an Alan I. Kay legacy for the Washington area for years to come.

Alan Kay was among the first Washington-area developers to recognize the full impact of the Metrorail system. "More than a decade ago we saw the potential of the Metro system," he says. "We recognized its impact on the growth of Montgomery County, and made a commitment to be part of that growth."

The firm has several major developments along the Metrorail Red Line that runs from Silver Spring through downtown Washington and out past Shady Grove in Montgomery County.

Employees of The Alan I. Kay Companies refer to its office parks as "prime environments for doing business." They should know. The firm is responsible for some of the region's most impressive projects, including the Tysons Commerce Center in Fairfax, the Twinbrook Metro Plaza, the Bethesda Metro Center, and many more.

The recently opened Bethesda Metro Center dominates the new "downtown" of the Montgomery County suburb. We see the Bethesda Metro Center as a focal point for community vitality, helping to provide a clear urban identity for Bethesda," says Alan Kay. The project includes a 17-story office building, the 12-story Hyatt Regency Hotel, and a 3-story, glass-enclosed shopping arcade.

Other projects recently completed are its Tysons-Dulles Office Plaza, Fairfax County; Ballston Common Office Center, Arlington; and Woodmont Office Center, Rockville.

Hotel construction is also an Alan I. Kay Companies interest. Hotels built by the corporation include the Hyatt Regency at Bethesda Metro Center, the Hyatt Orlando Hotel in Kissimmee, Florida, and the Holiday Inn Crowne Plaza in Rockville.

Success breeds success. With the desire to build superior quality developments in prime locations, The Alan I. Kay Companies recently announced major expansions into national markets. New projects totaling more than one million square feet and $200 million in construction value have been launched in La Jolla, California, and Atlanta, Georgia. Additional projects in such areas as Hartford, Connecticut, and Chicago, Illinois, are also contemplated.

The Alan I. Kay Companies' executive offices are located at 4520 East West Highway in Bethesda. Alan Kay's office is filled with antiques, original sculptures, and paintings by Renoir, Chagall, and other masters. He and his family live at Merrywood, the Potomac River estate in Virginia where Jacqueline Kennedy Onassis grew up and where John F. Kennedy wrote *Profiles in Courage*.

He has given vital support to the American Cancer Society. As chairman of the Washington Cancer Ball for five years, he has raised more than $5 million, and the ball is now the world's largest single-night fund-raising event for cancer.

Kay is a member of the board of directors of Wolf Trap Farm Park for the Performing Arts, the Washington Ballet, and the Corcoran Art Gallery, and serves as a trustee of the Washington Opera. He is a member of the National Board of the American Cancer Society. He is chairman of the Holy Cross Hospital Hospice Steering Committee, and a supporter of the Hebrew Home for the Aged and the National Conference for Christians and Jews.

Alan I. Kay has made himself as much a personal part of the Washington scene as his buildings are part of the skyline.

This complex is located at the intersection of Wisconsin Avenue and Old Georgetown Road, Bethesda, Maryland, and was built over the Bethesda Metro stop of the Washington Metropolitan Area Transit Authority's Red Line. A 387-room Hyatt Regency Hotel and a 36,000-square-foot office complex, which encompasses an eatery, retail space, and public plaza, are built on 3.48 acres of land leased from WMATA.

THE ACACIA GROUP

The Acacia Group is a Washington, D.C.-based financial services organization managing assets of over $3 billion. Founded in 1869 to meet the basic needs of a simpler era, The Acacia Group has made itself a complex modern corporation equipped to provide its clients with the full range of financial services—insurance, investments, savings, and management.

The seven companies of The Acacia Group include the parent company, Acacia Mutual Life; Acacia National Life; Calvert Group, Ltd.; Calvert Securities Corporation; Acacia Financial Corporation; and Enterprise Resources, Inc., the business services and management consulting arm of Acacia.

The group's newest corporation is Acacia Federal Savings Bank, located in Annandale, Virginia. Formed in 1984, the bank enables The Acacia Group to provide its clients with savings plans, checking accounts, money market accounts, trust services, and consumer loans.

Acacia was created as the Masonic Mutual Relief Association of the District of Columbia to benefit the widows and orphans of Masons. Members paid $3.10 to join and $1.10 whenever a member died. The assessment was divided, with one dollar for the beneficiary of the deceased, and 10 cents to pay expenses of the association. The first beneficiary of the plan received $204.

By 1893 the association had grown enough to require it to hire its first full-time employee, William Montgomery. His greatest challenge was to find a way to keep the company growing. Many of its members were elderly, and by 1895 the increasing death rate forced the directors to consider closing down. Instead, they hired a sales agent and adopted a plan of assessments based on age. Younger members paid only 50 cents instead of the $1.10 still charged members over 60. The board also instituted a physical examination for new members.

By the turn of the century the association and its mutual benefit plan began to resemble a modern insurance organization. New offices opened in Virginia, North Carolina, and Pennsylvania, all strongholds of Freemasonry. By 1903 the association had sufficient funds of its own to begin an investment program and to set aside a reserves fund to pay claims. Five years later its name was changed to the Masonic Mutual Life Association of the District of Columbia.

The company changed its name in 1922 to Acacia Mutual Life Association (the Acacia tree is a symbol of long life or immortality). In 1932 the organization expanded its marketing efforts beyond the limits of the Masonic brotherhood and became known as Acacia Mutual Life Insurance Company. The marketing base expanded again in 1936, with the decision to issue insurance policies to women and the hiring of the firm's first female agent.

Acacia was the first insurance company in America to adopt the monthly payment mortgage reduction plan to finance home mortgages. While many other insurance companies had financed home mortgages, most worked by collecting semiannual payments of interest only, with the full amount of the mortgage coming due at the end of a preagreed time, typically three years.

The Acacia plan, similar to that now commonly used by virtually all housing lenders, allowed a borrower to pay off the mortgage gradually by making monthly payments that included both principal and interest. At the same time Acacia acquired its own home at 51 Louisiana Avenue, NW.

By 1950 Acacia had more than one billion dollars of life insurance in force. The $2-billion milestone was reached in 1963. Eight years later the company topped the $3-billion mark and formed its first subsidiary: Acacia Equity Sales Corporation was created to market mutual funds and

The Acacia Group was founded in 1869 in a simpler era as the Masonic Mutual Relief Association of the District of Columbia. Today the corporation is headquartered in this imposing structure at 51 Louisiana Avenue, NW, in Washington, D.C.

other equity-based financial products. Acacia National Life Insurance Company was added in 1974 to market more competitive annuity and other variable income products.

The following year Duane B. Adams, CLU, became chief marketing officer. Under his direction the organization shifted and intensified its marketing focus, and quickly reached new milestones of business volume.

In 1976 the firm strengthened its marketing and research efforts and changed its entire field structure, aligning agencies into mutual support groups with similar needs and markets. Its Dynamics of Life Insurance Selling program developed the concept that successful sales depend on understanding human behavior and improving communications between agents and clients.

Adams was elected president of Acacia in 1980. Under his guidance, the company introduced its universal life product in 1981 under the name Flex-Account Life®. Public acceptance of the new policy brought Acacia to $4 billion in sales in 1981, and $5 billion in 1983—the year Adams became chairman of the board and chief executive officer.

In recognition of its diversified product lines and expanded services, the company adopted a new name, The Acacia Group. In 1984 Acacia purchased Calvert Group, Ltd., an investment management organization established in 1976 to offer a money market fund investing in variable U.S. government guaranteed instruments. Under Acacia ownership Calvert Group has developed an extensive range of money market accounts, mutual funds, and additional investment services.

"The 1,000 employees of Acacia share an enthusiastic vision of the years ahead," states Duane Adams. "The 'New Acacia' represents both anticipation of and a response to change. Meeting client needs is the justification for all we do."

In 1985 Acacia launched its newest initiative by opening full-service Acacia Financial Centers across the country. Each center offers the total family of Acacia products and services, including insurance, investment, banking, and financial planning services.

Achieving security and growth for its clients, The Acacia Group celebrated its own success in 1987 when it achieved one billion dollars in assets. "Such an achievement," notes chairman Adams, "marks a watershed from old to modern forms of financial services in America. Acacia, as before, found herself in the vanguard of that movement and, as before, prospered herself because she helped her clients prosper. There are no finer rewards for those who remain 'dedicated to service.'"

The group's newest corporation is Acacia Federal Savings Bank, located in Annandale, Virginia. The bank enables the Acacia Group to provide its clients with savings plans, checking accounts, money market accounts, trust services, and consumer loans.

The Calvert Group in Bethesda, Maryland, one of the seven companies of the Acacia Group, is an investment management organization specializing in an extensive range of money market accounts, mutual funds, and additional investment services.

SHANNON & LUCHS COMPANY

Throughout the twentieth century Washington's real estate market has reflected national events. Similarly, the history of Shannon & Luchs, the giant Washington-based real estate firm, has mirrored the unique, rapidly changing environment of the national capital region.

"The Washington real estate field has been invaded during the past week by an energetic young firm, which proposes to be heard from and whose friends say the community will soon have to sit up and take notice," reported a newspaper on March 4, 1906. They were right.

Herbert T. Shannon was a carpenter and home-building foreman; Morton J. Luchs was a real estate salesman. Their first commission was $1.25, earned by collecting the $25.50 monthly rent (including 50 cents for the water bill) on a six-room house that had just been placed under their management.

More than 80 years later their two families continue to share ownership and control of the organization—now among the nation's top privately owned real estate brokerage firms, with annual sales and leasing volume in the billions and an insurance division that has become one of the area's largest business insurance agencies. Foster Shannon, a son of one co-founder, is now president and chief executive officer; Kenneth J. Luchs, grandson of the other co-founder, is executive vice-president.

The company's four diverse divisions--commercial brokerage (leasing and sales), property management (commercial and residential), insurance, and residential sales has a combined staff of more than 3,000 employees and associates. The firm's residential sales division comprises 60 percent of its business. As of early 1988 it included more than 2,500 agents in more than 50 offices scattered throughout the region.

Morton J. Luchs, co-founder.

Herbert T. Shannon, co-founder.

The corporation first forged its place in Washington not only by selling houses but by developing real estate and arranging financing and property insurance as well. In an era when mortgages typically took the form of three-year, interest-only loans by private investors, Shannon & Luchs worked with lenders to create long-term, self-amortizing home financing.

Automobiles began to drive the national economy in the 1920s, and Shannon & Luchs built the region's first shopping center—a Park & Shop at Wisconsin Avenue and Ordway Street, NW. The firm also developed the city's first major parking garage, the 10-story Capital Garage at 13th Street and New York Avenue. The new company was cruising in high gear.

The high times crashed with the Great Depression, which halted real estate development in Washington and almost ended the history of Shannon & Luchs. Residential sales volume neared zero, and the firm faced major debts from its construction and development activities. Bankruptcy was a real possibility.

The partners saved their venture by using personal funds and income from the property management division to obtain long-term loans, stay in business, and keep their staff employed. The hard years strengthened both their commitment to a diversified approach to real estate brokerage and their decision to cease speculative development activities. In 1938 Morton Luchs' son, Frank, succeeded his father as executive vice-president.

World War II brought increased demand for housing and office space in Washington, but no new construction and few sales. Military priorities took first claim on materials and laborers. The firm's principals themselves joined the armed forces; division managers ran Shannon & Luchs for the duration. Once again its property management activities carried the business through a difficult period.

With peace came a critical housing and commercial building shortage as returning veterans, federal home financing, and a growing bureaucracy drove up demand. Herbert Shannon's eldest son, William, became president of the company in 1946.

Foster Shannon, William's younger brother, opened the firm's first suburban residential sales branch office on Wilson Boulevard in Arlington in 1949. Area families were growing out of their apartments, the first effect of the postwar baby boom. They needed more and larger housing. To serve them Shannon & Luchs opened branches in Wheaton, Maryland, and northwest Washington in the early 1950s.

The latter part of the decade brought integrated housing. Shannon & Luchs managed the city's first integrated development, and made it a success. As commercial development became part of planned suburban communities, the corporation's growing commercial division helped assemble large land packages for such innovative real estate concepts as Reston, Virginia. Since the end of the decade the organization has opened at least one new sales office every year.

The turbulence of the 1960s dampened real estate activity in the District of Columbia and accelerated growth in the suburbs. The company went through changes, too. In 1966 Ken Luchs became vice-president, representing the third generation of his family's involvement with the firm. Foster Shannon followed his brother as president in 1968.

To Washington realtors the 1970s were the era of office development. Shannon & Luchs made good use of the opportunity to expand and refine its commercial divisions. Residential prices and mortgage rates soared, sales dropped, and condominiums became part of the real estate market. By the 1980s creative financing was the watchword, and Shannon & Luchs helped develop new financial instruments to help clients buy new housing.

The 1980s are still an unfinished story, but Shannon & Luchs principals see continued growth for Washington's dynamic real estate market. As computerized data-base systems and market research reports have become vital parts of the real estate business, Shannon & Luchs takes a leading position. The firm's commercial market research department publishes regular reports on market statistics and trends, and its quarterly market newsletter provides coverage of current real estate and insurance issues.

Current expansion plans will increase Shannon & Luchs activity in Prince Georges and Anne Arundel counties in Maryland, but the firm will continue its concentration on Washington. "The future of Washington-area real estate continues to be bright," says Foster Shannon. So does the future of the Shannon & Luchs Company.

Foster Shannon and Kenneth J. Luchs, president and executive vice-president, respectively.

The first home of Shannon & Luchs, at 704 Thirteenth Street, NW, as it appeared in 1906.

B.F. SAUL COMPANY

The severe depression that gripped the United States in the early 1890s closed factories throughout the nation. Hungry, unemployed workers lined up behind Colonel Jacob Coxey and marched on Washington, D.C. The times seemed hardly propitious for starting a real estate business, but that is exactly what B.F. Saul did.

The seeds for B.F. Saul's dream were rooted in nursery property held by his father. John Saul, a noted Irish horticulturist, had come to the United States from County Cork at the request of Andrew Jackson Downing, the landscaper of the United States Capital. John Saul helped landscape the area around what is now Walter Reed Hospital, the Smithsonian Institution, and Lafayette Square. Within a few years he became the first chairman of Washington's Parks Commission. Later he opened 140 acres of nurseries in Washington.

In 1892 B.F. Saul inherited a portion of these properties from his father. He planned to subdivide the area and develop it in stages. Subsequently, he bought additional land, laid out plans, worked with home builders, and convinced the city to put in streets. To facilitate the sales of these lots, B.F. Saul took back notes from buyers and resold them to friends and associates. The notes carried terms of three years, and were secured by real estate mortgages. B.F. Saul's solid reputation enabled him to place them easily. The Saul business world was changing—from flowers to finance.

By 1900 the firm had prospered sufficiently to require augmenting the staff and acquiring more spacious business quarters. To house its increasingly complex affairs, B.F. Saul founded the Home Savings Bank with its main office at Seventh Street and New York Avenue, NW. Just as

B.F. Saul, founder.

he had sold notes to individual investors, B.F. Saul sought to attract small depositors as retail customers. He attracted large accounts as well, including that of Malcolm Gibbs, the founder of People's Drug Stores. In 1919 Home Savings merged with American Security and Trust Company.

From its founding in 1892 through the 1930s, the B.F. Saul Company's primary business activity was syndicating home mortgages by selling smaller notes to the public. A typical $5,000 mortgage might have notes ranging in size from $100 to $1,000 issued against it. Like the stan-

B.F. Saul II, grandson of the founder, has been president of the firm since 1969.

LEFT: The original B.F. Saul building was located at Seventh Street and New York Avenue, NW, in Washington, D.C.

RIGHT: The company moved into its new headquarters on Connecticut Avenue in Chevy Chase in 1971. Photo by Nancy Jamieson

dard mortgages of the era, Saul's notes were interest bearing only and matured after three years. Investors generally received 6 percent interest, an excellent return at a time when most area banks paid no interest at all to depositors.

By the Roaring '20s, as Model T Fords kicked up dust in the company's new row house developments throughout Washington, B.F. Saul had about $60 million in outstanding notes. The firm also financed, constructed, and managed office buildings and apartment complexes throughout Washington. When B.F. Saul died in 1931, 38 years after forming his business, the company was in a strong enough financial position to not only weather the Great Depression, but also to build on the financial and housing reforms of the New Deal and emerge even stronger.

The investment funds channeled by B.F. Saul helped to fuel the tremendous post-World War II growth of the Washington metropolitan area. The enterprise had several presidents during this era, including B.F. Saul's son, Andrew Maguire Saul. In 1969 B.F. Saul II, a grandson of the founder, took control of the organization and introduced changes that significantly altered its direction and growth.

Through the Real Estate Investment Trust, founded in 1961, B.F. Saul II allowed the company to expand its developments beyond the Washington area into the southeastern and southwestern sections of the United States. He drove his talented financial team in several new directions, one of which was to found Chevy Chase Savings & Loan Association.

After nearly 80 years of operating in Washington, the firm moved in 1971 to new headquarters on Connecticut Avenue in Chevy Chase.

The B.F. Saul Company is among the oldest continuing developers in Montgomery County, having developed such subdivisions as Springfield, Walnut Hills, Windemere, and Bradley Hills. The firm is continuing to expand its role as a commercial developer, mortgage banker, property manager, and financial adviser. Employing more than 3,000 people in 14 states as it approaches its 100th anniversary, the B.F. Saul Company has joined the top rank of America's privately owned real estate finance and development businesses.

CHEVY CHASE SAVINGS BANK, F.S.B.

In its first 18 years of operation Chevy Chase Savings Bank has grown from a one-room operation housed in a trailer to become the largest savings institution headquartered in Maryland, with 2,000 employees and over $3 billion in assets.

The company was founded by B. Francis Saul II, president of the B.F. Saul Company, a Washington mortgage banking and real estate development firm that was founded in 1892 and is now based in Chevy Chase. Chevy Chase Savings Bank was founded because B.F. Saul II saw the need for a financial institution that would pay interest on members' deposits at above market rates.

When it opened in 1969 Chevy Chase Savings Bank offered just one type of account—6-percent passbook savings. At the time 6 percent was well above the interest rate being paid by neighboring institutions, and customers happily welcomed the new venture.

In 1971 the main office of Chevy Chase Savings Bank moved into the Chevy Chase Lake Building on Connecticut Avenue, near the Capital Beltway. In November 1972 the first branch was opened on the west side of Western Avenue in the Friendship Heights area. By 1981 Chevy Chase Savings Bank had grown to 18 locations throughout Montgomery and Prince Georges counties.

In November 1982 Chevy Chase acquired Government Services Savings and Loan. The combined branch network offered customers their choice of 26 locations.

Community consciousness and the desire to enhance historical awareness have been a part of Chevy Chase's activities from the beginning. When the savings and loan opened its Aspen Hill branch in 1974, it sponsored a week-long arts festival called "The Arts and Aspen Hill." More than 5,000 area residents came to see and hear performances by the Opera Society of Washington, the District of Columbia Youth Orchestra, the Festival Arts Orchestra (under the direction of William Radford-Bennett), the Palisades Theatre Company, Adventure Theatre In-School Players, and two National Symphony orchestra ensembles.

The program continued through the month of October with an art exhibition featuring eight paintings by Washington artists, loaned by the Corcoran Art Gallery. To further promote both Chevy Chase Savings Bank and the arts in Washington, new customers were offered an unusual premium. They would receive a free membership in the Corcoran

Gathering for the fox hunt at the Chevy Chase Club, circa 1900. This is one of the historical drawings commissioned by Chevy Chase Savings Bank in 1974.

Locust Grove, home of Samuel Wade Magruder, revolutionary patriot, before restoration by Chevy Chase Savings Bank.

The interior of the firm's main office. Courtesy, Max Mackenzie

Gallery of Art (then worth $15) for opening an account with $250. The five-week Corcoran promotion brought 1,000 new members to the gallery, and a substantial volume of new business for Chevy Chase Savings Bank.

In another 1974 cultural promotion Chevy Chase Savings Bank commissioned a prominent local artist to create a series of 12 original pen-and-ink drawings capturing the colorful life and times of Maryland in the year 1875. These original prints, together with historically documented text, were brought together in a limited-edition 1975 calendar that was given to customers of the institution.

As a more recent community project the institution has undertaken the restoration of Locust Grove, Samuel Wade Magruder's home near Potomac, Maryland. One of Montgomery County's oldest surviving brick houses, Locust Grove was built in 1783 and remained in the Magruder family for 70 years. In 1853 it was sold at public auction to pay off existing debts.

Subsequent owners made no significant repairs to the house, although the land was farmed and the sawmill and gristmill were kept in operation. By 1890 the house was nearing collapse, and one wall had to be shored up.

Locust Grove continued to deteriorate until 1972, when Chevy Chase Savings Bank acquired it and opened a branch office nearby. The company has restored the house to represent its original period and form, and is operating a branch office in the restored building. The firm is legitimately proud that this grand structure will take its place beside other major historic sites in Montgomery County.

The key to the bank's success has always been its orientation toward the individual depositor, offering above-market rates of interest on deposits, providing all the advantages of a full-service financial institution, and making loans at reasonable rates. Today Chevy Chase Savings Bank offers more than 15 types of savings accounts, including passbook and statement savings, interest checking, an insured money market fund account, and certificates of deposit. A wide variety of consumer loans, home mortgages, and personalized investment services have also been introduced over the years.

The original main office of Chevy Chase Savings Bank.

THE SIGAL/ZUCKERMAN COMPANY

An active renovator of historic properties since its inception, the firm has brought new life to the Bond Building at 1400 New York Avenue. Built in 1901, the structure is a prized example of classic Beaux Arts architecture.

Shelton Zuckerman (left) and Ellen Sigal, the team that founded the real estate development firm, The Sigal/Zuckerman Company, in 1981.

Ellen Sigal and Shelton Zuckerman founded The Sigal/Zuckerman Company in 1981, thereby bringing together the complementary skills and perspectives of two distinguished real estate careers, as well as more than 25 years of business experience in Washington, D.C. Their innovative ideas and fresh approaches to development problems have enabled the company to grow tenfold over the past five years, as well as to build and renovate more than 3 million square feet of space in commercial and multifamily residential projects.

The firm's project portfolio presents a balance between commercial and residential development and between urban and suburban locations. Among Sigal/Zuckerman's recent commercial projects are such historic landmarks as the Bond Building at 1400 New York Avenue, the Riggs Building at 900 F Street, The Papermill Complex in Georgetown, and the former Alice Roosevelt Longworth residence on Massachusetts Avenue. The company's recent suburban commercial projects include Montgomery Village Professional Center and 8027 Leesburg Pike in Tysons Corner.

The Sigal/Zuckerman Company's strong commitment to multifamily residential housing is reflected in its garden apartment communities in Montgomery and Fairfax counties. These communities include Windsor Court, Windsor Tower, Hampton Court, and Beacon Hill apartments.

Ellen Sigal handles architectural direction, promotion, leasing, and administrative policy for the firm. She is a director of the Greater Washington Board of Trade and chairs its Planning and Development Committee. She also chairs the Mayor's Commission on Downtown Housing for the District of Columbia, is vice-president of the D.C. Preservation League, serves as a director of Metropolitan Bank, and is a trustee of the Lincoln Theatre.

Shelton Zuckerman directs the acquisition, construction, financing, and management of Sigal/Zuckerman projects. He serves as a director of Maximum Savings & Loan and of the Franklin Square Park Association. He also continues to be actively involved as a general partner in the development of Westfarm Technology Park, a 4-million-square-foot mixed-use development in Montgomery County, Maryland.

By maintaining a highly individualistic approach and exacting standards, The Sigal/Zuckerman Company has established for itself a well-defined niche in a highly competitive regional market. The firm's solid reputation and business skills have attracted major joint-venture partners for a variety of substantial projects. Locally owned and exclusively committed to the long-term potential of the Washington, D.C., metropolitan community, the firm has established a solid record for achieving both financial and aesthetic goals. On that foundation Washington can anticipate the continued delivery of noteworthy projects by this outstanding corporate citizen.

Another of the firm's recent renovation projects is the historic Riggs Building at 900 F Street.

JAMES MADISON LIMITED

James Madison Limited, one of the Washington region's leading full-service financial corporations, was formed in 1980 as the new parent company of Madison National Bank, which has been serving Washington residents and businesses since 1963.

Louis C. Paladini was the first president and founder of Madison National Bank. The organization quickly gained Washington's confidence, recording more than $3 million in deposits on its first day in business, and over $7.5 million by the end of the month. By 1969 Madison's assets exceeded $50 million.

Madison National Bank continued to experience remarkable growth throughout the 1970s, adding branch offices, introducing computer technology to its customer services, and reaching out from the historic Market section in Northeast to the affluent Spring Valley neighborhood of Northwest.

A leader in innovative banking technology, Madison was among the earliest area banks to adopt automatic teller machines (ATMs), and was the first area bank to link its ATMs with its central computer. It created Washington's first free-standing, 24-hour banking terminal (at The American University) in 1980.

The 1980 formation of James Madison Limited enabled the company to take advantage of new opportunities created by deregulation in the financial service industry. JML subsidiaries include A.E. Landvoigt, Inc., an established mortgage company; Madison Bank of Maryland in Montgomery County; The McLean Bank, N.A., in northern Virginia; and the United National Bank of Washington, one of Washington's most important minority-managed financial institutions.

James Madison Limited has also created JML Communications, Inc., and James Madison Financial Corporation (JMFC). The communications subsidiary markets The Office and Home Teller, micro-computer programs that allow customers to carry out banking operations from their offices or homes. JMFC is a leasing company, assisting clients in procuring business equipment.

K. Donald Menefee, chairman of the board and president.

Continuing its tradition of innovation and progressive industry leadership, JML will open in early 1988 a Financial Service Center in Annapolis, Maryland. This venture brings together under one roof a broad range of financial activities, including full-service banking, investment counseling and brokerage, mortgage placement, insurance, and travel services—all for the convenience of JML customers. JML Financial Service Centers will eventually be available in other regional locations.

In 1987 JML joined with the National Trust for Historic Preservation to celebrate the Bicentennial of the Constitution and pay tribute to its author, James Madison. A JML-sponsored video production on the life and accomplishments of Madison can be viewed by visitors to the newly restored Madison family estate, Montpelier.

MNB annually joins with The Catholic University of America to sponsor "Thanksgiving Tuesday," an event which honors individuals who have given of themselves to benefit the Washington community.

James Madison Limited has total assets exceeding $758 million, 23 bank branches throughout the national capital region, and more than 600 employees. The company has grown to become a comprehensive family of financial service companies, all locally owned and deeply committed to the capital region. K. Donald Menefee, a native Washingtonian and one of the founding members of Madison National Bank, is chairman of the board and president of JML. He is currently a director of the Federal Reserve Bank of Richmond.

WASHINGTONINC

First they were Wonderful Weddings, then Washington WhirlAround, and now, WashingtonInc, but no matter what name they use, the four partners and their dedicated staff have built one of America's foremost meeting, special events, and convention service organizations.

Barbara Boggs, Gretchen Poston, and Ellen Proxmire started the business in 1967. All three have strong ties to the Washington establishment as does Harriet Schwartz, who joined the enterprise three years later. Barbara Boggs is married to the prominent lawyer and lobbyist Tommy Boggs; her mother-in-law is Congresswoman Lindy Boggs. Gretchen Poston was social secretary to the White House in the Carter Administration, and her husband is a prominent lawyer. Ellen Proxmire is the wife of Senator William Proxmire (D-Wisconsin). Harriet Schwartz was a former aide to Edward and Robert Kennedy.

What started as a nuptial planning firm 20 years ago and netted the participants $400 each that first year has grown to WashingtonInc, a meeting and convention planning service, under the able direction of partners (seated, from left) Gretchen Poston and Barbara Boggs, and (standing, from left) Ellen Proxmire and Harriet Schwartz.

The group's announcement that they were opening a wedding consulting business was greeted with extensive publicity. "It came long before we deserved it," admits Ellen Proxmire. "I guess we had a lot of nerve." And enthusiasm.

But they were short of office space, supplies, equipment, and expertise. Working out of the Postons' library, they learned the ropes and acquired business acumen with long hours and tough on-the-job training. Over the next two years the company coordinated arrangements for nearly 100 nuptial affairs.

In 1969, tired of weddings and of emotional parents, the firm switched to business and professional meeting arrangements. Its big break came when it won a bid to run a "spouse tours" program for the American Society of Association Executives. The event proved to be a great showcase. After that they took the "WW" logo from Washington Weddings and became Washington Whirl-Around.

The renamed organization set up business in a one-bedroom Georgetown apartment directly across the street from WashingtonInc's second office at 2233 Wisconsin Avenue, NW. The company was new, and the partners all handled every conceivable task. One conventioneer even tipped his tour bus guide, Ellen Proxmire, 50 cents. "He felt sorry for me; he asked why my senator husband was making me work."

WashingtonInc, currently housed at 1990 M Street, is now among the oldest convention service businesses in the country, and among the most successful. Clients include giants of the corporate and association worlds. Assignments have included such demanding functions as the 1984 convention of the 28,000-member Radiological Society of North America, the largest yet held in Washington. The concern has staged special events for the queen of Jordan, the king of Nepal, and ace industrialist Armand Hammer.

The secret of this success is no secret in Washington where the reputation is that the firm "delivers." WashingtonInc receives, too. The partners have gone from business meetings at the kitchen table and spending the quarterly profits on a nice dinner out to grossing more than $6 million. As for Senator Proxmire, Tommy Boggs, and their other distinguished relatives—they're increasingly likely these days to find themselves being introduced as the husbands of those dynamic Washington businesswomen, the partners in WashingtonInc.

THE NATIONAL CAPITAL BANK OF WASHINGTON

Step inside the gracious banking house of The National Capital Bank of Washington at 316 Pennsylvania Avenue, SE, and rediscover banking as a customer-oriented business. The building opened in 1978, yet from the triple-tiered reproduction Queen Anne chandelier to the Chippendale-style cherry wood traditional banking furniture, to the broadloom carpeting, it speaks of a less hectic era. Only the glowing video display computer terminals remind one that National Capital Bank is just as technologically sophisticated as the interstate giants.

The National Capital Bank of Washington was founded in 1889 by John E. Herrell and a group of associates. Its first office was at the same Capitol Hill location currently occupied by the institution. From its inception it has been neighborhood bank, loyally patronized by Capitol Hill residents and devoting a substantial portion of its assets to improving the local residential and business community.

Among the founders of National Capital Bank was Albert Carry, a German-born brewmaster who built a substantial fortune in Washington. Flexible and responsive to the times, Carry responded to Prohibition by converting his National Capital Brewery to the Carry Ice Cream Company.

The National Capital Brewery/Carry Ice Cream Company filled the block bounded by D and E streets and 13th and 14th streets, SE. For many years it was among the most important businesses in the section then known as East Washington. Carry was also a director of both American Security & Trust Company and East Washington Savings Bank. His son, Charles A. Carry, later served as a vice-president of National Capital Bank.

The current president and chairman of the board of directors is George A. Didden, Jr., a grandson of

George A. Didden, Jr., president and chairman of the board.

Albert Carry and nephew of Charles Carry. A lawyer and general counsel of the bank, Didden assumed the presidency in 1943. He has served as an active bank president longer than any other individual in Washington. Under his leadership the institution increased its activities on Capitol Hill.

National Capital's only branch is at 2701 Pennsylvania Avenue, SE. Founded in 1946 at 2337 Pennsylvania Avenue, SE, it moved to its current location in 1957. "We have remained small as a philosophic commitment," says Didden. "We wanted to remain a community bank, and we wanted to keep our operations completely under our own control."

Prudent management and a conservative business philosophy have

A National Capital Bank note signed by H.H. McKee, president of the bank from 1917 to 1943. Notes of this type were often used as local currency.

consistently kept National Capital among Washington's "most secure" banks and among the 100 strongest banks in the nation. It holds total assets well in excess of $75 million.

The Didden family influence seems likely to continue at The National Capital Bank of Washington, a closely held private corporation. Four sons—George Didden III, Richard Didden, James Didden, and Donald Didden—are all vice-presidents.

THE LENKIN COMPANY

The Griffin Condominium, 955 Twenty-sixth Street, NW.

Back in the early days of the twentieth century, two brothers learned to do a wide variety of things to make ends meet in their newly adopted hometown of Washington, D.C. They ran a grocery and picked up a few extra dollars now and then by selling paint and wallpaper, and occasionally by performing a remodeling job.

By the early 1920s Harry and Morris Lenkin had acquired a neighborhood reputation as pretty fair businessmen. Soon, in addition to the remodeling work, they managed to obtain work as general contractors and to set savings aside for investments. In working with various partners they became involved in construction and real estate development.

The Lenkin Company is a real estate investment, development, building, and management firm. Still a family-owned business, it is a streamlined operation with only a dozen or so employees in the corporate offices. Melvin Lenkin, Harry's son, runs it in partnership with his own son, Edward. The firm works out of spacious, Art Deco-inspired headquarters in Bethesda, but most of its projects are in downtown Washington. As Melvin Lenkin says, "If your own backyard is nice and green, there's no need to look elsewhere."

The corporation still owns and manages three northwest Washington apartment complexes that Harry and Morris Lenkin built in the 1940s: Parkhill Apartments, at 1610 Park Road; The Yorkshire House, at 3355 Sixteenth Street; and the Lencshire House, at 3140 Wisconsin Avenue. The company's offices in those days were above the old Tivoli Theater at 14th Street and Park Road, NW.

During World War II the Lenkin brothers were busy managing the properties they already owned, and happy enough with their successes to sit back and enjoy the fruits of their hectic salad days. Their buildings were all fully leased, most by state department workers—although Melvin Lenkin recalls that a good subtenant of the State Department at the time was a Soviet trade mission.

Melvin Lenkin became a partner with his father and uncle in the early 1950s. He brought extensive experience to the company, having worked for several years in construction and as the manager of the family's properties.

Under his leadership the partnership developed 2121 Pennsylvania Avenue, NW, now the headquarters of the Group Health Association. The project helped launch the modern era of The Lenkin Company. Some of the projects that followed included the Jefferson Building at 1225 Nineteenth Street, NW, the Penn Branch Shopping Center in Southeast, and the Association of American Railroads Building at 1920 L Street, NW.

The organization's residential projects of the same era included the 142-unit Pennsylvania House at 2424 Pennsylvania Avenue, NW (which became its own home base in 1962), the 10-story Garfield House at 2844 Wisconsin Avenue, and Cathedral West Apartments at 4100 Cathedral Avenue, NW, among others.

In 1970 the corporation moved its offices to Bethesda. Its most impor-

1818 N Street, NW.

ABOVE: 1130 Connecticut Avenue, NW.

LEFT: 1133 Connecticut Avenue, NW.

tant new direction at the time included a partnership called Central Management, which purchased garden apartment complexes and rehabilitated them. In 1981 Central Management was dissolved. Eddie Lenkin joined the firm in 1975. "Actually," recalls Eddie Lenkin, "all I wanted was a job. I'd been working construction since 1966 and building houses in partnership with a cousin since 1972. In 1975 interest rates took off, and we ran out of financing, so I came looking for work."

"I've never believed that a father and son should have an employer/employee relationship," states Melvin Lenkin. "I wanted to work with him, so I made him a partner. I've had a lot of partners through the years, but Eddie is the best."

Among the projects developed and built by father and son is 1775 Pennsylvania Avenue, NW, now the headquarters of Citicorp Savings. The building won a 1981 national design award from the American Institute of Architects, an achievement that still brings pleasure to the developers. Some of the other projects developed by The Lenkin Company during the 1970s include the headquarters of the Air Transport Association, 1709 New York Avenue; the ABC Building, 1717 DeSales Street, NW; and the 12-story office building at 818 Connecticut Avenue. Lenkin was the first to build mixed residential and commercial uses into the same structure.

The Lenkin Company's most recent residential project is The Griffin, a condominium at 955 Twenty-sixth Street, NW. Recent commercial projects include Spring Valley Center, 4801 Massachusetts Avenue; and the 1400 Eye Street, NW, headquarters of United Press International (over the McPherson Square MetroRail station). The next project in line is a 12-story building scheduled for construction at Connecticut Avenue and DeSales streets, where Raleigh's will return with its downtown flagship store.

The Lenkin firm has long been a low-profile operation, without elaborate brochures or massive banners at construction sites to spread the company name. "Nobody really needs to know who we are," explains Melvin Lenkin. "Our management and leasing customers know us, and our subcontractors know us. We've been doing business with most of them for at least 20 years. For anybody else, we'll let our buildings speak for us."

In addition to its real estate investment, development, construction, and management, the Lenkins have been involved with several outside businesses. They briefly owned controlling interests in Security National Bank (1984-1985), and in radio station WAVA, which the Lenkins operated during the mid-1970s. The Lenkin Company currently owns the Aspen Hill Racket Club with its 15 tennis courts, 8 racketball courts, and 15,000-square-foot fitness center.

"Washington is our city," says Eddie Lenkin. "My family has been part of it for three generations. We're really proud of our family and its contribution to the Washington community."

JONES LANG WOOTTON USA

Jones Lang Wootton USA, part of an international real estate management firm, leases and manages such buildings in the Washington, D.C., area as the Army and Navy Club Building (left), where the firm's offices are located; 1701 Pennsylvania Avenue (below); 1225 Connecticut Avenue (right); and 1015 Eighteenth Street (below right).

Jones Lang Wootton USA is a leading investment and corporate real estate services organization, offering a comprehensive range of integrated services to institutions, corporations, investors, and property owners. These services include investment management, debt and equity financing, corporate real estate services, property management, development and project management, leasing, investment research and consulting, and valuation.

The company traces its origins to London, England, in 1783, and an auctioneer named Richard Winstanley. His modest but profitable business was property, which he bought and sold for his clients. He also checked inventories of contents at the termination of leases, acted as arbitrator, and advertised available premises.

The sons of Richard Winstanley followed in their father's path and became partners of another London estate agent and auctioneer, James Jones, in 1839. James Jones' son Frederick succeeded his father's place in the firm in 1871. The following year Frederick Jones was joined by C.A. Lang, and the organization changed its name to Jones Lang & Company. In 1939 the firm merged with Wootton and Sons and became known as Jones Lang Wootton.

From its base in London, Jones Lang Wootton grew rapidly following World War II. By 1958 it comprised 74 staff personnel, including the partners; by 1966 its staff had soared to 385, and to more than 750 by 1973. Today Jones Lang Wootton has 45 offices in 15 countries with an international staff of approximately 2,000.

The U.S. partnership affiliate, Jones Lang Wootton USA, was established in 1975 in New York City. Additional U.S. locations were established in Los Angeles (1978), Houston (1980), San Francisco (1982), and Washington, D.C. (1983).

At first the Washington office employed only two people, but it soon

built an active and successful full-service operation that quickly became an important component of the Washington real estate community. By 1987 the Washington staff had grown to more than 70, including five senior executives.

The Washington, D.C., office leases and manages more than 3 million square feet of space for national and international clients, and has accrued more than one billion dollars in sales, acquisitions, and financings since its inception.

As a coast-to-coast operation in the United States, Jones Lang Wootton USA has a staff of more than 500, 35 of whom are senior executives. As part of a worldwide organization, the company offers its clients access to equity capital, financing sources, and investment opportunities, as well as offering a truly national and international corporate real estate capability.

Jones Lang Wootton USA is distinguished by the exceptional qualification and depth of its professional staff. The high level of information, education, and multidisciplinary technical skills these professionals bring to their assignments is enhanced by research and computer support that is unique in the industry.

Traditionally an international leader in real estate investment management for overseas institutions and entrepreneurs, Jones Lang Wootton is now also recognized as a premier adviser to pension funds in the United States. A wholly owned subsidiary of the firm, Jones Lang Wootton Realty Advisors, is registered with the Security Exchange Commission and serves a clientele of major and public pension funds for whom it creates individually managed, separate account property portfolios.

In serving these clients Jones Lang Wootton Realty Advisors has created a national portfolio of office buildings, shopping centers, industrial properties, and hotels valued at more than one billion dollars for its investment accounts.

Throughout its 200-year history Jones Lang Wootton has maintained the highest professional standards and sensitivity to the precise requirements of each individual client. This mandate remains the cornerstone of all its investment and corporate activities.

CHILDREN'S HOSPITAL NATIONAL MEDICAL CENTER

Children's Hospital National Medical Center is a private, nonprofit medical institution. The main hospital is located on Michigan Avenue, NW. There are two suburban clinics: one in Fairfax, Virginia, and the other in Rockville, Maryland.

The 2,480-person staff of Children's Hospital National Medical Center is dedicated to the care of children. Whether treating young victims of shock trauma, transporting critically ill infants, performing kidney transplants, performing eye surgery, or providing care from its many other services, CHNMC staff and facilities combine outstanding care and the latest medical technology.

ABOVE: After the Civil War the infant mortality rate in Washington, D.C., was dreadful. Children's Hospital was born in 1870 in this rented house in northwest Washington to fulfill an overwhelming need.

LEFT: Today Children's Hospital, at 111 Michigan Avenue, NW, is renowned worldwide for outstanding care of its young patients and use of the latest in medical technology.

The hospital was created in response to critical local needs—needs that had arisen out of a national crisis.

Five years after Robert E. Lee's surrender at Appomattox Court House, the city of Washington still overflowed with victims of the Civil War. Many were the orphans and children of soldiers, others the victims of poverty in a community overcrowded with refugees and displaced persons. The city was experiencing a horrifying infant mortality rate. Fully half of its children were dying before they reached age 21. The greatest killers were disease and neglect.

In 1879 Dr. Samuel Clagett Busey, along with other community leaders, founded a medical institution specifically for the care of children. Children's Hospital was born as a 12-bed facility in a rented northwest Washington house. By the turn of the century it had quadrupled in size and had become a nationally recognized institution for medical education in pediatric care.

Researchers at Children's Hospital were among the first in the nation to recognize that the trauma of intensive medical treatment may have a direct impact on the recovery of a child. Consequently, they pioneered the development of programs designed to minimize problems caused by hospitalization.

Recognizing that recovery could be enhanced by having a parent nearby, the hospital provided sleeping space for parents. Approximately 200 of Children's Hospital's 279 patient beds have sleeping accommodations for parents. Similarly, the Child Life Department, established in 1972, helps children continue with play, development, and education while in the hospital.

Children's Hospital National Medical Center affiliated with The George Washington University School of Medicine in 1968. Today students of 10 university nursing programs as well as other technical and medical educational programs receive part of their training at Children's Hospital. The institution is now international in scope, treating children referred from hospitals nationwide and from many foreign countries.

GEORGETOWN UNIVERSITY

At Georgetown University, long and distinguished liberal arts and professional traditions combine with the political awareness and intellectual excitement of Washington, producing a unique approach and contribution to American education.

Founded in 1789 by John Carroll, the first Catholic bishop in the United States, Georgetown College was chartered by the first Congress of the United States. Its mission was to provide training in the liberal arts, philosophy, religion, and morality.

From its founding Georgetown has been witness to much of the nation's history. The young college was threatened by the British invasion of 1812 and the burning of the Capitol and the White House.

Students and alumni fought on both sides of the Civil War, and Union troops occupied the campus. At the end of that conflict, the university adopted as its colors blue and gray—signifying the unification of the nation.

"The heights in this neighborhood, above the Potomac River, are very picturesque," wrote Charles Dickens of a visit to Georgetown in 1842. The hilltop campus, which has grown to some 60 buildings spread over 100 acres, still dominates the river skyline today.

Father Patrick Healy, the son of a sea captain and a black bondswoman, directed the university in the postwar era. He revolutionized the curriculum, combining a concentration on the physical sciences with the traditional study of the liberal arts and a continued Jesuit emphasis on philosophy and religious studies. Father Healy's Georgetown model was widely admired and imitated throughout the nation.

The institution's School of Medicine was established in 1849. The School of Law was established in 1869. The University Hospital opened in 1898, the School of Dentistry in 1901, and the School of Nursing in 1903.

World War I taught the world that nations must, for their salvation, seek to cooperate through international trade and diplomacy. Recognizing that dictate, Father Edmund A. Walsh led Georgetown's creation of its School of Foreign Service in 1919.

World War II brought other demands on American educational institutions and new expectations from a more mature student body. In the years immediately following the war, Georgetown revived its graduate school. Under the leadership of Father J. Hunter Guthrie, it became an advanced school of teaching and research.

Dahlgren Chapel, built in 1892, occupies a prominent spot in the central courtyard. Georgetown University enrolls 12,000 students from all 50 states and more than 100 foreign countries.

The School of Business Administration was instituted in 1957. In recognition of the essential need to use languages as links and not as barriers between peoples, the School of Languages and Linguistics became part of the university eight years later.

Georgetown University's main campus on the heights above the Potomac River shelters historic and modern structures. In 1797 President George Washington spoke to Georgetown students in Old North Hall. Dahlgren Chapel, the center of liturgical life of the university, was dedicated in 1893 and completely renovated in 1976. The Lombardi Cancer Research Center and the Intercultural Center, which now houses all of Georgetown's international programs, were dedicated in 1982. An imposing university center and a clinical science building are scheduled for completion in 1988. They are two of seven building projects currently in progress.

Father Timothy S. Healy, S.J., is the president of Georgetown University.

WASHINGTON CONVENTION CENTER

Washington, D.C., always had the potential to be a great convention town. It had the location, it had transportation facilities, it had attractions for conventioneers and their families. But it lacked the giant exposition facilities and overabundance of hotel rooms required to become a major convention city.

The solution was obvious, at least to the city's planners, business leaders, and politicians. Build a convention center. Build it in Washington's decayed downtown area where it would attract redevelopment and help recreate the elegance that had once been part of downtown Washington. A major complex would bring expositions and conventions to Washington, and with them would come hotels, jobs, and new economic vitality for the depressed inner city.

But if the solution was obvious, so were the problems. Such a project would severely strain the already overburdened local tax base. Also, the project would have to win approval from Congress—a Congress made up of representatives from places that would compete with Washington for convention and exposition business.

In the era before home rule, few people saw Washington as a community in its own right. Fewer still believed that the diverse interest groups of Washington could lay aside their differences and work together long enough and hard enough to complete such a complex project.

Critics of a convention center said it couldn't be done, but a few local leaders said they could do it. They first drew up the plans in 1969, naming the proposed complex the Eisenhower Civic Center. The campaign to build it started in 1970, endorsed by economic consultants working for the city's Downtown Renewal Program and by the National Capital Planning Commission.

The critics said the road to a convention center in Washington would be too long and too difficult. The doubters said it would never be approved, never be built, never be finished. A few others—individuals and organizations—knew enough to take things one step at a time.

The White House first publicly supported the building of a convention center in Washington in 1972, and Congress authorized the District to develop plans for a facility to be built by a private corporation, then leased back to the city. Center supporters enthusiastically developed a series of plans, but throughout the following year each in turn was rejected either by corporate sponsors or by Congress. By the end of the year the campaign had been abandoned. It looked as if the visionaries had been wrong and their critics right.

Dreams and good ideas die hard. Three years later the District's first home rule administration under the leadership of Mayor Walter E. Washington revived the convention center concept. The Economic Development Administration of the U.S. Department of Commerce provided new

Exterior views of the Washington Convention Center.

planning funds, and the mayor appointed a Convention Center Task Force.

Public hearings in 1977 showed strong support for the center, and the city council voted to include the convention center in its 1978 budget. After extended negotiations and several compromises, Congress approved the plans, and the initial convention center appropriation was funded in November 1978.

In 1979 the city purchased the Ninth Street and New York Avenue site for the complex. In August the Washington City Council passed the Washington Convention Center Management Act of 1979, creating the five-person board of directors for the center.

On April 23, 1980, Mayor Marion Barry, Jr., along with many local and civic business leaders, broke ground for the Washington Convention Center. The actual construction began that August, more than 10 years after the initial plans had first gained the approval of Washington's leaders.

On December 10, 1982, Mayor Barry cut the ribbon that officially opened the center. Washington Convention Center board chairman Edward A. Singletary politely understated the triumph. "For the last 22 years," he told the crowd, "people have had doubts about this center being completed. But today it is a reality, and it was built on time and on budget."

That evening the center hosted a gala reception for more than 300 top association executives. The Washington Convention Center was in business and showing off for its potential clients.

The first official event was the mayor's 1983 inauguration on January 3. Three days later the National Capital Area International Auto Show became its first exposition, and drew an audience of nearly a quarter-million people.

The center's first national convention and trade show, the annual meeting of the American Society of Association Executives, was held March 23-27. The nation's top convention planners were among the people who attended that meeting. By the time they had left the ASAE convention, many had selected the Washington Convention Center as the site of their own future meetings.

One guest summed up the general reaction to the convention center after a 1983 meeting: "We're coming back because the town's a terrific draw for both domestic and foreign exhibitors and visitors, the facility is a dandy, and the staff is upbeat."

With more than 350,000 square feet of available space, the Washington Convention Center is one of America's 15 largest convention and exhibition halls. Forty flexible meeting rooms can accommodate groups of 100 to 1,400 people. The main meeting hall can seat between 10,000 and 12,000 guests. Its audiovisual systems, telecommunications, catering and banquet services, security, and logistics are among the most advanced and efficient in the world.

It has worked for the city, too. The convention center has helped make Washington one of the leading convention locations in America. Original estimates and projections of new jobs and businesses, downtown revitalization, and hotel construction have been realized and exceeded.

Each year now more and more convention delegates come to town intent on doing business. The Washington Convention Center is pleased to accommodate them.

BLACKIE'S HOUSE OF BEEF

The specialty of the house is the Prime Rib of Beef Au Jus. It is carefully selected and aged, top-quality roast beef served with bleu cheese and crackers, baked potato or French fries, tossed green salad, and assorted breads and butter.

This is Blackie's House of Beef on 22nd Street, NW, in Washington, D.C., the Capital City of the United States of America. From its ornate cast-iron portico and balconies to its Wild West interiors, half New Orleans, half Dodge City, there is no other place in the world quite like it.

The dinner menu typically includes offerings for seafood lovers, but people come to Blackie's for the beef. Single cut, heavy cut, or double cut, the prime rib tops the menu. Spareribs, top sirloin, chopped sirloin, filet mignon, New York sirloin, and "Blackie's Choice," a children's (under 12) special, fill out the main choices. The restaurant has a full-service bar, but Blackie recommends wine with dinner. The menu offers a selection of popular California and imported wines.

From the entryway of the restaurant, which is a Washington landmark and an American tradition, one can watch the chefs slicing thick slabs of top-quality beef with their long sharp knives. The meat is selected and purchased especially for Blackie's directly from Monfort of Greeley, Colorado.

The saddle above the beef bar is a gift from a group of saddle-sore horsemen who rode into town one day in 1961 to publicize the centennial of the Pony Express. They rode 3,000 miles to the White House, then headed to Blackie's for a beef dinner. They gave him the saddle and proclaimed his place a repository of Western Americana before riding off into the sunset.

For lunch Blackie's offers a variety of sandwiches, steaks, vegetables, hot luncheon platters, burgers, and cold plates. The entire menu is available for carry out, but most folks like to enjoy the meals amidst the exotic, eclectic decor of the House of Beef.

In celebration of the 1954 opening night, the Augers hosted a party featuring prime ribs, which have been a tradition at Blackie's ever since.

The cocktail lounge was designed by Blackie himself. Much of the red velvet upholstered furniture came from the old Capitol Theater on F Street. The stained glass came from Providence Hospital, and the rustic wood bar was obtained from the O'Donnell farm in Maryland.

The Boot Hill Room provides a gallery of mementos provided by a former congressman, including a photo of Chief Sitting Bull and one of his rifles. When Blackie opened the Boot Hill Room in 1959, Marshall Ramon House of Dodge City was the guest of honor.

Celebrities are part of the scene at Blackie's. Photographs in the menu and on the walls commemorate the visits of uncounted numbers of politicians, journalists, and entertainers. The list includes Jimmy Durante, Art Linkletter, Walter Winchell, John Kennedy, Jonathan Winters, Russell Long, Hubert Humphrey, Julius La Rosa, Art Buchwald, Estes Kefauver, George Hamilton, and many, many others. Sooner or later everybody comes to Washington, and everybody in Washington comes to Blackie's.

Blackie (his real name is Ulysses G. Auger; "Blackie" is a World War II Army nickname) is a native of Pennsylvania, but his father, Gregory Auger, brought him to Washington when he was only seven days old.

Blackie's father also owned a Washington restaurant, the Expert Lunch at 2919 M Street. Blackie left Washington for military service in 1942. He had met Louie Hansen, a secretary in the Department of the Treasury, before the war. He married her in 1946 in Hollywood, California, shortly after his discharge.

The young couple headed east later that year, with all their possessions and hopes fitting easily in an aging Chevrolet. They hoped to open a small restaurant of their own in Washington. Blackie borrowed the start-up money from his mother and opened a small cafe, the Minute Grille, at 22nd and M streets. Today the California license plate from the

Chevrolet hangs above the bar of the House of Beef.

Washington proved to be a tough market to crack. Louie ran the restaurant while Blackie rolled a food-vending cart through the offices of the *U.S. News and World Report* building, Capitol Cadillac, the U.S. Weather Bureau, and the Bureau of National Affairs. In 1949 they lost their lease on the restaurant site and moved to new quarters across the street.

Blackie and Louie worked as cooks, waiters, dishwashers—whatever was needed. To supplement their income they opened a dry cleaning establishment next door. Then, in 1953, after some informal market research, Blackie decided to offer top-quality beef at reasonable prices. Traditionally available only in fine hotel restaurants and at finer prices, the move required a major investment and commitment.

Hard times ended for the Auger family in 1954. Since then a series of expansions have been necessary to handle the ever-increasing crowds that come to eat at a restaurant that is recommended by folks as far away as New Orleans and Dodge City. By 1981 Blackie's was handling 1,200 customers.

A second Blackie's opened in 1983 in Springfield, Virginia, complete with an ambience and capacity similar to Blackie's in Washington.

The original Blackie's bar showing one of the seven wood-burning fireplaces, which burn brightly throughout the winter. The stained glass windows are from the Providence Hospital, which was chartered by Congress in 1844, and the hand-carved velvet chair by the fireplace is from the old Capitol Theatre. One of many paintings throughout the restaurant, the painting over the bar reflects the Rembrandt School.

Both restaurants also include one of Washington's (and Springfield's) most popular night spots, Deja Vu, featuring dancing and music of the 1950s and 1960s.

And now, how about some dessert? Why not try Blackie's famous cheesecake? Or maybe one of the homemade pies.

C&P TELEPHONE COMPANY

On the morning of February 14, 1868, Alexander Graham Bell walked into the U.S. Patent Office and applied for a patent on a new invention called the telephone. That afternoon, just before closing, attorneys representing inventor Elisha Gray rushed in to file a caveat describing a "speaking telephone" that Gray had in progress.

Nine hours separated the two events—nine hours that determined the course of telecommunications history. The office awarded the patent to Bell in March 1876.

Although there have been changes in the basic workings and usage of the telephone since its invention, it is still the easiest and the swiftest way to say "hi" to someone you care for or someone who depends on your caring. It is now also the fastest way to send information—across town or across the world.

Everything else about the telephone company and the people behind this vital utility has changed dramatically—and changed for the better.

As Mikhail Gorbachev, General Secretary of the Soviet Communist Party, and President Ronald Reagan met in the Oval Office on that historic afternoon, December 8, 1987, the entire world waited to hear the good word—about reducing the nuclear arsenals of the two superpowers. And thanks to C&P Telephone, the two leaders didn't have to "yell." They used the "telephone"—in more ways than one.

Between midnight of December 6 and 8:00 a.m. of December 7, C&P Telephone crews had installed hundreds of telephone lines in the International Press Center (at the J.W. Marriott), from where the word was flashed to the entire world. C&P's radio and television experts had installed audio and video circuits that brought sharp images of the historic event to the homes of millions around the globe. Under normal circumstances, the total work volume would have required a couple of months to finish. But this job was done in a matter of days.

C&P is aware of the fact that a "telephone" plays an important role in the lives of everyone. People depend on their telephone service. There is individual as well as institutional sensitivity toward this reality.

C&P Telephone helped in solving the problems associated with the operation of Washington's E-911 emergency service. It trained the telephone answering personnel on techniques of obtaining information from the caller quickly and efficiently.

The company's concern is not limited to the life that might be saved. C&P participates actively in events and enterprises that enliven and improve the quality of life in this city.

C&P employees are active in almost all major civic and community organizations and the firm also patronizes such cultural organizations as the Washington Performing Arts Society.

It also supports the process of grooming future generations through an active educational relations program that includes both students and teachers. C&P's volunteer speakers are available to help groups make deci-

By 1900 operators sat at the switchboard on specially designed chairs to support their backs, the chest transmitter had replaced suspended boxes, and more than 17,000 women had found the telephone company a good place to work.

AT&T Company Photo Center plant construction. An aerial lineman gasses an aerial cable in 1932.

sions on the hottest and most complex telecommunications issues or to help 15-year-olds decide what career may be more suitable for them.

The C&P Telephone Company (of Washington) was incorporated in June 1883, but its roots go back to April 1876 when George C. Maynard received a Bell license to operate a telephone business. He began installation in early 1877, probably with a line from the office of chief signal officer of the U.S. Army to Fort Whipple (now known as Fort Myer), Virginia.

From that one line grew more than 120 lines by July 1878. The company operated from a small room in Maynard's electrical supplies store on G Street, NW. In January 1879 it was moved to 1420 New York Avenue, NW. A month earlier the telephone company had been reorganized as National Capital Telephone Company (NCTC). Two years later the NCTC was incorporated in West Virginia.

During World War I President Woodrow Wilson wanted to "use the telephone" and the federal government "took possession and assumed control and supervision of the telephone and telegraph system" under a special wartime emergency act. It was returned to private control in August 1919.

The giant Bell System was divested on January 1, 1984, through an agreement signed by AT&T and the Justice Department in early 1982. The Bell System was divided into seven regional holding companies and AT&T kept the long-distance service, the Western Electric Company, and Bell Laboratories.

C&P is owned by the holding company called Bell Atlantic, which owns the four C&P companies (Washington, Virginia, Maryland, West Virginia), Bell of Pennsylvania, New Jersey Bell, and the Diamond State Telephone Company.

Today C&P faces a dual challenge: It must live up to the image of its glorious past, and it must meet the future expectations of its customers—from John Q. Public to President Ronald Reagan—whether they live in Washington or just visit for a few days.

President Dwight D. Eisenhower once heard someone talking loudly in the room next to the Oval Office. He asked what was going on. He was told that the person next door was "talking to New York."

"For God's sake," quipped the president, "tell him to use the telephone!"

If some folks still yell while talking on the phone, it is simply a habit, not a necessity.

In a little more than 100 years since the first telephone patent was awarded to its inventor, Alexander Graham Bell, the telephone has become an example of the saying: "The more things change, the more they remain the same."

Communications technician Rudy Quijada can fix a trouble on the all-electronic super switcher by simply plugging in a preassembled circuit pack. This method replaces the more tedious and time-consuming task of rewiring that was necessary on the previous electromechanical equipment.

Arthur Killion, communications technician, uses this test console to check the quality of transmission paths that link local exchanges and distant locations to the super switcher.

AMERICAN SECURITY BANK

The roots of American Security Bank go back to the Bank of the Metropolis, founded in 1814. Rechartered under the national banking act in 1865 as the National Metropolitan Bank of Washington, this venerable institution played an important role in the financial history of Washington. It became part of American Security Bank in 1958.

District of Columbia law had no provision for chartering trust companies when American Security and Trust was founded in 1889, so the founders obtained a Virginia charter. Officially the bank was based in Virginia, but its office was at 1419 G Street NW. The following year American Security reincorporated under the newly passed District of Columbia Trust Company Act.

The new organization quickly established several departments: the Money Department "for the receipt of deposits and payment of checks"; a Safe Deposit Department with a vault "protected by the most modern electrical safeguards"; and a Real Estate Department. In 1893, as America struggled through a severe economic crisis, American Security declared its first dividend.

The bank took its place among Washington's financial leaders in 1905, when it opened its headquarters at 15th Street and Pennsylvania Avenue, NW, opposite the United States Treasury Building. One banking journal hailed the new structure as "the handsomest banking building in the United States."

Traditionally a conservative financial institution, American Security has nonetheless often been an innovator. As automobiles started rolling off early assembly lines, American Security gave the green light to installment credit, the first Washington bank to help customers purchase expensive necessities.

After World War II, as returning GIs and burgeoning bureaucracy brought boom times to Washington, American Security became a regional leader in real estate financing, helping to reshape the Washington area skyline. In 1948 the institution purchased Columbia National Bank, leading to a significant expansion of its branch office network.

The bank created its holding company, American Security Corporation, in 1958. The new organization facilitated the purchase of National Metropolitan and, in 1959, the City Bank, and made it possible for the company to hold real estate and engage in such nonbanking businesses as insurance and travel.

American Security Bank, founded in 1889, is prominently located on the corner of 15th Street and Pennsylvania Avenue, directly across from the U.S. Treasury.

In 1983 American Security reorganized its institutional accounts and investments group as ASB Capital Management, Inc., a wholly owned subsidiary of American Security Corporation. As a registered investment adviser, ASB Capital Management offers a full range of money-management services to institutional clients. It was the first such investment subsidiary in Washington.

With 1986 assets exceeding $4.6 billion and 30 banking offices, American Security ranks among Washington's most substantial financial institutions. Chairman of the board and chief executive officer is Daniel J. Callahan III; William G. Tull is president.

On March 16, 1987, American Security merged with Maryland National Corporation. With combined assets of $16 billion, the new organization will continue to be a leader in Washington-area banking.

Photographed from the U.S. Capitol, commercial construction projects changed the face of the city during the 1930s—American Security financed many of the projects in the area known as the Federal Triangle.

GLASSIE, PEWETT, DUDLEY, BEEBE & SHANKS

The Washington law firm of Glassie, Pewett, Dudley, Beebe & Shanks is one of Washington's most respected and admired general law partnerships. Moderate in size with only 10 partners and six associates, Glassie, Pewett is surprisingly well known and influential, especially in the fields of historical preservation and real estate investment and financing.

Henry Glassie began his law career with Chadbourne & Parke in New York City. A native of Chevy Chase, Maryland, he founded this firm in Washington in 1949 with Henry B. Weaver. Weaver later withdrew to become general counsel of Atlantic Richfield Corporation.

The firm is headquartered in the historic Sun Building, one of the oldest, if not the oldest, surviving "skyscrapers" in the United States. While its distinction became less visible when it lost its spire in a 1950 renovation, the nine-story structure at 1317 F Street, NW, was the first steel-frame office building erected in Washington. Designed by architect Alfred B. Mullett (whose other works include the old Executive Office Building), and built by the Baltimore-based Sun Newspaper Corporation in 1885, it is listed on the National Register of Historic Places and frequently visited by architectural historians.

The Sun Building's 48 fireplaces, intricate wrought-iron railings, paneling, elaborate plaster decoration, and other outstanding handwork provide an appropriate setting to a law firm that has become deeply involved in the constructive reuse of historic Washington structures.

"We've taken wonderful old buildings that had been allowed to deteriorate and restored them to creative life," says Glassie. Among other Glassie, Pewett renovation projects that have previously served as the firm's headquarters are 1737 H Street, NW, which was among the first District buildings to be remodeled under special taxation provisions, and 1527 New Hampshire Avenue, NW, now the home of the National Political Science Association.

"We practice law in an old-fashioned way," says Glassie. "Our partners all have their own specialties and their own interests—often interests that take them to other areas." Glassie is a historian and art expert. He is on the board of directors of the Columbia Historical Association and the author of several books, including *Victorian Homes in Washington* and *The Capitol Image: Painters in Washington, 1800-1915.*

Senior partner Hershel Shanks, a litigator, is also known to an international audience as the editor of the *Biblical Archaeology Review.* Michael J. Ruane, one of the firm's experts on real estate financing, is managing partner. Henry A. Dudley serves on the Board of Visitors of the University of Virginia, Roanoke College, and other public institutions.

"We like to practice in the small-firm atmosphere," says Glassie. "It allows us each to be ourselves, to serve the law and our community as we see best. Our law practice and our historic preservation work are similar. Both go far deeper than the facade. We see ourselves as making an important contribution to the cultural life of Washington."

The Sun Building, once the Washington headquarters of the Sun Newspapers, is now the home of Glassie, Pewett, Dudley, Beebe & Shanks.

Partners in the law firm (from left, seated) are David S. Kahn, Michael J. Ruane, Henry H. Glassie, Henry A. Dudley, Joseph P. Hart, and (standing, from left) James Bramer, Hershel Shanks, Charles A. Trainum, James M. Kefauver, and Joseph W. O'Malley.

Patrons

The following individuals, companies, and organizations have made a valuable commitment to the quality of this publication. Windsor Publications and The Columbia Historical Society gratefully acknowledge their participation in *Washington at Home: An Illustrated History of Neighborhoods in the Nation's Capital.*

The Acacia Group*
American Security Bank*
The American University*
Arnold & Porter*
AT&T*
The Begg Companies*
Blackie's House of Beef*
Blue Cross and Blue Shield of the National Capital Area*
Brenneman Associates, Inc.
C&P Telephone Company*
Caterpillar Inc.
Chevy Chase Historical Society
Chevy Chase Savings Bank, F.S.B.*
Children's Hospital National Medical Center*
Citizens Savings & Loan Association
James U. Clemons
Cleveland Park Historical Society
Columbia First Federal Savings and Loan Association*
Columbia Hospital for Women Medical Center*
Covington & Burling*
District of Columbia Chamber of Commerce*
The Donohoe Companies, Inc.*
Gallaudet University*
Georgetown University*
The George Washington University*
H.A. Gill & Son Realtors
M.S. Ginn Company*
Glassie, Pewett, Dudley, Beebe & Shanks*
Government Employees Insurance Company*
Mark G. Griffin
Randall H. Hagner & Co.
Howard University*
Howard University Hospital*
Ingersoll and Bloch, Chartered*
Johnson & Higgins of Washington, D.C.*
Carlton D. Jones
Jones Lang Wootton USA*
The Alan I. Kay Companies*
The Kiplinger Washington Editors*
The Lenkin Company*
James Madison Limited*
Mones-Yglesias Architects
Mount Vernon College*
The National Bank of Washington*
The National Capital Bank of Washington*
Old Town Trolley Tours of Washington
Omni Construction, Inc.*
Dr. William D. Pederson, LSU-S
Riggs National Bank*
B.F. Saul Company*
Shannon & Luchs Company*
The Sigal/Zuckerman Company*
Syscon Corporation*
Helen M. Toomey
USAir*
Washington Convention Center*
WashingtonInc*
In memory of Norma Aronson Wegner
Woodward & Lothrop*
WTOP Newsradio 15*
Wynmark Development Corporation*

*Partners in Progress of *Washington at Home: An Illustrated History of Neighborhoods in the Nation's Capital.* The histories of these companies and organizations appear in Part Six, beginning on page 271.

About the Contributors

Robert McQuail Bachman has been active in Takoma Park preservation efforts and made its history the subject of a master's thesis in American Studies at George Washington University. He presently works in health-care advocacy as executive director of the National Council on Patient Information and Education.

Olivia Cadaval has conducted research and participated in cultural programming in the Washington, D.C., Latino community for more than eight years. She is currently a predoctoral Smithsonian Fellow and a doctoral candidate in the American Studies Folklife Program at George Washington University.

Marvin Caplan is a writer and journalist as well as a community activist who has been a resident of Shepherd Park and the immediate area for 30 years: he was a founding member and first president of Neighbors, Inc. His articles have appeared in such publications as the *Washington Post, Atlantic Monthly, New Republic,* and *Washington Jewish Week.*

Emily Hotaling Eig is an architectural historian and partner in the firm of Traceries. A graduate of Brandeis University, with a graduate degree from George Washington University, she has focused her professional efforts on Washington architecture of the late nineteenth and twentieth centuries.

Howard Gillette, Jr., is Professor of American Civilization and Director of the American Studies Program at George Washington University, where he teaches courses on Washington and urban history. He is co-editor of *American Urbanism* (1987) and second vice-president of the Columbia Historical Society.

Maria Goodwin is a native Washingtonian and a resident of Benning Heights who has pursued local history as an avocation, authoring the Columbia Historical Society's *Special Research Series,* among other projects. She is employed in arts administration and research at the National Endowment for the Arts.

Katherine Grandine explored the development of Brightwood in a 1983 master's thesis for George Washington University. She has done historical surveys for the Historic American Buildings Survey and presently works as a historical consultant with Traceries in Washington, D.C.

Marcia M. Greenlee is a consultant for history, historic preservation, and museum education projects in the area of Washington, D.C., where she has pursued a special interest in local history. She holds degrees from Willamette University in Salem, Oregon, and Howard University and a Ph.D from George Washington University in Washington, D.C.

Judith Beck Helm is a third-generation Washingtonian whose history of Tenleytown, *Tenleytown, D.C.: Country Village into City Neighborhood,* was published in 1981. She is presently pastor of Zion Lehigh Lutheran Church in Alburtis, Pennsylvania.

Alison K. Hoagland coordinated a volunteer survey of historic buildings in Washington's old downtown for the preservation group Don't Tear It Down; that survey resulted in a downtown historic district. She is employed as an architectural historian at the Historic American Buildings Survey of the U.S. National Park Service.

Ronald M. Johnson is a professor of American history at Georgetown University who has published frequently in the fields of race relations and urban affairs. He co-authored *Propaganda and Aesthetics,* a study of Afro-American literary politics in the twentieth century. He holds a Ph.D. from the University of Illinois.

Linda Low, as a history teacher and as a preservation consultant, has been involved in a variety of history and preservation projects, including Mount Pleasant's successful historic district application. A Mount Pleasant resident since 1970, she is presently a realtor in the Washington area.

Keith Melder, a specialist in American social and political history, has published many articles and books, including *City of Magnificent Intentions,* a D.C. history text he edited for the D.C. Public Schools. Employed as a curator in the Smithsonian Institution's Museum of American History, he holds a Ph.D. in American Studies from Yale University.

Ruth Ann Overbeck, an American social historian, is the co-author of *Houses and Homes: Exploring Their History* and the founder and president of the public history firm, Washington Perspectives, Inc. She has conducted extensive research on Capitol Hill, and headed the historical research team that recently completed an official survey of Deanwood for the D.C. Historic Preservation Office.

John N. Pearce studied Brookland while a professor at the George Washington University in Washington, D.C., where he co-edited with George W. McDaniel and Martin Aurand *Images of Brookland: The History and Architecture of a Washington Suburb.* He presently teaches in the Department of Historic Preservation at Mary Washington College in Fredericksburg, Virginia.

Judith Helm Robinson is a professional architectural historian, preservation consultant, and publications specialist. She is the president of the Chevy Chase Historical Society and a founding partner in the firm of Traceries, where she specializes in the history and architecture of the D.C. area.

Suzanne Sherwood Unger holds an M.A. from George Washington University, where her thesis on Foggy Bottom was published in 1978. She worked for the National Trust for Historic Preservation for seven years before moving to Phoenix, Arizona, where she now resides.

Linda Wheeler is a reporter and photographer, working for the *Washington Post* since 1968 and specializing in coverage of Washington, D.C., neighborhoods. She is a former resident of Dupont Circle and now owns a house in Shaw.

Kathleen Sinclair Wood, executive director of the Cleveland Park Historical Society, is an architectural historian involved in teaching, researching, and writing about American art and architecture in Washington, D.C. A resident of Cleveland Park, she was responsible for the application that led to its listing on the National Register.

Additional Acknowledgments

The authors wish to thank the following individuals and organizations, as well as many unnamed neighborhood residents, for their enthusiasm and generous help with this project. They assisted with research, found photographs, read manuscripts, and shared expertise and information—efforts that have made this book truly a community effort.

Adams Morgan: David Bosserman, Jan Fleming, Dr. Marcia Greenlee, and Rene Horacio Quintanilla.

Benning Heights: James and Lena Ferguson, Thomas and Sarajane Goodwin, Gladys and William Holmes, Jr., Dr. George Young, and Dr. Marilyn W. Nickels.

Brightwood: Jean Alexander.

Brookland: Dr. George W. McDaniel and Martin Aurand who co-edited with the author two editions of *Images of Brookland,* upon which this essay is based, as well as many former colleagues and students at George Washington University who assisted with the research for that volume.

Capitol Hill: Melissa McLoud and Arline Roback.

Chevy Chase: Gavin Farr, Eleanor Ford, Alice Kinter, Joan Marsh, Julie Mueller, Mary Ann Tuohey, Marjorie Zapruder, and the Chevy Chase Historical Society.

Cleveland Park: Rives Carroll, Dorothy Provine, Richard Longstreth, and Richard Striner.

Deanwood: This essay is based on a Department of Interior multi-cultural resources survey funded through the D.C. Historic Preservation Division, and the Far East Community Services Inc. The team included Laura Henley, John Lee, Dr. Julia C. Parks, Dr. John Ross, and Dr. Robert Verrey. Thanks also to Robert Hughes and the descendants of the Sheriff-Lowrie-Dean family.

Dupont Circle: The staff and volunteers of the Columbia Historical Society.

Foggy Bottom: Inez Pulver and Rhea Radin.

Georgetown: Robert Lyle, Mary Mitchell, Ann Satterthwaite, and Niente Smith.

Kalorama: The Kalorama Citizens' Association, Sheridan-Kalorama Historical Association, Sheridan-Kalorama Neighborhood Council, and the D.C. Historic Preservation Division, all of which funded projects that provided data for this essay. Thanks also to Alison Stone Blanton and Katherine Grandine.

LeDroit Park: Theresa Brown.

Old Anacostia: John Kinard and Dorn McGrath.

7th Street Downtown: Don't Tear It Down survey volunteers.

Shepherd Park: F. Merle Bollard, Brice Clagett, Robert Melende, Musindo Mwinyipembe, John Richardson, Marion Reid, and James Walker.

Southwest: Delores Smith.

Takoma Park: Karen Fishman, Mary Lou Friebele, Ellen R. Marsh, and the staffs of the Takoma Park, Maryland, Library and the Takoma Park Branch of the D.C. Library.

For help of all kinds with the photographs: James Ballard, James DeMersman, Ronald Elbert, Dennis Gale, Dr. Kenneth Gorelick, Sharon Reinckens, Millie Riley, Judy Smith, Douglas Sprunt, Mary Ternes, Haddasah Thurz, Robert Truax, and Keith Washington.

Bibliography

The essays in this book are based largely on primary sources. Rather than listing the detailed and voluminous references of the authors, of limited use to the general reader, this section provides a description of the materials available to researchers pursuing neighborhood studies of their own. The footnotes and bibliographies for each chapter in this book are available at the Library of the Columbia Historical Society and in the Washingtoniana Division of the D.C. Public Library.

Primary Sources

• *Maps.* The real estate atlases created for the purposes of private insurance companies from the 1870s to the 1960s are the best sources with which to begin neighborhood research. The specific information they contain gives the researcher an overview of a locality's physical growth and suggests avenues of research. These plat maps locate all buildings in the city, name the streets, and identify each property by square and lot number; this information is invaluable for further research in tax assessment records and building permits. Comparison of maps issued in different years reveals patterns of growth and change in every section of the city. The maps also include the names of many major institutions, businesses, and land- owners—names that can be used to begin the search for information on the neighborhood.

The atlases are available at the Columbia Historical Society, the Washingtoniana Division of the D.C. Public Library (hereafter cited simply as the Washingtoniana Division), and the Geography and Map Division of the Library of Congress. The years of issue available at each place vary. The earliest atlas is Faehtz and Pratt, 1873-1874, but the 1887 Griffith M. Hopkins atlas is the first to show buildings. All three libraries also have collections of individual historical maps useful to the neighborhood historian, as does the Special Collections section of the Gelman Library of The George Washington University (hereafter, Gelman Library).

• *City Directories.* City directories list the names of most people residing in the city, along with their addresses, occupations, and sometimes places of work. Each directory also includes lists of businesses by type. Advertisements for local businesses, some with illustrations, provide additional information. The directories are available at the Columbia Historical Society and the Washingtoniana Division.

The earliest directory was published in 1822, but annual volumes are not available until after 1865. They become irregular after 1942; the last was published in 1973. The books become most useful for neighborhood research after 1914 when residents began to be listed for the first time by address as well as alphabetically, making it possible to construct a profile of a particular block or entire neighborhood. The directories have limitations. They often left out people, most often poor, black, or transient. Names are sometimes misspelled.

• *Tax Assessment Records.* The most complete records of the tax assessor are at the National Archives, although many volumes are also available in the Washingtoniana Division. These records include lists of all the landowners in the city and the value of the land and improvements, organized by lot and square number (which can be obtained from the plat maps). These records allow the researcher to determine when buildings were constructed, to identify landowners, and to ascertain the relative value of buildings and land in a neighborhood.

• *Building Permits.* Permits for the construction of buildings or additions, for demolition, and for new land uses that could be considered nuisances were required by the city government beginning in 1877. These building permits are available on microfilm in Room 400 of the National Archives. They are filed by date, and within each date by square and lot number. An index by square number allows the researcher to identify all building permits for specific blocks. These documents include the size, materials, and purpose of buildings to be built; the name of the builder and/or architect; and sometimes accompanying permits for plumbing, lists of signers of petitions for special uses, and architectural drawings (filed separately in the Cartography and Architecture Branch).

• *Newspapers.* Newspaper articles provide one of the richest sources of information for neighborhood research. The Washingtoniana Division, the Columbia Historical Society, and the Gelman Library have "vertical files" of clippings organized by neighborhood as well as by the names of institutions within the neighborhoods. The clipping files of the *Washington Star,* which ceased publication in 1981, have been deposited in the Washingtoniana Division, which also has copies of every major newspaper published in Washington, D.C., since 1800. An index to the *Star* begins in 1906, with partial indexing before that date. Most of the items related to neighborhoods are listed under the heading Real Estate. The *Washington Post* is indexed from 1971 to the present. These newspapers are also available on microfilm in the Periodicals Division of the Library of Congress.

The Washingtoniana Division has a variety of neighborhood newspapers and newsletters for selected dates.

• *Federal Manuscript Census.* The manuscript schedules of the federal census are the original documents created by the census takers. They provide specific information on individuals or families in increasing detail from 1790 to 1910, the most recent schedule to be opened for public inspection. The first to be truly useful for neighborhood research, however, is the 1880 census, which lists households by address. The 1890 manuscript census was destroyed by fire. The 1880, 1900, and 1910 manuscript schedules provide the data necessary to create a demographic profile of a particular street or neighborhood.

Information in the 1880 manuscript census includes the names of all members of the household and their relationships to one another, race, sex, age, marital status, occupation, unemployment information, whether ill or disabled, whether literate, and place of birth of each individual and the parents of the individual. The 1900 census adds date of birth, number of years married, number of children born and number living, dates of immigration and naturalization, whether in school, and home ownership information. The 1910 census includes workplace as well as occupation for the first time. These materials are available on microfilm in Room 400 of the National Archives.

• *Photographs.* Photographs are being appreciated increasingly as sources of historical information. Of all the sources on Washington neighborhoods, photographs are the most scattered. The major repositories are the Columbia Historical Society, the Washingtoniana Division, the Prints and Photographs Division of the Library of Congress, and the Still Pictures Division of the National Archives. Images related to the history of black Washingtonians are available at the Moorland-Spingarn Research Center of Howard University. The Gelman Library also has a small collection of Washington, D.C., photographs.

The images at the Columbia Historical Society are filed primarily by location, and at the Washingtoniana Division by location and subject matter. The Library of Congress has a large Washingtoniana collection filed by subject; in 1988 the Library of Congress will publish a catalog by Kathleen Collins, *Washingtoniana Photographs,* describing 750,000 of its Washington-related images. Washington photographs are most difficult to locate at the National Archives, where the images are filed by the government agency that created them.

Collections particularly rich in images useful for neighborhood research include the *Washington Star* collection in the Washingtoniana Division and, at the Columbia Historical Society, the Wymer collection, the Federal Reservation collection, and the Emil Press collection.

• *Manuscript Collections.* The letters, diaries, and other personal papers of individuals associated with particular neighborhoods can sometimes be located in manuscript collections. The most likely repositories of such material are the Manuscripts Division of the Library of Congress, the Moorland-Spingarn Research Center of Howard University, the Columbia Historical Society, and the Gelman Library. The Gelman Library manuscripts collection includes the archives of the Greater Washington Board of Trade, the Jewish Community Council of Greater Washington, the Committee of 100 on the Federal City, as well as papers on the history of Metrorail in Washington.

• *D.C. Commissioners' Annual Reports.* These volumes include the annual reports of all departments of the District of Columbia government from 1874 to 1960. The late nineteenth and early twentieth century volumes are particularly valuable for neighborhood research because they contain information on public improvements (such as street grading, paving, and cleaning), public schools, public health, and other issues that affected all parts of the city. These early volumes include a variety of large fold-out maps illustrating the extent of public improvements, the incidence of fatal diseases, and the extent of suburbanization.

• *Other Records.* Documents compiled by churches, civic and citizens associations, businesses, and other institutions are a rich but elusive resource. These records are still almost entirely in private hands, where they exist at all. When available, they can provide valuable information about the neighborhoods they served, as well as about the institutions themselves.

• *Oral History.* The taped reminiscences of residents or former residents of Washington neighborhoods can often provide information available nowhere else. Small but growing collections of oral history interviews now exist at the Columbia Historical Society, the Washingtoniana Division, and the Gelman Library. Particularly useful are the tapes created by *The Washington Ear* project and the Oral History Project of the Jewish Historical Society of Greater Washington at the Washingtoniana Division. The Columbia Historical Society has notable collections related to Dupont Circle.

Researchers creating their own oral history resources are directed to *Oral History for the Local Historical Society* by Willa K. Baum, cited below. Oral history is best done after research in all other available resources is complete. The interviewer is then able to ask good questions, to check the responses against other sources, and to use materials already collected, especially interesting photographs, maps, and documents, to prompt reminiscences.

GUIDES TO THE USE OF PRIMARY SOURCES

Baum, Willa K. *Oral History for the Local Historical Society.* 2nd ed., rev. Nashville: American Association for State and Local History, 1974.

Hoagland, Kim. *Guide to Resources for Researching Historic Buildings in Washington, D.C.* Washington, D.C.: Don't Tear It Down, 1982.

Kyvig, David E., and Myron Marty. *Nearby History: Exploring the Past Around You.* Nashville: American Association for State and Local History, 1982.

Smith, Kathryn S. *You in History.* Washington, D.C.: Associates for Renewal in Education, 1983.

Neighborhood Titles

The following is a selected list of published and unpublished materials related to specific Washington neighborhoods. They range widely in scope and type, including master's theses and doctoral dissertations, journal articles, government reports, church histories, reminiscences, walking tours, and promotional publications of real estate development companies. Many of the articles are drawn from the *Records of the Columbia Historical Society,* published from 1894 to the present, the most extensive collection of published work on the history of local Washington, D.C. They are cited here as *RCHS.* Indexes are available.

The list cannot be all inclusive. It is intended rather to suggest the variety of approaches available to the researcher interested in a particular locality. Most of the titles listed here are available at the Columbia Historical Society, the Washingtoniana Division of the D.C. Public Library, or the Special Collections of the Gelman Library of The George Washington University. Additional materials are listed in *Neighborhood History in Washington, D.C.: A Survey and Checklist of Selected Projects and Sources of Information,* compiled by Keith Melder (Washington, D.C.: Museum of the City of Washington, 1982), available at the Columbia Historical Society and the Washingtoniana Division.

COLLECTIONS OF NEIGHBORHOOD MATERIALS

Applications for historic district status for Washington neighborhoods may be studied at the D.C. Historic Preservation Division, Department of Consumer and Regulatory Affairs.

Cityscape. Magazine published by students at the Duke Ellington School for the Arts, 8 volumes published from 1974 to 1981.

D.C. Deputy Mayor for Economic Development. *Draft Ward Plans.* Washington, D.C.: Government of the District of Columbia, 1986.

D.C. Office of Planning and Development. *Ward Notebooks.* Washington, D.C.: Government of the District of Columbia, 1982.

Footsteps: Historical Walking Tours of Chevy Chase, Cleveland Park, Tenleytown, Friendship. Washington, D.C.: Neighborhood Planning Councils 2 and 3, 1976.

Proctor, John Clagett. Series of articles on Washington localities in the *Sunday Star,* 1928-1952. Indexed at the Washingtoniana Division of the D.C. Public Library and at the Columbia Historical Society.

Protopappas, John J., and Lin Brown, eds. *Washington on Foot.* 3rd ed. rev. Washington, D.C.: National Area Chapter American Planning Association and Smithsonian Institution Press, 1984.

Shannon, J. Harry. Series of articles by "The Rambler" on localities in Washington and vicinity in the *Sunday Star,* 1912-1927. Indexed at the Washingtoniana Division of the D.C. Public Library and at the Columbia Historical Society.

ADAMS MORGAN

D.C. Office of Urban Renewal. *Adams Morgan, Democratic Action to Save a Neighborhood.* Washington, D.C.: Government Printing Office, 1964.

Henig, Jeffrey R. *Gentrification in Adams Morgan: Political and Commercial Consequences of Neighborhood Change.* George Washington Studies No. 9. Washington, D.C.: George Washington University, 1982.

U.S. Commission of Fine Arts. *Sixteenth Street Architecture.* Vol 1. Washington, D.C.: Government Printing Office, 1978.

BRIGHTWOOD

Cox, William Van Zandt. "Matthew Gault Emery, The Last Mayor of Washington, 1870-1871." *RCHS* 20 (1917) 19-59.

Grandine, Katherine. "Brightwood, Its Development and Suburbanization, 1800-1915." M.A. thesis, George Washington University, 1983.

BROOKLAND

McDaniel, George W., and John N. Pearce, eds. *Images of Brookland: The History and Architecture of a Washington Suburb.* George Washington Studies No. 10. Washington, D.C.: George Washington University, 1982.

CAPITOL HILL

Capitol Hill Prospectus. A report prepared by a committee from the Capitol Hill community. Washington, D.C.: Capitol Hill Restoration Society, 1967.

Clark, Allen C. "Daniel Carroll of Duddington." *RCHS* 39 (1938) 1-48.

Davis, Madison. "The Navy Yard During the Life of Rev. William Ryland." *RCHS* 4 (1901) 199-221.

Downing, Margaret Brent. "The Earliest Proprietors of Capitol Hill." *RCHS* 21 (1918) 1-23.

Ennis, Robert Brooks. "Christ Church, Washing-

ton Parish." *RCHS* 1969-1970 (1971) 126-177.
Myers, Susan H. "Capitol Hill, 1870-1900: The People and Their Homes." *RCHS* 1973-1974 (1976) 276-299.
Paullin, Charles O. "History of the Site of the Congressional and Folger Libraries." *RCHS* 37-38 (1937) 173-194.
Taylor, Frank A. "Growing Up on Capitol Hill." RCHS *50 (1980) 508-521.*

CHEVY CHASE

Atwood, Albert W. *Francis G. Newlands, a Builder of the Nation.* Washington D.C.: Newlands Co., 1969.
----------. "The Romance of Senator Francis G. Newlands and Chevy Chase." *RCHS* 1966-1968 (1969) 294-310.
Fisher, Thos. J., & Co. *Chevy Chase for Homes.* Washington, D.C.: Thos. J. Fisher & Co., 1916.
French, Roderick S. "Chevy Chase Village in the Context of the National Suburban Movement, 1870-1900." *RCHS* 1973-1974 (1976) 300-329.
Origins and *Origins II.* Washington, D.C.: Neighborhood Planning Councils 2 and 3, 1975, 1976.
Stafford, Edward T. *Fifty Years in Chevy Chase, 1909-1959.* Washington, D.C.: Chevy Chase Citizens Association, 1959.
Sween, Jane C. *Montgomery County: Two Centuries of Change.* Northridge, CA: Windsor Publications, 1984.
See the collections of the Chevy Chase Historical Society. For information call the Chevy Chase Village Hall in Chevy Chase, Maryland.

CLEVELAND PARK

Carroll, Rives, ed. *Cleveland Park Voices.* Washington, D.C.: John Eaton Public School, 1984.
Citizens Northwest Suburban Association. *Suburban Washington as a Place of Residence.* Washington, D.C.: Citizens Northwest Suburban Association, 1901.
Hamilton, Sara White, Louise Mann Madden, and Sheila Dressner Ruffine, eds. *Historic Preservation Study of Cleveland Park, Washington, D.C.* Washington, D.C.: American University, 1977.
Matteson, William F. *Connecticut Avenue Highlands, Cathedral Highlands, Richmond Park.* Washington, D.C.: by the author, 1910.
Moore, David, and William A. Hill. *Cleveland Park.* Washington, D.C.: by the authors, 1904. Reprinted with an introduction by Kathleen Sinclair Wood. Washington, D.C.: Columbia Historical Society, 1982.
Peter, Grace Dunlop, and Joyce D. Southwick. *Cleveland Park: An Early Residential Neighborhood of the Nation's Capital.* Washington, D.C.: Cleveland Park Community Library Committee, 1958.

DOWNTOWN

Clark, Allen C. "More about the Fourth Ward." *RCHS* 33-34 (1932) 71-86.
Conn, Stetson. *Washington's Epiphany: Church and Parish, 1842-1972.* Washington, D.C.: Church of the Epiphany, 1976.
Davis, Henry E. "Ninth and F Streets and Thereabout." *RCHS* 5 (1902) 238-258.
Garrow, Patrick H., ed. *Archeological Investigations on the Washington, D.C. Civic Center Site.* Washington, D.C.: Soil Systems, Inc., 1982.
McArdle, Walter F. "The Development of the Business Sector in Washington, D.C., 1800-1973." *RCHS* 1973-1974 (1976) 556-594.
Milburn, Page. "Fourth Ward." *RCHS* 33-34 (1932) 61-69.
Miller, Elizabeth Jane. "The Dry Goods Trade in Washington, D.C." M.A. thesis, George Washington University, 1977.
Nordlinger, Bernard I. "A History of the Washington Hebrew Congregation." *The Record* of the Jewish Historical Society of Greater Washington 4 (November 1969) 1-82.
Stanley, Joan H. *Judiciary Square, Washington, D.C., a Park History.* Washington, D.C.: Division of History, U.S. Office of Archeology and Historic Preservation, 1968.
Topham, Washington. "Centre Market and Vicinity." *RCHS* 26 (1924) 1-88.
----------. "The Benning-McGuire House: E St. and Neighborhood." *RCHS* 33-34 (1932) 87-131.
----------. "Northern Liberty Market." *RCHS* 24 (1922) 43-66.
----------. "Business Washington: A Survey of the Commercial and Industrial Development of the District of Columbia." In John Clagett Proctor, ed., *Washington: Past and Present.* New York: Lewis Historical Publishing Co., 1930.
U.S. National Capital Planning Commission. *Downtown Urban Renewal Area Landmarks, Washington, D.C.* Washington, D.C.: Government Printing Office, 1970.
Zevely, Douglass. "Old Houses on C Street and Those Who Lived There." *RCHS* 5 (1902) 151-175.
----------. "Old Residences and Family History in the City Hall Neighborhood." *RCHS* 6 (1903) 104-142.

DUPONT CIRCLE

Albano, Walter S. "History of the Dupont Circle Neighborhood, Washington, D.C. 1880-1900." M.A. thesis, University of Maryland, 1982.
Cherkasky, Mara. "Slices of the Pie: Black and White Dupont Circle from the 1920s to the 1950s." M.A. thesis, George Washington University, 1985.
Olszewski, George J. *Dupont Circle, Washington, D.C.* Washington, D.C.: Division of History, U.S. Office of Archeology and Historic Preservation, 1967.
Rubicam, Milton. "Mr. Christian Heurich and His Mansion." *RCHS* 1960-1962 (1963) 167-205.

FOGGY BOTTOM

Easby-Smith, Maria Wilhelmine. *Personal Recollections of Early Washington and a Sketch of the Life of Captain William Easby.* Washington, D.C.: Beresford, 1913.
Gatti, Lawrence P. *Historic St. Stephen's: An Account of Its Eighty-Five Years, 1867-1952.* Washington, D.C.: privately printed, 1952.
Harkness, Robert H. "The Old Glass House." *RCHS* 18 (1915) 201-238.
Herman, Jan K. *A Hilltop in Foggy Bottom: Home of the Old Naval Observatory and the Navy Medical Department.* Washington, D.C.: Naval Medical Command, Department of the Navy, 1984.
Heurich, Gary F. "The Christian Heurich Brewing Company, 1872-1956." *RCHS* 1973-1974 (1976) 604-615.
Kayser, Elmer Louis. *Bricks Without Straw: The Evolution of George Washington University.* New York: Appleton-Century-Crofts, 1970.
Langley, Harold D. *St. Stephen Martyr Church and the Community, 1867-1967.* Washington, D.C.: St. Stephen's Centennial Committee, 1968.
Sherwood, Suzanne Berry. *Foggy Bottom 1800-1975: A Study in the Use of an Urban Neighborhood.* George Washington Studies No. 7. Washington, D.C.: George Washington University, 1978.

GEORGETOWN

Durkin, Joseph T. *Georgetown University, First in the Nation's Capital.* Washington, D.C.: Georgetown University, 1964.
Gale, Dennis. "Restoration in Georgetown, Washington, D.C., 1915-1965." Ph.D. dissertation, George Washington University, 1982.
Garrow, Patrick H., and Mary Beth Reed. *In Search of Suters Tavern.* Atlanta: Garrow & Associates, 1986.
Gordon, William A. "Recollections of a Boyhood in Georgetown." *RCHS* 20 (1917) 121-140.
Holmes, Oliver W. "The City Tavern: A Century of Georgetown History, 1797-1898." *RCHS* 50 (1980) 1-35.
Hurst, Harold W. "Businesses and Businessmen in Pre-Civil War Georgetown, 1840-1860." *RCHS* 50 (1980) 161-171.
Jackson, Richard P. *The Chronicles of Georgetown, D.C. from 1751 to 1878.* Washington, D.C.: R.O. Polkenhorn, 1878.
MacMaster, Richard K. "Georgetown and the

Tobacco Trade, 1751-1783." *RCHS* 1966-1968 (1969) 1-33.

Mitchell, Mary. *Chronicles of Georgetown Life 1865-1900.* Washington, D.C.: Seven Locks Press, 1986.

----------. *Divided Town, A Study of Georgetown During the Civil War.* Barre, MA: Barre Publishers, 1968.

Mitchell, Pauline Gaskins. "The History of Mt. Zion United Methodist Church and Mt. Zion Cemetery." *RCHS* 51 (1984) 103-118.

Peter, Grace Dunlop. *Portrait of Old Georgetown.* Richmond, VA: Dietz Press, 1951.

Ritzenberg, Albert. "A Study in the Resettlement of an Urban Area: An Ecological Analysis of Georgetown." M.A. thesis, George Washington University, 1951.

Sanderlin, Walter S. *The Great National Project: A History of the Chesapeake and Ohio Canal.* Baltimore: Johns Hopkins Press, 1946.

Smith, Kathryn Schneider. "The Georgetown Waterfront, 1880-1920: A Study of Neighborhood Change." M.A. thesis, George Washington University, 1986.

Sullivan, Eleanore C. *Georgetown Visitation Since 1799.* Washington, D.C.: Georgetown Visitation, 1975.

Taggart, Hugh T. "Old Georgetown." *RCHS* 11 (1908) 120-224.

U.S. Commission of Fine Arts. *Georgetown Historic Waterfront, Washington, D.C.: A Review of Canal and Riverside Architecture.* Issued jointly by the U.S. Commission of Fine Arts and the Office of Archeology and Historic Preservation, Department of the Interior. Washington, D.C.: Government Printing Office, 1974.

----------. *Georgetown Architecture: Northwest, Northwest Washington, District of Columbia.* Washington, D.C.: U.S. Commission of Fine Arts, 1970.

----------. *Georgetown Architecture: The Waterfront.* Washington, D.C.: U.S. Commission of Fine Arts, 1968.

----------. *Georgetown Commercial Architecture: M Street, Northwest Washington, District of Columbia.* Arlington, VA: U.S. Commission of Fine Arts, 1967.

----------. *Georgetown Commercial Architecture: Wisconsin Avenue, Northwest Washington, District of Columbia.* Arlington, VA: U.S. Commission of Fine Arts, 1967.

----------. *Georgetown Residential Architecture: Northeast, Northwest Washington, District of Columbia.* Washington, D.C.: U.S. Commission of Fine Arts, 1969.

Williams, Mathilde. "Old Georgetown as Chronicled in the Peabody Collection." *RCHS* 1960-1962 (1963) 54-74.

---------. "Georgetown: The Twentieth Century, A Continuing Battle." *RCHS* 1971-1972 (1973) 783-796.

See also the collections in the Peabody Room of the Georgetown Public Library, the indexes to the *Records of the Columbia Historical Society,* and library card-catalogs for additional materials on Georgetown.

KALORAMA

Bacon-Foster, Corra. "The Story of Kalorama." *RCHS* 13 (1910) 98-118.

Mitchell, Mary. "Kalorama: Country Estate to Washington Mayfair." *RCHS* 1971-1972 (1973) 164-189.

U.S. Commission of Fine Arts. *Massachusetts Avenue Architecture.* 2 vols. Washington, D.C.: U.S. Commission of Fine Arts, 1973, 1975.

LEDROIT PARK

A.L. Barber and Co. *LeDroit Park Illustrated.* Washington, D.C.: F. Beresford, 1877.

Carr, Lynch Associates. *LeDroit Park Conserved.* Washington, D.C.: D.C. Department of Housing and Community Development, 1979.

Hamilton, Charles A. "Washington's First Residential Suburb." *The Nation's Capital Magazine* 1 (December 1930) 29.

Hightower, Barbara. "LeDroit Park: The Making of a Suburb, 1872-1888." M.A. thesis, George Washington University, 1982.

Johnson, Ronald M. "From Romantic Suburb to Racial Enclave: LeDroit Park, Washington, D.C., 1880-1920." *Phylon* XLV, no. 4 (1984) 264-270.

Logan, Rayford Whittingham. *Howard University: The First Hundred Years, 1867-1967.* New York: New York University Press, 1969.

Terrell, Mary Church. *A Colored Woman in a White World.* Washington, D.C.: Ransdell, Inc., 1940.

MASSACHUSETTS AVENUE HEIGHTS

Trustees, Massachusetts Heights. *Massachusetts Avenue Heights, Washington, D.C.* Washington, D.C.: by the author, 1911.

MOUNT PLEASANT

Battaglia, Barbara Jean. "Neighborhood Change and Revitalization in Mount Pleasant: The Long Time Homeowner's Perspective." M.A. thesis, George Washington University, 1978.

Emery, Fred A. "Mount Pleasant and Meridian Hill." *RCHS* 33-34 (1932) 187-223.

See also the Mount Pleasant materials at the Mount Pleasant Public Library.

OLD ANACOSTIA

Cantwell, Thomas J. "Anacostia: Strength in Adversity." *RCHS* 1973-1974 (1976) 330-370.

D.C. Department of Housing and Community Development. *Anacostia Conserved.* Washington, D.C.: Government of the District of Columbia, 1979.

Hutchinson, Louise Daniel. *The Anacostia Story, 1608-1930.* Washington, D.C.: Smithsonian Institution Press, 1977.

Office of the Mayor for Housing Programs. *Washington's Far Southeast 70.* Washington, D.C.: Government of the District of Columbia, 1970.

Senkevitch, Anatole, Jr., ed. *Old Anacostia, Washington, D.C.* Washington, D.C.: School of Architecture, University of Maryland and Metropolitan Washington Planning and Housing Association, 1975.

----------. *Design Guide for the Exterior Rehabilitation of Buildings in Old Anacostia.* Washington, D.C.: School of Architecture, University of Maryland and Metropolitan Washington Planning and Housing Association, 1975.

SHAW

Robinson, Henry S. "The M Street High School, 1891-1916." *RCHS* 51 (1984) 119-143.

Turner Associates. *The Logan Circle Historic Preservation Area: A Report Prepared for the District of Columbia Redevelopment Land Agency.* Washington, D.C.: by the author, 1973.

SOUTHWEST

Groves, Paul A. "The Development of a Black Residential Community in Southwest Washington: 1860-1897." *RCHS* 1973-1974 (1976) 260-275.

Huddleson, Sarah M. "The Sunny Southwest." *RCHS* 26 (1924) 157-187.

Mattingly, Judge Robert E. "Early Recollections and Reminiscences of South Washington—The Island." *RCHS* 37-38 (1937) 101-122.

Thursz, Daniel. *Where Are They Now?* Washington, D.C.: Health and Welfare Council of the National Capital Area, 1966.

Ward, Richard F. *South and West of the Capitol Dome.* New York: Vantage Press, 1978.

SWAMPOODLE

Press, Emil A. "Growing up in Swampoodle." Also, William H. Press, "Another View of Swampoodle." *RCHS* 1973-1974 (1976) 618-626.

TAKOMA PARK

Bachman, Robert M. "Takoma Park, Maryland: 1883-1942. A Case Study of an Early Railroad Suburb." M.A. thesis, George Washington University, 1975.

"Fifty Years of Progress in Takoma Park." *Program for the Fiftieth Anniversary Celebration of the Founding of Takoma Park, Md.-D.C.* Takoma Park, D.C.: Pioneer Press, 1933.

B.F. Gilbert Real Estate. *The Villa Lots of Takoma Park: A Suburb of Washington City.* Washington, D.C.: A.G. Gedney, 1886.

Hecht, Arthur. "The Takoma Park Public Library." *RCHS* 1966-1968 (1969) 318-335.

Marsh, Ellen R., and Mary Anne O'Boyle. *Takoma Park, Portrait of a Victorian Suburb.* Takoma Park, MD: Historic Takoma, Inc., 1984.

Mauck, Elwyn A. *Improving the Government of Takoma Park.* College Park, MD: University of Maryland, 1948.

See also the Takoma Park materials at the Takoma Park branch of the D.C. Public Library and the Takoma Park, Maryland, Public Library. For some materials permission is required from Historic Takoma, Inc., or the Takoma Park Historical Society.

TENLEYTOWN

Helm, Judith Beck. *Tenleytown, D.C.: Country Village into City Neighborhood.* Washington, D.C.: Tennally Press, 1981.

City-wide Titles

BIBLIOGRAPHIES

Calavan, Rita A., comp. *Selected Theses & Dissertations on the Washington, D.C. Region.* Washington, D.C.: Center for Washington Area Studies, George Washington University, 1982.

Fisher, Perry G., and Linda J. Lear, comps. *A Selected Bibliography for Washington Studies and Descriptions of Major Local Collections.* George Washington Studies No. 8. Washington, D.C.: George Washington University, 1981.

GENERAL HISTORIES

Federal Writers' Project. *Washington City and Capital, American Guide Series.* Washington, D.C.: Government Printing Office, 1937.

Green, Constance McLaughlin. *Washington: A History of the Capital, 1800-1950.* Princeton: Princeton University Press, 1962. Paperback ed., 1976.

Gutheim, Frederick. *Worthy of the Nation: The History of Planning for the National Capital.* Washington, D.C.: Smithsonian Institution Press, 1977.

Junior League of Washington. *An Illustrated History: The City of Washington.* Thomas Froncek, ed. New York: Alfred A. Knopf, 1977.

Melder, Keith, ed. *City of Magnificent Intentions: A History of the District of Columbia.* 2nd ed., rev. Washington, D.C.: Associates for Renewal in Education, 1983.

TRANSPORTATION

Boettjer, John W. "Street Railways in the District of Columbia." M.A. thesis, George Washington University, 1963.

Emery, Fred A. "Washington's Historic Bridges." *RCHS* 39 (1938) 49-70.

Formwalt, Lee W. "Benjamin Henry Latrobe and the Development of Transportation in the District of Columbia, 1802-1817." *RCHS* 50 (1980) 36-66.

King, LeRoy O. *100 Years of Capital Traction: The Story of Streetcars in the Nation's Capital.* Dallas: Taylor Publishing Company, 1972.

Merrill, E.D. "Changing Fashions in Transportation." *RCHS* 48-49 (1949) 159-170.

Myer, Donald B. *Bridges and the City of Washington.* Washington, D.C.: U.S. Commission of Fine Arts, 1974. Rpt. 1983.

Tindall, William. "Beginnings of Street Railways in the National Capital." *RCHS* 21 (1918) 24-86.

White, John H., Jr. "Public Transport in Washington Before the Great Consolidation of 1902." *RCHS 1966-1968 (1969) 216-229.*

MISCELLANEOUS

Afro-American Bicentennial Corp. "A Study of Historic Sites in the District of Columbia of Special Significance to Afro-Americans. "2 vols. Unpublished ms. in the Washingtoniana Division of the D.C. Public Library.

Altshuler, David, ed. *The Jews of Washington, D.C.: A Communal History Anthology.* Washington, D.C.: Jewish Historical Society of Greater Washington, 1985.

Borchert, James. *Alley Life in Washington: Family, Community, Religion, and Folklife in the City, 1850-1970.* Urbana: University of Illinois Press, 1980.

Both, Deborah. "A Study of the Residential Integration Process in the Washington Metropolitan Area." M.A. thesis, George Washington University, 1974.

Brown, Letitia. *Free Negroes in the District of Columbia, 1790-1846.* New York: Oxford University Press, 1972.

Brown, Letitia, and Elsie M. Lewis. *Washington from Banneker to Douglass, 1791-1870.* Washington, D.C.: National Portrait Gallery, Smithsonian Institution, 1971.

---------. *Washington in the New Era, 1870-1970.* Washington, D.C.: National Portrait Gallery, Smithsonian Institution, 1972.

Cooling, Benjamin Franklin. *Symbol, Sword and Shield: Defending Washington During the Civil War.* Hamden, CN: Archon Books, 1975.

Dabney, Lillian G. "The History of Schools for Negroes in the District of Columbia 1807-1947." Ph.D. dissertation, Catholic University of America, 1949.

Ethridge, Harrison M. "The Black Architects of Washington, D.C., 1900-Present." D.A. dissertation, Catholic University of America, 1979.

Fant, Barbara Gale Howick. "Slum Reclamation and Housing Reform in the Nation's Capital, 1890-1940." Ph.D. dissertation, George Washington University, 1982.

Gillette, Howard, Jr. "A National Workshop for Urban Policy: The Metropolitanization of Washington, 1946-1968." *Public Historian* 7 (Winter 1985) 7-27.

Gillette, Howard, Jr., and Alan M. Kraut. "The Evolution of Washington's Italian-American Community, 1890-World War II." *Journal of American Ethnic History* 6 (Fall 1986) 7-27.

Goode, James M. *Capital Losses: A Cultural History of Washington's Destroyed Buildings.* Washington, D.C.: Smithsonian Institution Press, 1979.

Green, Constance McLaughlin. *The Secret City: A History of Race Relations in the Nation's Capital.* Princeton: Princeton University Press, 1967.

Harley, Sharon. "Black Women in the District of Columbia, 1890-1920: Their Economic, Social and Institutional Activities." Ph.D. dissertation, Howard University, 1981.

Hines, Christian. *Early Recollections of Washington City.* Washington, D.C.: Chronicle Book and Job Print, 1866. Rpt. Junior League of Washington, 1981.

A History of the City of Washington: Its Men and Institutions. Washington, D.C.: *Washington Post,* 1903.

Ibanga, Ufota A. "Residential Segregation and Neighborhood Change in Washington, D.C. between 1960 and 1970." M.A. thesis, Howard University, 1972.

Lee, Richard M. *Mr. Lincoln's City. An Illustrated Guide to the Civil War Sites of Washington.* McLean, VA: EPM Publications, 1981.

Maury, William M. "Alexander Shepherd and the Board of Public Works." *RCHS* 48 (1971-1972) 394-410.

Milburn, Page. "How Washington Grew in Spots." *RCHS* 26 (1924) 106-120.

Overbeck, Ruth Ann, and Melissa McLoud. ". . . in a workmanlike manner . . . The Building of Residential Washington, 1790-1900." A catalog. Washington, D.C.: The Charles M. Sumner School Museum and Archives, 1987.

Reiff, Daniel. *Washington Architecture 1791-1861: Problems in Development.* Washington, D.C.: U.S. Commission of Fine Arts, 1971.

Schmeckebier, Laurence F. "The Ward Boundaries of Washington and Georgetown, 1801-1871." *RCHS* 51-52 (1955) 66-77.

Sessford, John. "The Sessford Annals." Rpt. *RCHS* 11 (1908) 271-388.

Smith, Sam. *Captive Capital: Colonial Life in Modern Washington.* Bloomington: Indiana University Press, 1974.

Thurber, Bert H. "The Negro at the Nation's Capital, 1913-1931." Ph.D. dissertation, Yale University, 1973.

Young, James Sterling. *The Washington Community, 1800-1828.* New York: Harcourt, Brace & World, 1966.

Index

Partners in Progress Index

General Index

Italics indicate illustrations.